THE COMPLETE WORKS OF ROBERT BROWNING, VOLUME III

Photo by Chalue

Portrait of Robert Browning by William Fisher, 1854

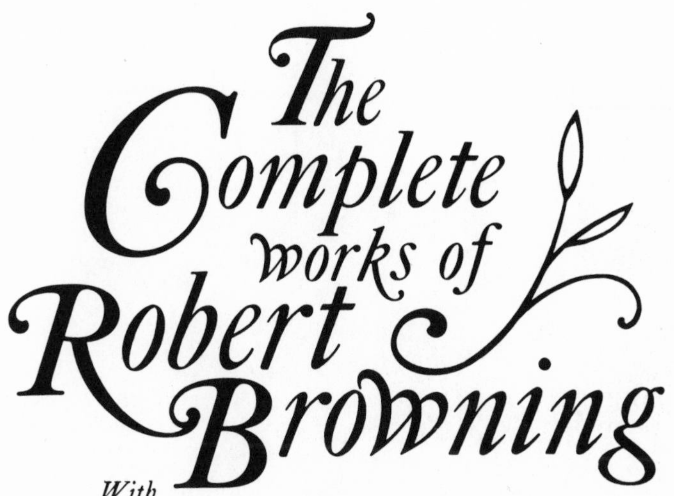

With Variant Readings & Annotations

VOLUME III

OHIO UNIVERSITY PRESS

ATHENS, OHIO 1971

Library of Congress Catalog Card Number: 68-18389
ISBN 8214-74-6

Printed in the United States of America

CONTENTS

Preface

I CONTENTS

This edition of the works of Robert Browning is intended to be complete. It is expected to run to thirteen volumes and will contain:

1. The full contents of the first editions of Browning's work, arranged in chronological order. The poems included in *Dramatic Lyrics, Dramatic Romances and Lyrics,* and *Men and Women* appear in the order of their first publication rather than the order in which Browning rearranged them for later publication.

2. All prefaces, dedications, and advertisements which Browning wrote for his own works or for those of Elizabeth Barrett Browning and others.

3. The two known prose essays which Browning published: the review of a book on Tasso, generally referred to as "The Essay on Chatterton," and the preface for a collection of letters supposed to have been written by Percy Bysshe Shelley, generally referred to as "The Essay on Shelley."

4. The front matter and the table of contents of each of the collected editions (1849, 1863, 1868, 1888–89a, and 1889) which Browning himself saw through the press. The table of contents will include both the pagination of the first edition and of this edition.

5. Poems by Browning published during his lifetime but not collected by him.

6. Unpublished poems by Browning which have come to light since his death.

7. John Forster's *Thomas Wentworth, Earl of Strafford* to which Browning contributed significantly, though to what precise extent so far cannot be determined.

8. Variants from secondary materials (see section six of this preface).

II GENERAL TEXTUAL PRINCIPLES: COPY-TEXT AND VARIANTS

It is increasingly recognized that methods of editing nineteenth-century texts need to be reexamined and probably revised. The old fashioned notion that a nineteenth- or twentieth-century text could be simply reprinted from either the first or last edition is no longer tenable. Recent examination of the works of Hawthorne, Melville, Twain, Cooper, Mill and others, for example, reveal problems different from those arising from texts of earlier centuries, and also differing problems among recent writers which distinguish any one from the others.

Before we published Volume One of this edition, and after three years of intensive study of both the specific problems connected with Browning's texts and the adequacy of prevailing theory to solve them, we arrived at certain basic principles which we felt would produce an authoritative, useful edition of Browning's work. We recognized at that time, however, that after further practical experience with the text and with new information that would undoubtedly become available, we might want to elaborate upon and further document our initial statement of textual principles. We now feel that the time has come for a restatement. We are convinced that the principles and methods outlined in Volume One are basically sound. We will attempt here, however, to clarify any vagueness which might have existed in our original effort and to provide additional evidence which, we believe, will further increase the reasonableness of our choices and procedures.

Our first problem was to select an authoritative text, and to determine what was and what was not a legitimate variant to it. We have manuscripts for nineteen of Browning's thirty-four book publications. Others may become available during the time we are working on this edition. None, however, with the possible exception of *Asolando*, published on the day of Browning's death, can be said to represent the author's final intentions. Each of Browning's works went through a series of editions during his lifetime and each was revised by Browning himself. If, indeed, the manuscript and each successive edition were under Browning's control and if it can be established that in all probability the changes made in each were his own, then each represents Browning's final decision at the time, and must be considered as a possible copy-text. Thus the establishment of authorial control becomes the central concern of the editors. That Browning did exercise control over the publication of his works we shall demonstrate in due course.

Clearly in the case of a poet who was revising his work over a period of more than fifty years neither the original manuscript nor the first edition published from it can meet the accepted requirements for the copy-text. Nor would any one text, produced by a process of emendation and conflation, result in a single text more representative than any one we now have of what might be called the "real" Browning. To attempt to construct such a text would indicate not editorial responsibility, but flagrant violation of the editorial principle that the author's own decisions are, to the extent they are discernible, to be respected. Indeed, the position we found ourselves in—that of producing *a* text carrying the authority of *an* author—forced us to reconsider the commonly accepted understanding of the terms *text* and *author*.

Too often both text and author are considered as static entities, Platonic archetypes. We do not have space here to consider fully the philosophical implications of such an assumption and must of necessity restrict ourselves to a brief statement of a more practical nature. For those interested, we suggest that they read Morse Peckham's article "Reflections on the Foundations of Textual Criticism: Human Behavior and Better Editions," *Proof* 1 (1971). For a work that varies in a series of documents and editions, each having authorial authority, clearly there is no such empirical entity as *the* text. Indeed, grasp of this simple fact raises questions about the author himself. Which author—or the author at which stage in the process—is meant? Upon what basis can we ascribe greater authenticity to one than to the others? The young Browning who wrote *Pauline* in 1832, the maturing poet who revised it in 1863 and 1868, and the old man who put it in final form in 1888 and 1889 differ greatly. Each of these editions represented Browning's final decisions as he understood himself at the time. Each has its own authority, representing the author as he existed at that particular time. Clearly, to reduce the Browning of those diverse stages to a static entity renders him no less an artificial construction than to reduce a number of versions of a work to a similar artificially constructed single text. Neither of such constructions can be regarded as an empirical entity.

Our focus shifts, necessarily, from the *text* and the *author* considered as static metaphysical entities to the process of creating and editing involved in the compilation of a series of documents; and concern about the transmission of the text is redirected to the problem of understanding the character of the decisions by which the successive and varying versions of the work came to be.

It follows, therefore, that we are concerned more about authorial *function* and editorial *function* than about *author* and *editor*. Any writer's work consists of two processes: he generates a work, and he corrects or edits it by balancing his current conceptions of the coherence of what he has written, and his grasp of the conventions applicable to the kind of discourse he is composing as they then obtain and as he understands them. The two functions are not necessarily isolated and sequential. That is, he does not generate a statement once and then forever after merely edit it. The text itself remains fluid, subject to continuous recreation. The manuscript that goes to the printer for the first edition, no doubt, already represents a series of generations and revisions; likewise, the marked copy for each subsequent edition may and probably does represent both editing and recreation. The second and subsequent editions of *Pauline*, for example, containing as they do, material which not only clarifies and corrects but elaborates upon and, in some cases, changes the meaning of the original, represent more than editing. Following are characteristic examples of genuinely substantive changes that Browning made in the first edition:

525| *1833*: As would encircle me with praise and love;
1888: As straight encircle men with praise and love,
543–544| *1833*: First in the struggle, and again would make
All bow to it; and I would sink again.
1888: First in the struggle, fail again to make
All bow enslaved, and I again should sink.
564| *1833*: I was most happy, sweet, for all delights
1888: I seemed defiant, sweet, for old delights
875–876| *1833*: No less I feel that thou hast brought me bliss,
And that I still hope to win it back.
1888: No less song proves one word has brought me bliss,
Another still may win bliss surely back.

The cumulative impact of numerous such small changes have a profound effect upon the meaning of the revised poem.

This process of revision Browning continued throughout his life. One of the most curious alterations occurred in his revision of *Paracelsus*. In 1835, lines 649–650 of Part Two read:

Who in his own person acts his own creations.
Had you but told me this at first! . . . Hush! hush!

In 1849, Browning expanded this passage to include a statement of belief in the Christian doctrine of Incarnation which radically altered the meaning of the original:

Who in creation acts his own conceptions.
Shall man refuse to be aught less than God?
Man's weakness is his glory—for the strength
Which raises him near to heaven and near God's self,
Came spite of it: God's strength his glory is,
For thence came with our weakness sympathy
Which brought God down to earth, a man like us.
Had you but told me this at first! . . . Hush! hush!

In 1863, Browning restored the original reading, changing only capitalization and punctuation.

The inspiration to place Pompilia's rescue on St. George's Day came after the first draft of *The Ring and the Book* was written and is recorded as a revision on the manuscript that went to the printer. Other significant changes in the text of this work suggest that the process of creation continued long after the first edition was published. For the second edition of 1872 he added seventeen new lines and made hundreds of changes in both wording and punctuation, many of which went far beyond the scope of mere editing. For the final editions in 1888 and again in 1889 he made still other changes.

It appears to us, therefore, that in exercising his authorial-editorial functions the author's basis for his activity is continually changing, and may continue to change throughout his life. His grasp of both the coherence of his work and of the conventions may improve or deteriorate; he may come to feel that the conventions are either more or less binding on him. Author, then, as we use the term, refers not to a stable entity but to an unstable and continuously innovating continuum.

We recognize, of course, that individuals other than the author exercise, directly or indirectly, an editorial function. Sometimes, more common in the past than now, their intervention was direct and decisive. In the history of printing, the compositor, the printer, and the copyreader have been responsible for variants, and insofar as such variants reflect a grasp of the coherence of the work and of current conventions, they cannot be classified as errors. Nevertheless, they do not have authorial authority and in practice must be distinguished from those known to derive from the author himself. An error, in contrast, is a variant which self-evidently damages the coherence of the text and departs from the conventions, as the textual critic himself understands both factors as they were at work in the historical situation from which the work emerged. The history of printing has moved in the direction of trying to limit printers' errors, to train compositors to set only what is before them, and to restrict the copyreader to the detection of errors by requiring him to refer questionable variants to the editor or author. Both errors and arbitrary changes, originating other than with the author, cannot be regarded as legitimate parts of the text.

There is also the matter of house styling which may induce changes for which the author is not responsible, or only nominally so. The extent to which house styling is reflected in Browning's poetry will be discussed later. Still another kind of editorial assistance is that of the professional copyreader or the friend who reads the manuscript and suggests changes in it. To what extent do changes so made have authority? The question is a delicate one, almost incapable of irrefutable answer. If the author has no opportunity to reject or if he accepts the changes perfunctorily their status is dubious. If, however, the evidence indicates clearly that he was free to accept or reject them and does one or the other after careful deliberation, the decision must be regarded as his own.

At this point we may summarize. All changes in the text which are not obvious errors and for which the author himself is responsible are to be considered authoritative and accepted as legitimate parts of an authoritative text. This eliminates arbitrary changes by anyone other than the author, but includes those which might have originated with someone other than the author but deliberately accepted by him. This principle provides the basis both for the selection of the copy-text and for the recording of variants.

We question the theory that automatically regards all spelling and punctuation as accidentals, that is, as matters affecting the formal presentation of a text but not its meaning. To be genuinely accidental a variant must be one that in *no way* alters the meaning of the text. On the other hand, anything—word, syntax, punctuation, typography, for example—that might affect the meaning must be considered substantive. Likewise anything which affects the phonic character of the line must be regarded as substantive.

Spelling can delay the recognition of a semantic function, but if the current standards of spelling can be unequivocably substituted, then it is truly accidental, and so with word divisions and the like. Spelling may, however, alter the meaning of a poem by distorting the intended rhythm or sound pattern of a line, and in such a case, modernization would be a violation of the author's intention. No simple application of a theory which regards spelling automatically as an accidental is acceptable to a sensitive editor of poetic texts.

Punctuation is still a different matter, however. Whatever its meaning may be—and this is a matter very little understood—everyone feels that it is meaningful. Punctuation, under which we include paragraphing, does not merely affect the meaning but is part of the meaning. One reason is that punctuation is at least in part an attempt to record the character of junctures in the spoken language. Since Browning's mature poetic style is far closer to the spoken language than is normal expository prose and much other poetry, punctuation and all variants in punctuation in his works are of particular interest. It would seem to us irresponsible to ignore them.

Thus the study of a series of editorial decisions in a passage involving only punctuational variants can, and surely must, have both an interesting and important effect upon the interpretation of the passage. It seems to us, therefore, that particularly in the works of a nineteenth- or twentieth-century poet, punctuation variants must be considered a part of meaning and so recorded. Browning was especially sensitive to the rhetorical function of punctuation; and, many of the changes in punctuation which he made in his various editions reflect his concern to heighten or clarify meaning. A dramatic example is the way in which he replaced the indeterminate dash—so frequently used in the earlier drafts and early editions of his work—by other more precise marks of punctuation. Whatever else may be said about the signification of the dash, it is clear that its use suggests between the elements thus marked off and the rest of the sentence a looser relationship than that achieved by other marks of punctuation. It also signals a more radical break in the rhythmic pattern of the line than that suggested by commas, for example. In the 1833 edition of *Pauline,* there are 292 dashes. In the heavily revised edition of 1868 these have been reduced to 77. In the manuscript of *The Ring and the Book* there are considerably more dashes than there are in the first and subsequent editions. The number in Book I are reduced from 146 to 127 in the final edition; those in Book VIII, from 447 to 218. In almost every case the dash is replaced by some other mark of punctuation. The following examples, all taken from *Pauline,* but characteristic of Browning's practice elsewhere, illustrate how this revision in punctuation substantially alters the relation between the involved elements and certainly results in a very different rhythmic pattern and, most likely, in a different meaning.

700| *1833*: I am prepared—I have made life my own—
1868: I am prepared: I have made life my own.
703| *1833*: Thro' all conjuncture—I have lived all life
When it is most alive—when strangest fate
1868: Thro' all conjuncture, I have lived all life
When it is most alive, where strangest fate
740| *1833*: No—we will pass to morning—
Morning—the rocks and valleys and old woods.
1868: No, we will pass to morning—
Morning, the rocks and valleys and old woods.
788| *1833*: Air, air—fresh life-blood—thin and searching air—
1868: Air, air, fresh life-blood, thin and searching air,

The only serious question that remains, as we see it, is whether or not Browning was indeed responsible for the changes in punctuation that occur in the various stages of his work. Once that fact is established, we have no choice but to include them as substantive readings.

III THE BASIC MATERIALS

Aside from a handful of uncollected poems, all short, everything but *Asolando* went through two or more editions during Browning's lifetime. Except for *Pauline, Strafford,* and *Sordello,* everything published before 1849 was republished in newly edited form in the 1849 collection. *Strafford* and *Sordello* were newly edited for the collection of

1863, as were all other works in that edition. The 1868 collection added a newly revised *Pauline* and *Dramatis Personae* to the other works, which were themselves revised. The 1888–89a collection in sixteen volumes included everything so far published in volumes (certain poems published only in periodicals were not included; *Asolando* was added as Volume XVII after Browning's death). The printing of this edition was completed in July, 1889, and the exhaustion of some of the early volumes led Browning to correct the first ten volumes before he left for Italy in late August. The second edition of this sixteen volume collection is dated 1889 on the title pages; the first eight volumes of the first edition are dated 1888, the rest, 1889. We have designated Volumes IX to XVI of the first edition 1889a.

We have designated the existing manuscripts and editions either as primary or secondary materials. The primary materials include:

1. The manuscript of each volume (when such exists; see table at the end of preface);

2. The proof sheets (when such exist);

3. The original edition of each volume (and subsequent separate editions when such exist);

4. The collected editions over which Browning exercised editorial control:

1849—*Poems by Robert Browning.* Two Volumes. London: Chapman and Hall.

1863—*The Poetical Works.* Three Volumes. London: Chapman and Hall.

1868—*The Poetical Works.* Six Volumes. London: Smith, Elder and Company.

1888—*The Poetical Works.* Volumes 1–8. London: Smith, Elder and Company.

1889a—*The Poetical Works.* Volumes 9–16. London: Smith, Elder and Company.

1889—*The Poetical Works.* Volumes 1–16. London: Smith, Elder and Company.

(Vols. 1–10, a revision of 1888–1889a; Vols. 11–16, a reprint of 1889a.)

All other relevant materials now known to exist or which may be discovered while this edition is being prepared will be called secondary. Examples of such materials are: the copy of the first edition of *Pauline* which contains annotations by Browning and John Stuart Mill; the copies of the first edition of *Paracelsus* which contain corrections in Browning's hand; Elizabeth Barrett's suggestions for the revision of *A Soul's Tragedy* and certain poems in *Dramatic Romances and Lyrics* (1845); and the edition of *Strafford* by Miss Emily Hickey for which Browning made suggestions.

IV AUTHORIAL CONTROL

Given these diverse materials, we must first determine the nature of the decisions for the variants in order to establish the extent to which each may be given authorial authority. Any variant clearly an error we have corrected. This includes all obvious misprints, particularly dropped end line punctuation, and also inadvertent errors in paragraphing which are revealed when the printed versions of a text are compared with the manuscript. When, for example, a paragraph, indicated in the manuscript, comes between two lines the first of which falls in the first edition at the bottom of the page but in subsequent editions within the page of text, the paragraph may very well not be indicated in the latter. In such cases, we have restored what was unquestionably the author's intention, even though he himself failed to detect the error in proof.

Matters of spelling and typography present no real problems. Discrepancies between Browning's spelling and modern practices are few indeed and require no emendation. There are some discrepancies in the use of two possible spellings for the same word. For example, in the manuscript of *The Ring and the Book* Browning uses both *honour* and *honor*. In the first and subsequent editions, however, the form *honour* is used consistently. Whether Browning himself decided in proof to regularize his spelling or whether consistency was imposed upon him by the publisher we cannot say. In either case, however, the matter is immaterial since it in no way alters the meaning of Browning's statement. Similarly, the plural of *folk* in the manuscript and in the first and second edition of *The Ring and the Book* is *folks*. In the 1888 edition it has been changed to *folk*. That Browning himself was responsible for this change is suggested by the fact that one such example not corrected (*In a Balcony*, l. 184) in the 1888 edition is changed in Browning's hand for the 1889 reprinting. With such words we have accepted the form used in the 1888–1889 edition and recorded all variants therefrom because, in such instances, the phonic character of the line is changed. Materials of this sort are valuable not only to readers of Browning's poetry but also to students of language, particularly of orthography.

Typography is less a problem than it might be with poets whose meaning depends partly on the appearance of their poetry on the page. The issue, however, is not entirely irrelevant. The manner of printing the long lines of *La Saisiaz*, whether on one- or two-line spaces, for example, might control to some degree the reader's response to them. Nowhere, however, does Browning indicate that he wished to use typography to control meaning, and the inference is that whatever changes occur from edition to edition are the responsibility of the printer. We have made no effort to record them.

Changes in typography along with a number of others may reasonably be considered matters of house styling. A number of variants occur in the plays in the presentation of characters, place location, stage directions, and character designations all of which we record except: (1) accidentals for stage directions which involve only change in manner of statement such as *Enter Hampden* instead of *Hampden enters* (such accidentals are standardized to the 1889 text when they are used as drop words); (2) accidentals for stage directions such as *Aside* instead of *aside,* [*Aside.*] instead of [*Aside*], [STRAFFORD.] instead of [STRAFFORD]; (3) accidentals for character designations such as *Lady Carlisle* instead of *Car* or *Carlisle.*

During most of Browning's career, a space was left in the contraction of two words; thus "it's" was printed "it 's." These we have closed up in accordance with modern practices. Another matter almost certainly the result of house styling is the manner of indicating quotations. In the first edition of *Christmas Eve and Easter Day,* for example, and in the collected edition of 1863, each line of a quotation is preceded by a quotation mark. In contrast, in *Sordello* in both the first edition and in the collected edition of 1863, quotation marks are placed only at the beginning and end of a quotation. The first edition of *Sordello,* published by Edward Moxon, and that of *Christmas Eve and Easter Day,* published by Chapman and Hall, were both printed by Bradbury and Evans. It would seem in this case at least that the compositors printed the material they were given without attempting to make it conform to house styling. One might assume that the different publishers imposed their own practices upon the manuscript before submitting it to the printer. The 1863 collected edition, where these differences are maintained, serves only to confuse the issue, however. This edition also was published by Chapman and Hall, but printed by John Edward Taylor. Clearly here neither publisher nor printer bothered to follow a consistent practice. Browning too, presumably having read the proof, was content to let the inconsistencies stand. It was not until 1868 when Smith, Elder and Company both printed and published the new collected edition that a fairly consistent policy of indicating quotations was adopted for Browning's work. In general after the appearance of this edition, quotations are indicated by a quotation mark both at the beginning and end of the quotation and at the beginning of each new line within the quotation. Smith, Elder and Company printed the four titles following the 1868 collected edition. After those, the remaining were printed by Spottiswoode and Company. It would seem, therefore, that Browning's new and last publisher imposed house styling upon the poet in the manner of indicating quotations. The matter is not entirely clear, however, since some inconsistencies remain even in the last collected edition. The weight of the evidence, nevertheless, is that Browning deferred to his publisher on this matter. We regard the quotation marks, therefore, as genuine accidentals and in our text follow the modern practice—also that of Browning in many cases—of indicating a quotation with marks only at the beginning and the end.

The manuscript of *The Ring and the Book* throws considerable light upon not only this subject but related ones, all of which can best be discussed together. *The Ring and the Book* was printed and published by Smith, Elder and Company. The manuscript, in two bound volumes, is now in the British Museum. The first volume contains the material published in 1868; the second, that published in 1869. The first volume contains relatively few corrections, although those which do appear are undoubtedly in Browning's hand. Between the manuscript and the first edition, however, there are extensive differences, both in wording and punctuation. Clearly Browning or someone made extensive corrections, perhaps in the proofs. Unfortunately those proofs, as far as can now be determined, no longer exist. The second volume, in contrast, is very heavily corrected in Browning's hand, and the differences between the corrected manuscript and the first edition are considerably fewer. The second volume presumably received the revision that was made in the first volume only after the proofs had been printed. The corrected manuscript of the second volume is consistent with the printed first edition of volume one. The changes in both the first edition of books one through six and of volume two of the manuscript suggest that Browning himself made them in order to be more precise and expressive in his choice of words, to reflect more sensitively the nature of the juncture between rhetorical units, or better to utilize phonic and rhythmic patterns as part of his meaning. It appears that Browning wrote hurriedly, giving primary attention to wording and less to punctuation, being satisfied, as I have already suggested, to use a dash to indicate almost any break in thought or rhythm. Later, either in proof (the first six books) or on the manuscript itself (the last six books) he changed the dashes to other, more expressive marks of punctuation. The punctuation of the printed first six books and that of the manuscript of the last six books is consistent; both are consistent with Browning's practices elsewhere. The punctuational changes in *The Ring and the Book* we must conclude are those of Browning's own choice and not of house-styling.

In the matter of indicating quotations, however, the evidence, as we have already suggested, is that Browning accepted house styling. In the manuscript for the first six books, quotations begin and end with a quotation mark. In the first edition, however, quotation marks also precede each line of a quotation. In the last six books the latter practice is followed both in the manuscript and in the first edition. The inference is that Browning prepared his manuscript following one procedure and then changed it, perhaps in response to his new publisher's policies established in the 1868 edition of his collected poetry, in proof for the first six books and in the manuscript for the last six books.

Having eliminated obvious errors and having decided not to record variants clearly arising from house styling, we arrive finally at those variants, both word and punctuation, which are substantive, and which if they are Browning's, should be recognized as authoritative and recorded. Let us begin where the evidence is clear and irrefutable. Browning had complete control over the text for the 1888–1889 edition of his works. Professor Michael Hancher, editor of the correspondence between Browning and his publisher George Smith, has published an enlightening article in which he summarizes the relevant information contained in these letters. He concludes: "The evidence is clear that Browning undertook the 1888–1889 edition of his *Poetical Works* intent on controlling even the smallest minutiae of the text. Though he at one time considered supplying biographical and explanatory notes to the poems, he finally decided against such a scheme, concluding in his letter to Smith of 12 November 1887, 'I am correcting them carefully, and *that* must suffice.' " On January 13, 1888, he wrote, regarding the six-volume edition of his collected works published in 1868 which was to serve as the printer's copy for the final edition: "I have thoroughly corrected the six volumes of the Works, and can let you have them at once." Hancher continues: "Browning evidently kept a sharp eye on the production of all sixteen of the volumes, including those later volumes. . . . Browning returned proof for Volume 3 on 6 May 1888, commenting, 'I have had, as usual, to congratulate myself on the scrupulous accuracy of the Printers'; on 31 December he returned proofs of Volume II, 'corrected carefully'; and he returned 'the corrected Proofs of Vol. XV' on 1 May 1889." (All quotations are from Michael Hancher's "Browning and the Poetical Works of 1888–1889." *Browning Newsletter*, (Spring 1971):25–27.

These letters certainly establish Browning's intent to control the text of the final edition of his work. There is concrete evidence that what he intended he achieved. By spring of 1889, it was evident that a new printing would be required. Browning informed James Dykes Campbell that he was making corrections which the publisher would incorporate in the new printing. Browning offered to transcribe the corrections into Campbell's own set. The copies of the volumes corrected in Browning's hand are now in the British Museum and contain on the fly leaf of volume one a note by Campbell which explains precisely what happened. Browning proposed to correct the entire edition before reprinting. Before he left for Italy on August 29, 1889, he had completed his corrections for the first ten volumes. His death in Venice a few months later prevented him from finishing the task as far as we presently know. When the new printing appeared in 1889 the first ten volumes incorporated Browning's emendations. Campbell says that the corrections numbered "upwards of 250" (there are 247). It should be recognized, of course, that this marked copy was not the one used by the printer and that even Browning in transferring the changes from one text to another might have erred. Nevertheless, these changes are indisputably Browning's and are those which, according to his own statement, he proposed to make in the new edition. They are, therefore, unquestionably authoritative. To what extent, we then ask, were these authorial requests recognized, and were there changes in the 1889 text which suggest that anyone other than Browning altered the text?

The evidence is overwhelming that Browning's proposed changes were made as he directed. Two hundred thirty-two of them appear precisely as they are marked in the Campbell text. Of the twelve which are omitted all except two are end of line punctuation marks and appear, since Browning's changes are obviously corrections in the 1888 edition required by the meaning of the line, to be simple printers' errors. The two exceptions are failures to change *Utopia* to *Eutopia* and *they* to *then*. The latter is certainly an error since the meaning of the text requires the change.

There are three examples in which the printers made changes other than those designated by Browning:

King Victor and King Charles, Second Year, Part I, l. 31:
1888: give pretext
B's Correction: give a pretext
1889: give the pretext
Pauline, l. 332:
1888: caves
B's Correction: caves,
1889: caves:
The Ring and the Book, IX, l. 1492:
1888: afterward
B's Correction: afterward.
1889: afterward!

There is no certain way to account for these discrepancies. Browning himself might have made an error in transcribing the changes in Campbell's copy or the printers might unconsciously have made substitutions. There is nothing, however, to suggest that the changes were made deliberately by someone who wished to alter the meaning of the text. They remain isolated examples more logically accounted for as errors than as anything else. It seems conclusive, both from Browning's stated intention and his practice, that for this final edition Browning and Browning alone was responsible.

The strong probability exists that by at least 1863 Browning had principle control over the editorial function. Writing to Chapman in the 1850s he shows concern for punctuation ("I attach importance to the mere stops . . ."). Hancher cites evidence of Browning's close supervision of the 1868 edition of his collected works. Mrs. Orr reports his resentment of those who garbled his text by misplacing his stops (*Life*, 357–358). She continues that his punctuation "was always made with the fullest sense of its significance to any but the baldest style, and of its special importance to his own (*Life*, 360)." We note also that she says he sent proof sheets to his French friend Joseph Milsand for correction (*Life*, 265). There is no evidence, however, that in seeking such help, Browning relinquished his own final editorial function.

That he was solely responsible from the beginning for all changes of words and lines seems obvious. In 1847 Elizabeth Barrett made suggestions for numerous changes in *A Soul's Tragedy* and some of the poems which compose *Dramatic Romances and Lyrics* (for a full list see *New Poems by Robert Browning and Elizabeth Barrett Browning*, ed. Sir Frederick G. Kenyon [New York, 1915], pp. 140–76). Some of these Browning accepted and others he rejected. Obviously he did not defer automatically even to her, although he professes great confidence in her literary judgment. Those which he accepted after deliberation, we regard as his own. Careful examination of the manuscripts and the first editions reveal no information to suggest that anyone other than Browning tampered with his wording between submission of the manuscript and the appearance of the first edition. Such changes as do occur are consistent with what we know of Browning's practices and suggest that in every case he himself made the change. In the case of *Paracelsus* and *The Ring and the Book*, if these two sizable manuscripts may be regarded as representative, there is every reason to indicate that such changes as appear in the first edition were those which Browning himself made.

The history of the *Paracelsus* text is of the highest interest and importance. The manuscript of that poem exhibits either an ignorance of punctuation conventions or a refusal to consider them very seriously. For whatever reason, Browning exhibits in this manuscript a wide latitude of innovation even from a variety of conflicting current punctuational conventions. The manuscript shows, however, house styling, or the exercise of the editorial function by someone other than Browning for one leaf in Act I and all but the first and last pages of Act III. Several other pages show editorial changes in punctuation which may be Browning's. What precisely happened to the styling of some of the manuscript before it was finally printed is uncertain. Either a new manuscript was prepared, or proof was set up from the manuscript as it stood after partial editing and was then thoroughly revised. The manuscript shows signs of heavy use, indications for the signatures (corrected for one signature), and what are compositors' names. The second possibility, then, seems the more likely. The results are significant. First, although the printed punctuation of the edited portions of the manuscript does not correspond with that editing, it is in the same style as that editing. Second, the printed punctuation of the unedited portions is in the same style as the printed versions of the edited portions, and thus of the editing in the manuscript. Third, subsequent published works for which no manuscript exists are in the same style as the printed 1835 *Paracelsus.*

The next available manuscript of major significance, that for *Christmas Eve and Easter Day*, prepared for the printer by Elizabeth and Robert, shows virtually no variation from the first edition of 1850. All evidence indicates that from 1835 onward Browning was responsible for variants to be found in the several editions of his work over which he had nominal supervision except those listed above as excluded.

V CHOICE OF TEXT

One cannot reasonably say that the 1889 text or any single one of the others best represents the "real" Robert Browning. There is no way of establishing objectively the greater accuracy or the greater artistic merit of any one of these various texts. We prefer the 1889 edition (amended to conform to the Campbell text and corrected for obvious error) because, in addition to being indisputably authoritative it has other recommendable characteristics. Although we cannot say that it represents the final intentions of *an* author, conceived as a static entity, it does represent the final decisions of Robert Browning who remained to the end of his life an author capable of continual change. Moreover, by 1889, Browning was the most experienced editor of his own poetic discourse. It seems to us, therefore, that the 1889 edition of his work provides the most satisfactory basic text because the possibility is that in 1889 he had a better grasp of the coherence of individual works and of the poetic convention, including the conventions of punctuation, than anyone else.

We propose, therefore, to print the 1889 text (amended to conform with the Campbell text) for the first ten volumes; the 1888 text for the second six volumes; the 1889 edition of *Aslando*, all corrected to eliminate both errors and the consequences of house styling. The only alterations which we have made in the arrangement of the copy-text is to rearrange the materials so that they appear in the order of their first publication. This involves restoring to their original order the poems included in *Dramatic Lyrics, Dramatic Romances and Lyrics*, and *Men and Women.*

By presenting this text accompanied by the variant readings from manuscripts and subsequent editions, we provide the reader not only an acceptable text but the materials necessary to reconstruct any portion of

Browning's work as it developed over the years. This enables him both to study the work in its variant forms and the poetic process by which it came into existence.

VI PRESENTATION OF VARIANTS

The presentation of variants is not entirely conventional. Indeed, there is no one way to offer variants. We feel justified, therefore, in having developed a method consistent with the principles of good textual practice and appropriate to the particular requirements of our present task. We believe that it has the advantage of presenting the history of the variants in the order in which they appeared, from the first form through the final one, and in a way in which the full text of each line of each edition is most accurately and readily reconstructed.

In presenting the variants from the 1889 text we print at the bottom of the page variants found in the manuscripts, when available, and in the first and subsequent editions—that is, variants found in the primary materials. It seems to us that we can give a clearer, more concise notion of Browning's editorial function if we separate primary materials from secondary materials as these are defined in item III. Moreover, we must assume that additional manuscripts may become available between now and the time the last volume of this edition is published, making a supplemental volume of variants necessary. We have decided, therefore, that it would be logical to place all variants derived from secondary materials together in a final volume. This final volume will also include *Thomas Wentworth, Earl of Strafford* by John Forster, to which Browning's contribution was apparently considerable but is so far indeterminable.

TABLE OF SIGNS

All signs used by Browning himself have been avoided. The symbols essential to an understanding of the variant notes are set out in the following table of signs:

§ . . . §	Editor's note
<>	Words omitted
/	Line break
//,///, . . .	Line break plus one or more lines without internal variants

All variants are placed at the bottom of the page of text to which they refer. A variant is generally preceded and followed by a pickup and a drop word (example *a*). No note terminates with a punctuation mark unless the punctuation mark comes at the end of a line. If a variant drops or adds a punctuation mark, the next word is added (example *b*).

If the normal pickup word has appeared previously in the same line, the note begins with the word preceding it. If the normal drop word appears subsequently in the line, the next word is added (example *c*). If a single capitalized pickup word occurs within the line, it is accompanied by the preceding word. No pickup word, however, is used for any variant consisting of an internal change, for example, a hyphen in a compounded word, an apostrophe, a tense change, or a spelling change. Nor is a drop word used when the variant comes at the end of a line (example *e*). Illustrations from *Sordello*:

a 611| *1840:* but that appeared *1863:* but this appeared
b 1) at end of line:
109| *1840:* it, "taken <> intrigue:" *1863:* it, taken <> intrigue.
2) 82| *1840:* forests like *1863:* forests, like
c 183| *1840:* after clue and *1863:* after clue, and
77| *1840:* Who managed <> that night by
1863: She managed <> that, night by night, *1888:* by night
d 1) a single capitalized pickup word:
61| *1840:* Now—nor, this *1863:* Now—not this
2) a single capitalized pickup word within line:
295| *1840:* at Padua to repulse the
1863: at Padua who repulsed the
e 1) 285| *1840:* shall *1863:* should
2) at end of line:
86| *1840:* sky: *1863:* sky.

Each recorded variant will be assumed to be incorporated in the next edition if there is no indication otherwise.

All character designations which appear in variant entries will conform to the 1889 text as it appears in this edition. In typing variants in the plays, we ignore character designations unless the designation comes within a numbered line, in which case we treat it as any other word. In such cases, therefore, it is used as pickup or drop word. When it is used as a pickup word, however, the general rule regarding pickup words which begin with a capital letter does not apply.

VII ANNOTATIONS

Browning scholarship is not yet fully mature. The notes we have presented, therefore, are not intended to be exhaustive or final. The format of the edition has been planned to allow for revision of the notes without disturbing the text. If the text proves satisfactory, it can be reprinted indefinitely with new sets of notes.

As a general principle, we have annotated proper names, phrases that function as proper names, and words or groups of words the full meaning of which requires factual, historical, or literary background.

Thus, we have attempted to hold interpretation to a minimum, although we realize that the act of selection itself is to some extent interpretative.

Specifically, we have annotated the following: (1) proper names; (2) geographical locations; (3) allusions to Biblical and other literature; (4) words not included in *Webster's Collegiate Dictionary*, Seventh Edition (since some limits must be imposed upon our work and because this dictionary is generally accepted and readily available. We annotate words used by Browning in a sense other than that given in this dictionary. For a more accurate understanding we have relied heavily upon Samuel Johnson's dictionary); and (5) other items requiring factual information which is not of current common knowledge or easily available. All passages in a language other than English are translated into English. Occasional quotations from Browning's sources are included when such source quotations seem especially pertinent and are of difficult access.

For notes, particularly on historical figures and events, we have tended to prefer fullness and even to risk the tangential and unessential. As a result, some of the information provided may be perhaps unnecessary for the mature scholar. On the other hand, it is impossible to assume that all who use this edition—the ordinary reader and the undergraduate and graduate student, for example—will be fully equipped to assimilate unaided all of Browning's copious literary, historical, and mythological allusions. Thus we have directed our efforts toward an audience conceived as a continuum from the relatively uninformed to the trained.

TABLE OF ABBREVIATIONS AND SHORT TITLES USED IN ANNOTATIONS

B	Browning
DeVane, *Hdk.*	William C. DeVane. *A Browning Handbook.* New York: Appleton-Century-Croft, 1955.
Griffin and Minchin	W. H. Griffin and H. C. Minchin. *The Life of Robert Browning.* New York: Macmillan, 1910.
Hood, *Ltrs.*	Thurman L. Hood, ed. *Letters of Robert Browning Collected by T. J. Wise.* New Haven: Yale University Press, 1933.
Orr, *Hkb.*	Mrs. Sutherland Orr. *Handbook to the Works of Robert Browning.* New Edition. Revised and in part Part Rewritten by Fredric G. Kenyon. Boston and New York: Houghton Mifflin Company, 1891.
P-C	Charlotte Porter and Helen A. Clarke, eds. *The Complete Works of Robert Browning.* 12 vols. Issued first in 1898 and reissued frequently. It appeared in 1910 as the De Luxe Edition and in 1912 as the Pocket Edition. New York: Crowell and Company.

VIII TABLE OF MANUSCRIPTS

The following manuscripts are known to exist in the locations indicated:

Paracelsus
Forster and Dyce Collection,
Victoria and Albert Museum, Kensington

Christmas-Eve and Easter-Day
Forster and Dyce Collection,
Victoria and Albert Museum, Kensington

Dramatis Personae
Pierpont Morgan Library, New York

The Ring and the Book
British Museum

Balaustion's Adventure
Balliol College Library, Oxford

Prince Hohenstiel-Schwangau
Balliol College Library, Oxford

Fifine at the Fair
Balliol College Library, Oxford

Red Cotton Night-Cap Country
Balliol College Library, Oxford

Aristophanes' Apology
Balliol College Library, Oxford

The Inn Album
Balliol College Library, Oxford

Of Pacchiarotto and How He Worked in Distemper
Balliol College Library, Oxford

The Agamemnon of Aeschylus
Balliol College Library, Oxford

La Saisaiz and The Two Poets of Croisic
Balliol College Library, Oxford

Dramatic Idyls First Series
Balliol College Library, Oxford

Dramatic Idyls Second Series
Balliol College Library, Oxford

Jocoseria
Balliol College Library, Oxford

Ferishtah's Fancies
Balliol College Library, Oxford

Parleyings With Certain People of Importance in Their Day
Balliol College Library, Oxford
Asolando
Pierpont Morgan Library, New York
Each manuscript is fully described in this edition in the section given to annotations on the corresponding text.

The following manuscripts are not known to be extant:

Pauline
Strafford
Sordello
Pippa Passes
King Victor and King Charles
"The Essay on Chatterton"
Dramatic Lyrics
The Return of the Druses
A Blot in the 'Scutcheon
Colombe's Birthday
Dramatic Romances and Lyrics
Luria
A Soul's Tragedy
"The Essay on Shelley"
Men and Women

We should like to request that anyone with information about any of the manuscripts which are presently unknown to the scholarly world communicate with the Director of the Ohio University Press, Athens, Ohio.

IX REQUEST FOR CORRECTIONS

We have tried to make this edition free from error, but we know that the history of printing proves that such an ambition is impossible of fulfillment. We urgently request that whoever discovers errors will report them to the Ohio University Press, Athens, Ohio, where a file of such errors will be kept so that any future printings can take advantage of such reports.

X ACKNOWLEDGMENTS

We express our appreciation especially to the following: the Ohio University Press, the Ohio University Library, and the Ohio University English Department for providing money and services which have made it possible for us to assemble the vast materials required for preparation of this edition; The Armstrong Browning Library, Baylor University, Waco, Texas, and its director Professor Jack Herring for various favors.

We have also received valuable assistance in securing and preparing materials to appear in later volumes from the British Museum; Balliol College Library, Oxford, and its librarian Mr. E. V. Quinn; Mr. Philip Kelley, New York; and Mr. John Murray, London.

We are indebted to Wellesley College Library, Wellesley College, and to the research librarian Miss Hannah D. French, for our frontispiece. This portrait of Robert Browning, painted at Rome by William Fisher in 1854, was presented to the English Poetry Collection, Wellesley College Library, by George Herbert Palmer, June 8, 1915 (see Sotheby, Wilkingson and Hodge, Catalogue of Pictures, Drawings and Engravings, Autograph Letters and Manuscripts, Books, and Works of Art, The Property of R. W. Barrett Browning, Esq. (deceased), 1913, no. 60).

The Editors
Athens, Ohio

TABLE OF EDITIONS REFERRED TO IN VOLUME III

1841 *Bells and Pomegranates,* No. I. *Pippa Passes.*
London: Edward Moxon.

1842 *Bells and Pomegranates,* No. II. *King Victor and King Charles.*
London: Edward Moxon.

1842 *Bells and Pomegranates,* No. III. *Dramatic Lyrics.*
London: Edward Moxon.

1843 *Bells and Pomegranates,* No. IV. *The Return of the Druses.*
London: Edward Moxon.

1849 *Poems*
Two Volumes. London: Chapman and Hall.

1863 *The Poetical Works.*
Three Volumes. London: Chapman and Hall.

1868 *The Poetical Works.*
Six Volumes. London: Smith, Elder, and Company.

1888 *The Poetical Works.*
Volumes 1–8. London: Smith, Elder, and Company.

1889a *The Poetical Works.*
Volumes 9–16. London: Smith, Elder, and Company.

1889 *The Poetical Works.*
Sixteen Volumes. London: Smith, Elder, and Company.

A description of each of these may be found in Section A, pp. 1–60 of *Robert Browning: A Bibliography, 1830–1950.* Compiled by Leslie Nathan Broughton, Clark Sutherland Northrup, and Robert Pearsall (Ithaca: Cornell University Press, 1953). A complete descriptive bibliography of all of Browning's works will appear in Volume XIII of the Ohio edition.

PIPPA PASSES

Edited by Morse Peckham

KING VICTOR AND KING CHARLES

Edited by Park Honan

ESSAY ON CHATTERTON

Edited by Donald Smalley

DRAMATIC LYRICS

Edited by John Hulsman

THE RETURN OF THE DRUSES

Edited by Morse Peckham

ADVERTISEMENT

Two or three years ago I wrote a Play, about which the chief matter I much care to recollect at present is, that a Pit-full of goodnatured people applauded it:—ever since, I have been desirous of doing something in the same way that should better reward their attention. What follows I mean for the first of a series of Dramatical Pieces, to come out at intervals, and I amuse myself by fancying that the cheap mode in which they appear will for once help me to a sort of Pit-audience again. Of course such a work must go on no longer than it is liked; and to provide against a certain and but too possible contingency, let me hasten to say now—what, if I were sure of success, I would try to say circumstantially enough at the close—that I dedicate my best intentions most admiringly to the Author of "Ion"—most affectionately to Serjeant Talfourd.

ROBERT BROWNING.

ADVERTISEMENT.: § in 1841 only §

I DEDICATE MY BEST INTENTIONS, IN THIS POEM,

ADMIRINGLY TO THE AUTHOR OF 'ION,'

AFFECTIONATELY TO MR. SERGEANT TALFOURD.

R. B.

LONDON: 1841.

1849: § adds dedication; no place or date § this Poem, most admiringly <> of "Ion,"—most affectionately to Mr. Serjeant Talfourd. R. B. *1863:* poem, admiringly <> of "Ion,"—affectionately <> Talfourd. London, 1841. R. B. *1868:* of "Ion," affectionately *1888:* Sergeant <> London: 1841. R. B.

PERSONS.

PIPPA.

OTTIMA.

SEBALD.

Foreign Students.

GOTTLIEB.

SCHRAMM.

JULES.

PHENE.

Austrian Police.

BLUPHOCKS.

LUIGI *and his* Mother.

Poor Girls.

MONSIGNOR *and his Attendants.*

PERSONS <> *Attendants.*: § added 1888 §

PIPPA PASSES

1841

INTRODUCTION

NEW YEAR'S DAY AT ASOLO IN THE TREVISAN

SCENE—*A large mean airy chamber. A girl,* PIPPA, *from the Silk-mills, springing out of bed.*

Day!
Faster and more fast,
O'er night's brim, day boils at last:
Boils, pure gold, o'er the cloud-cup's brim
Where spurting and suppressed it lay,
For not a froth-flake touched the rim
Of yonder gap in the solid gray
Of the eastern cloud, an hour away;
But forth one wavelet, then another, curled,
Till the whole sunrise, not to be suppressed,
Rose, reddened, and its seething breast
Flickered in bounds, grew gold, then overflowed the world.

Oh, Day, if I squander a wavelet of thee,
A mite of my twelve hours' treasure,
The least of thy gazes or glances,

---

§ Ed. 1841, MS (see Annotations), 1849, 1863, 1868, 1888, 1889. § Part-title and stage directions / *1841: New <> Trevisan. A large, mean, airy* *MS:* bed— *1849: the Trevisan.—A <> bed.* *1863:* THE TREVISAN. *A* *1868: large mean airy* *1888:* INTRODUCTION. / NEW <> TREVISAN. / SCENE.—*A* 2| *1841:* fast *MS:* fast, 3| *1841:* brim day <> last *MS:* brim, day *1888:* last: 5| *1841:* suppress it lay— *1868:* suppressed it lay; *1888:* lay, 8| *1841:* Of eastern cloud an <> away— *MS:* Of the eastern cloud, an <> away; 9| *1841:* wavelet then another curled, *MS:* wavelet, then another, curled, 10| *1841:* suppress, *1868:* suppressed, 11| *1841:* Rose-reddened *MS:* Rose, reddened 12–13| *1841:* § no space § *1849:* § space § 13| *1841:* Day, if I waste a *MS:* Oh, Day, if I squander a 14| *1841:* Aught of my twelve-hours' treasure— *MS:* A mite of my twelve-hours treasure, *1849:* twelve-hours' 15| *1841:* One of thy gazes, one of thy

(Be they grants thou art bound to or gifts above measure)
One of thy choices or one of thy chances,
(Be they tasks God imposed thee or freaks at thy pleasure)
—My Day, if I squander such labour or leisure,
Then shame fall on Asolo, mischief on me!

Thy long blue solemn hours serenely flowing,
Whence earth, we feel, gets steady help and good—
Thy fitful sunshine-minutes, coming, going,
As if earth turned from work in gamesome mood—
All shall be mine! But thou must treat me not
As prosperous ones are treated, those who live
At hand here, and enjoy the higher lot,
In readiness to take what thou wilt give,
And free to let alone what thou refusest;
For, Day, my holiday, if thou ill-usest
Me, who am only Pippa,—old-year's sorrow,
Cast off last night, will come again to-morrow:
Whereas, if thou prove gentle, I shall borrow
Sufficient strength of thee for new-year's sorrow.
All other men and women that this earth

---

glances, *MS:* The least of thy gazes or glances, 16| *1841:* (Grants <> to, gifts above measure,) *MS:* (Be they grants <> to, or gifts <> measure) *1863:* measure *1868:* to or <> measure) 17| *1841:* choices, one *MS:* choices, or one *1868:* choices or 18| *1841:* (Tasks <> thee, freaks <> pleasure,) *MS:* (Be they tasks <> thee, or freaks <> pleasure) *1868:* thee or 19| *1841:* Day, if I waste such <> leisure *MS:*—My Day, if I squander such <> leisure, 20–25| *1841:* Shame betide Asolo, mischief to me! / § no space § / But in turn, Day *MS:* Then shame fall on Asolo, mischief on me! / § space § / Thy long blue solemn hours serenely flowing, / Whence earth, we feel, gets steady help and good— / Thy fitful sunshine minutes, coming, going, / That show § cancelled by § In which, earth turns from work in gamesome mood— / All shall be mine! But thou must treat 23| *1863:* sunshine-minutes 24| *1863:* As if earth turned 26| *1841:* As happy tribes—so happy tribes! who *MS:* As the prosperous are treated, those who *1888:* As prosperous ones are 27| *1841:* hand—the common, other creatures' lot— *MS:* hand here, and enjoy the higher lot, 28| *1841:* Ready to take when thou *MS:* In readiness to take what thou 29| *1841:* Prepared to pass what *MS:* And free to let alone what 30| *1841:* Day, 'tis but Pippa thou *MS:* For, Day, my holiday, if thou 31| *1841:* If thou prove sullen, me, whose old year's sorrow *MS:* Me, who am only Pippa—old-year's sorrow, *1863:* Pippa,—old-year's 32| *1841:* Who except thee can chase before to-morrow, *MS:* Cast off last night, will come again to-morrow— *1868:* to-morrow: 33| *1841:* Seest thou, my day? Pippa's—who mean to borrow *MS:* Whereas, if thou prove gentle, I shall borrow 34–43| *1841:* Only of thee strength against new year's sorrow: / For let thy morning scowl on 35–42| § added *MS*,

Belongs to, who all days alike possess,
Make general plenty cure particular dearth,
Get more joy one way, if another, less:
Thou art my single day, God lends to leaven
What were all earth else, with a feel of heaven,—
Sole light that helps me through the year, thy sun's!
Try now! Take Asolo's Four Happiest Ones—
And let thy morning rain on that superb
Great haughty Ottima; can rain disturb
Her Sebald's homage? All the while thy rain
Beats fiercest on her shrub-house window-pane,
He will but press the closer, breathe more warm
Against her cheek; how should she mind the storm?
And, morning past, if midday shed a gloom
O'er Jules and Phene,—what care bride and groom
Save for their dear selves? 'Tis their marriage-day;
And while they leave church and go home their way,
Hand clasping hand, within each breast would be
Sunbeams and pleasant weather spite of thee.
Then, for another trial, obscure thy eve
With mist,—will Luigi and his mother grieve—
The lady and her child, unmatched, forsooth,
She in her age, as Luigi in his youth,
For true content? The cheerful town, warm, close
And safe, the sooner that thou art morose,
Receives them. And yet once again, outbreak

---

variants from 1889 § 38| *MS:* joy, one *1868:* joy one 40| *MS:* heaven; *1863:* heaven,— 43| *1841:* For let thy morning scowl on, *MS:* And let thy morning rain on 44| *1841:* haughty Ottima—can scowl disturb *MS:* haughty Ottima; can rain disturb 45–49| *1841:* homage? And if noon shed gloom *MS:* homage? All the while thy rain / Beats fiercest on her shrub-house window-pane, / He will but press the closer, breathe more warm / Against her cheek; how should she mind the storm? / And, morning past, if mid-day shed a gloom 50| *1841:* Phene—what *MS:* Phene,—what 51–55| *1841:* selves? Then, obscure *MS:* selves? 'Tis their marriage-day; / And while they leave church, and go home their way / Hand clasping hand,—within each breast would be / Sunbeams and pleasant weather spite of thee! / Then, for another trial, obscure 52| *1863:* way, 53| *1868:* hand, within 54| *1868:* thee. 56| *1841:* mist—will <> and Madonna grieve *MS:* mist,—will <> and his mother grieve— 57| *1841:*—The mother and the child—unmatched *MS:* Madonna § cancelled by § The Lady and her child, unmatched *1868:* lady 58| *1841:* age as *MS:* age, as 59–61| *1841:* content? And once *MS:* content? The cheerful town, warm, close, / And safe, the sooner that thou art morose / Receives them! And

In storm at night on Monsignor, they make
Such stir about,—whom they expect from Rome
To visit Asolo, his brothers' home,
And say here masses proper to release
A soul from pain,—what storm dares hurt his peace?
Calm would he pray, with his own thoughts to ward
Thy thunder off, nor want the angels' guard.
But Pippa—just one such mischance would spoil
Her day that lightens the next twelvemonth's toil
At wearisome silk-winding, coil on coil!
   And here I let time slip for nought!
Aha, you foolhardy sunbeam, caught
With a single splash from my ewer!
You that would mock the best pursuer,
Was my basin over-deep?
One splash of water ruins you asleep,
And up, up, fleet your brilliant bits
Wheeling and counterwheeling,
Reeling, broken beyond healing:
Now grow together on the ceiling!
That will task your wits.
Whoever it was quenched fire first, hoped to see
Morsel after morsel flee
As merrily, as giddily . . .
Meantime, what lights my sunbeam on,

---

yet once 60| *1863:* morose, 61| *1868:* them. And 62| *1841:* Monsignor they *MS:* Monsignor, they 63| *1841:* stir to-day about, who foregoes Rome *MS:* stir about,—whom they expect from Rome 64| *1841:* brother's *MS:* brothers' 65| *1841:* say there masses *MS:* say here masses 66–69| *1841:* The soul <> pain—what <> hurt that peace? / <> spoil, *MS:* A soul <> pain,—what <> hurt his peace? / Calm would he pray, with his own thoughts to ward / Thy thunder off, nor want the angels' guard! / But <> spoil 68| *1868:* guard. 70| *1841:* Bethink thee, utterly next *MS:* Her day that lightens the next 71–72| *1841:* § space § *1849:* § end of page § *1863:* § no space § 72| *1841:* § space § And here am I letting *MS:* am I letting the § cancelled by § I let *1868:* § ¶ § 73| *1841:* You fool-hardy sunbeam—caught *MS:* Aha, you foolhardy *1868:* sunbeam, caught 75| *1841:* that mocked *MS:* that would mock 77| *1841:* asleep *MS:* asleep, 80| *1841:* Reeling, crippled beyond healing— *MS:* Reeling, broken beyond *1868:* healing: 81| *1841:* Grow <> ceiling, *MS:* Now grow <> ceiling! 82| *1841:* wits! *1868:* wits. 83| *1841:* was first quenched fire hoped *MS:* Whoever quenched fire first, hoped *1868:* Whoever it was quenched 85–86| *1841:* As merrily, / As giddily . . . what lights he on— *MS:* As

Where settles by degrees the radiant cripple?
Oh, is it surely blown, my martagon?
New-blown and ruddy as St. Agnes' nipple,
Plump as the flesh-bunch on some Turk bird's poll!
Be sure if corals, branching 'neath the ripple
Of ocean, bud there,—fairies watch unroll
Such turban-flowers; I say, such lamps disperse
Thick red flame through that dusk green universe!
I am queen of thee, floweret!
And each fleshy blossom
Preserve I not—(safer
Than leaves that embower it,
Or shells that embosom)
—From weevil and chafer?
Laugh through my pane then; solicit the bee;
Gibe him, be sure; and, in midst of thy glee,
Love thy queen, worship me!

—Worship whom else? For am I not, this day,
Whate'er I please? What shall I please today?
My morn, noon, eve and night—how spend my day?
Tomorrow I must be Pippa who winds silk,
The whole year round, to earn just bread and milk:
But, this one day, I have leave to go,
And play out my fancy's fullest games;
I may fancy all day—and it shall be so—

---

merrily, as giddily . . . / Meantime, what lights my sunbeam on, 87| *1841:* settles himself the cripple? *MS:* settles by degrees the radiant cripple? 88| *1841:* Oh never surely *MS:* Oh, is it surely 89| *1841:* New-blown, though!—ruddy as a nipple, *MS:* New-blown and ruddy as St. Agnes' nipple, 90| *1841:* flesh bunch *1849:* flesh-bunch 93| *1841:* turban flowers . . I *MS:* turban-flowers; I 94| *1841:* thro' *MS:* through 95–103| *1841:* § indented § *1868:* § indentation cancelled § 95| *1841:* Queen <> floweret, *MS:* I am queen <> floweret; 96| *1841:* Each *MS:* And each 97| *1841:* Keep I not, safer *MS:* Preserve I not—(safer 98| *1841:*it *MS:* it, 99| *1841:* embosom, *MS:* embosom) 100| *1841:* From *MS:*—From 101| *1841:* thro' <> then, solicit the bee, *MS:* through <> then; solicit the bee; 102| *1841:* sure, and in <> glee *MS:* sure; and, in <> glee, 103| *1841:* Worship *MS:* Love thy queen, worship 104| *1841:* Worship <> not this Day *MS:*—Worship <> not, this day, 105| *1841:* please? Who shall I seem to-day? *MS:* please? What shall I please to-day? 106| *1841:* Morn, Noon, Eve, Night—how must I spend my Day? / § space § *MS:* My morning, noon, eve, night—how spend my day? / § no space § *1868:* morn <> eve and night 107–113| § added *MS*, variants from 1889 § 107| *MS:* To-morrow I am § cancelled by § To-morrow I must be 109–113| *MS:*

That I taste of the pleasures, am called by the names
Of the Happiest Four in our Asolo!
See! Up the hillside yonder, through the morning,
Some one shall love me, as the world calls love:
I am no less than Ottima, take warning!
The gardens, and the great stone house above,
And other house for shrubs, all glass in front,
Are mine; where Sebald steals, as he is wont,
To court me, while old Luca yet reposes:
And therefore, till the shrub-house door uncloses,
I . . . what now?—give abundant cause for prate
About me—Ottima, I mean—of late,
Too bold, too confident she'll still face down
The spitefullest of talkers in our town.
How we talk in the little town below!
   But love, love, love—there's better love, I know!
This foolish love was only day's first offer;
I choose my next love to defy the scoffer:
For do not our Bride and Bridegroom sally
Out of Possagno church at noon?
Their house looks over Orcana valley:
Why should not I be the bride as soon
As Ottima? For I saw, beside,
Arrive last night that little bride—
Saw, if you call it seeing her, one flash

---

§ indented § *1868:* § indentation cancelled § 114| *1841:* Up the hill-side, thro' *MS:* See! Up the Hill-side yonder, through *1888:* hill-side 115| *1841:* Love me as I love! *MS:* Someone shall love me, as the world calls love: *1849:* Some one 116| *1841:* I am Ottima, take warning, *MS:* I am no less than Ottima, take warning! 117| *1841:* And the gardens, and stone *MS:* The gardens, and the great stone 119| *1841:* mine, and Sebald steals as <> wont *MS:* mine; where Sebald steals, as <> wont, 120| *1841:* me, and old <> reposes, *MS:* me, while old <> reposes; *1868:* reposes: 121| *1841:* therefore till <> uncloses *MS:* therefore, 'till <> uncloses, *1849:* till 122| *1841:* now? give *MS:* what, now?—give *1868:* what now 123| *1841:* Of me (that's Ottima)—too bold of *MS:* About me—Ottima, I mean—of 124| *1841:* By far too *MS:* Too bold, too 125| *1841:* town— *1868:* town. 126–127| *1841:* § space § *1849:* § end of page § *1863:* § no space § 127| *1841:* love, love, love, there's <> love I *1841:* love, love, love—there's <> love, I *1863:* § ¶ § 128| *1841:* This love's only <> offer— *MS:* This foolish love was only <> offer; 129| *1841:* Next love shall defy *MS:* I choose my next love to defy 130| *1841:* not bride and bridegroom *MS:* not our Bride and Bridegroom 132| *1841:* valley— *1868:* valley: 133| *1841:* Why not be *MS:* Why should I not *1863:* should not I be 134| *1841:* As Ottima? I saw, myself, beside, *MS:* As Ottima? For I saw, beside, 135| *1841:* that bride— *MS:* that little

Of the pale snow-pure cheek and black bright tresses,
Blacker than all except the black eyelash;
I wonder she contrives those lids no dresses!
—So strict was she, the veil
Should cover close her pale
Pure cheeks—a bride to look at and scarce touch,
Scarce touch, remember, Jules! For are not such
Used to be tended, flowerlike, every feature,
As if one's breath would fray the lily of a creature?
A soft and easy life these ladies lead:
Whiteness in us were wonderful indeed.
Oh, save that brow its virgin dimness,
Keep that foot its lady primness,
Let those ankles never swerve
From their exquisite reserve,
Yet have to trip along the streets like me,
All but naked to the knee!
How will she ever grant her Jules a bliss
So startling as her real first infant kiss?
Oh, no—not envy, this!

—Not envy, sure!—for if you gave me
Leave to take or to refuse,
In earnest, do you think I'd choose
That sort of new love to enslave me?
Mine should have lapped me round from the beginning;
As little fear of losing it as winning:
Lovers grow cold, men learn to hate their wives,

---

bride— 137| *1841:* blacker tresses *MS:* pale, snow-pure <> black bright tresses, *1868:* pale snow-pure 138| *1841:* Than . . . not the *MS:* Blacker than all except the 139| *1841:* A wonder <> dresses *MS:* I wonder <> dresses! 140| *1841:* she the *MS:* she, the 143| *1841:* Remember Jules!—for *MS:* Scarce touch, remember, Jules *1868:* remember, Jules! For 145–148| *1841:* creature? / Oh *MS:* creature? / A soft and easy life these ladies lead! / Whiteness in us were wonderful indeed— / Oh 146| *1868:* lead: 147| *1863:* indeed. 148–156| *MS:* § indented § *1868:* § indentation cancelled § 150| *1841:* ancles *1863:* ankles *1868:* ancles *1888:* ankles 152| *1841:* me *MS:* me, 156| *1841:* Oh—no—not envy this! / § no space § *MS:* Oh, no—not envy, this! / § space § 157| *1841:* Not <> sure, for, if *MS:*—Not <> sure!—for if 158| *1841:* refuse *MS:* refuse, 161| *1841:* beginning *MS:* beginning; 162–165| *1841:* winning— / Why look you! when at eve the pair *MS:* winning; § cancelled by § / Lovers grow cold, men learn to hate their wives, / And only parents' love can last our lives: / So, look you!—when at § cancelled by § At eve the son and mother, gentle Pair, 162| *1868:*

And only parents' love can last our lives.
At eve the Son and Mother, gentle pair,
Commune inside our turret: what prevents
My being Luigi? While that mossy lair
Of lizards through the winter-time is stirred
With each to each imparting sweet intents
For this new-year, as brooding bird to bird—
(For I observe of late, the evening walk
Of Luigi and his mother, always ends
Inside our ruined turret, where they talk,
Calmer than lovers, yet more kind than friends)
—Let me be cared about, kept out of harm,
And schemed for, safe in love as with a charm;
Let me be Luigi! If I only knew
What was my mother's face—my father, too!
   Nay, if you come to that, best love of all
Is God's; then why not have God's love befall
Myself as, in the palace by the Dome,
Monsignor?—who to-night will bless the home
Of his dead brother; and God bless in turn
That heart which beats, those eyes which mildly burn
With love for all men! I, to-night at least,
Would be that holy and beloved priest.

Now wait!—even I already seem to share
In God's love: what does New-year's hymn declare?

---

winning: 164| *1863:* lives. 165| *1849:* pair, *1868:* the Son and Mother 166| *1841:* turret, what *MS:* our Turret; what *1868:* turret *1888:* turret: what 167| *1841:* being Luigi?—While *MS:* being Luigi? while *1868:* While 168| *1841:* thro' the winter-time, is *MS:* through *1888:* winter-time is 170–175| *1841:* new year <> / I will be <> harm *MS:* new-year <> / (For I observe of late, the evening walk / Of Luigi and his mother, always ends / Inside our ruined turret, where they talk, / Calmer than lovers, yet more kind than friends) / Let me be <> harm, 175| *1863:*—Let 176| *1841:* charm, *MS:* charm; 177| *1841:* I will be Luigi . . . if *MS:* Let me be Luigi! . . . If *1863:* Luigi! If 178| *1841:* my father like . . . my mother too! § space § *MS:* my mother's face—my father, too! *1863:* too! / § end of page § *1868:* too! § no space § 179| *1841:* § no ¶ § <> that, the greatest love *MS:* that, best love *1888:* § ¶ § 180| *1841:* Is God's: well then, to have *MS:* Is God's; then why not have 181| *1841:* Oneself as in <> dome *MS:* Myself as, in the Palace <> Dome, *1888:* palace 182| *1841:* Where Monsignor to-night *MS:* Monsignor?—who to-night 183–185| *1841:* brother! I *MS:* brother; and God will bless in turn / That heart which beats, those eyes which mildly burn / With love for all men: I *1888:* and God bless 186| *1841:* Will be *MS:* Would be <> priest! *1868:* priest. 188–190| *1841:* In that—why else

What other meaning do these verses bear?

All service ranks the same with God:
If now, as formerly he trod
Paradise, his presence fills
Our earth, each only as God wills
Can work—God's puppets, best and worst,
Are we; there is no last nor first.

Say not "a small event!" Why "small"?
Costs it more pain that this, ye call
A "great event," should come to pass,
Than that? Untwine me from the mass
Of deeds which make up life, one deed
Power shall fall short in or exceed!

And more of it, and more of it!—oh yes—
I will pass each, and see their happiness,
And envy none—being just as great, no doubt,
Useful to men, and dear to God, as they!
A pretty thing to care about
So mightily, this single holiday!
But let the sun shine! Wherefore repine?
—With thee to lead me, O Day of mine,

---

should new year's hymn declare / § space § / *All* *MS:* In that § cancelled by § In God's love: what does New-year's Hymn declare? / What other meaning do these verses bear? / § space § / *All* *1849:* hymn 191| *MS:* formerly *He* *1868: he* 192| *1841: Paradise, God's presence* *MS: Paradise, His presence* *1868: his* 193| *1841: earth, and each but as* *MS: earth, then each but as* § cancelled by § *earth, each only as* 196| *1841: not, a <> event! Why small?* *MS: not "a <> event"! Why "small"?* *1849: event!" Why "small?"* *1888: event!" Why "small"?* 197| *1841: pain this thing ye* *MS: pain that this, ye* *1841: pain than this* *1888: pain that this* 198| *1841: A great event should <> pass* *MS: A "great event," should <> pass,* 199| *1841: me, from* *MS: me from* 201| *1841: in, or* *1868: in or* 202| *1841:* And more of it, and more of it—oh, yes! *MS:* And more of it, and more of it!—oh, yes— 203–204| *1841:* So that my passing, and each happiness / I pass, will be alike important—prove / That true! oh yes—the brother, / The bride, the lover, and the mother,— / Only to pass whom will remove— / Whom a mere look at half will cure / The Past, and help me to endure / The Coming . . . I am just *MS:* I will pass by, and see their happiness, / And envy none—being just *1868:* pass each, and 205| *1841:* As they! *MS:* Useful to men, and dear to God, as 207| *1841:* mightily—this *MS:* mightily, this 208–214| *MS:* § indented § *1868:* § indentation cancelled § 208| *1841:* Why repine? *MS:* But let the sun shine! Wherefore repine? 209| *1841:* With <>

Down the grass path grey with dew,
Under the pine-wood, blind with boughs,
Where the swallow never flew
Nor yet cicala dared carouse—
No, dared carouse! [*She enters the street.*]

---

me, Day *MS:*—With <> me, O Day 210| *MS:* grass-path *1888:* grass path 211| *1841:* 'Neath the *MS:* Under the 213| *1841:* As yet, nor cicale <> carouse: *MS:* carouse— *1863:* cicala *1868:* Nor yet cicala 214| *MS:* Dared *1868:* No, dared

PART I. [i] MORNING

SCENE—*Up the Hillside, inside the Shrub-house.* LUCA'S *wife,* OTTIMA, *and her paramour, the German* SEBALD.

SEBALD [*sings*].

Let the watching lids wink!
Day's a-blaze with eyes, think!
Deep into the night, drink!

OTTIMA Night? Such may be your Rhine-land nights perhaps;
But this blood-red beam through the shutter's chink
—We call such light, the morning: let us see!
Mind how you grope your way, though! How these tall
Naked geraniums straggle! Push the lattice
Behind that frame!—Nay, do I bid you?—Sebald,
It shakes the dust down on me! Why, of course
The slide-bolt catches. Well, are you content,
Or must I find you something else to spoil?
Kiss and be friends, my Sebald! Is't full morning?
Oh, don't speak then!
SEBALD Ay, thus it used to be.
Ever your house was, I remember, shut

Part-title and stage directions/ *1841:* I.—*Morning. Up the Hill-side. The Shrub House.* LUCA'S *Wife* OTTIMA, *and Her Paramour the* *MS: the Hill-side, inside the Shrub-house. Luca's Wife, Ottima and her Paramour, the* *1849: the Shrub-house.* LUCA'S *Wife,* OTTIMA, *and* *1888:* PART I / MORNING. / SCENE.—*Up* 2| *1841: think,—* *MS: think—* *1868: think!* 3| *1841: night drink!* *MS: night, drink!* 4–7| *1841:* Night? What, a Rhineland night, then? How *MS:* Night? Such may be your Rhine-land nights, perhaps; / But this blood-red beam through the shutter's chink, / —We call such light, the morning's: let us see! / Mind how you grope your way, though! How *1868:* nights perhaps; / <> chink / <> morning 8| *1841:* lattice— *1868:* lattice 9| *1841:* frame.—Nay *MS:* frame!—Nay 11| *1841:* catches—Well *MS:* catches.—Well *1868:* catches. Well 13| *1841:* my Sebald. Is it *1888:* my Sebald!

Till mid-day; I observed that, as I strolled
On mornings through the vale here; country girls
Were noisy, washing garments in the brook,
Hinds drove the slow white oxen up the hills:
But no, your house was mute, would ope no eye.
And wisely: you were plotting one thing there,
Nature, another outside. I looked up—
Rough white wood shutters, rusty iron bars,
Silent as death, blind in a flood of light.
Oh, I remember!—and the peasants laughed
And said, "The old man sleeps with the young wife."
This house was his, this chair, this window—his.
OTTIMA Ah, the clear morning! I can see St. Mark's;
That black streak is the belfry. Stop: Vicenza
Should lie . . . there's Padua, plain enough, that blue!
Look o'er my shoulder, follow my finger!
SEBALD Morning?
It seems to me a night with a sun added.
Where's dew, where's freshness? That bruised plant, I bruised
In getting through the lattice yestereve,
Droops as it did. See, here's my elbow's mark
I' the dust o' the sill.
OTTIMA Oh, shut the lattice, pray!
SEBALD Let me lean out. I cannot scent blood here,
Foul as the morn may be.
There, shut the world out!
How do you feel now, Ottima? There, curse
The world and all outside! Let us throw off

Is't 16| *1841:* mid-day—I *1868:* mid-day; I 17| *1841:* thro' <> here: country *1863:* through *1868:* here; country 18| *1841:* brook–– *1863:* brook, 19| *1841:* Herds drove <> hills— *MS:* Hinds drove *1863:* hills, *1868:* hills: 20| *1841:* eye— *1863:* eye! *1888:* eye. 21| *1841:* wisely—you *1868:* wisely: you 22| *1841:* Nature another outside: I *MS:* Nature, another *1868:* outside. I 24| *1841:* light, *MS:* light; *1863:* light. 26| *1841:* wife!" *1863:* wife." 28| *1841:* see St. Mark's: *1888:* see St. Mark's; 29| *1841:* belfry—stop *MS:* belfry. Stop 30| *1841:* lie—there's <> blue. *MS:* lie . . . There's <> blue! 31| *1841:* shoulder—follow my finger— SEBALD *1863:* shoulder, follow my finger. SEBALD *1868:* finger! SEBALD 32| *1841:* added: *1863:* added. 33| *1841:* dew? where's <> plant I *MS:* plant, I *1868:* dew, where's 36| *1841:* In <> on <> Oh shut *1868:* sill. OTTIMA Oh, shut *1888:* I' <> o' 37| *1841:* here *1849:* here, *1868:* out! I *1888:* out. I 38| *1841:* be—¶ There *1863:* be. ¶ There 39| *1841:* now, Ottima? There—curse *1863:* now, Ottima? There, curse 40| *1841:* world, and *1863:* world and 42| *1841:*

This mask: how do you bear yourself? Let's out
With all of it.
OTTIMA Best never speak of it.
SEBALD Best speak again and yet again of it,
Till words cease to be more than words. "His blood,"
For instance—let those two words mean "His blood"
And nothing more. Notice, I'll say them now,
"His blood."
OTTIMA Assuredly if I repented
The deed—
SEBALD Repent? Who should repent, or why?
What puts that in your head? Did I once say
That I repented?
OTTIMA No, I said the deed . . .
SEBALD "The deed" and "the event"—just now it was
"Our passion's fruit"—the devil take such cant!
Say, once and always, Luca was a wittol,
I am his cut-throat, you are . . .
OTTIMA Here's the wine;
I brought it when we left the house above,
And glasses too—wine of both sorts. Black? White then?
SEBALD But am not I his cut-throat? What are you?
OTTIMA There trudges on his business from the Duomo
Benet the Capuchin, with his brown hood
And bare feet; always in one place at church,
Close under the stone wall by the south entry.
I used to take him for a brown cold piece
Of the wall's self, as out of it he rose
To let me pass—at first, I say, I used:
Now, so has that dumb figure fastened on me,
I rather should account the plastered wall
A piece of him, so chilly does it strike.

---

it! OTTIMA *1888:* it. OTTIMA 46| *1841:* more. Notice—I'll *1863:* more. Notice, I'll 50| *1841:* OTTIMA No—I <> deed— *1863:* OTTIMA No, I *1868:* deed . . . 51| *1841:* event"—and just *1849:* deed," and "the event"—just *1888:* deed" and 54| *1841:* are— OTTIMA Here is the wine— *1863:* wine; *1868:* are . . . OTTIMA *1888:* OTTIMA Here's 55| *1841:* above— *1863:* above, 56| *1841:* white, then? *1868:* sorts. Black? White then? 58| *1841:* Duomo, *1849:* Duomo 60| *1841:* feet—always *1868:* feet; always 61| *1841:* entry; *1863:* entry. 64| *1841:* used— *1868:* used: 65| *1841:* Now—so <> me— *1863:*

This, Sebald?
SEBALD No, the white wine—the white wine!
Well, Ottima, I promised no new year
Should rise on us the ancient shameful way;
Nor does it rise. Pour on! To your black eyes!
Do you remember last damned New Year's day?
OTTIMA You brought those foreign prints. We looked at them
Over the wine and fruit. I had to scheme
To get him from the fire. Nothing but saying
His own set wants the proof-mark, roused him up
To hunt them out.
SEBALD 'Faith, he is not alive
To fondle you before my face.
OTTIMA Do you
Fondle me then! Who means to take your life
For that, my Sebald?
SEBALD Hark you, Ottima!
One thing to guard against. We'll not make much
One of the other—that is, not make more
Parade of warmth, childish officious coil,
Than yesterday: as if, sweet, I supposed
Proof upon proof were needed now, now first,
To show I love you—yes, still love you—love you
In spite of Luca and what's come to him
—Sure sign we had him ever in our thoughts,
White sneering old reproachful face and all!
We'll even quarrel, love, at times, as if
We still could lose each other, were not tied
By this: conceive you?
OTTIMA Love!
SEBALD Not tied so sure.

Now, so <> me, 68| *1841:* SEBALD No—the white wine—the *1868:* SEBALD No, the white wine—the 70| *1841:* way, *1868:* way; 71| *1841:* rise—pour on—To *1849:* rise: pour on! To *1888:* rise. Pour 76| *1841:* proof-mark roused *1849:* proof-mark, roused 77| *1841:* SEBALD Faith *1849:* SEBALD 'Faith 78| *1849:* face! OTTIMA *1868:* face. OTTIMA 79| *1841:* then: who *1849:* me, then! who *1868:* me then! Who 80| *1841:* you, Ottima, *1868:* you, Ottima! 81| *1841:* thing's *1868:* thing 84| *1841:* yesterday—as *1863:* if, Sweet *1868:* yesterday: as if, sweet 85| *1841:* was *1868:* were 86| *1841:* you—still *1849:* you—yes, still 87| *1841:* him. *1849:* him 89| *1841:* all— *1849:* all! 90| *1863:* Love *1868:* love 91| *1841:* other—were *1863:* other; were 92| *1841:* this—conceive <> Love— SEBALD <> sure— *1863:* OTTIMA Love!

Because though I was wrought upon, have struck
His insolence back into him—am I
So surely yours?—therefore forever yours?
OTTIMA Love, to be wise, (one counsel pays another)
Should we have—months ago, when first we loved,
For instance that May morning we two stole
Under the green ascent of sycamores—
If we had come upon a thing like that
Suddenly . . .
SEBALD "A thing"—there again—"a thing!"
OTTIMA Then, Venus' body, had we come upon
My husband Luca Gaddi's murdered corpse
Within there, at his couch-foot, covered close—
Would you have pored upon it? Why persist
In poring now upon it? For 'tis here
As much as there in the deserted house:
You cannot rid your eyes of it. For me,
Now he is dead I hate him worse: I hate . . .
Dare you stay here? I would go back and hold
His two dead hands, and say, "I hate you worse,
"Luca, than . . ."
SEBALD Off, off—take your hands off mine,
'Tis the hot evening—off! oh, morning is it?
OTTIMA There's one thing must be done; you know what thing.
Come in and help to carry. We may sleep
Anywhere in the whole wide house to-night.
SEBALD What would come, think you, if we let him lie
Just as he is? Let him lie there until
The angels take him! He is turned by this
Off from his face beside, as you will see.

<> sure! *1868:* this: conceive *1888:* sure. 93| *1841:* tho' <> upon—have *1863:* though <> upon, have 95| *1841:* therefore, forever *1868:* therefore forever 97| *1841:* ago—when *1868:* ago, when 101| *1841:* Suddenly— SEBALD "A thing" . . there *1863:* Suddenly . . . SEBALD "A thing"—there 106| *1841:* here— *1863:* here 107| *1841:* house— *1863:* house: 108| *1841:* it: for *1863:* it. For 109| *1841:* worse—I hate— *1863:* hate . . . *1868:* worse: I 111| *1841:* say, I <> worse *1868:* say, "I <> worse, 112| *1841:* than— SEBALD Off, off; take <> mine! *1863:* than . . . SEBALD *1868:* than . . ." SEBALD Off, off—take <> mine, 113| *1841:* morning, is *1868:* morning is 114| *1841:* done—you *1863:* done; you 119| *1841:* him: he *1868:* him! He 120| *1841:*

OTTIMA This dusty pane might serve for looking glass.
Three, four—four grey hairs! Is it so you said
A plait of hair should wave across my neck?
No—this way.
SEBALD Ottima, I would give your neck,
Each splendid shoulder, both those breasts of yours,
That this were undone! Killing! Kill the world
So Luca lives again!—ay, lives to sputter
His fulsome dotage on you—yes, and feign
Surprise that I return at eve to sup,
When all the morning I was loitering here—
Bid me despatch my business and begone.
I would . . .
OTTIMA See!
SEBALD No, I'll finish. Do you think
I fear to speak the bare truth once for all?
All we have talked of, is, at bottom, fine
To suffer; there's a recompense in guilt;
One must be venturous and fortunate:
What is one young for, else? In age we'll sigh
O'er the wild reckless wicked days flown over;
Still, we have lived: the vice was in its place.
But to have eaten Luca's bread, have worn
His clothes, have felt his money swell my purse—
Do lovers in romances sin that way?
Why, I was starving when I used to call
And teach you music, starving while you plucked me
These flowers to smell!

---

face, beside *1868:* face beside 121| *1841:* looking-glass. *1888:* looking glass. 122| *1841:* is *1849:* hairs! Is 124| *1841:* way! SEBALD *1868:* way. SEBALD 126| *1841:* undone! Killing?—Let the world die *1849:* undone! Killing?—Kill the world *1868:* undone! Killing? Kill the world, *1888:* undone! Killing! Kill <> world 127| *1841:* again!—Ay *1849:* again!—ay 129| *1841:* returned *1868:* return 131| *1841:* dispatch *1888:* despatch 132| *1841:* would— OTTIMA *1849:* finish! Do *1863:* would . . . OTTIMA *1888:* finish. Do 134| *1841:* talked of is at bottom fine *1849:* is, at *1863:* bottom, fine *1888:* of, is 135| *1841:* suffer—there's <> in that: *1849:* in guilt; *1868:* suffer; there's a recompence *1888:* recompense 136| *1841:* fortunate— *1863:* fortunate: 137| *1841:* for else *1849:* for, else 138| *1841:* wild, reckless, wicked <> over: *1849:* over; *1868:* wild reckless wicked 140| *1841:* bread—have *1849:* bread, have 141–143| *1841:* purse—/ Why *1849:* purse—/ Do lovers in romances sin that way? / Why 144–145| *1841:* music—starving <> pluck'd / Me flowers *1849:* plucked me / These

OTTIMA My poor lost friend!

SEBALD He gave me
Life, nothing less: what if he did reproach
My perfidy, and threaten, and do more—
Had he no right? What was to wonder at?
He sat by us at table quietly:
Why must you lean across till our cheeks touched?
Could he do less than make pretence to strike?
'Tis not the crime's sake—I'd commit ten crimes
Greater, to have this crime wiped out, undone!
And you—O how feel you? Feel you for me?

OTTIMA Well then, I love you better now than ever,
And best (look at me while I speak to you)—
Best for the crime; nor do I grieve, in truth.
This mask, this simulated ignorance,
This affectation of simplicity,
Falls off our crime; this naked crime of ours
May not now be looked over: look it down!
Great? let it be great; but the joys it brought,
Pay they or no its price? Come: they or it!
Speak not! The past, would you give up the past
Such as it is, pleasure and crime together?
Give up that noon I owned my love for you?
The garden's silence: even the single bee
Persisting in his toil, suddenly stopped,
And where he hid you only could surmise

---

flowers *1868:* music, starving 146| *1841:* Life—nothing *1863:* Life, nothing 148–150| *1841:* at? / Why <> touch'd? *1849:* at? / He sate by us at table quietly— / Why *1863:* sat / <> / <> touched? *1868:* quietly: 151| *1841:* strike me? *1868:* strike? 152| *1849:* not for the *1868:* not the 153| *1841:* out—undone! *1863:* out, undone! 154| *1841:* you—O, how <> you? feel *1868:* you—O how <> you? Feel 155| *1841:* Well, then—I <> ever— *1863:* then, I <> ever, *1868:* Well then 157| *1841:* crime—nor <> grieve in truth *1849:* grieve, in truth, *1863:* crime; nor 159| *1841:* simplicity *1849:* simplicity, 161| *1841:* not be <> over—look it down, then! *1849:* not, now, be *1863:* over: look *1868:* not now be <> down then! *1888:* down! 162| *1841:* great—but <> brought *1849:* brought, *1863:* great; but 163| *1841:* price? Come—they *1863:* price? Come: they 164| *1863:* not! The Past <> Past *1868:* past <> past 166| *1841:* you— *1863:* you? 167| *1841:* silence—even *1863:* silence! even *1888:* silence: even 168| *1841:* stopt *1863:* stopt; *1868:* stopped: *1888:* stopped,

By some campanula chalice set a-swing.
Who stammered—"Yes, I love you?"
SEBALD And I drew
Back; put far back your face with both my hands
Lest you should grow too full of me—your face
So seemed athirst for my whole soul and body!
OTTIMA And when I ventured to receive you here,
Made you steal hither in the mornings—
SEBALD When
I used to look up 'neath the shrub-house here,
Till the red fire on its glazed windows spread
To a yellow haze?
OTTIMA Ah—my sign was, the sun
Inflamed the sere side of yon chestnut-tree
Nipped by the first frost.
SEBALD You would always laugh
At my wet boots: I had to stride thro' grass
Over my ankles.
OTTIMA Then our crowning night!
SEBALD The July night?
OTTIMA The day of it too, Sebald!
When heaven's pillars seemed o'erbowed with heat,
Its black-blue canopy suffered descend
Close on us both, to weigh down each to each,
And smother up all life except our life.
So lay we till the storm came.
SEBALD How it came!
OTTIMA Buried in woods we lay, you recollect;
Swift ran the searching tempest overhead;
And ever and anon some bright white shaft
Burned thro' the pine-tree roof, here burned and there,

170| *1841:* campanula's <> a-swing *1863:* a-swing: *1868:* campanula *1888:* a-swing. 171| *1841:* As he clung there—"Yes <> you" SEBALD *1849:* you!" SEBALD *1863:* Who stammered—"Yes <> you?" SEBALD 172| *1841:* Back: put *1849:* Back; put 177| *1841:* here *1849:* here, 179| *1841:* Into *1849:* To 181| *1841:* Nipt <> frost— SEBALD *1849:* frost. SEBALD *1868:* Nipped 182| *1841:* boots—I *1863:* boots: I 183| *1841:* ancles <> night— *1863:* ankles <> night! *1868:* ancles. OTTIMA *1888:* ankles 185| *1849:* When the heaven's *1868:* When heaven's 186| *1841:* canopy seemed let descend *1868:* canopy suffered descend 193| *1841:* Burnt <> roof—here burnt *1863:* roof, here *1868:* Burned

As if God's messenger thro' the close wood screen
Plunged and replunged his weapon at a venture,
Feeling for guilty thee and me: then broke
The thunder like a whole sea overhead—
SEBALD Yes!
OTTIMA —While I stretched myself upon you, hands
To hands, my mouth to your hot mouth, and shook
All my locks loose, and covered you with them—
You, Sebald, the same you!
SEBALD Slower, Ottima!
OTTIMA And as we lay—
SEBALD Less vehemently! Love me!
Forgive me! Take not words, mere words, to heart!
Your breath is worse than wine! Breathe slow, speak slow!
Do not lean on me!
OTTIMA Sebald, as we lay,
Rising and falling only with our pants,
Who said, "Let death come now! 'Tis right to die!
Right to be punished! Nought completes such bliss
But woe!" Who said that?
SEBALD How did we ever rise?
Was't that we slept? Why did it end?
OTTIMA I felt you
Taper into a point the ruffled ends
Of my loose locks 'twixt both your humid lips.
My hair is fallen now: knot it again!
SEBALD I kiss you now, dear Ottima, now and now!
This way? Will you forgive me—be once more

<> burned 196| *1841:* me—then *1849:* me, then 198| *1841:* Yes. OTTIMA While *1849:* Yes! OTTIMA —While 200| *1841:* them. *1849:* them— 201| *1841:* same you— SEBALD <> Ottima— *1863:* same you! SEBALD *1868:* same you! SEBALD <> Ottima! 202| *1841:* vehemently—Love me *1849:* vehemently! Love *1863:* me! 203| *1841:* me—take not words—mere words—to heart— *1863:* me! take not words, mere words, to heart! *1868:* me! Take 204| *1841:* wine—breathe <> slow— *1849:* wine! Breathe *1863:* wine. Breathe <> slow! *1888:* wine! Breathe 205| *1841:* me— OTTIMA *1863:* me! OTTIMA 207| *1841:* now—'tis *1863:* now! 'tis *1868:* now! 'Tis 208| *1841:* punished—nought *1863:* punished! nought *1868:* punished! Nought 210| *1841:* felt *1849:* felt you, *1868:* you 211| *1841:* You tapering to a *1849:* Fresh tapering *1863:* Tapering into a *1868:* Taper into 212| *1841:* lips— *1868:* lips. 213| *1841:* (My <> knot it again). *1849:* again!) *1863:* now: knot *1868:* My <> again! 214| *1841:* and now; *1849:* dear Ottima, now, and now! *1868:* dear Ottima, now 215| *1841:* will *1849:*

My great queen?
OTTIMA Bind it thrice about my brow;
Crown me your queen, your spirit's arbitress,
Magnificent in sin. Say that!
SEBALD I crown you
My great white queen, my spirit's arbitress,
Magnificent . . .

[*From without is heard the voice of* PIPPA, *singing—*]

The year's at the spring
And day's at the morn;
Morning's at seven;
The hillside's dew-pearled;
The lark's on the wing;
The snail's on the thorn:
God's in his heaven—
All's right with the world!

[PIPPA *passes.*]

SEBALD God's in his heaven! Do you hear that? Who spoke?
You, you spoke!
OTTIMA Oh—that little ragged girl!
She must have rested on the step: we give them
But this one holiday the whole year round.
Did you ever see our silk-mills—their inside?
There are ten silk-mills now belong to you.
She stoops to pick my double heartsease . . . Sh!
She does not hear: call you out louder!
SEBALD Leave me!
Go, get your clothes on—dress those shoulders!
OTTIMA Sebald?
SEBALD Wipe off that paint! I hate you.
OTTIMA Miserable!

Will 220–221| *1841:* Magnificent—/ [Without.] The year's <> spring, *1849:* Magnificent—/ [*From without is heard the voice of* PIPPA, *singing*—/ *The year's* *1868: of Pippa singing*— *1888: spring* 224| *1841:* dew-pearled: *1863: dew-pearled;* 225| *1841: wing,* *1849: wing;* 226| *1841: thorn;* *1868: thorn:* 230| *1841:* girl: *1849:* girl! 231| *1841:* step—we give *1849:* give them *1863:* step: we 232| *1841:* Them but one <> round— *1849:* But this one <> round. 233| *1841:* e'er *1849:* ever 236| *1841:* hear—you call out *1863:* hear: call you out 237| *1841:* shoulders. OTTIMA *1849:* shoulders! OTTIMA 238| *1841:* paint. I hate you! OTTIMA *1868:* paint! I hate you.

SEBALD My God, and she is emptied of it now!
Outright now!—how miraculously gone
All of the grace—had she not strange grace once?
Why, the blank cheek hangs listless as it likes
No purpose holds the features up together,
Only the cloven brow and puckered chin
Stay in their places: and the very hair,
That seemed to have a sort of life in it.
Drops, a dead web!
OTTIMA Speak to me—not of me!
SEBALD —That round great full-orbed face, where not an angle
Broke the delicious indolence—all broken!
OTTIMA To me—not of me! Ungrateful, perjured cheat!
A coward too: but ingrate's worse than all.
Beggar—my slave—a fawning, cringing lie!
Leave me! Betray me! I can see your drift!
A lie that walks and eats and drinks!
SEBALD My God!
Those morbid olive faultless shoulder-blades—
I should have known there was no blood beneath!
OTTIMA You hate me then? You hate me then?
SEBALD To think
She would succeed in her absurd attempt,
And fascinate by sinning, show herself
Superior—guilt from its excess superior
To innocence! That little peasant's voice
Has righted all again. Though I be lost,
I know which is the better, never fear,
Of vice or virtue, purity or lust,

OTTIMA 239| *1841:* My God! and *1868:* My God, and 245| *1841:* places—and *1868:* places: and 247| *1841:* Drops a *1849:* Drops, a 248| *1841:* That *1849:*—That 250| *1841:* Ungrateful—to me—not of me—perjured cheat— *1849:* To me—not of me!—ungrateful, perjured *1863:* cheat! *1868:* of me! Ungrateful 251| *1841:* too—but <> all: *1849:* coward, too <> all! *1863:* too: but *1868:* coward too *1888:* all. 253| *1841:* me!—betray me!—I <> drift— *1863:* me! Betray me! I <> drift! 254| *1841:* walks, and eats, and *1868:* walks and eats and 255| *1841:* morbid, olive, faultless *1868:* morbid olive faultless 257| *1841:* me, then? you *1849:* then? You *1863:* then? You hate me, then? *1868:* me then? You hate me then? 258| *1841:* attempt *1849:* attempt, 259| *1841:* fascinate with sin! and show *1849:* fascinate by sinning; and *1868:* sinning, and *1888:* sinning, show 260| *1841:* Superior—Guilt <> excess, superior *1868:* guilt <> excess superior 261| *1841:* To Innocence. That *1863:*

Nature or trick! I see what I have done,
Entirely now! Oh I am proud to feel
Such torments—let the world take credit thence—
I, having done my deed, pay too its price!
I hate, hate—curse you! God's in his heaven!

OTTIMA —Me!

Me? no, no, Sebald, not yourself—kill me!
Mine is the whole crime. Do but kill me—then
Yourself—then—presently—first hear me speak!
I always meant to kill myself—wait, you!
Lean on my breast—not as a breast; don't love me
The more because you lean on me, my own
Heart's Sebald! There, there, both deaths presently!

SEBALD My brain is drowned now—quite drowned: all I feel
Is . . . is, at swift-recurring intervals,
A hurry-down within me, as of waters
Loosened to smother up some ghastly pit:
There they go—whirls from a black fiery sea!

OTTIMA Not me—to him, O God, be merciful!

[I.ii.]

Talk by the way, while PIPPA *is passing from the hill-side to Orcana.* Foreign STUDENTS *of painting and sculpture, from Venice, assembled opposite the house of* JULES, *a young French statuary, at Possagno.*

1 STUDENT Attention! My own post is beneath this window, but the pomegranate clump yonder will hide three or four of you with a lit-

---

To Innocence! That *1868:* innocence 265| *1841:* Nature, or trick—I <> done *1849:* done, *1863:* trick! I *1868:* Nature or 266| *1841:* now. Oh, I *1849:* now! Oh *1868:* now! Oh I 267| *1841:* credit that *1849:* credit thence— 269| *1841:* heaven OTTIMA Me! *1849:* heaven! OTTIMA —Me! *1863:* His *1868:* his 270| *1841:* no, no Sebald—not *1849:* no, no, Sebald *1863:* no, no, Sebald, not *1888:* me 271| *1841:* crime—do *1868:* crime. Do 272| *1841:* crime—do *1868:* crime. Do 273| *1841:* wait you! *1849:* wait, you! 274| *1841:* breast . . not *1849:* breast—not 276| *1841:* Heart's Sebald. There—there—both *1849:* Heart's Sebald! There—there *1868:* Heart's Sebald! There, there, both 278| *1841:* Is . . . is at *1863:* Is . . . is, at 279| *1841:* hurrying-down *1868:* hurry-down 280| *1841:* pit— *1863:* pit: 281| *1841:* black, fiery sea. *1849:* sea! *1868:* They—they <> black fiery *1888:* There they 282| *1841:* him oh God be *1849:* Not to me, God—to him be *1868:* Not me—to him, O God, be

Stage directions / *1841: way in the mean time.* FOREIGN <> *Statuary. 1849: way, while* PIPPA *is passing from the hill-side to Orcana.* FOREIGN *1868: statuary, at Possagno.*
1| *1841:* Attention: my *1849:* Attention! my 2| *1841:* pomegranate-clump

tle squeezing, and Schramm and his pipe must lie flat in the balcony. Four, five—who's a defaulter? We want everybody, for Jules must not be suffered to hurt his bride when the jest's found out.

2 STUDENT All here! Only our poet's away—never having much meant to be present, moonstrike him! The airs of that fellow, that Giovacchino! He was in violent love with himself, and had a fair prospect of thriving in his suit, so unmolested was it,—when suddenly a woman falls in love with him, too; and out of pure jealousy he takes himself off to Trieste, immortal poem and all: whereto is this prophetical epitaph appended already, as Bluphocks assures me,—*"Here a mammoth-poem lies, Fouled to death by butterflies."* His own fault, the simpleton! Instead of cramp couplets, each like a knife in your entrails, he should write, says Bluphocks, both classically and intelligibly. —*Æsculapius, an Epic. Catalogue of the drugs: Hebe's plaister—One strip Cools your lip. Phœbus' emulsion—One bottle Clears your throttle. Mercury's bolus—One box Cures . . .*

3 STUDENT Subside, my fine fellow! If the marriage was over by ten o'clock, Jules will certainly be here in a minute with his bride.

2 STUDENT Good!—only, so should the poet's muse have been universally acceptable, says Bluphocks, *et canibus nostris* . . . and Delia not better known to our literary dogs than the boy Giovacchino!

1 STUDENT To the point, now. Where's Gottlieb, the new-comer? Oh, —listen, Gottlieb, to what has called down this piece of friendly vengeance on Jules, of which we now assemble to witness the winding-up. We are all agreed, all in a tale, observe, when Jules shall burst

---

1849: pomegranate clump 4| *1841:* defaulter? Jules *1849:* defaulter? We want everybody, for Jules 5| *1841:* bride. *1849:* bride when the jest's found out. 6| *1841:* The poet's *1849:* All here! Only our poet's 7–8| *1841:* him! He was in love *1849:* him! The airs of that fellow, that Giovacchino! He was in violent love 9| *1841:* suit, when *1849:* suit, so unmolested was it,—when 10| *1841:* fell <> him too, and <> jealousy, he *1849:* falls <> him, too; and <> jealousy he 11| *1841:* all—whereto *1868:* all: whereto 12–13| *1841:* assured me:—*"The author on the author. Here so and so, the mammoth, lies, Fouled* *1849:* assures me—*"Here a mammoth-poem lies,—Fouled* *1863: lies, Fouled* *1868:* me,—*"Here* 16| *1841: epic <> drugs:—Hebe's* *1849: Epic <> drugs: Hebe's* 17| *1841: lip; Phoebus' <> throttle;* *1849: lip. Phoebus' <> throttle.* 19| *1841:* fellow; if *1849:* fellow! If 21–22| *1841:* So <> been acceptable, says Bluphocks, and *1849:* Good!—Only, so <> been universally acceptable, says Bluphocks, *et canibus nostris* . . . and *1888:* only 23| *1841:* our dogs <> boy. *1849:* our literary dogs <> boy—Giovacchino! *1868:* boy Giovacchino! 24| *1841:* now. Where's Gottlieb? Oh, *1849:* now. Where's Gottlieb, the new-comer? Oh, 25| *1841:* listen, Gottlieb—What called *1849:*—listen, Gottlieb, to what has called 27| *1841:* all in <> Jules bursts *1849:* all agreed, all <> Jules shall

out on us in a fury by and by: I am spokesman—the verses that are to undeceive Jules bear my name of Lutwyche—but each professes himself alike insulted by this strutting stone-squarer, who came alone from Paris to Munich, and thence with a crowd of us to Venice and Possagno here, but proceeds in a day or two alone again—oh, alone indubitably!—to Rome and Florence. He, forsooth, take up his portion with these dissolute, brutalized, heartless bunglers!—so he was heard to call us all: now, is Schramm brutalized, I should like to know? Am I heartless?

GOTTLIEB Why, somewhat heartless; for, suppose Jules a coxcomb as much as you choose, still, for this mere coxcombry, you will have brushed off—what do folks style it?—the bloom of his life. Is it too late to alter? These love-letters now, you call his—I can't laugh at them.

4 STUDENT Because you never read the sham letters of our inditing which drew forth these.

GOTTLIEB His discovery of the truth will be frightful.

4 STUDENT That's the joke. But you should have joined us at the beginning: there's no doubt he loves the girl—loves a model he might hire by the hour!

GOTTLIEB See here! "He has been accustomed," he writes, "to have Canova's women about him, in stone, and the world's women beside him, in flesh; these being as much below, as those above, his soul's aspiration: but now he is to have the reality." There you laugh again! I say, you wipe off the very dew of his youth.

---

burst 28–29| *1841:* us by and bye: I shall be spokesman, but *1849:* us in a fury by and bye: I am spokesman—the verses that are / to undeceive Jules bear my name of Lutwyche—but *1863:* by-and-by *1868:* by and by 30| *1841:* came singly *1868:* came alone 31| *1841:* to Munich, thence *1849:* to Munich, and thence 32| *1841:* alone, oh! alone, *1849:* alone again—oh, alone, *1868:* oh, alone 33| *1841:* indubitably—to <> Florence. He take *1849:* indubitably!—to <> Florence. He, forsooth, take 35–36| *1841:* bunglers! (Is <> brutalized? Am I heartless?) *1849:* bunglers!—So he was heard to call us all: now, is <> brutalised, I should like to know? Am I heartless? *1863:* brutalized *1868:* so 37| *1841:* for, coxcomb *1849:* for, suppose Jules a coxcomb 38| *1841:* choose, you *1849:* choose, still, for this mere coxcombry, you 40| *1841:* alter? These letters, now <> his. I *1849:* alter? These love-letters, now <> his . . . I *1863:* his—I *1868:* love-letters now 45–47| *1841:* beginning; there's <> girl. *1849:* beginning: there's <> girl—loves a model he might hire by the hour! 48| *1841:* here: "He has *1849:* here! "He has 50| *1849:* above—his *1868:* above his *1888:* above, his 51| *1841:* aspiration; but <> have" . . . There *1849:* aspiration: but <> have the real."

1 STUDENT Schramm! (Take the pipe out of his mouth, somebody!) Will Jules lose the bloom of his youth?

SCHRAMM Nothing worth keeping is ever lost in this world: look at a blossom—it drops presently, having done its service and lasted its time; but fruits succeed, and where would be the blossom's place could it continue? As well affirm that your eye is no longer in your body, because its earliest favourite, whatever it may have first loved to look on, is dead and done with—as that any affection is lost to the soul when its first object, whatever happened first to satisfy it, is superseded in due course. Keep but ever looking, whether with the body's eye or the mind's, and you will soon find something to look on! Has a man done wondering at women?—there follow men, dead and alive, to wonder at. Has he done wondering at men?—there's God to wonder at: and the faculty of wonder may be, at the same time, old and tired enough with respect to its first object, and yet young and fresh sufficiently, so far as concerns its novel one. Thus . . .

1 STUDENT Put Schramm's pipe into his mouth again! There, you see! Well, this Jules . . . a wretched fribble—oh, I watched his disportings at Possagno, the other day! Canova's gallery—you know: there he marches first resolvedly past great works by the dozen without vouchsafing an eye: all at once he stops full at the *Psiche-fanciulla* —cannot pass that old acquaintance without a nod of encouragement —"In your new place, beauty? Then behave yourself as well here as at Munich—I see you!" Next he posts himself deliberately before the

---

. . . There *1863:* real." There *1868:* reality 53| *1841:* Schramm (take <> somebody), *1849:* Schramm! (Take <> somebody)— *1863:* somebody.) *1868:* somebody!) 54| *1841:* will *1863:* Will 56–58| *1841:* presently and fruits succeed: as *1849:* presently, having done its service and lasted its time; but fruits succeed, and where would be the blossom's place could it continue? As 59–60| *1841:* body because <> favourite is dead <> with, as *1849:* body, because <> favourite, whatever it may have first loved to look on, is dead <> with—as 61–64| *1841:* object is <> course. Has *1849:* object, whatever happened first to satisfy it, is <> course. Keep but ever looking, whether with the body's eye or the mind's, and you will soon find something to look on! Has a man done wondering at women?—There *1868:* there 65| *1841:* men? *1863:* men?— 66| *1841:* There's <> be at *1849:* be, at *1868:* there's 67| *1841:* time grey enough <> its last object *1849:* time, old and tired enough <> its first object 68| *1841:* yet green sufficiently so <> one: *1849:* yet young and fresh sufficiently, so <> one. 69| *1841:* thus . . . *1849:* Thus . . . 70| *1841:* again—There you *1849:* again! There, you 71| *1841:* well this Jules . . a *1849:* see! Well, this—Jules . . . a *1849:* this Jules 72–73| *1841:* at Possagno the <> day! The Model-Gallery—you know: he *1849:* at Possagno, the <> day! Canova's gallery—you know: there he 77| *1841:* you!"—Next posts *1849:* you!" Next he

unfinished *Pietà* for half an hour without moving, till up he starts of a sudden, and thrusts his very nose into—I say, into—the group; by which gesture you are informed that precisely the sole point he had not fully mastered in Canova's practice was a certain method of using the drill in the articulation of the knee-joint—and that, likewise, has he mastered at length! Good-bye, therefore, to poor Canova—whose gallery no longer needs detain his successor Jules, the predestinated novel thinker in marble!

5 STUDENT Tell him about the women: go on to the women!

1 STUDENT Why, on that matter he could never be supercilious enough. How should we be other (he said) than the poor devils you see, with those debasing habits we cherish? He was not to wallow in that mire, at least: he would wait, and love only at the proper time, and meanwhile put up with the *Psiche-fanciulla.* Now, I happened to hear of a young Greek—real Greek girl at Malamocco; a true Islander, do you see, with Alciphron's "hair like sea-moss"—Schramm knows!—white and quiet as an apparition, and fourteen years old at farthest,—a daughter of Natalia, so she swears—that hag Natalia, who helps us to models at three *lire* an hour. We selected this girl for the heroine of our jest. So first, Jules received a scented letter—somebody had seen his Tydeus at the Academy, and my picture was nothing to it: a profound admirer bade him persevere—would make herself known to him ere long. (Paolina, my little friend of the *Fenice,* transcribes divinely.) And in due time, the mysterious correspondent gave certain hints of her peculiar charms—the pale cheeks, the black hair—whatever, in short, had

---

posts 79| *1841:* sudden and <> into . . I say into <> group— *1849:* sudden, and <> into—I say, into <> group; 80| *1841:* which you *1849:* which gesture you 81| *1841:* in Canova was *1849:* in Canova's practice was 82–84| *1841:* that, even, has <> to Canova <> longer contains Jules, *1849:* that, likewise, has <> to poor Canova <> longer need detain his successor Jules, *1863:* needs *1868:* length! Good bye therefore *1888:* length! Good-bye, therefore 85| *1841:* predestinated thinker *1849:* predestinated novel thinker 86| *1841:* women—go <> women. *1849:* to the women! *1863:* women: go 88| *1841:* other than *1849:* other (he said) than 90| *1841:* would love at *1849:* would wait, and love only at 91| *1841: fanciulla.* Now *1868: fanciulla.* Now, 92–94| *1841:* at Malamocco, a <> Alciphron hair like sea-moss—you know! White *1849:* real Greek—girl at Malamocco; a <> Alciphron's "hair like sea-moss"—Schramm knows!—white *1863:* real Greek girl 95–97| *1841:* farthest; daughter, so she swears, of that <> hour. So first Jules *1849:* farthest,—a daughter of Natalia, so she swears—that <> hour. We selected this girl for the heroine of our jest. So, first, Jules *1868:* jest. So first 99| *1841:* it—bade *1849:* it—a profound admirer bade *1868:* it: a 100| *1841:* long—(Paolina *1868:* long. (Paolina 101–105| *1841:* friend, transcribes divinely.) Now think *1849:* friend of

struck us in our Malamocco model: we retained her name, too—Phene, which is, by interpretation, sea-eagle. Now, think of Jules finding himself distinguished from the herd of us by such a creature! In his very first answer he proposed marrying his monitress: and fancy us over these letters, two, three times a day, to receive and despatch! I concocted the main of it: relations were in the way—secrecy must be observed—in fine, would he wed her on trust, and only speak to her when they were indissolubly united? St—st—Here they come!

6 STUDENT Both of them! Heaven's love, speak softly, speak within yourselves!

5 STUDENT Look at the bridegroom! Half his hair in storm and half in calm,—patted down over the left temple,—like a frothy cup one blows on to cool it: and the same old blouse that he murders the marble in.

2 STUDENT Not a rich vest like yours, Hannibal Scratchy!—rich, that your face may the better set it off.

6 STUDENT And the bride! Yes, sure enough, our Phene! Should you have known her in her clothes? How magnificently pale!

GOTTLIEB She does not also take it for earnest, I hope?

1 STUDENT Oh, Natalia's concern, that is! We settle with Natalia.

6 STUDENT She does not speak—has evidently let out no word. The only thing is, will she equally remember the rest of her lesson, and repeat correctly all those verses which are to break the secret to Jules?

---

the *Fenice,* transcribes divinely). And in due time, the mysterious correspondent gave certain hints of her peculiar charms—the pale cheecks, the black hair—whatever, in short, had struck us in our Malamocco model: we retained her name, too—Phene, which is by interpretation, sea-eagle. Now, think 101| *1868:* divinely.) And 107| *1841:* monitress; and *1849:* monitress: and 108| *1841:* letters two <> day to *1849:* letters, two <> day, to 109| *1841:* dispatch *1868:* despatch 110| *1841:* observed—would <> trust and *1849:* observed—in fine, would <> trust, and 111–112| *1841:* united? St—St! *1849:* united? St—st—Here they come! 113| *1841:* softly! speak *1868:* softly, speak 115| *1841:* the Bridegroom—half his *1849:* bridegroom! Half his <> storm, and *1868:* storm and 116| *1841:* calm—patted <> temple, like *1849:* calm,—patted <> temple,—like 117| *1841:* it; and <> blouse he *1849:* it! and <> blouse that he *1868:* it: and 118| *1841:* in! *1868:* in. 119| *1841:* yours, Hannibal Scratchy, rich that *1849:* yours, Hannibal Scratchy!—rich, that 121–122| *1841:* And the bride—and the bride—how *1849:* And the bride! Yes, sure enough, our Phene! Should you have known her in her clothes? How 124| *1841:* is; we *1849:* is! We 125–129| *1841:* word. GOTTLIEB *1849:* word. The only thing is, will she equally remember the rest of her lesson, and repeat

GOTTLIEB How he gazes on her! Pity—pity!

1 STUDENT They go in: now, silence! You three,— not nearer the window, mind, than that pomegranate: just where the little girl, who a few minutes ago passed us singing, is seated!

---

correctly all those verses which are to break the secret to Jules? GOTTLIEB 129| *1841:* her! *1849:* her! Pity—pity! 130–132| *1841:* in—now, silence! *1849:* silence! You three,—not nearer the window, mind, than that pomegranate—just where the little girl, who a few minutes ago passed us singing, is seated! 130| *1868:* in: now 131| *1868:* pomegranate: just

PART II. [i] NOON

SCENE—*Over Orcana. The house of* JULES, *who crosses its threshold with* PHENE: *she is silent, on which* JULES *begins*—

Do not die, Phene! I am yours now, you
Are mine now; let fate reach me how she likes,
If you'll not die: so, never die! Sit here—
My work-room's single seat. I over-lean
This length of hair and lustrous front; they turn
Like an entire flower upward: eyes, lips, last
Your chin—no, last your throat turns: 'tis their scent
Pulls down my face upon you. Nay, look ever
This one way till I change; grow you—I could
Change into you, beloved!

You by me,
And I by you; this is your hand in mine,
And side by side we sit: all's true. Thank God!
I have spoken: speak you!

O my life to come!
My Tydeus must be carved that's there in clay;
Yet how be carved, with you about the room?
Where must I place you? When I think that once

Part-title and stage directions / *1841:* II.—*Noon. Over* <> *with* PHENE—*she* *1863:* *with* PHENE: *she* *1888:* PART II. / NOON. / SCENE.—*Over* [1]| *1841:* die, Phene—I <> now—you *1863:* die, Phene! I <> now, you [2]| *1841:* now—let <> likes *1849:* likes, *1863:* now; let [3]| *1841:* die—so never *1849:* so, never *1868:* die: so [4]| *1841:* seat—I do lean over *1849:* seat: I over-lean *1863:* seat. I [5]| *1841:* front—they *1863:* front; they [6]| *1841:* upward—eyes—lips—last *1863:* upward: eyes *1868:* eyes, lips, last [7]| *1841:* turns—'tis *1868:* turns: 'tis [8]| *1849:* you! Nay *1868:* you. Nay [9]| *1841:* That one *1849:* This one [10]| *1841:* beloved! ¶ Thou by me *1849:* beloved! ¶ You by me, *1863:* Beloved *1868:* beloved [11]| *1841:* by thee—this <> mine— *1849:* by you—this *1863:* you; this <> mine, [12]| *1841:* sit—all's *1849:* sit: all's [13]| *1841:* spoken—speak thou! ¶ —O, my *1849:* speak, you *1863:* spoken: speak, you! ¶ O *1868:* you! ¶ O my [14]| *1841:* clay, *1849:* carved, that's <> clay; *1868:* carved that's [15]| *1841:* And how be carved with <> the chamber? *1849:* Yet how be

This room-full of rough block-work seemed my heaven
Without you! Shall I ever work again,
Get fairly into my old ways again,
Bid each conception stand while, trait by trait,
My hand transfers its lineaments to stone?
Will my mere fancies live near you, their truth—
The live truth, passing and repassing me,
Sitting beside me?

Now speak!

Only first,

See, all your letters! Was't not well contrived?
Their hiding-place is Psyche's robe; she keeps
Your letters next her skin: which drops out foremost?
Ah,—this that swam down like a first moonbeam
Into my world!

Again those eyes complete

Their melancholy survey, sweet and slow,
Of all my room holds; to return and rest
On me, with pity, yet some wonder too:
As if God bade some spirit plague a world,
And this were the one moment of surprise
And sorrow while she took her station, pausing
O'er what she sees, finds good, and must destroy!
What gaze you at? Those? Books, I told you of;
Let your first word to me rejoice them, too:
This minion, a Coluthus, writ in red
Bistre and azure by Bessarion's scribe—

---

carved, with *1868:* the room? 18| *1841:* again— *1863:* again, 19| *1841:* again— *1863:* again, 20| *1841:* while trait by trait *1849:* while, trait by trait, 22| *1841:* Will they, my fancies, live near you, my truth— *1849:* Will my mere fancies live *1868:* you, their truth— 23| *1841:* truth—passing <> me— *1863:* truth, passing <> me, 24| *1841:* speak! ¶ Only, first, *1868:* speak! ¶ Only first, 25| *1841:* Your letters to me—was't *1849:* See, all your letters! Was't 26| *1841:* A hiding-place in Psyche's robe—there lie *1849:* Their hiding-place is Psyche's robe; she keeps 27| *1841:* Next to her skin your letters: which comes foremost? *1849:* Your letters next her skin: which drops out foremost? 28| *1841:* Good—this *1849:* Ah,—this 29–37| *1841:* world. ¶ Those? Books I <> of. 29| *1849:* world! ¶ Again those eyes complete 30–36| § added 1849, variants from 1889 § 32| *1849:* too— *1868:* too: 37| *1849:* What gaze you at? Those? Books, I <> of; 38| *1841:* too— *1849:* too: 39| *1841:* minion of Coluthus *1849:*

Read this line . . . no, shame—Homer's be the Greek
First breathed me from the lips of my Greek girl!
This Odyssey in coarse black vivid type
With faded yellow blossoms 'twixt page and page,
To mark great places with due gratitude;
"*He said, and on Antinous directed*
A bitter shaft" . . . a flower blots out the rest!
Again upon your search? My statues, then!
—Ah, do not mind that—better that will look
When cast in bronze—an Almaign Kaiser, that,
Swart-green and gold, with truncheon based on hip.
This, rather, turn to! What, unrecognized?
I thought you would have seen that here you sit
And I imagined you,—Hippolyta,
Naked upon her bright Numidian horse.
Recall you this then? "Carve in bold relief"—
So you commanded—"carve, against I come,
A Greek, in Athens, as our fashion was,
Feasting, bay-filleted and thunder-free,
Who rises 'neath the lifted myrtle-branch.
'Praise those who slew Hipparchus!' cry the guests,
'While o'er thy head the singer's myrtle waves
As erst above our champion: stand up, all!' "
See, I have laboured to express your thought.
Quite round, a cluster of mere hands and arms,

---

minion, a Coluthus 41–43| *1841:* line . . no <> Greek! / My Odyssey *1849:* the Greek / First breathed me from the lips of my Greek girl! / My *1868:* This Odyssey *1888:* line . . . no 44–46| *1841:* and page; / "He *1849:* and page, / To mark great places with due gratitude; / *"He* 46–47| *1841:* "He <> / <> shaft" § in roman § *1849:* § in italics § 47–49| *1841:* shaft"—then blots a flower the rest! / —Ah *1849: shaft"* . . . a flower blots out the rest! / Again upon your search? My statues, then! / —Ah 50| *1841:* bronze . . an <> Kaiser that, *1849:* bronze—an <> Kaiser, that, 51| *1841:* gold with <> hip— *1849:* gold, with <> hip. 52| *1841:* This rather, turn to . . but a check already— *1849:* This, rather, turn to! What, unrecognized? 53| *1841:* Or you had recognized that *1849:* I thought you would have seen that 54| *1841:* you, Hippolyta *1849:* you,—Hippolyta 55| *1841:* horse! *1868:* horse. 56| *1841:* —Forget you this then? "carve <> relief" . . . *1849:* Recall you this, then? "Carve <> relief"— *1868:* this then 57| *1841:* command me—"carve against I come *1849:* commanded—"carve, against I come, 58–59| *1841:* A Greek, bay-filleted *1849:* A Greek, in Athens, as our fashion was, / Feasting, bay-filletted 60–65| *1841:* Rising beneath <> myrtle-branch, / Whose turn arrives to praise Harmodius."—Praise him! / Quite <> arms *1849:* Who rises 'neath <> myrtle-branch: / '*Praise those who slew Hipparchus,*' cry the guests, / '*While o'er thy head the singer's*

(Thrust in all senses, all ways, from all sides,
Only consenting at the branch's end
They strain toward) serves for frame to a sole face,
The Praiser's, in the centre: who with eyes
Sightless, so bend they back to light inside
His brain where visionary forms throng up,
Sings, minding not that palpitating arch
Of hands and arms, nor the quick drip of wine
From the drenched leaves o'erhead, nor crowns cast off,
Violet and parsley crowns to trample on—
Sings, pausing as the patron-ghosts approve,
Devoutly their unconquerable hymn.
But you must say a "well" to that—say "well!"
Because you gaze—am I fantastic, sweet?
Gaze like my very life's-stuff, marble—marbly
Even to the silence! Why, before I found
The real flesh Phene, I inured myself
To see, throughout all nature, varied stuff
For better nature's birth by means of art:
With me, each substance tended to one form
Of beauty—to the human archetype.
On every side occurred suggestive germs
Of that—the tree, the flower—or take the fruit,—
Some rosy shape, continuing the peach,
Curved beewise o'er its bough; as rosy limbs,
Depending, nestled in the leaves; and just

---

myrtle waves / As erst above our champions': stand up, all!' " / See, I have laboured to express your thought! / Quite <> arms, *1869:* myrtle-branch. / 'Praise <> Hipparchus!' <> // <> all!' " § in roman § / <> thought. 66| *1841:* Thrust *1849:* (Thrust 67| *1841:* branches' *1863:* branch's 68| *1841:* towards, serves <> face— *1849:* toward) serves *1863:* face, 69| *1841:* (Place your own face)—the Praiser's, who *1849:* The Praiser's—in the centre—who *1863:* The Praiser's, in *1868:* centre: who 71–72| *1841:* up, / (Gaze—I am your Harmodius dead and gone,) / Sings, minding nor the palpitating *1849:* up, / Sings, minding not that palpitating 74| *1841:* nor who cast off *1849:* nor crowns cast off, 75| *1841:* Their violet crowns for him to *1849:* Violet and parsley crowns to 77| *1841:* hymn— *1849:* hymn! *1868:* hymn. 78| *1841:* that—say "well" *1849:* that—say, "well!" *1868:* that—say "well!" 81| *1841:* silence—and before *1849:* silence! why before *1863:* why, before *1868:* silence! Why 83| *1841:* see throughout all nature varied *1849:* see, throughout all nature, varied 84| *1863:* art. *1868:* art: 86| *1841:* human Archetype— *1863:* archetype. 87| *1841:* And every *1849:* On every 88| *1841:* flower—why, take the fruit, *1849:* flower—or take the fruit,— 90| *1841:* bough, as rosy limbs *1849:* bough; as rosy limbs, 91| *1841:* Depending nestled

From a cleft rose-peach the whole Dryad sprang.
But of the stuffs one can be master of,
How I divined their capabilities!
From the soft-rinded smoothening facile chalk
That yields your outline to the air's embrace,
Half-softened by a halo's pearly gloom;
Down to the crisp imperious steel, so sure
To cut its one confided thought clean out
Of all the world. But marble!—'neath my tools
More pliable than jelly—as it were
Some clear primordial creature dug from depths
In the earth's heart, where itself breeds itself,
And whence all baser substance may be worked;
Refine it off to air, you may,—condense it
Down to the diamond;—is not metal there,
When o'er the sudden speck my chisel trips?
—Not flesh, as flake off flake I scale, approach,
Lay bare those bluish veins of blood asleep?
Lurks flame in no strange windings where, surprised
By the swift implement sent home at once,
Flushes and glowings radiate and hover
About its track?
                                        Phene? what—why is this?
That whitening cheek, those still dilating eyes!
Ah, you will die—I knew that you would die!

PHENE *begins, on his having long remained silent.*

Now the end's coming; to be sure, it must
Have ended sometime! Tush, why need I speak

<> leaves—and *1849:* Depending, nestled *1863:* leaves; and 92| *1841:* sprung! *1849:* sprang! *1863:* sprang. 94| *1841:* capabilities *1849:* capabilities! 96–98| *1841:* embrace, / Down *1849:* embrace, / Half-softened by a halo's pearly gloom; / Down 100| *1841:* world: but *1863:* world. But 102| *1841:* from deep *1849:* from depths 103| *1841:* the Earth's heart where itself <> itself *1849:* heart, where itself <> itself, *1863:* earth's 105| *1841:* air you may—condense *1849:* air, you *1863:* may,—condense 106| *1841:* there *1849:* there, 107| *1841:* specks *1868:* speck 108| *1841:* flesh—as *1863:* flesh, as 109| *1841:* blueish *1863:* bluish 113–115| *1841:* track?— ¶ Phene <> this? / Ah *1849:* this? / That whitening cheek, those still-dilating eyes! / Ah *1863:* track? ¶ Phene 116| *1841:* coming—to be sure it *1849:* sure, it *1863:* coming; to 117| *1841:* sometime!—Tush—I will not speak *1849:* sometime! Tush—why need I

Their foolish speech? I cannot bring to mind
One half of it, beside; and do not care
For old Natalia now, nor any of them.
Oh, you—what are you?—if I do not try
To say the words Natalia made me learn,
To please your friends,—it is to keep myself
Where your voice lifted me, by letting that
Proceed: but can it? Even you, perhaps,
Cannot take up, now you have once let fall,
The music's life, and me along with that—
No, or you would! We'll stay, then, as we are:
Above the world.
                    You creature with the eyes!
If I could look for ever up to them,
As now you let me,—I believe, all sin,
All memory of wrong done, suffering borne,
Would drop down, low and lower, to the earth
Whence all that's low comes, and there touch and stay
—Never to overtake the rest of me,
All that, unspotted, reaches up to you,
Drawn by those eyes! What rises is myself,
Not me the shame and suffering; but they sink,
Are left, I rise above them. Keep me so,
Above the world!
                    But you sink, for your eyes
Are altering—altered! Stay—"I love you, love" . . .

---

speak *1863:* sometime! Tush, why 118| *1841:* speech—I *1849:* speech? I 119| *1841:* Half—so the whole were best unsaid—what care *1849:* One half of it, besides; and do not care *1868:* beside 120| *1841:* I for Natalia now, or all of them? *1849:* For old Natalia now, nor any of them. 121| *1841:* you . . what are you?—I do not attempt *1849:* you—what are you?—if I do not try 122| *1841:* words Natalia bade me learn *1849:* words Natalia made me learn, 123| *1841:* friends, that I may keep *1849:* friends,—it is to keep 124| *1841:* me—by letting you *1849:* me, by letting it *1868:* letting that 125| *1841:* Proceed . . but can you?—even you perhaps *1849:* Proceed—but can it? Even you, perhaps, 127| *1841:* with it? *1849:* with that— 128| *1841:* No—or you would . . we'll stay then as we are *1849:* No, or you would! We'll stay, then, as *1863:* are: 129–139| § added 1849, variants from 1889 § 129| *1849:* —Above *1863:* Above 132| *1849:* done or suffering *1868:* done, suffering 138| *1849:* Not so the *1868:* Not me the 139| *1849:* them—Keep me so *1863:* them. Keep me so, 140| *1841:* world— ¶ Now you sink—for *1849:* world! ¶ But you sink, for 141| *1841:* altered . . altering—stay <> you, love you." *1849:* altering—altered! Stay <> you, love you" . . . *1868:* you, love" . . .

I could prevent it if I understood:
More of your words to me: was't in the tone
Or the words, your power?
Or stay—I will repeat
Their speech, if that contents you! Only change
No more, and I shall find it presently
Far back here, in the brain yourself filled up.
Natalia threatened me that harm should follow
Unless I spoke their lesson to the end,
But harm to me, I thought she meant, not you.
Your friends,—Natalia said they were your friends
And meant you well,—because, I doubted it,
Observing (what was very strange to see)
On every face, so different in all else,
The same smile girls like me are used to bear,
But never men, men cannot stoop so low;
Yet your friends, speaking of you, used that smile,
That hateful smirk of boundless self-conceit
Which seems to take possession of the world
And make of God a tame confederate,
Purveyor to their appetites . . . you know!
But still Natalia said they were your friends,
And they assented though they smiled the more,
And all came round me,—that thin Englishman
With light lank hair seemed leader of the rest;
He held a paper—"What we want," said he,
Ending some explanation to his friends—
"Is something slow, involved and mystical,
Only when on the lips or loathing tongue."
To hold Jules long in doubt, yet take his taste

143| *1841:* me . . was't *1849:* me—was't *1863:* me: was't 144| *1841:* Of the voice, your power? ¶ Stay, stay, I *1849:* Or the words, your power? ¶ Or stay—I 145| *1841:* that affects you! only *1849:* that contents you! Only, change *1868:* you! Only change 146| *1841:* more and <> presently— *1849:* more, and <> presently 147| *1841:* here in <> up: *1849:* —Far back here, in <> up. *1868:* Far 148| *1841:* Natalia said (like Lutwyche) harm would follow *1849:* Natalia threatened me that harm *1868:* should 150| *1841:* thought, not you: and so *1849:* thought she meant, not you. 151–176| § added 1849, variants from 1889 § 155| *1849:* like us are *1868:* like me are 159| *1849:* of this world *1868:* of the world 160| *1849:* of God their tame *1868:* of God a tame 161| *1849:* appetites . . you *1888:* appetites . . . you 162| *1849:* But no—Natalia *1868:* But still Natalia 163| *1849:* assented while they *1868:* assented though they 165| *1849:* light, lank *1868:* light lank 170| *1849:* on, so that, at

And lure him on until, at innermost
Where he seeks sweetness' soul, he may find—this!
—As in the apple's core, the noisome fly:
For insects on the rind are seen at once,
And brushed aside as soon, but this is found
And so he read what I have got by heart:
I'll speak it,—"Do not die, love! I am yours."
No—is not that, or like that, part of words
Yourself began by speaking? Strange to lose
What cost such pains to learn! Is this more right?
I am a painter who cannot paint;
In my life, a devil rather than saint;
In my brain, as poor a creature too:
No end to all I cannot do!
Yet do one thing at least I can—
Love a man or hate a man
Supremely: thus my lore began.
Through the Valley of Love I went,
In the lovingest spot to abide,
And just on the verge where I pitched my tent,
I found Hate dwelling beside.
(Let the Bridegroom ask what the painter meant,
Of his Bride, of the peerless Bride!)
And further, I traversed Hate's grove,
In the hatefullest nook to dwell;

1868: on until, at 176| *1849:* heart— *1868:* heart: 177| *1841:* die, Phene, I am yours" . . *1849:* die, love! I am yours" . . . *1888:* yours." 178| *1841:* Stop—is <> of what *1849:* of words *1868:* No—is 179| *1841:* You spoke? 'Tis not my fault—that I should lose *1849:* Yourself began by speaking? Strange to lose
180–185| *1841:* pains acquiring! is this right? / The Bard said, do one thing I can— *1849:* cost such pains to learn! Is this more right? / *I am a painter who cannot paint;* / *In my life, a devil rather than saint,* / *In my brain, as poor a creature too*— / *No end to all I cannot do!* / *Yet do one thing at least I* 182| *1888: saint;* 183| *1863: too:*
186–199| § in roman 1841 only § 186| *1841:* man and hate *1849: man, or hate* *1868: man or hate* 187| *1849: my love began.* *1863: my lore began.*
188| *1841:* Thro' *1849: Through* 189| *1841:* In its lovingest <> abide; *1849: abide,* *1868: In the lovingest* 190| *1841:* tent *1849: tent,* 191| *1841:* Dwelt Hate beside— *1849: I found Hate dwelling beside.* 192| *1841:* (And the bridegroom asked what the bard's smile meant *1849: (Let the Bridegroom ask what the painter meant,* 193| *1841:* his bride.) *1849: Of his Bride, of the peerless Bride!)* 194| *1841:* Next Hate I traversed, the Grove, *1849: And further, I traversed Hate's grove,* 195| *1841:* In its hatefullest <> dwell— *1849: dwell;*

But lo, where I flung myself prone, couched Love
Where the shadow threefold fell.
(The meaning—those black bride's-eyes above,
Not a painter's lip should tell!)

"And here," said he, "Jules probably will ask,
'You have black eyes, Love,—you are, sure enough,
My peerless bride,—then do you tell indeed
What needs some explanation! What means this?' "
—And I am to go on, without a word—

So, I grew wise in Love and Hate,
From simple that I was of late.
Once, when I loved, I would enlace
Breast, eyelids, hands, feet, form and face
Of her I loved, in one embrace—
As if by mere love I could love immensely!
Once, when I hated, I would plunge
My sword, and wipe with the first lunge
My foe's whole life out like a sponge—
As if by mere hate I could hate intensely!
But now I am wiser, know better the fashion
How passion seeks aid from its opposite passion:
And if I see cause to love more, hate more

1868: In the hatefullest 196| *1841:* And lo *1849: But lo* 197| *1841:* Next cell. *1849: Where the deepest shadow fell.* *1868: the shadow threefold fell.* 198| *1841:* (For not I, said the bard, but those black bride's eyes above *1849: (The meaning—those black bride's-eyes above,* 199| *1841:* Should tell!) *1849: Not the painter's lip should tell!)* *1868: Not a painter's* 200| *1841:* (Then Lutwyche said you probably would ask, *1849:* "And here," said he, "Jules probably will ask, 201–203| § in italics 1849 and 1863 only § 201| *1841:* "You <> love <> are sure enough *1849: You <> are, sure enough,* *1868:* 'You <> Love 202| *1841:* My beautiful bride—do you, as he sings, tell *1849: My peerless bride,—so do you tell, indeed,* *1863: so, do* *1868:* bride,—then do you tell indeed 203| *1841:* some exposition—what is this?" *1849: some explanation—what means this?"* *1868:* explanation! What <> this?' " 204–207| *1841:* . . . And <> word, / Once when I loved I *1849:* —And <> word— / *So I grew wiser in Love and Hate, / From simple, that I was of late. / For once, when I loved, I* 205| *1863: So, I* 206–07| *1868: wise <> simple that* 207| *1888: Once* 207–233| § in roman 1849 only § 209–211| *1841:* loved in <> / And, when *1849: loved, in <> / As if by mere love I could love immensely! / And when* 211| *1888: Once, when* 213–217| *1841:* spunge: / —But if I would love and hate *1849: out, like a sponge— / As if by mere hate I could hate intensely! / But now I am wiser, know better the fashion / How passion seeks aid from its opposite passion, / And if I see cause to love more, or hate* 213| *1863: spunge—* *1868: out like a sponge—* 216| *1868: passion* 217| *1868: more, hate*

Than ever man loved, ever hated before—
And seek in the Valley of Love,
The nest, or the nook in Hate's Grove,
Where my soul may surely reach
The essence, nought less, of each,
The Hate of all Hates, the Love
Of all Loves, in the Valley or Grove,—
I find them the very warders
Each of the other's borders.
When I love most, Love is disguised
In Hate; and when Hate is surprised
In Love, then I hate most: ask
How Love smiles through Hate's iron casque,
Hate grins through Love's rose-braided mask,—
And how, having hated thee,
I sought long and painfully
To reach thy heart, nor prick

218| *1841:* man hated or loved before— *1849: man loved, ever hated, before— 1868: hated before—* 219| *1841:* Would seek in the valley of Love *1849: And seek in the Valley of Love,* 220| *1841:* The spot, or in Hatred's grove *1849: spot, or the spot in Hate's Grove, 1868: The nest, or the nook in* 221| *1841:* The spot where my soul may reach *1849: Where my soul may the sureliest reach 1868: may surely reach* 222–223| *1841:* each . . . (Here he said, if you interrupted me / With, "There must be some error,—who induced you / To speak this jargon?"—I was to reply / Simply—"Await till . . . until . ." I must say / Last rhyme again—) / . . The essence, nought less, of each— / The <> all Hates, or the § (Here <> //// <> again—) not indented § *1849: each, / The Hate of all 1868: all Hates, the* 224| *1841:* all Loves in its glen or its grove, *1849: all Loves, in its Valley or Grove,— 1868: in the Valley* 225| *1841:* —I *1849: I* 227| *1841:* So most I love when Love's disguised *1849: I love most, when Love is disguised 1868: When I love most, Love* 228| *1841:* In Hate's garb—'tis when Hate's surprised *1849: In Hate; and when Hate is surprized 1863:* surprised 229| *1841:* In Love's weed that I hate most; ask *1849: In Love, then I hate most: ask* 230| *1841:* How Love can smile thro' Hate's barred iron *1849: How Love smiles through Hate's iron casque,* 231–232| *1841:* grin thro' <> mask, Of thy bride, Giulio! (Then you, "Oh, not mine— / Preserve the real name of the foolish song!" / But I must answer, "Giulio—Jules 'tis Jules!) / Thus, I, Jules, hating thee § Preserve <> / <> Jules!) not indented § *1849: grins through <> mask,— / And how, having hated thee,* 233–238| *1841:* Sought <> painfully . . . / [JULES *interposes*] / Lutwyche—who *1849: I sought <> painfully / To wound thee, and not prick / The skin, but pierce to the quick— / Ask this, my Jules, and be answered straight / By thy bride—how the painter Lutwyche can hate! //* Lutwyche—who 234| *1868: To reach thy heart,*

The skin but pierce to the quick—
Ask this, my Jules, and be answered straight
By thy bride—how the painter Lutwyche can hate!

JULES *interposes.*

Lutwyche! Who else? But all of them, no doubt,
Hated me: they at Venice—presently
Their turn, however! You I shall not meet:
If I dreamed, saying this would wake me.
Keep
What's here, the gold—we cannot meet again,
Consider! and the money was but meant
For two years' travel, which is over now,
All chance or hope or care or need of it.
This—and what comes from selling these, my casts
And books and medals, except . . . let them go
Together, so the produce keeps you safe
Out of Natalia's clutches! If by chance
(For all's chance here) I should survive the gang
At Venice, root out all fifteen of them,
We might meet somewhere, since the world is wide.
[*From without is heard the voice of* PIPPA, *singing*—]

Give her but a least excuse to love me!
When—where—
How—can this arm establish her above me,
If fortune fixed her as my lady there,
There already, to eternally reprove me?

---

nor prick 235| *1868: skin but* 238| *1863:* Lutwyche! who 239| *1841:* me—them at *1849:* me: they at 240| *1841:* For them, however <> meet— *1849:* Their turn, however <> meet: 241| *1841:* saying that would <> § no ¶ § Keep *1849:* saying this would wake me! ¶ Keep *1868:* me. ¶ Keep 242| *1841:* here—this too—we <> again *1849:* here, this gold—we <> again, *1868:* here, the gold 243| *1841:* Consider—and *1868:* Consider! and 244| *1841:* now *1849:* now, 245| *1841:* chance, or hope, or care, or <> it! *1868:* chance or hope or care or <> it. 246| *1841:* these—my *1849:* these, my 247| *1841:* books, and medals except *1849:* medals, except *1868:* books and 248| *1841:* Together—so *1849:* Together, so <> safe, *1868:* safe 249| *1849:* clutches!—If *1888:* clutches! If 252–253| *1841:* somewhere since <> / 1. / [*Without.*] *Give* *1849:* somewhere, since <> wide— / [*From without is heard the voice of* PIPPA, *singing*— / *Give* *1863:* wide. 253–257| § in roman 1841 only § 255| *1841:* me *1849: me,* 256| *1841:* fixed my lady there— *1849: fixed her as my lady there,* 257| *1841:*

("Hist!"—said Kate the Queen;
But "Oh!"—cried the maiden, binding her tresses,
" 'Tis only a page that carols unseen,
Crumbling your hounds their messes!")

Is she wronged?—To the rescue of her honour,
My heart!
Is she poor?—What costs it to be styled a donor?
Merely an earth to cleave, a sea to part.
But that fortune should have thrust all this upon her!
("Nay, list!"—bade Kate the Queen;
And still cried the maiden, binding her tresses,
" 'Tis only a page that carols unseen,
Fitting your hawks their jesses!")

[PIPPA *passes.*]

JULES *resumes.*

What name was that the little girl sang forth?
Kate! The Cornaro, doubtless, who renounced
The crown of Cyprus to be lady here
At Asolo, where still her memory stays,
And peasants sing how once a certain page
Pined for the grace of her so far above
His power of doing good to, "Kate the Queen—
She never could be wronged, be poor," he sighed,

—There *1849: There* 258–261| § not indented farther 1841, 1849, 1863 § 258–260| *1841: (Hist, said Kate the queen: / —Only a page who carols unseen 1849: ("Hist"—said <> queen; / But "Oh—" cried the maiden, binding her tresses, / " 'Tis only a page that carols* *1868:* ("Hist!"—said Kate the Queen; // *unseen,* 261–262| *1841: messes!* / 2. / She's wronged <> honor, *1849: messes!") / Is she wronged <> honour,* 262–266| § in roman 1841 only § 264| *1841:* She's poor *1849: Is she poor* 265| *1841:* An earth's <> sea's to part! *1849: Merely an earth's 1868: earth <> sea to part.* 266| *1841:* —But *1849: But* 267–270| § not indented farther 1841, 1849, 1863 § 267–269| *1841: (Nay, list, bade <> queen: / Only 1849: ("Nay, list,—bade <> queen; / And still cried the maiden, binding her tresses, / " 'Tis only <> unseen* 267| *1868: the Queen;* 269| *1868: unseen,* 270–272| *1841: jesses!) /* [PIPPA passes. / Kate? Queen Cornaro doubtless *1849: jesses!") /* <> / JULES *resumes.* / What name was that the little girl sang forth? / Kate? The Cornaro, doubtless 273| *1841:* Cyprus to live and die the lady *1849:* The crown of Cyprus to be lady 274–282| *1841:* At Asolo—and whosoever loves 274| *1849:* At Asolo, where still the peasants keep *1868:* her memory stays, 275–281| § added 1849, variants from 1889 § 275| *1849:* Her memory; and songs tell how many a page *1868:* And peasants sing how once a certain page 276| *1849:* of one so *1868:* of her so 277| *1849:* to, as a queen— *1868:* to, "Kate the Queen— 278| *1849:* "She *1868:*

"Need him to help her!"
Yes, a bitter thing
To see our lady above all need of us;
Yet so we look ere we will love; not I,
But the world looks so. If whoever loves
Must be, in some sort, god or worshipper,
The blessing or the blest one, queen or page,
Why should we always choose the page's part?
Here is a woman with utter need of me,—
I find myself queen here, it seems!
How strange!
Look at the woman here with the new soul,
Like my own Psyche,—fresh upon her lips
Alit, the visionary butterfly,
Waiting my word to enter and make bright,
Or flutter off and leave all blank as first.
This body had no soul before, but slept
Or stirred, was beauteous or ungainly, free
From taint or foul with stain, as outward things
Fastened their image on its passiveness:
Now, it will wake, feel, live—or die again!
Shall to produce form out of unshaped stuff
Be Art—and further, to evoke a soul
From form be nothing? This new soul is mine!

Now, to kill Lutwyche, what would that do?—save
A wretched dauber, men will hoot to death
Without me, from their hooting. Oh, to hear
God's voice plain as I heard it first, before
They broke in with their laughter! I heard them
Henceforth, not God.
To Ancona—Greece—some isle!

She 279| *1849:* For him *1868:* Need him 282| *1849:* But the world looks so. If whoever loves 283| *1841:* be in <> sort god *1849:* be, in <> sort, god 284–287| *1841:* blessing, or the <> page— / I <> here it *1849:* blessing or the <> page, / Why should we always choose the page's part? / Here is a woman with utter need of me,— / I <> here, it 288–298| § added 1849, variants from 1889 § 289| *1849:* own Psyche's *1868:* own Psyche 298| *1841:* of shapelessness *1849:* of unshaped stuff 299| *1841:* art—and, further *1863:* Be Art *1868:* and further 300–301| *1841:* mine— / § no space § / Now to kill Lutwyche what <> do?—Save *1849:* mine! / § space § / Now, to kill Lutwyche, what <> save 302| *1841:* dauber men *1849:* dauber, men 303–306| *1841:* me. ¶ To Ancona *1849:* me, from their laughter!—Oh, to hear

I wanted silence only; there is clay
Everywhere. One may do whate'er one likes
In Art: the only thing is, to make sure
That one does like it—which takes pains to know.
Scatter all this, my Phene—this mad dream!
Who, what is Lutwyche, what Natalia's friends,
What the whole world except our love—my own,
Own Phene? But I told you, did I not,
Ere night we travel for your land—some isle
With the sea's silence on it? Stand aside—
I do but break these paltry models up
To begin Art afresh. Meet Lutwyche, I—
And save him from my statue meeting him?
Some unsuspected isle in the far seas!
Like a god going through his world, there stands
One mountain for a moment in the dusk,
Whole brotherhoods of cedars on its brow:
And you are ever by me while I gaze
—Are in my arms as now—as now—as now!
Some unsuspected isle in the far seas!
Some unsuspected isle in far-off seas!

[II.ii.]

Talk by the way, while PIPPA *is passing from Orcana to the Turret. Two or three of the Austrian Police loitering with* BLUPHOCKS, *an English vagabond, just in view of the Turret.*

BLUPHOCKS* So, that is your Pippa, the little girl who passed us singing? Well, your Bishop's Intendant's money shall be honestly earned:—

* "He maketh his sun to rise on the evil and on the good, and sendeth rain on the just and on the unjust."

/ God's voice plain as I heard it first, before / They broke in with that laughter! / I heard them / Henceforth, not God! ¶ To *1863:* laughter! Oh *1868:* their hooting. Oh // <> with their laughter 307| *1841:* only—there *1863:* only: there *1888:* only; there 308| *1841:* Every where *1863:* Everywhere 309| *1841:* In Art—the <> to be sure *1849:* to make sure *1863:* In Art: the 312| *1841:* Who—what is Lutwyche—what Natalia— *1849:* is Lutwyche—what Natalia's friends, *1863:* Who, what is Lutwyche, what 313| *1841:* own *1849:* own, 318| *1841:* art afresh. Shall I meet Lutwyche, *1868:* begin Art afresh. Meet Lutwyche, I— 319| *1841:* statue's *1868:* statue 321| *1841:* thro' his world I trace *1849:* world there stands *1863:* through *1868:* world, there 323| *1841:* brow— *1863:* brow: 324| *1841:* while I trace *1849:* while I gaze 327| *1841:* far off *1863:* far-off

Stage directions / *1841: way in the mean time. Two* *1849: way, while* PIPPA *is passing from Orcana to the Turret. Two* **1863:* maketh His *1868:* maketh his

1–6| § to *Oh were* first appear 1849 §

now, don't make me that sour face because I bring the Bishop's name into the business; we know he can have nothing to do with such horrors: we know that he is a saint and all that a bishop should be, who is a great man beside. *Oh were but every worm a maggot, Every fly a grig, Every bough a Christmas faggot, Every tune a jig!* In fact, I have abjured all religions; but the last I inclined to, was the Armenian: for I have travelled, do you see, and at Koenigsberg, Prussia Improper (so styled because there's a sort of bleak hungry sun there), you might remark over a venerable house-porch, a certain Chaldee inscription; and brief as it is, a mere glance at it used absolutely to change the mood of every bearded passenger. In they turned, one and all; the young and lightsome, with no irreverent pause, the aged and decrepit, with a sensible alacrity: 'twas the Grand Rabbi's abode, in short. Struck with curiosity, I lost no time in learning Syriac—(these are vowels, you dogs,—follow my stick's end in the mud—*Celarent, Darii, Ferio!*) and one morning presented myself, spelling-book in hand, a, b, c,—I picked it out letter by letter, and what was the purport of this miraculous posy? Some cherished legend of the past, you'll say—*"How Moses hocus-pocussed Egypt's land with fly and locust,"*—or, *"How to Jonah sounded harshish, Get thee up and go to Tarshish,"*—or, *"How the angel meeting Balaam, Straight his ass returned a salaam,"* In no wise! *"Shackabrack—Boach—somebody or other—Isaach, Re-cei-ver, Pur-cha-ser and Ex-chan-ger of—Stolen Goods!"* So, talk to me of the religion of a bishop! I have renounced all bishops save Bishop Beveridge—mean to live so—and die—*As some Greek dog-sage, dead and merry, Hellward bound in Charon's wherry, With food for both worlds, under and upper, Lupine-seed and Hecate's supper, And never an obolus . . .* (Though thanks to you, or this Intendant through you, or this Bishop

---

4–5| *1841:* business—we <> horrors—we <> that a Bishop *1868:* business; we <> horrors: we <> bishop 6| *1849:* besides. *1868:* beside. 6| *1841: Oh! were 1868: Oh were* 7| *1841:* christmas *1863: Christmas* 8| *1841:* religions,—but <> to was the Armenian—for *1849:* religions; but <> to, was *1868:* the Armenian: for 10| *1841:* there,) you *1868:* there), you 13| *1841:* all, the *1849:* all; the 15–16| *1841:* alacrity,—'twas <> short. I <> Syriac—(vowels, you dogs,— *1849:* short. Struck with curiosity, I <> Syriac—(these are vowels, you dogs,— *1868:* alacrity: 'twas 18–19| *1841:* myself spelling-book <> c,—what *1849:* c,—I picked it out letter by letter, and what *1868:* myself, spelling-book 20| *1863:* Past *1868:* past 21| *1841: pocust 1868: pocussed* 23| *1841: salaam,"—in 1849: salaam;"—in 1863: salaam." In 1888: salaam," In* 25–26| *1841: of—Stolen goods."* So talk to me of obliging a bishop! I *1849: goods!"* So talk to me of the religion of a bishop! I *1863: of—Stolen Goods!"* So, talk 28| *1841: in Charon's ferry*—With *1849: in Charon's wherry—With 1868: wherry, With* 29–32| *1841: obolus . .* (it might be got in somehow) *Tho' Cerberus should gobble us—To*

through his Intendant—I possess a burning pocketful of *zwanzigers*) . . . *To pay the Stygian Ferry!*

1 POLICEMAN There is the girl, then; go and deserve them the moment you have pointed out to us Signor Luigi and his mother. [*To the rest.*] I have been noticing a house yonder, this long while: not a shutter unclosed since morning!

2 POLICEMAN Old Luca Gaddi's, that owns the silk-mills here: he dozes by the hour, wakes up, sighs deeply, says he should like to be Prince Metternich, and then dozes again, after having bidden young Sebald, the foreigner, set his wife to playing draughts. Never molest such a household, they mean well.

BLUPHOCKS Only, cannot you tell me something of this little Pippa, I must have to do with? One could make something of that name. Pippa—that is, short for Felippa—rhyming to *Panurge consults Hertrippa—Believest thou, King Agrippa?* Something might be done with that name.

2 POLICEMAN Put into rhyme that your head and a ripe musk-melon would not be dear at half a *zwanziger!* Leave this fooling, and look out; the afternoon's over or nearly so.

3 POLICEMAN Where in this passport of Signor Luigi does our Principal instruct you to watch him so narrowly? There? What's there beside a simple signature? (That English fool's busy watching.)

2 POLICEMAN Flourish all round—"Put all possible obstacles in his way;" oblong dot at the end—"Detain him till further advices reach you;" scratch at bottom—"Send him back on pretence of some informality in the above;" ink-spirt on right-hand side (which is the case

---

pay the Stygian ferry—or you might say, *Never an obol To pay for the coble*. . . . Though <> thro' <> thro' <> burning pocket-full of *zwanzigers*. *1849: obolus* . . . (Though <> burning pocket full of *zwanzigers*) . . *To pay the Stygian ferry!* *1863:* through <> through *1868: the Stygian Ferry!* *1888:* pocketful of *zwanzigers*) . . . To
33–34| § added 1849 § 35| *1841:* yonder this <> while—not *1849:* yonder, this *1863:* while: not 36| *1841:* morning *1849:* morning! 38| *1841:* hour—wakes *1863:* hour, wakes 39| *1841:* again after *1849:* again, after 40| *1841:* draughts: never *1868:* draughts. Never 42| *1841:* Only tell me who this little Pippa is I *1849:* Only, cannot you tell me something of this little Pippa, I 43| *1841:* with—one *1849:* with?—one *1863:* with? One 44| *1841:* for Felippa—*Panurge* *1849:* for Felippa—rhyming to—*Panurge* *1863:* to *Panurge* 45| *1841: Believ'st* *1868: Believest* 47| *1841:* Your *1849:* Put into rhyme that your 48| *1841:* fool *1849:* fooling 49| *1841:* out—the *1863:* out: the *1888:* out; the 50| *1841:* does the principal *1849:* does our principal *1863:* Principal 51| *1841:* what's *1868:* What's 52| *1841:* signature? That <> watching. *1849:* signature? (That <> watching.) 53| *1841:* put *1863:* Put 55| *1841:* send *1863:* Send 56| *1841:* above." Ink-spirt <> side,

here)—"Arrest him at once." Why and wherefore, I don't concern myself, but my instructions amount to this: if Signor Luigi leaves home to-night for Vienna—well and good, the passport deposed with us for our *visa* is really for his own use, they have misinformed the Office, and he means well; but let him stay over to-night—there has been the pretence we suspect, the accounts of his corresponding and holding intelligence with the Carbonari are correct, we arrest him at once, to-morrow comes Venice, and presently Spielberg. Bluphocks makes the signal, sure enough! That is he, entering the turret with his mother, no doubt.

(which *1849:* above;" ink-spirt *1888:* side (which 57| *1841:* once," why *1863:* once." Why 59| *1841:* for Vienna, well and good—the *1868:* for Vienna—well and good, the 61| *1841:* but, let *1849:* but let 62| *1841:* suspect—the *1863:* suspect, the 63| *1841:* correct—we <> once—to-morrow *1863:* correct, we <> once, to-morrow 64| *1841:* comes Venice—and presently, Spielberg <> signal *1863:* comes Venice, and <> signal, *1868:* presently Spielberg 65| *1841:* enough! *1849:* enough! That is he, entering the turret with his mother, no doubt.

PART III. [i.] EVENING

SCENE—*Inside the Turret on the Hill above Asolo.* LUIGI *and his* MOTHER *entering.*

MOTHER If there blew wind, you'd hear a long sigh, easing
The utmost heaviness of music's heart.
LUIGI Here in the archway?
MOTHER Oh no, no—in farther,
Where the echo is made, on the ridge.
LUIGI Here surely, then.
How plain the tap of my heel as I leaped up!
Hark—"Lucius Junius!" The very ghost of a voice
Whose body is caught and kept by . . . what are those?
Mere withered wallflowers, waving overhead?
They seem an elvish group with thin bleached hair
That lean out of their topmost fortress—look
And listen, mountain men, to what we say,
Hand under chin of each grave earthly face.
Up and show faces all of you!—"All of you!"
That's the king dwarf with the scarlet comb; old Franz,

Part-title and stage directions / *1841:* III.—Evening. *Inside the Turret.* LUIGI *1868: the Turret on the Hill above Asolo.* LUIGI *1888:* PART III / EVENING / SCENE—*Inside* 1| *1841:* wind you'd *1849:* wind, you'd 3| *1841:* further. *1849:* farther, 4| *1841:* made—on <> surely then! *1849:* surely, then. *1863:* made, on 5–6| *1841:* up: / Aristogeiton! "ristogeiton"—plain / Was't not? Lucius Junius! The <> voice— *1849:* up! / Hark—*"Lucius Junius!"* The <> voice, *1868:* Lucius Junius!" <> voice 7–9| *1841:* Whose flesh is <> by those withered wall-flowers, / Or by the elvish *1849:* Whose body is <> by . . . what are those? / Mere withered wall-flowers, waving overhead? / They seem an elvish *1868:* wallflowers 10| *1841:* Who lean *1849:* looking *1868:* That lean <> look 11| *1841:* men and women, to what *1849:* listening <> men, to what we say, *1868:* listen 12| *1841:* We say—chins under each <> face: *1849:* Hands under chin of each *1888:* face. 13| *1849: All of you!" 1868:* All of you!" 14–16| *1841:* king with <> comb: come down!—"Come down." / Do not kill that Man, my *1849:* king's dwarf with <> comb; now hark— / Come down and meet your fate! Hark—*"Meet your fate!"* / Let him not meet

Come down and meet your fate? Hark—"Meet your fate!"
MOTHER Let him not meet it, my Luigi—do not
Go to his City! Putting crime aside,
Half of these ills of Italy are feigned:
Your Pellicos and writers for effect,
Write for effect.
LUIGI Hush! Say A. writes, and B.
MOTHER These A.s and B.s write for effect, I say.
Then, evil is in its nature loud, while good
Is silent; you hear each petty injury,
None of his virtues; he is old beside,
Quiet and kind, and densely stupid. Why
Do A. and B. not kill him themselves?
LUIGI They teach
Others to kill him—me—and, if I fail,
Others to succeed; now, if A. tried and failed,
I could not teach that: mine's the lesser task.
Mother, they visit night by night . . .
MOTHER —You, Luigi?
Ah, will you let me tell you what you are?
LUIGI Why not? Oh, the one thing you fear to hint,
You may assure yourself I say and say
Ever to myself! At times—nay, even as now
We sit—I think my mind is touched, suspect
All is not sound: but is not knowing that,
What constitutes one sane or otherwise?

---

it, my *1868:* king <> comb; old Franz, / <> Meet your fate!" 15| *1888:* fate? Hark 17| *1841:* to the City! putting *1849:* to his City *1868:* his City! Putting 18| *1841:* feigned— *1863:* feigned: 19| *1841:* effect *1849:* effect, 20| *1841:* say *1868:* effect. LUIGI <> Say 21| *1841:* These A's and B's <> effect I *1849:* effect, I *1863:* These A.'s and B.'s. *1868:* These A.s and B.s 22| *1841:* Then evil *1849:* Then, evil 23| *1841:* silent—you <> injury— *1863:* silent; you <> injury, 24| *1841:* his daily virtues <> old, *1868:* his virtues <> old beside, 25| *1841:* Quiet, and <> stupid—why *1863:* stupid. Why *1868:* Quiet and 26| *1841:* Do A and B not *1849:* Do A. and B. not 27| *1841:* and if I fail *1849:* and, if I fail, 28| *1841:* now if A tried and failed *1849:* now, if A. tried *1863:* failed, 29| *1841:* not do that <> *lesser* *1849:* not teach that <> lesser 30| *1841:* by night . . . MOTHER You Luigi? *1849:* by night . . . MOTHER —You, Luigi? 31| *1841:* Ah will *1849:* Ah, will 32| *1841:* not? Oh the <> hint *1849:* not? Oh, the <> hint, 34| *1841:* Often to myself; at times—nay, now—as now *1849:* Ever to <> nay, even as now *1868:* myself! At 35| *1841:* sit, I <> touched—suspect *1868:* sit—I <> touched, suspect 36| *1841:* sound—but <>

I know I am thus—so, all is right again.
I laugh at myself as through the town I walk.
And see men merry as if no Italy
Were suffering; then I ponder—"I am rich,
Young, healthy; why should this fact trouble me,
More than it troubles these?" But it does trouble.
No, trouble's a bad word: for as I walk
There's springing and melody and giddiness,
And old quaint turns and passages of my youth,
Dreams long forgotten, little in themselves,
Return to me—whatever may amuse me:
And earth seems in a truce with me, and heaven
Accords with me, all things suspend their strife,
The very cicala laughs "There goes he, and there!
Feast him, the time is short; he is on his way
For the world's sake: feast him this once, our friend!"
And in return for all this, I can trip
Cheerfully up the scaffold-steps. I go
This evening, mother!
MOTHER   But mistrust yourself—
Mistrust the judgment you pronounce on him!
LUIGI Oh, there I feel—am sure that I am right!
MOTHER Mistrust your judgment then, of the mere means
To this wild enterprise. Say, you are right,—
How should one in your state e'er bring to pass
What would require a cool head, a cold heart,
And a calm hand? You never will escape.

---

that *1849:* sound: but <> that, 38| *1841:* so all <> again! *1868:* so, all <> again. 39| *1841:* thro' <> walk *1849:* through <> walk, 40| *1841:* see the world merry *1849:* see men merry 41| *1841:* suffering—then I ponder—I *1849:* suffering; then I ponder—"I 42| *1841:* healthy, happy, why <> me . . . *1849:* healthy; why <> me, 43| *1841:* these? But <> trouble me *1849:* these?" But <> me! *1863:* trouble! *1868:* trouble. 44| *1841:* No—trouble's <> word—for *1868:* No, trouble's <> word: for 46| *1841:* youth— *1868:* youth, 47| *1841:* themselves— *1868:* themselves, 48| *1841:* may recreate me, *1849:* may amuse me, *1868:* me; *1888:* me: 51| *1841:* cicales laugh <> he and there— *1849:* cicalas <> he, and there! *1863:* cicale *1868:* cicala laughs 52| *1841:* short—he *1863:* short; he 53| *1841:* sake—feast *1863:* sake: feast 55| *1841:* scaffold-steps: I *1863:* scaffold-steps. I 56| *1841:* mother. MOTHER *1849:* mother! MOTHER 57| *1841:* him. *1868:* him! 58| *1841:* right. *1849:* right! 59| *1841:* then of *1849:* judgment, then, of *1868:* judgment then 60| *1841:* Of this wild enterprise: say you *1863:* say, you *1868:* To this *1888:* enterprise. Say 62| *1868:* heart *1888:* heart, 63| *1841:* hand? you *1849:*

LUIGI Escape? To even wish that, would spoil all.
The dying is best part of it. Too much
Have I enjoyed these fifteen years of mine,
To leave myself excuse for longer life:
Was not life pressed down, running o'er with joy,
That I might finish with it ere my fellows
Who, sparelier feasted, make a longer stay?
I was put at the board-head, helped to all
At first; I rise up happy and content.
God must be glad one loves his world so much.
I can give news of earth to all the dead
Who ask me:—last year's sunsets, and great stars
Which had a right to come first and see ebb
The crimson wave that drifts the sun away—
Those crescent moons with notched and burning rims
That strengthened into sharp fire, and there stood,
Impatient of the azure—and that day
In March, a double rainbow stopped the storm—
May's warm slow yellow moonlit summer nights—
Gone are they, but I have them in my soul!
MOTHER (He will not go!)
LUIGI   You smile at me? 'Tis true,—
Voluptuousness, grotesqueness, ghastliness,
Environ my devotedness as quaintly
As round about some antique altar wreathe
The rose festoons, goats' horns, and oxen's skulls.
MOTHER See now: you reach the city, you must cross
His threshold—how?
LUIGI   Oh, that's if we conspired!
Then would come pains in plenty, as you guess—

You   64| *1841:* Escape—to wish that even would <> all! *1849:* to even wish that, would *1868:* Escape? To <> all.   65| *1841:* it—I have *1849:* it. Too much 66| *1841:* Enjoyed <> mine too much *1849:* Have I enjoyed <> mine, 67| *1841:* life— *1868:* life: 70| *1841:* Who sparelier feasted make *1849:* Who, sparelier feasted, make   71| *1841:* board head *1849:* board-head   72| *1841:* first: I *1849:* first; I   73| *1841:* much— *1863:* loves His <> much! *1868:* his <> much.   75| *1841:* sunsets and *1849:* sunsets, and   76| *1841:* That had *1888:* Which had   79| *1841:* fire and <> stood *1849:* fire, and <> stood, 81| *1841:* In March a *1849:* In March, a   82| *1841:* warm, slow, yellow *1868:* warm slow yellow   83| *1841:* they—but *1849:* they, but   84| *1841:* me—I know *1849:* me! 'Tis true,— *1868:* me? 'Tis   89| *1841:* now—you reach <> city—you *1849:* now: you reach *1863:* city, you   90| *1841:* conspire! *1849:* conspired!   91| *1841:* Then come the pains in plenty you foresee *1849:* Then

But guess not how the qualities most fit
For such an office, qualities I have,
Would little stead me, otherwise employed,
Yet prove of rarest merit only here.
Every one knows for what his excellence
Will serve, but no one ever will consider
For what his worst defect might serve: and yet
Have you not seen me range our coppice yonder
In search of a distorted ash?—I find
The wry spoilt branch a natural perfect bow.
Fancy the thrice-sage, thrice-precautioned man
Arriving at the palace on my errand!
No, no! I have a handsome dress packed up—
White satin here, to set off my black hair;
In I shall march—for you may watch your life out
Behind thick walls, make friends there to betray you;
More than one man spoils everything. March straight—
Only, no clumsy knife to fumble for.
Take the great gate, and walk (not saunter) on
Thro' guards and guards——I have rehearsed it all
Inside the turret here a hundred times.
Don't ask the way of whom you meet, observe!
But where they cluster thickliest is the door
Of doors; they'll let you pass—they'll never blab
Each to the other, he knows not the favourite,
Whence he is bound and what's his business now.

---

would come pains in plenty, as you guess— 92| *1841:* —Who guess <> qualities required *1849:* But guess *1863:* qualities most fit 93| *1841:* office—qualities I have— *1863:* office, qualities I have, 94| *1841:* stead us otherwise *1849:* stead me otherwise *1868:* me, otherwise 95| *1841:* merit here—here only. *1863:* here, here *1868:* merit only here. 96| *1841:* excellences *1849:* excellence 98| *1841:* defects <> serve; and *1849:* defect *1888:* serve: and 100| *1841:* ash?—it happens *1868:* ash?—I find 101| *1841:* branch's <> bow: *1849:* bow! *1868:* branch <> bow. 102| *1841:* thrice sage, thrice precautioned *1849:* thrice-sage, thrice-precautioned 103| *1841:* the city on *1849:* the palace on 104| *1841:* No, no—I *1863:* No, no! I 105| *1841:* here to <> hair— *1849:* here, to *1863:* hair. *1868:* hair; 107| *1841:* walls—binding friends to *1849:* walls—make friends there to *1863:* walls, make <> you: *1868:* you; 108| *1841:* every thing—March *1849:* everything. March 109| *1841:* Only no <> for— *1849:* Only, no *1863:* for. 112| *1841:* the Turret <> times— *1863:* times! *1868:* turret <> times. 113| *1841:* observe, *1863:* observe! 115| *1841:* doors: they'll <> pass . . they'll *1849:* doors; they'll <> pass—they'll 117| *1841:*

Walk in—straight up to him; you have no knife:
Be prompt, how should he scream? Then, out with you!
Italy, Italy, my Italy!
You're free, you're free! Oh mother, I could dream
They got about me—Andrea from his exile,
Pier from his dungeon, Gualtier from his grave!
MOTHER Well, you shall go. Yet seems this patriotism
The easiest virtue for a selfish man
To acquire: he loves himself—and next, the world—
If he must love beyond,—but nought between:
As a short-sighted man sees nought midway
His body and the sun above. But you
Are my adored Luigi, ever obedient
To my least wish, and running o'er with love:
I could not call you cruel or unkind.
Once more, your ground for killing him!—then go!
LUIGI Now do you try me, or make sport of me?
How first the Austrians got these provinces . . .
(If that is all, I'll satisfy you soon)
—Never by conquest but by cunning, for
That treaty whereby . . .
MOTHER Well?
LUIGI (Sure, he's arrived,
The tell-tale cuckoo: spring's his confidant,
And he lets out her April purposes!)
Or . . . better go at once to modern time,
He has . . . they have . . . in fact, I understand
But can't restate the matter; that's my boast:

---

now— *1863:* now. 118| *1841:* him—you <> knife— *1863:* him; you <> knife: 121| *1841:* You're free, you're free—Oh <> I believed *1849:* You're free, you're free! Oh <> I could dream 124| *1841:* Well you <> go. If patriotism were not *1849:* Well, you <> go. Yet seems this patriotism 126| *1841:* acquire! he <> and then, the *1849:* acquire! He <> and next, the *1868:* acquire: he 127| *1841:* beyond, but *1849:* beyond,—but 130| *1841:* adored Luigi—ever *1868:* adored Luigi, ever 131| *1841:* love— *1868:* love: 132| *1841:* unkind! *1863:* unkind. 133| *1863:* him?—then *1868:* him!—then 134| *1841:* you ask me, or *1868:* you try me, or 135| *1841:* provinces— *1863:* provinces . . . 137| *1841:* . . . Never by warfare but by treaty, for *1849:* by conquest but by cunning, for *1863:* —Never 138| *1841:* Sure he's arrived— *1849:* arrived, *1888:* Sure, he's 139| *1841:* cuckoo—spring's *1863:* cuckoo: spring's 141| *1841:* Or . . better <> times— *1863:* times. *1868:* time. *1888:* Or . . . better 142| *1841:* has . . they have . . in fact I *1849:* fact, I *1888:* has . . . they have . . . in 143| *1841:* re-state <> boast; *1863:* restate <> boast:

Others could reason it out to you, and prove
Things they have made me feel.

MOTHER Why go to-night?
Morn's for adventure. Jupiter is now
A morning-star. I cannot hear you, Luigi!

LUIGI "I am the bright and morning-star," saith God—
And, "to such an one I give the morning-star."
The gift of the morning-star! Have I God's gift
Of the morning-star?

MOTHER Chiara will love to see
That Jupiter an evening-star next June.

LUIGI True, mother. Well for those who live through June!
Great noontides, thunder-storms, all glaring pomps
That triumph at the heels of June the god
Leading his revel through our leafy world.
Yes, Chiara will be here.

MOTHER In June: remember,
Yourself appointed that month for her coming.

LUIGI Was that low noise the echo?

MOTHER The night-wind.
She must be grown—with her blue eyes upturned
As if life were one long and sweet surprise:
In June she comes.

LUIGI We were to see together
The Titian at Treviso. There, again!

[*From without is heard the voice of* PIPPA, *singing*—]

A king lived long ago,

147| *1841:* morning-star. . . . I *1849:* morning star. I *1888:* morning-star
148| *1841:* morning-star, "God saith— *1868:* morning-star," saith God—
149| *1841:* And, "such <> morning-star!" *1849:* And, "to such *1868:* morning-star." *1888:* morning-star. 150| *1841:* morning-star—have *1868:* morning-star! Have 153| *1841:* live June over. *1849:* live through June! 154| *1841:* noontides—thunder storms—all *1849:* noontides, thunder storms, all *1863:* thunder-storms 155| *1841:* Which triumph <> the God *1849:* of sovereign June *1863:* of the god June *1868:* That triumph <> of June the god 156| *1841:* thro' *1849:* his glorious revel thro' our world. *1863:* his revel through our leafy world. 157| *1841:* here—MOTHER In June—remember *1849:* remember, *1863:* here. MOTHER In June: remember, 158| *1841:* coming— *1863:* coming.
161| *1841:* surprise— *1849:* surprise: 162| *1841:* LUIGI We are to *1849:* LUIGI We were to 163–164| *1841:* at Treviso—there again! / [*Without.*] A *1849:* there, again! / [*From without is heard the voice of* PIPPA, *singing*— / *A* *1868:* at Treviso. There 164–177| § in roman 1841 only § 167| *1841:* curled *1868:*

In the morning of the world,
When earth was nigher heaven than now:
And the king's locks curled,
Disparting o'er a forehead full
As the milk-white space 'twixt horn and horn
Of some sacrificial bull—
Only calm as a babe new-born:
For he was got to a sleepy mood,
So safe from all decrepitude,
Age with its bane, so sure gone by,
(The gods so loved him while he dreamed)
That, having lived thus long, there seemed
No need the king should ever die.

LUIGI No need that sort of king should ever die!

Among the rocks his city was:
Before his palace, in the sun,
He sat to see his people pass,
And judge them every one
From its threshold of smooth stone.
They haled him many a valley-thief
Caught in the sheep-pens, robber-chief
Swarthy and shameless, beggar-cheat,
Spy-prowler, or rough pirate found
On the sea-sand left aground;
And sometimes clung about his feet,
With bleeding lip and burning cheek,
A woman, bitterest wrong to speak
Of one with sullen thickset brows:
And sometimes from the prison-house

---

curled, 174| *1841:* bane so *1849: bane, so* 175| *1841:* (The Gods <> dreamed,) *1868: gods <> dreamed)* 178| *1841:* die. *1849:* die!
179–203| § in roman 1841 only § 179| *1841:* [*Without.*] Among *1849:* [*From without.*] *Among* *1863: Among* 181| *1841:* sate *1863: sat* 185| *1841:* robber-chief, *1868: robber-chief* 186| *1841:* shameless—beggar-cheat— *1868: shameless, beggar-cheat,* 187| *1841:* Spy-prowler—or some pirate *1849: or rough pirate* *1868: Spy-prowler, or* 188| *1841:* sea sand *1849: sea-sand*
189| *1841:* Sometimes there clung <> feet *1849: And sometimes clung <> feet,*
190| *1841:* cheek *1849: cheek,* 192| *1841:* sullen, thickset *1888: sullen thickset* 193| *1841:* Sometimes from out the *1849: And sometimes from the*

The angry priests a pale wretch brought,
Who through some chink had pushed and pressed
On knees and elbows, belly and breast,
Wormlike into the temple,—caught
He was by the very god,
Who ever in the darkness strode
Backward and forward, keeping watch
O'er his brazen bowls, such rogues to catch!
These, all and every one,
The king judged, sitting in the sun.

LUIGI That king should still judge sitting in the sun!

His councillors, on left and right,
Looked anxious up,—but no surprise
Disturbed the king's old smiling eyes
Where the very blue had turned to white.
'Tis said, a Python scared one day
The breathless city, till he came,
With forky tongue and eyes on flame,
Where the old king sat to judge alway;
But when he saw the sweepy hair
Girt with a crown of berries rare
Which the god will hardly give to wear
To the maiden who singeth, dancing bare
In the altar-smoke by the pine-torch lights,
At his wondrous forest rites,—
Seeing this, he did not dare
Approach that threshold in the sun,

195| *1841:* pressed, *1868: pressed* 196| *1841:* Knees and *1849: On knees* 198| *1841:* very God, *1868: god,* 201| *1841:* catch: *1849: catch!* 202| *1841:* These *1849: And these* *1868: These* 204| *1841:* sun. *1849:* sun! 205–222| § in roman 1841 only § 205| *1841:* [*Without.*] His *1849:* [*From without.*] *His* *1863: His* 207| *1841:* eyes, *1868: eyes* 209| *1841:* A python passed one *1849: 'Tis said, a Python scared one* 210| *1841:* The silent streets—until he *1849: The breathless city, till he* 212| *1841:* king judged alway; *1849: king sate to judge* *1863: sat* *1888: alway,* 213| *1841:* hair, *1868: hair* 215| *1841:* The God *1849: Which the* *1868: god* 218–219| *1841:* rites,— / But which the God's self granted him / For setting free each felon limb / Because of earthly murder done / Faded till other hope was none;— / Seeing <> dare, *1849: rites,— / Beholding this* *1863: dare* *1868: Seeing this*

Assault the old king smiling there.
Such grace had kings when the world begun!

[PIPPA *passes.*]

LUIGI And such grace have they, now that the world ends!
The Python at the city, on the throne,
And brave men, God would crown for slaying him,
Lurk in bye-corners lest they fall his prey.
Are crowns yet to be won in this late time,
Which weakness makes me hesitate to reach?
'Tis God's voice calls: how could I stay? Farewell!

[III.ii.]

Talk by the way, while PIPPA *is passing from the Turret to the Bishop's Brother's House, close to the Duomo S. Maria. Poor* GIRLS *sitting on the steps.*

1 GIRL There goes a swallow to Venice—the stout seafarer!
Seeing those birds fly, makes one wish for wings.
Let us all wish; you wish first!
2 GIRL I? This sunset
To finish.
3 GIRL That old—somebody I know,
Greyer and older than my grandfather,
To give me the same treat he gave last week—
Feeding me on his knee with fig-peckers,
Lampreys and red Breganze-wine, and mumbling
The while some folly about how well I fare,
Let sit and eat my supper quietly:
Since had he not himself been late this morning
Detained at—never mind where,—had he not . . .

221–229| *1841:* there. [PIPPA *passes.* / Farewell, farewell—how 222–228| § added 1849, variants from 1889 § 224| *1849:* The Python in the *1868:* The Python at the 227| *1849:* won, in this late trial, *1863:* late time, *1868:* won in 229| *1841:* Farewell, farewell—how *1849:* 'Tis God's voice calls, how *1868:* calls: how Stage directions / *1841: way in the mean time. Poor* Girls *sitting on the steps of* MONSIGNOR*'s brother's house, close to the Duomo S. Maria. 1849: way, while* PIPPA *is passing from the Turret to the Bishop's Brother's House* <> *Maria. Poor* Girls *sitting on the steps.* 1–3| *1841:* sea-farer! / Let <> first. 2*nd* GIRL *1849:* sea-farer! / Seeing those birds fly, makes one wish for wings. / Let <> you, wish first! 2*nd* GIRL *1863:* seafarer! *1888:* you wish 4–6| *1841:* old . . . somebody I know, / To *1849:* know, / Greyer and older than my grandfather, / To *1863:* old—somebody 8| *1841:* Lampreys, and *1868:* Lampreys and 9–11| *1841:* fare— / Since *1849:* fare, / To be let eat my supper quietly— / Since *1863:* quietly: *1868:* Let sit and eat 12| *1841:*

"Eh, baggage, had I not!"—
2 GIRL How she can lie!
3 GIRL Look there—by the nails!
2 GIRL What makes your fingers red?
3 GIRL Dipping them into wine to write bad words with
On the bright table: how he laughed!
1 GIRL My turn.
Spring's come and summer's coming. I would wear
A long loose gown, down to the feet and hands,
With plaits here, close about the throat, all day;
And all night lie, the cool long nights, in bed;
And have new milk to drink, apples to eat,
Deuzans and junetings, leather-coats . . ah, I should say,
This is away in the fields—miles!
3 GIRL Say at once
You'd be at home: she'd always be at home!
Now comes the story of the farm among
The cherry orchards, and how April snowed
White blossoms on her as she ran. Why, fool,
They've rubbed the chalk-mark out, how tall you were,
Twisted your starling's neck, broken his cage,
Made a dung-hill of your garden!
1 GIRL They, destroy
My garden since I left them? well—perhaps!
I would have done so: so I hope they have!
A fig-tree curled out of our cottage wall;
They called it mine, I have forgotten why,
It must have been there long ere I was born:
Cric—cric—I think I hear the wasps o'erhead
Pricking the papers strung to flutter there

---

where—had he not . . *1849:* where,—had *1888:* net . . . 13| *1841:* Eh <> not!— 2*nd* GIRL *1849:* "Eh <> not!"— 2*nd* GIRL 14| *1841:* nails— 2*nd* GIRL *1863:* nails! 2*nd* GIRL 15| *1849:* with, *1868:* with 16| *1841:* table—how <> turn: *1863:* table: how <> turn. 17| *1841:* coming: I *1868:* coming. I 18| *1841:* gown—down <> hands— *1863:* gown, down <> hands, 20| *1841:* bed— *1868:* bed; 21| *1841:* drink—apples *1868:* drink, apples 22| *1841:* say *1849:* say, 24| *1841:* home—she'd *1868:* home: she'd 27| *1841:* ran: why fool, *1849:* why, fool, *1868:* ran. Why 28| *1841:* out how <> were, *1849:* rubbed out the chalk-mark of how *1868:* rubbed the chalk-mark out, how *1888:* were 30| *1841:* garden— 1*st* GIRL They destroy *1849:* 1*st* GIRL They, destroy *1868:* garden! 1*st* GIRL 32| *1841:* so—so *1863:* so: so 33| *1841:* wall— *1863:* wall; 35| *1841:* born, *1849:* born; *1863:* born: 36| *1841:*

And keep off birds in fruit-time—coarse long papers,
And the wasps eat them, prick them through and through.
3 GIRL How her mouth twitches! Where was I?—before
She broke in with her wishes and long gowns
And wasps—would I be such a fool!—Oh, here!
This is my way: I answer every one
Who asks me why I make so much of him—
(If you say, "you love him"—straight "he'll not be gulled!")
"He that seduced me when I was a girl
 Thus high—had eyes like yours, or hair like yours,
 Brown, red, white,"—as the case may be: that pleases!
See how that beetle burnishes in the path!
There sparkles he along the dust: and, there—
Your journey to that maize-tuft spoiled at least!
1 GIRL When I was young, they said if you killed one
Of those sunshiny beetles, that his friend
Up there, would shine no more that day nor next.
2 GIRL When you were young? Nor are you young, that's true.
How your plump arms, that were, have dropped away!
Why, I can span them. Cecco beats you still?
No matter, so you keep your curious hair.
I wish they'd find a way to dye our hair
Your colour—any lighter tint, indeed,
Than black: the men say they are sick of black,
Black eyes, black hair!
4 GIRL Sick of yours, like enough.
Do you pretend you ever tasted lampreys
And ortolans? Giovita, of the palace,
Engaged (but there's no trusting him) to slice me

Criq—criq *1849:* Cric—cric *1863: Cric—cric* 38| *1841:* papers *1849:* papers, 40| *1841:* where was I before *1849:* twitches! Where was I?—before 43| *1841:* way—I *1868:* way: I 45| *1841:* (Say, you love him—he'll <> gulled, he'll say) *1849:* (If you say <> him—straight "he'll <> gulled") *1863:* gulled!" *1868:* say, "you <> him"—straight 48| *1841:* be—that *1868:* be: that 49| *1841:* (See <> path— *1863:* See *1868:* path! 50| *1841:* dust—and there— *1849:* dust! and, there— 51| *1841:* maize-tuft's spoilt *1849:* least!) *1863:* least! *1868:* maize-tuft spoiled 52| *1841:* young they *1849:* young, they 54| *1841:* there would <> day or next. *1849:* there, would <> day nor next. 55| *1841:* true! *1868:* true. 57| *1841:* Why I <> them! Cecco *1849:* Why, I *1868:* them. Cecco 58| *1841:* matter so *1849:* matter, so 61| *1841:* black—the *1863:* black: the 62| *1841:* enough, *1849:* enough! *1868:*

Polenta with a knife that had cut up
An ortolan.
2 GIRL Why, there! Is not that Pippa
We are to talk to, under the window,—quick,—
Where the lights are?
1 GIRL That she? No, or she would sing.
For the Intendant said . . .
3 GIRL Oh, you sing first!
Then, if she listens and comes close . . I'll tell you,—
Sing that song the young English noble made,
Who took you for the purest of the pure,
And meant to leave the world for you—what fun!
2 GIRL [*sings*].

You'll love me yet!—and I can tarry
Your love's protracted growing:
June reared that bunch of flowers you carry,
From seeds of April's sowing.

I plant a heartful now: some seed
At least is sure to strike,
And yield—what you'll not pluck indeed,
Not love, but, may be, like.

You'll look at least on love's remains,
A grave's one violet:
Your look?—that pays a thousand pains.
What's death? You'll love me yet!

---

enough. 66| *1849:* has *1863:* had 67| *1841:* 2*nd* GIRL Why—there! is *1849:* 2*nd* GIRL Why, there / *1868:* there! Is 68| *1841:* window, quick *1849:* window,—quick,— 69| *1841:* 1*st* GIRL No—or <> sing *1849:* sing; *1868:* 1*st* GIRL That she? No, or <> sing. 70| *1841:* —For <> first— *1849:* said . . 3*rd* GIRL *1863:* For *1868:* first! *1888:* said . . . 3*rd* GIRL 71| *1841:* you, *1868:* you,— 73| *1841:* of the pure *1849:* of the pure, 75–86| § in roman 1841, 1849, 1863; no alternate indentation of lines 1841, 1849 § 77| *1841:* carry *1863:* carry, 79| *1841:* heartfull now—some *1863:* now: some *1868: heartfull* 80| *1841:* strike *1863:* strike, 81| *1841:* not care, indeed, *1849:* not pluck indeed, 82| *1841:* To pluck, but, may be like *1849:* Not love, but, may be, like! *1868: like.* 83| *1841:* To look upon . . my whole remains, *1849:* You'll look at least

3 GIRL [*to* PIPPA *who approaches*]. Oh, you may come closer—we shall not eat you! Why, you seem the very person that the great rich handsome Englishman has fallen so violently in love with. I'll tell you all about it.

---

on love's remains, 86| *1841:* death?—You'll *1868: death? You'll*
88–90| *1841:* eat you! § end § *1849:* eat you! Why, you seem the very person that the great rich handsome Englishman has fallen so violently in love with! I'll tell you all about it. 89| *1868:* with. I'll.

PART IV. [i.] NIGHT

SCENE—*Inside the Palace by the Duomo.* MONSIGNOR, *dismissing his* ATTENDANTS.

MONSIGNOR Thanks, friends, many thanks! I chiefly desire life now, that I may recompense every one of you. Most I know something of already. What, a repast prepared? *Benedicto benedicatur* . . . ugh, ugh! Where was I? Oh, as you were remarking, Ugo, the weather is mild, very unlike winter-weather: but I am a Sicilian, you know, and shiver in your Julys here. To be sure, when 'twas full summer at Messina, as we priests used to cross in procession the great square on Assumption Day, you might see our thickest yellow tapers twist suddenly in two, each like a falling star, or sink down on themselves in a gore of wax. But go, my friends, but go! [*To the* Intendant.] Not you, Ugo! [*The others leave the apartment.*] I have long wanted to converse with you, Ugo.

INTENDANT Uguccio—

MONSIGNOR . . . 'guccio Stefani, man! of Ascoli, Fermo and Fossombruno; —what I do need instructing about, are these accounts of your administration of my poor brother's affairs. Ugh! I shall never get through a third part of your accounts: take some of these dainties before we attempt it, however. Are you bashful to that degree? For me, a crust and water suffice.

INTENDANT Do you choose this especial night to question me?

Stage directions / *1841: Night. The* *1868: Night. Inside the* *1888:* NIGHT / SCENE—*Inside* 1–2| *1841:* many thanks. I desire life now chiefly that *1849:* many thanks. I chiefly desire life now, that *1868:* many thanks! I 3| *1841:* already. *Benedicto benedicatur* . . ugh . . ugh! *1849:* already. What, a repast prepared? *Benedicto* *1868: benedicatur* . . . ugh, ugh! 5| *1841:* winter-weather,—but *1868:* winter-weather: but 6| *1841:* here: To *1863:* here. To 11| *1841: apartment, where a table with refreshments is prepared.*] I *1849: apartment.*] I 12| *1841:* you, Ugo! *1868:* you, Ugo. 14| *1841:* of Ascoli, Fermo, and Fossombruno: *1849:* and Fossombruno; *1868:* of Ascoli, Fermo and 15| *1841:* about are *1849:* about, are 18| *1841:* however: are *1863:* however. Are

MONSIGNOR This night, Ugo. You have managed my late brother's affairs since the death of our elder brother: fourteen years and a month, all but three days. On the Third of December, I find him . . .

INTENDANT If you have so intimate an acquaintance with your brother's affairs, you will be tender of turning so far back: they will hardly bear looking into, so far back.

MONSIGNOR Ay, ay, ugh, ugh,—nothing but disappointments here below! I remark a considerable payment made to yourself on this Third of December. Talk of disappointments! There was a young fellow here, Jules, a foreign sculptor I did my utmost to advance, that the Church might be a gainer by us both: he was going on hopefully enough, and of a sudden he notifies to me some marvellous change that has happened in his notions of Art. Here's his letter,—"He never had a clearly conceived Ideal within his brain till to-day. Yet since his hand could manage a chisel, he has practised expressing other men's Ideals; and, in the very perfection he has attained to, he foresees an ultimate failure: his unconscious hand will pursue its prescribed course of old years, and will reproduce with a fatal expertness the ancient types, let the novel one appear never so palpably to his spirit. There is but one method of escape: confiding the virgin type to as chaste a hand, he will turn painter instead of sculptor, and paint, not carve, its characteristics,"—strike out, I dare say, a school like Correggio: how think you, Ugo?

INTENDANT Is Correggio a painter?

MONSIGNOR Foolish Jules! and yet, after all, why foolish? He may—probably will—fail egregiously; but if there should arise a new painter, will it not be in some such way, by a poet now, or a musician (spirits who have conceived and perfected an Ideal through some other channel), transferring it to this, and escaping our conventional roads by

22| *1841:* brother—fourteen *1863:* brother: fourteen 23| *1841:* days. The 3rd *1849:* days. On the 3rd *1868:* the Third 25| *1841:* back—they *1863:* back: they 26| *1841:* into so *1849:* into, so 28| *1841:* 3rd *1868:* this Third 30| *1841:* sculptor, I <> church *1863:* Church *1868:* sculptor I 33| *1841:* art; here's *1863:* Art *1868:* of Art. Here's 35| *1841:* chisel he <> men's Ideals—and *1849:* chisel, he <> and, *1863:* men's Ideals; and, 36| *1841:* to he *1849:* to, he 37| *1841:* failure—his *1863:* failure: his 39| *1841:* spirit: there *1863:* spirit. There 40| *1841:* escape—confiding *1868:* escape: confiding 41| *1841:* will paint, not *1849:* will turn painter instead of sculptor, and paint, not 46| *1841:* will, fail *1888:* will—fail 47| *1841:* way—a poet, now <> musician, spirits *1849:* way by a poet <> musician, (spirits *1868:* way, by 48–49| *1841:* channel, transferring *1849:* channel) transferring *1888:* channel),

pure ignorance of them; eh, Ugo? If you have no appetite, talk at least, Ugo!

INTENDANT Sir, I can submit no longer to this course of yours. First, you select the group of which I formed one,—next you thin it gradually,—always retaining me with your smile,—and so do you proceed till you have fairly got me alone with you between four stone walls. And now then? Let this farce, this chatter end now: what is it you want with me?

MONSIGNOR Ugo!

INTENDANT From the instant you arrived, I felt your smile on me as you questioned me about this and the other article in those papers—why your brother should have given me this villa, that *podere,*—and your nod at the end meant,—what?

MONSIGNOR Possibly that I wished for no loud talk here. If once you set me coughing, Ugo!—

INTENDANT I have your brother's hand and seal to all I possess: now ask me what for! what service I did him—ask me!

MONSIGNOR I would better not: I should rip up old disgraces, let out my poor brother's weaknesses. By the way, Maffeo of Forli (which, I forgot to observe, is your true name), was the interdict ever taken off you, for robbing that church at Cesena?

INTENDANT No, nor needs be: for when I murdered your brother's friend, Pasquale, for him . . .

MONSIGNOR Ah, he employed you in that business, did he? Well, I must let you keep, as you say, this villa and that *podere,* for fear the world should find out my relations were of so indifferent a stamp? Maffeo, my family is the oldest in Messina, and century after century have my progenitors gone on polluting themselves with every wickedness under heaven: my own father . . . rest his soul!—I have, I know, a

---

transferring 50| *1841:* them, eh *1849:* them; eh 52| *1841:* yours: first, *1868:* yours. First, 55| *1841:* walls: *1863:* walls. 56| *1841:* and <> end now—what *1863:* And <> end now: what 58| *1841:* Ugo . . . *1863:* Ugo! 59| *1841:* arrived I *1849:* arrived, I 61| *1841:* why, your <> this manor, that liberty,—and *1849:* why your <> this villa, that *podere,*—and 63| *1841:* here—if *1849:* here: if *1868:* here. If 64| *1841:* coughing, Ugo! *1849:* coughing, Ugo!— 67| *1841:* I had better not—I <> disgraces—let *1863:* I would better <> disgraces, let *1868:* not: I 69| *1841:* name) was *1863:* name,) was *1888:* name), was 70| *1841:* you for *1849:* you, for 71| *1841:* be—for *1863:* be: for 73| *1841:* that matter, did *1849:* that business, did 74| *1841:* this manor and that liberty, for *1849:* this villa and that *podere,* for 75| *1841:* stamp: *1849:* stamp! *1868:* stamp? 78| *1841:* Heaven *1868:* heaven

chapel to support that it may rest: my dear two dead brothers were, —what you know tolerably well; I, the youngest, might have rivalled them in vice, if not in wealth: but from my boyhood I came out from among them, and so am not partaker of their plagues. My glory springs from another source; or if from this, by contrast only,—for I, the bishop, am the brother of your employers, Ugo. I hope to repair some of their wrong, however; so far as my brothers' illgotten treasure reverts to me, I can stop the consequences of his crime: and not one *soldo* shall escape me. Maffeo, the sword we quiet men spurn away, you shrewd knaves pick up and commit murders with; what opportunities the virtuous forego, the villainous seize. Because, to pleasure myself, apart from other considerations, my food would be millet-cake, my dress sackcloth, and my couch straw,—am I therefore to let you, the offscouring of the earth, seduce the poor and ignorant by appropriating a pomp these will be sure to think lessens the abominations so unaccountably and exclusively associated with it? Must I let villas and *poderi* go to you, a murderer and thief, that you may beget by means of them other murderers and thieves? No—if my cough would but allow me to speak!

INTENDANT What am I to expect? You are going to punish me?

MONSIGNOR —Must punish you, Maffeo. I cannot afford to cast away a chance. I have whole centuries of sin to redeem, and only a month or two of life to do it in. How should I dare to say . . .

INTENDANT "Forgive us our trespasses"?

MONSIGNOR My friend, it is because I avow myself a very worm, sinful beyond measure, that I reject a line of conduct you would applaud, perhaps. Shall I proceed, as it were, a-pardoning?—I?—who have no symptom of reason to assume that aught less than my strenuousest efforts will keep myself out of mortal sin, much less keep others out.

79| *1841:* may: my *1849:* may rest: my 80| *1841:* well: I *1849:* well; I 81| *1841:* wealth, but *1868:* wealth: but 83| *1841:* source, or *1849:* source; or 86| *1841:* crime, and *1849:* crime; and *1868:* crime: and 89| *1841:* myself, *1868:* myself 91| *1841:* straw, am <> let the *1849:* straw,—am <> let you, the *1868:* sackcloth and *1888:* sackcloth, and 92| *1841:* off-scouring <> earth seduce the ignorant *1849:* earth, seduce the poor and ignorant, by *1868:* ignorant by *1888:* offscouring 94| *1841:* let manors and *1849:* let villas and 95| *1841:* liberties go *1849:* *poderes* go *1863:* *poderi* 96| *1841:* thieves? No . . . if *1863:* thieves? No—if 99| *1841:* Must *1849:* —Must 101| *1841:* in! How *1868:* in. How 102| *1841:* trespasses." *1849:* trespasses"— *1863:* trespasses"? *1868:* trespasses?" *1888:* trespasses"? 104| *1841:* applaud, *1868:* applaud 105| *1841:* perhaps: shall *1863:* perhaps. Shall 107| *1841:* less,

No: I do trespass, but will not double that by allowing you to trespass.

INTENDANT And suppose the villas are not your brother's to give, nor yours to take? Oh, you are hasty enough just now!

MONSIGNOR 1, 2—N° 3!—ay, can you read the substance of a letter, N° 3, I have received from Rome? It is precisely on the ground there mentioned, of the suspicion I have that a certain child of my late elder brother, who would have succeeded to his estates, was murdered in infancy by you, Maffeo, at the instigation of my late younger brother—that the Pontiff enjoins on me not merely the bringing that Maffeo to condign punishment, but the taking all pains, as guardian of the infant's heritage for the Church, to recover it parcel by parcel, howsoever, whensoever, and wheresoever. While you are now gnawing those fingers, the police are engaged in sealing up your papers, Maffeo, and the mere raising my voice brings my people from the next room to dispose of yourself. But I want you to confess quietly, and save me raising my voice. Why, man, do I not know the old story? The heir between the succeeding heir, and this heir's ruffianly instrument, and their complot's effect, and the life of fear and bribes and ominous smiling silence? Did you throttle or stab my brother's infant? Come now!

INTENDANT So old a story, and tell it no better? When did such an instrument ever produce such an effect? Either the child smiles in his face; or, most likely, he is not fool enough to put himself in the employer's power so thoroughly: the child is always ready to produce—as you say—howsoever, wheresoever, and whensoever.

MONSIGNOR Liar!

INTENDANT Strike me? Ah, so might a father chastise! I shall sleep soundly to-night at least, though the gallows await me to-morrow; for what a life did I lead! Carlo of Cesena reminds me of his connivance, every time I pay his annuity; which happens commonly thrice a

---

keep *1868:* less keep 108| *1841:* No—I *1863:* No: I 109| *1841:* the manors are <> give, or yours *1849:* the villas are <> give, nor yours 111| *1841:* 1, 2—No. 3 *1849:* 1, 2—No. 3 *1863:* 1, 2—No. 3 112| *1841:* No. 3 <> is on the ground I there *1849:* No. 3 <> is precisely on the ground there *1863:* No 3 113| *1841:* mention of *1849:* mentioned, of 115| *1841:* late brother *1888:* late younger brother 116| *1841:* pontiff *1849:* Pontiff 117| *1841:* of that *1868:* of the 118| *1841:* church *1849:* Church 124| *1841:* and that heir's *1868:* and this heir's 125| *1841:* bribes, and *1868:* bribes and 126| *1841:* infant? Come, now *1868:* infant? Come now! 129| *1841:* face, or *1868:* face; or 130| *1841:* thoroughly—the *1863:* thoroughly: the 131| *1868:* wheresoever and *1888:* wheresoever, and 135–136| *1841:* lead? Carlo <> connivance every <> annuity (which *1849:* lead! Carlo <> connivance, every *1863:* annuity; which

year. If I remonstrate, he will confess all to the good bishop—you!

MONSIGNOR I see through the trick, caitiff! I would you spoke truth for once. All shall be sifted, however—seven times sifted.

INTENDANT And how my absurd riches encumbered me! I dared not lay claim to above half my possessions. Let me but once unbosom myself, glorify Heaven, and die!

Sir, you are no brutal dastardly idiot like your brother I frightened to death: let us understand one another. Sir, I will make away with her for you—the girl—here close at hand; not the stupid obvious kind of killing; do not speak—know nothing of her nor of me! I see her every day—saw her this morning: of course there is to be no killing; but at Rome the courtesans perish off every three years, and I can entice her thither—have indeed begun operations already. There's a certain lusty blue-eyed florid-complexioned English knave, I and the Police employ occasionally. You assent, I perceive—no, that's not it—assent I do not say—but you will let me convert my present havings and holdings into cash, and give me time to cross the Alps? 'Tis but a little black-eyed pretty singing Felippa, gay silk-winding girl. I have kept her out of harm's way up to this present; for I always intended to make your life a plague to you with her. 'Tis as well settled once and for ever. Some women I have procured will pass Bluphocks, my handsome scoundrel, off for somebody; and once Pippa entangled!—you conceive? Through her singing? Is it a bargain?

[*From without is heard the voice of* PIPPA, *singing*—]

Overhead the tree-tops meet,
Flowers and grass spring 'neath one's feet;

137| *1841:* year). If *1863:* year. If 138| *1841:* thro' *1863:* through 139| *1841:* once; all *1863:* once. All 143| *1841:* brutal, dastardly *1868:* brutal dastardly 144| *1841:* death . . . let *1849:* death—let *1863:* death: let 146| *1841:* her or me. I *1868:* me! I *1868:* her nor of me 147| *1841:* morning—of <> is no *1849:* morning: of <> is to be no 149| *1841:* have, indeed, begun <> already—there's *1849:* already. There's *1868:* have indeed begun 150–151| *1841:* lusty, blue-eyed, florid-complexioned, English knave I employ occasionally.—You *1849:* knave I and the Police employ *1863:* florid-complexioned English knave, I <> occasionally. You *1868:* lusty blue-eyed florid-complexioned 153–154| *1841:* black-eyed, pretty *1868:* black-eyed pretty 156| *1841:* her! 'Tis <> forever: *1849:* for ever: *1868:* her. 'Tis <> ever. 157| *1841:* some *1868:* Some 158| *1841:* somebody, and *1849:* somebody; and 159–160| *1841:* MONSIGNOR Why, if she sings, one might . . . / [*Without*] Over-head <> meet— *1849:* § INTENDANT § Through her singing? Is it a bargain? / [*From* <> *singing*—] / *Over-head* *1863:* *Overhead* <> *meet,* 160–175| § in roman 1841 § 161–164| *1841:* feet—/

There was nought above me, nought below,
My childhood had not learned to know:
For, what are the voices of birds
—Ay, and of beasts,—but words, our words,
Only so much more sweet?
The knowledge of that with my life begun.
But I had so near made out the sun,
And counted your stars, the seven and one,
Like the fingers of my hand:
Nay, I could all but understand
Wherefore through heaven the white moon ranges;
And just when out of her soft fifty changes
No unfamiliar face might overlook me—
Suddenly God took me.

[PIPPA *passes.*]

MONSIGNOR [*springing up*]. My people—one and all—all—within there! Gag this villain—tie him hand and foot! He dares . . . I know not half he dares—but remove him—quick! *Miserere mei, Domine!* Quick, I say!

[IV.ii.]

SCENE—PIPPA'S *chamber again. She enters it.*

The bee with his comb,
The mouse at her dray,
The grub in his tomb,
Wile winter away;
But the fire-fly and hedge-shrew and lobworm, I pray,
How fare they?
Ha, ha, thanks for your counsel, my Zanze!

What *1849: feet—/ There was nought above me, and nought below, / My childhood had not learned to know! / For, what* *1863: feet;* <> / <> *know:* 165| *1841:* and beasts, too—but words—our *1849: and of beasts,—but* *1868: words, our*
167| *1841:* That knowledge with <> begun! *1849: The knowledge of that with* *1868: begun.* 168| *1841:* sun— *1849: sun,* 169| *1841:* Could count <> Seven and One! *1849: And counted your* <> *One,* *1868: seven and one,* 170| *1841:* hand— *1849: hand:* 171| *1841:* Nay, could *1849: Nay, I could* *1868: Nay I* *1888: Nay, I* 172| *1841:* How and wherefore the moon ranges— *1849: Wherefore through heaven the white moon ranges;* 175| *1841:* me— *1849: me—*
177| *1841:* foot: he dares—I *1849:* foot! He dares—I *1863:* dares . . I *1888:* dares . . . I
Stage directions / *1841:* PIPPA'S *1888:* SCENE—PIPPA'S 3| *1841:* in its tomb *1849:* tomb, *1888:* in his tomb, 5| *1841:* lobworm *1849:* lob-worm
6| *1841:* Where be they? *1849:* How fare they? 7| *1841:* thanks my Zanze— *1849:* Ha, ha, best thanks for your counsel, my *1868:* Ha, ha, thanks <> Zanze!

"Feast upon lampreys, quaff Breganze"—
The summer of life so easy to spend,
And care for to-morrow so soon put away!
But winter hastens at summer's end,
And fire-fly, hedge-shrew, lobworm, pray,
How fare they?
No bidding me then to . . . what did Zanze say?
"Pare your nails pearlwise, get your small feet shoes
More like" . . (what said she?)—"and less like canoes!"
How pert that girl was!—would I be those pert
Impudent staring women! It had done me,
However, surely no such mighty hurt
To learn his name who passed that jest upon me:
No foreigner, that I can recollect,
Came, as she says, a month since, to inspect
Our silk-mills—none with blue eyes and thick rings
Of raw-silk-coloured hair, at all events.
Well, if old Luca keep his good intents,
We shall do better, see what next year brings.
I may buy shoes, my Zanze, not appear
More destitute than you perhaps next year!
Bluph . . . something! I had caught the uncouth name
But for Monsignor's people's sudden clatter
Above us—bound to spoil such idle chatter
As ours: it were indeed a serious matter
If silly talk like ours should put to shame
The pious man, the man devoid of blame,

8| *1849:* quaff the Breganze"— *1888:* quaff Breganze"— 9–11| *1841:* life's <> spend! / But *1849:* spend, / And care for to-morrow so soon put away! / But *1868:* life 13| *1841:* Where be they? *1849:* How fare they? 14| *1841:* bidding you then to . . what *1849:* bidding me then <> did she say? *1868:* did Zanze say? *1888:* to . . . what 16| *1841:* like . . (what said she?)—and <> canoes—" *1863:* canoes"— *1868:* like" . . (what said she?)—"and <> canoes!" 17| *1841:* Pert as a sparrow . . . would *1849:* How pert that girl was!—would 18| *1841:* staring wretches! it *1849:* staring women! it *1868:* It 20| *1841:* me.— *1849:* me: 22| *1841:* since to *1849:* since, to 24| *1841:* Of English-coloured hair *1868:* Of raw-silk-coloured hair 25| *1841:* Well—if <> keeps <> intents *1849:* intents, *1863:* Well, if *1868:* keep 26| *1841:* better—see <> brings— *1849:* better: see <> brings! *1868:* better, see *1888:* brings. 28| *1841:* So destitute, perhaps, next *1849:* More destitute than you, perhaps *1868:* you perhaps next 29| *1841: Bluf*—something—I *1849:* Bluph . . . something! I 31–34| *1841:* chatter, / The pious *1849:* chatter / As ours; it were, indeed, a serious matter / If silly talk like ours should put to shame / The pious 32| *1868:* ours: it were indeed a

The . . . ah but—ah but, all the same,
No mere mortal has a right
To carry that exalted air;
Best people are not angels quite:
While—not the worst of people's doings scare
The devil; so there's that proud look to spare!
Which is mere counsel to myself, mind! for
I have just been the holy Monsignor:
And I was you too, Luigi's gentle mother,
And you too, Luigi!—how that Luigi started
Out of the turret—doubtlessly departed
On some good errand or another,
For he passed just now in a traveller's trim,
And the sullen company that prowled
About his path, I noticed, scowled
As if they had lost a prey in him.
And I was Jules the sculptor's bride,
And I was Ottima beside,
And now what am I?—tired of fooling.
Day for folly, night for schooling!
New year's day is over and spent,
Ill or well, I must be content.
Even my lily's asleep, I vow:
Wake up—here's a friend I've plucked you:
Call this flower a heart's-ease now!
Something rare, let me instruct you,
Is this, with petals triply swollen,
Three times spotted, thrice the pollen;

35| *1841:* ah, but—ah, but *1868:* ah but—ah but 37| *1841:* carrry *1849:* carry 38| *1841:* quite— *1863:* quite: 39| *1841:* not worst people's *1849:* not the worst of people's 40| *1841:* devils <> that regard to *1849:* that proud look to *1863:* devil 41| *1841:* § no ¶ § Mere *1849:* Which is mere *1868:* § ¶ § 42| *1841:* been Monsignor! *1849:* been the holy Monsignor! *1868:* holy Monsignor: 43| *1841:* too, mother *1849:* too, Luigi's gentle mother, 45| *1841:* the Turret *1868:* turret 46–51| *1841:* some love-errand or another—/ And *1849:* some good errand or another, / For he past just now in a traveller's trim, / And the sullen company that prowled / About his path, I noticed, scowled / As if they had lost a prey in him. / And 47| *1863:* pass'd *1868:* passed 53| *1841:* fooling! *1868:* fooling. 54| *1841:* schooling— *1849:* schooling! 55–57| *1841:* over—over! / § no ¶ § Even *1849:* over and spent, / Ill or well, I must be content! / Even 56| *1868:* content. 57| *1868:* § ¶ § 58| *1841:* friend I pluckt you. *1849:* friend I've pluckt you! *1868:* plucked 59| *1841:* See—call this a *1849:* this flower a *1868:* Call 60| *1849:* And something *1868:* Something 61| *1841:* this—with *1868:* this, with 62| *1841:* pollen, *1868:* pollen;

While the leaves and parts that witness
Old porportions and their fitness,
Here remain unchanged, unmoved now;
Call this pampered thing improved now!
Suppose there's a king of the flowers
And a girl-show held in his bowers—
"Look ye, buds, this growth of ours,"
Says he, "Zanze from the Brenta,
I have made her gorge ploenta
Till both cheeks are near as bouncing
As her . . . name there's no pronouncing!
See this heightened colour too,
For she swilled Breganze wine
Till her nose turned deep carmine;
'Twas but white when wild she grew.
And only by this Zanze's eyes
Of which we could not change the size,
The magnitude of all achieved
Otherwise, may be perceived."

Oh what a drear dark close to my poor day!
How could that red sun drop in that black cloud?
Ah Pippa, morning's rule is moved away,
Dispensed with, never more to be allowed!
Day's turn is over, now arrives the night's.
Oh lark, be day's apostle
To mavis, merle and throstle,
Bid them their betters jostle
From day and its delights!
But at night, brother howlet, over the woods,

63| *1863:* witness, *1868:* witness 64| *1841:* The old <> fitness *1863:* fitness, *1868:* Old 65| *1841:* remain, unchanged unmoved now— *1863:* unchanged, unmoved *1868:* remain unchanged <> now; 66| *1849:* So call *1863:* So, call *1868:* Call 74| *1841:* too— *1868:* too, 76| *1841:* carmine— *1868:* carmine; 77| *1841:* grew! *1868:* grew. 80| *1841:* of what's achieved *1868:* of all achieved 81| *1841:* Elsewhere may be perceived!" *1849:* Otherwise, may *1868:* perceived." 82| *1841:* drear, dark *1868:* drear dark 83| *1841:* cloud! *1868:* cloud? 84| *1841:* Ah, Pippa *1868:* Ah Pippa 85| *1841:* allowed. *1849:* allowed, *1863:* allowed! 86| *1841:* turn's over—now's the night's— *1849:* turn is over—now arrives the *1863:* over: now <> night's. *1868:* over, now 87| *1841:* Oh Lark be *1849:* Oh, Lark, be *1868:* Oh lark 91| *1841:* brother Howlet *1849:* brother Howlet, far over *1868:* howlet, over

Toll the world to thy chantry;
Sing to the bats' sleek sisterhoods
Full complines with gallantry:
Then, owls and bats,
Cowls and twats,
Monks and nuns, in a cloister's moods,
Adjourn to the oak-stump pantry!

[*After she has begun to undress herself.*]

Now, one thing I should like to really know:
How near I ever might approach all these
I only fancied being, this long day:
—Approach, I mean, so as to touch them, so
As to . . . in some way . . . move them—if you please,
Do good or evil to them some slight way.
For instance, if I wind
Silk to-morrow, my silk may bind

[*Sitting on the bedside.*]

And border Ottima's cloak's hem.
Ah me, and my important part with them,
This morning's hymn half promised when I rose!
True in some sense or other, I suppose.

[*As she lies down.*]

God bless me! I can pray no more to-night.
No doubt, some way or other, hymns say right.
All service ranks the same with God—
With God, whose puppets, best and worst,
Are we: there is no last nor first.

[*She sleeps.*]

92| *1841:* chantry— *1863:* chantry; 94| *1841:* galantry— *1863:* gallantry: 95–96| *1841:* bats, cowls *1888:* bats, / Cowls 99| *1841:* Now one *1849:* Now, one <> like really to know: *1863:* like to really know: 101| *1841:* being this long day— *1849:* being, this *1863:* day! *1868:* day: 102| *1841:* . . . Approach <> them—so *1849:* —Approach *1863:* them, so 103| *1841:* to . . in some way . . move *1888:* to . . . in some way . . . move 106| *1841:* to-morrow, silk *1849:* to-morrow, my silk 107| *1841:* And broider Ottima's <> hem— *1863:* hem. *1868:* And border Ottima's 108| *1841:* Ah, me and my important passing them *1849:* important part with them, *1868:* Ah me, and 110–111| *1841:* suppose. / [*As she lies down.* / God <> me tho' I cannot pray to-night. *1849:* suppose, / Though I passed by them all, and felt no sign. / [*As she lies down.* / God <> me! I can pray no more to-night. *1868:* suppose. / [*As she lies down.* / God 113–115| § not indented 1841, 1849, 1863 § 113| *1841: service is the* *1868: service ranks the* 114| *1841: Whose* *1849: With God, whose* 115| *1841: Are we. . . . . .* *1849: Are we: there is no last nor first.—* *1863: first.*

BELLS AND POMEGRANATES. NUMBER II.

KING VICTOR AND KING CHARLES

Edited by Park Honan

KING VICTOR AND KING CHARLES;

A TRAGEDY.

1842: BELLS AND POMEGRANATES. / No. II.—KING VICTOR AND KING CHARLES. / BY ROBERT BROWNING, / AUTHOR OF "PARACELSUS." / LONDON: / EDWARD MOXON, DOVER STREET. / MDCCCXLII. *1849:* KING VICTOR AND KING CHARLES. / A TRAGEDY. *1863:* § on page with Note § *1888:* § on page preceding Note § CHARLES; / A

NOTE.

So far as I know, this Tragedy is the first artistic consequence of what Voltaire termed "a terrible event without consequences;" and although it professes to be historical, I have taken more pains to arrive at the history than most readers would thank me for particularizing: since acquainted, as I will hope them to be, with the chief circumstances of Victor's remarkable European career—nor quite ignorant of the sad and surprising facts I am about to reproduce (a tolerable account of which is to be found, for instance, in Abbé Roman's *Récit*, or even the fifth of Lord Orrery's Letters from Italy)—I cannot expect them to be versed, nor desirous of becoming so, in all the detail of the memoirs, correspondence, and relations of the time. From these only may be obtained a knowledge of the fiery and audacious temper, unscrupulous selfishness, profound dissumulation, and singular fertility in resources, of Victor—the extreme and painful sensibility, prolonged immaturity of powers, earnest good purpose and vacillating will of Charles—the noble and right woman's manliness of his wife—and the ill-considered rascality and subsequent better-advised rectitude of D'Ormea. When I say, therefore, that I cannot but believe my statement (combining as it does what appears correct in Voltaire and plausible in Condorcet) more true to person and thing than any it has hitherto been my fortune to meet with, no doubt my word will be taken, and my evidence spared as readily.

R.B.

LONDON: 1842

1842: ADVERTISEMENT. / So *1849:* So *1888:* NOTE. / So 1| *1842:* artistical *1868:* artistic 4| *1842:* particularising *1863:* particularizing 7| *1842:* reproduce (tolerable accounts of *1868:* reproduce (a tolerable account of 8| *1842:* are to *1868:* is to 10| *1842:* or desirous <> the detail of *1849:* nor desirous *1868:* detail 15| *1842:* will, of *1868:* will of 16| *1842:* woman's-manliness *1868:* woman's manliness *1842:* § no date § *1849:* § no signature § *1863:* readily.—R. B. / LONDON, 1842 *1868:* *London* *1888:* readily. / R. B. / LONDON: 1842

PERSONS.

VICTOR AMADEUS, *first King of Sardinia.*

CHARLES EMMANUEL, *his son, Prince of Piedmont.*

POLYXENA, *wife of Charles.*

D'ORMEA, *minister.*

SCENE.—*The Council Chamber of Rivoli Palace, near Turin, communicating with a Hall at the back, an Apartment to the left, and another to the right of the stage.*

TIME, 1730–1731.

1842: § follows title on first page of text § *1868:* § on page preceding text § SCENE / *1842:* left and *1888:* left, and

KING VICTOR AND KING CHARLES

1842

FIRST YEAR, 1730—KING VICTOR

PART I

CHARLES, POLYXENA

CHARLES You think so? Well, I do not.
POLYXENA My beloved,
All must clear up; we shall be happy yet:
This cannot last for ever—oh, may change
To-day or any day!
CHARLES —May change? Ah yes—
May change!
POLYXENA Endure it, then.
CHARLES No doubt, a life
Like this drags on, now better and now worse.
My father may . . . may take to loving me;
And he may take D'Ormea closer yet
To counsel him;—may even cast off her
—That bad Sebastian; but he also may
. . . Or no, Polyxena, my only friend,
He may not force you from me?
POLYXENA Now, force me
From you!—me, close by you as if there gloomed
No Sebastians, no D'Ormeas on our path—
At Rivoli or Turin, still at hand,

---

§ Ed. 1842, 1849, 1863, 1868, 1888, 1889. No MS extant. § 1| *1863:* Beloved, *1868:* beloved, 2| *1842:* up—we *1863:* up; we 3| *1842:* ever . . oh *1863:* ever—oh 5| *1842:* it then <> doubt a *1849:* it, then <> doubt, a 6| *1842:* worse; *1863:* worse. 8| *1842:* take, too, D'Ormea *1863:* take D'Ormea 11| *1842:* . . Or *1849:* . . Or, no *1868:* . . Or no *1888:* . . . Or 14| *1842:* No D'Ormeas, no Sebastians on *1868:* No Sebastians, no D'Ormeas on

Arch-counsellor, prime confidant . . . force me!
CHARLES Because I felt as sure, as I feel sure
We clasp hands now, of being happy once.
Young was I, quite neglected, nor concerned
By the world's business that engrossed so much
My father and my brother: if I peered
From out my privacy,—amid the crash
And blaze of nations, domineered those two.
'Twas war, peace—France our foe, now—England, friend—
In love with Spain—at feud with Austria! Well—
I wondered, laughed a moment's laugh for pride
In the chivalrous couple, then let drop
My curtain—"I am out of it," I said—
When . . .
POLYXENA You have told me, Charles.
CHARLES Polyxena—
When suddenly,—a warm March day, just that!
Just so much sunshine as the cottage child
Basks in delighted, while the cottager
Takes off his bonnet, as he ceases work,
To catch the more of it—and it must fall
Heavily on my brother! Had you seen
Philip—the lion-featured! not like me!
POLYXENA I know—
CHARLES And Philip's mouth yet fast to mine,
His dead cheek on my cheek, his arm still round
My neck,—they bade me rise, "for I was heir
To the Duke," they said, "the right hand of the Duke:"
Till then he was my father, not the Duke.
So . . . let me finish . . . the whole intricate
World's-business their dead boy was born to, I

23| *1842:* two; *1863:* two. 24| *1842:* now—England's friend— *1849:* now—England, friend— 25| *1842:* with Austria!—Well— *1863:* with Austria! · Well— 26| *1842:* wondered—laughed *1863:* wondered, laughed 27| *1842:* couple—then *1863:* couple, then 29| *1868:* me, Charles! ¶ CHARLES *1888:* me, Charles. ¶ CHARLES 30| *1842:* that *1849:* that! 31–33| *1842:* Sunshine the cottager's child basks in—he / Takes <> bonnet as <> work *1849:* Just so much sunshine as the <> child / Basks in delighted, while the cottager / Takes <> bonnet, as <> work, *1868:* the cottage child 35| *1842:* brother . . . had *1868:* brother! Had 36| *1842:* lion-featured!—not *1863:* lion-featured! not 37| *1868:* mine § Omission of comma apparently a printer's error. § *1888:* mine, 40| *1842:* of the Duke;" *1868:* of the Duke:" 41| *1842:* the Duke! *1888:* the Duke. 42| *1842:* So . . let me finish . . the *1888:* So . . . let me finish . . . the 45| *1842:*

Must conquer,—ay, the brilliant thing he was,
I, of a sudden must be: my faults, my follies,
—All bitter truths were told me, all at once,
To end the sooner. What I simply styled
Their overlooking me, had been contempt:
How should the Duke employ himself, forsooth,
With such an one, while lordy Philip rode
By him their Turin through? But he was punished,
And must put up with—me! 'Twas sad enough
To learn my future portion and submit.
And then the wear and worry, blame on blame!
For, spring-sounds in my ears, spring-smells about,
How could I but grow dizzy in their pent
Dim palace-rooms at first? My mother's look
As they discussed my insignificance,
She and my father, and I sitting by,—
I bore; I knew how brave a son they missed:
Philip had gaily run state-papers through,
While Charles was spelling at them painfully!
But Victor was my father spite of that.
"Duke Victor's entire life has been," I said,
"Innumerable efforts to one end;
And on the point now of that end's success,
Our Ducal turning to a Kingly crown,
Where's time to be reminded 'tis his child
He spurns?" And so I suffered—scarcely suffered,
Since I had you at length!

POLYXENA —To serve in place
Of monarch, minister, and mistress, Charles.

CHARLES But, once that crown obtained, then was't not like
Our lot would alter? "When he rests, takes breath,

---

sudden, must *1868:* sudden must 46| *1842:* once *1863:* once, 50| *1842:* one while *1863:* one, while 53| *1842:* submit— *1863:* submit. 55| *1842:* —For *1868:* For 58| *1842:* insignificance— *1868:* insignificance, 59| *1842:* (She <> father and <> by,)— *1849:* father, and *1863:* She <> by,— 60| *1842:* bore:—I *1863:* bore; I 61| *1842:* gaily passed state-papers o'er *1849:* o'er, *1868:* gaily run state-papers through, 64| *1842:* Duke <> been, I *1849:* "Duke <> been," I 65| *1842:* Innumerable *1849:* "Innumerable 66| *1842:* And, on *1868:* And on 69| *1842:* suffered . . hardly suffered, *1849:* suffered . . yet scarce suffered, *1863:* suffered—yet *1868:* suffered—scarcely suffered *1888:* scarcely suffered, 71| *1842:* minister and *1863:* mistress, Charles! *1888:* minister, and <> Charles. 73| *1842:* alter?—When *1849:* alter?—"When *1863:*

Glances around, sees who there's left to love—
Now that my mother's dead, sees I am left—
Is it not like he'll love me at the last?"
Well, Savoy turns Sardinia; the Duke's King:
Could I—precisely then—could you expect
His harshness to redouble? These few months
Have been . . . have been . . . Polyxena, do you
And God conduct me, or I lose myself!
What would he have? What is't they want with me?
Him with this mistress and this minister,
—You see me and you hear him; judge us both!
Pronounce what I should do, Polyxena!
POLYXENA Endure, endure, beloved! Say you not
He is your father? All's so incident
To novel sway! Beside, our life must change:
Or you'll acquire his kingcraft, or he'll find
Harshness a sorry way of teaching it.
I bear this—not that there's so much to bear.
CHARLES You bear? Do not I know that you, tho' bound
To silence for my sake, are perishing
Piecemeal beside me? And how otherwise
When every creephole from the hideous Court
Is stopped: the Minister to dog me, here—
The Mistress posted to entrap you, there!
And thus shall we grow old in such a life;
Not careless, never estranged,—but old: to alter
Our life, there is so much to alter!
POLYXENA Come—
Is it agreed that we forego complaint
Even at Turin, yet complain we here

---

alter? "When 74| *1842:* around, and sees who's left *1888:* around, sees who there's left 75| *1842:* Now *1849:* "Now 76| *1842:* Was it <> like he'd love <> last? *1849:* "Is it <> like he'll love <> last?" 77| *1842:* Well: Savoy <> Sardinia—the <> King! *1863:* Well, Savoy <> Sardinia; the <> King: 80| *1842:* Have been . . . have been . . Polyxena *1868:* Have been . . have *1888:* Have been . . . have been . . . Polyxena 81| *1842:* me or *1849:* me, or 86| *1842:* say *1849:* Say *1863:* Beloved *1868:* beloved 87| *1842:* That he's your Father *1868:* He is your father 89| *1842:* he'll learn *1849:* he'll find 90| *1842:* His own's a *1849:* Harshness a 91| *1842:* to bear— *1863:* to bear. 92| *1842:* bear it? Don't I *1849:* don't *1868:* bear? Do not I 94| *1842:* me? and how otherwise? *1868:* me? And how otherwise 95| *1842:* —When *1868:* When 96| *1842:* stopt; the *1868:* stopped *1888:* stopped: the 97| *1842:* you there! *1849:* you, there! *1868:* there? *1888:* there! 98| *1842:* life— *1868:* life; 99| *1842:* careless,—never *1868:* careless, never 101| *1842:* complaints *1868:*

At Rivoli? 'Twere wiser you announced
Our presence to the King. What's now afoot
I wonder? Not that any more's to dread
Than every day's embarrassment: but guess
For me, why train so fast succeeded train
On the high-road, each gayer still than each!
I noticed your Archbishop's pursuivant,
The sable cloak and silver cross; such pomp
Bodes . . . what now, Charles? Can you conceive?

CHARLES
Not I.

POLYXENA A matter of some moment.

CHARLES
There's our life!
Which of the group of loiterers that stare
From the lime-avenue, divines that I—
About to figure presently, he thinks,
In face of all assembled—am the one
Who knows precisely least about it?

POLYXENA
Tush!
D'Ormea's contrivance!

CHARLES
Ay, how otherwise
Should the young Prince serve for the old King's foil?
—So that the simplest courtier may remark
'Twere idle raising parties for a Prince
Content to linger the Court's laughing-stock.
Something, 'tis like, about that weary business

[*Pointing to papers he has laid down, and which* POLYXENA *examines.*]

—Not that I comprehend three words, of course,
After all last night's study.

POLYXENA
The faint heart!
Why, as we rode and you rehearsed just now
Its substance . . . (that's the folded speech I mean,

---

complaint 104| *1842:* the King—What's now a-foot, *1849:* the King. What's *1863:* afoot, *1868:* afoot 105| *1842:* wonder?—Not *1888:* wonder? Not 106| *1842:* embarrassment—but *1849:* guess, *1868:* embarrassment: but guess 107| *1842:* me why *1849:* me, why 108| *1842:* than each; *1868:* than each! 111| *1842:* Bodes . . what *1888:* Bodes . . . what 112| *1842:* moment— ¶ CHARLES *1888:* moment. ¶ CHARLES 113| *1842:* stared *1868:* stare 114| *1842:* lime-avenue divines *1849:* lime-avenue, divines 118| *1842:* CHARLES Ay—how *1868:* CHARLES Ay, how 120| *1849:* remark, *1868:* remark 122| *1842:* linger D'Ormea's laughing-stock! *1868:* laughing-stock. *1888:* linger the Court's laughing-stock. 123| *1863:* business: *1868:* business 127| *1842:* substance . .

Concerning the Reduction of the Fiefs)
—What would you have?—I fancied while you spoke,
Some tones were just your father's.
CHARLES Flattery!
POLYXENA I fancied so:— and here lurks, sure enough
My note upon the Spanish Claims! You've mastered
The fief-speech thoroughly: this other, mind,
Is an opinion you deliver,—stay,
Best read it slowly over once to me;
Read—there's bare time; you read it firmly—loud
—Rather loud, looking in his face,—don't sink
Your eye once—ay, thus! "If Spain claims . . ." begin
—Just as you look at me!
CHARLES At you! Oh truly,
You have I seen, say, marshalling your troops,
Dismissing councils, or, through doors ajar,
Head sunk on hand, devoured by slow chagrins
—Then radiant, for a crown had all at once
Seemed possible again! I can behold
Him, whose least whisper ties my spirit fast,
In this sweet brow, nought could divert me from
Save objects like Sebastian's shameless lip,
Or worse, the clipped grey hair and dead white face
And dwindling eye as if it ached with guile,
D'Ormea wears . . .
[*As he kisses her, enter from the* KING's *apartment* D'ORMEA.]
I said he would divert
My kisses from your brow!
D'ORMEA [*aside*]. Here! So, King Victor
Spoke truth for once: and who's ordained, but I

(that's *1888:* substance . . . (that's 128| *1842:* of the Fiefs . .) *1863:* of the Fiefs) 129| *1842:* spoke *1849:* spoke, 131| *1842:* enough, *1888:* enough 132| *1842:* you've *1849:* You've 133| *1842:* thoroughly—this *1863:* thoroughly: this 137| *1842:* loud-looking *1868:* loud, looking 139| *1842:* CHARLES At you! Oh, truly, *1868:* CHARLES At you! Oh truly, 140| *1842:* troops— *1868:* troops, 141| *1842:* councils—or *1868:* councils, or 146| *1842:* brow nought <> from, *1849:* brow, nought *1868:* from 148| *1842:* Or, worse, the clipt grey <> face, *1868:* Or worse, the clipped grey <> face 150| *1842:* Which D'Ormea </> D'ORMEA. ¶ . . I *1863:* D'Ormea </> D'ORMEA. ¶ I 151| *1842: aside*] Here! So King *1863: aside*] Here! So, King 152| *1842:* once, and <> ordained but I *1849:* once; and <> ordained, but I, *1868:*

To make that memorable? Both in call,
As he declared. Were't better gnash the teeth,
Or laugh outright now?
CHARLES [*to* POLYXENA]. What's his visit for?
D'ORMEA [*aside*]. I question if they even speak to me.
POLYXENA [*to* CHARLES]. Face the man! He'll suppose you fear him, else.
[*Aloud.*] The Marquis bears the King's command, no doubt?
D'ORMEA [*aside*]. Precisely!—If I threatened him, perhaps?
Well, this at least is punishment enough!
Men used to promise punishment would come.
CHARLES Deliver the King's message, Marquis!
D'ORMEA [*aside*]. Ah—
So anxious for his fate? [*Aloud.*] A word, my Prince,
Before you see your father—just one word
Of counsel!
CHARLES Oh, your counsel certainly!
Polyxena, the Marquis counsels us!
Well, sir? Be brief, however!
D'ORMEA What? You know
As much as I?—preceded me, most like,
In knowledge! So! ('Tis in his eye, beside—
His voice: he knows it, and his heart's on flame
Already.) You surmise why you, myself,
Del Borgo, Spava, fifty nobles more,
Are summoned thus?
CHARLES Is the Prince used to know,
At any time, the pleasure of the King,
Before his minister?—Polyxena,
Stay here till I conclude my task: I feel
Your presence (smile not) through the walls, and take

once: and <> I 154| *1842:* declared! Were't <> teeth *1849:* teeth, *1888:* declared. Were't 156| *1842:* if they'll even *1863:* if they even 157| *1842:* Face D'Ormea, he'll suppose *1863:* Face the man! he'll *1868:* He'll 158| *1842:* doubt. *1868:* doubt? 165| *1842:* certainly— *1868:* certainly!
167| *1842:* you *1868:* You 169| *1842:* knowledge? So! 'Tis *1849:* So! ('Tis *1863:* knowledge! So 170| *1842:* voice—he knows it and *1863:* voice: he knows it, and 171| *1842:* Already! You *1849:* Already!) You *1888:* Already.) You
173| *1842:* know *1849:* know, 174| *1842:* time the pleasure <> King *1849:* time, the pleasure <> King, 176| *1842:* task—I *1863:* task: I 177| *1842:*

Fresh heart. The King's within that chamber?

D'ORMEA [*passing the table whereon a paper lies, exclaims, as he glances at it.*] "Spain!"

POLYXENA [*aside to* CHARLES]. Tarry awhile: what ails the minister?

D'ORMEA Madam, I do not often trouble you.
The Prince loathes, and you scorn me—let that pass!
But since it touches him and you, not me,
Bid the Prince listen!

POLYXENA [*to* CHARLES]. Surely you will listen!
—Deceit?—those fingers crumpling up his vest?

CHARLES Deceitful to the very fingers' ends!

D'ORMEA [*who has approached them, overlooks the other paper* CHARLES *continues to hold.*]
My project for the Fiefs! As I supposed!
Sir, I must give you light upon those measures
—For this is mine, and that I spied of Spain,
Mine too!

CHARLES Release me! Do you gloze on me
Who bear in the world's face (that is, the world
You make for me at Turin) your contempt?
—Your measures?—When was not a hateful task
D'Ormea's imposition? Leave my robe!
What post can I bestow, what grant concede?
Or do you take me for the King?

D'ORMEA Not I!
Not yet for King,—not for, as yet, thank God,
One who in . . . shall I say a year, a month?
Ay!—shall be wretcheder than e'er was slave
In his Sardinia.—Europe's spectacle

---

presence . . (smile not) . . thro' *1849:* presence—(smile not)—thro' *1863:* through 178| *1842: it*] Spain! *1849: it*] "Spain!" 181| *1842:* loathes and you loathe me <> pass; *1849:* loathes, and *1863:* pass! *1888:* you scorn me 183| *1868:* will listen *1888:* will listen! 184| *1842:* Those *1888:* those 191| *1842:* You've made for *1868:* You make for 192| *1842:* was any hateful *1868:* —Your measure?—When was not any hateful *1888:* —Your measures?—When <> not a hateful 193| *1842:* Not D'Ormea's *1868:* D'Ormea's 196| *1842:* for King,—not for as *1849:* for King,—not for, as 197| *1842:* in . . shall <> year—a *1849:* One, who *1868:* One who <> year, a *1888:* in . . . shall 199| *1842:* his Sardinia,—Europe's *1849:* spectacle, *1868:* spectacle *1888:* his

And the world's bye-word! What? The Prince aggrieved
That I excluded him our counsels? Here
[*Touching the paper in* CHARLES's *hand.*]
Accept a method of extorting gold
From Savoy's nobles, who must wring its worth
In silver first from tillers of the soil,
Whose hinds again have to contribute brass
To make up the amount: there's counsel, sir,
My counsel, one year old; and the fruit, this—
Savoy's become a mass of misery
And wrath, which one man has to meet—the King:
You're not the King! Another counsel, sir!
Spain entertains a project (here it lies)
Which, guessed, makes Austria offer that same King
Thus much to baffle Spain; he promises;
Then comes Spain, breathless lest she be forestalled,
Her offer follows; and he promises . . .
CHARLES —Promises, sir, when he has just agreed
To Austria's offer?
D'ORMEA That's a counsel, Prince!
But past our foresight, Spain and Austria (choosing
To make their quarrel up between themselves
Without the intervention of a friend)
Produce both treaties, and both promises . . .
CHARLES How?
D'ORMEA Prince, a counsel! And the fruit of that?
Both parties covenant afresh, to fall
Together on their friend, blot out his name,
Abolish him from Europe. So, take note,
Here's Austria and here's Spain to fight against:

Sardinia.—Europe's 201| *1842:* That I've excluded *1863:* That I excluded
206| *1842:* amount—there's <> sir! *1868:* amount: there's *1888:* sir, 207| *1842:* counsel one *1849:* counsel, one 212| *1842:* Which guessed makes *1849:* Which, guessed, makes 215| *1842:* follows, and *1849:* follows; and 216| *1842:* Promises <> he before agreed *1849:* —Promises *1888:* he has just agreed
218| *1842:* But, past our foresight Spain and Austria, choosing *1849:* But past our foresight, Spain and Austria (choosing 220| *1842:* friend, *1849:* friend)
222| *1842:* counsel!—And *1888:* counsel! And 223| *1842:* afresh to *1849:* afresh, to 225| *1842:* from Europe. So take *1863:* from Europe. So, take 226| *1842:* against, *1863:* Here's Austria, and *1868:* Here's Austria and *1888:* against:

And what sustains the King but Savoy here,
A miserable people mad with wrongs?
You're not the King!

CHARLES Polyxena, you said
All would clear up: all does clear up to me.

D'ORMEA Clear-up! 'Tis no such thing to envy, then?
You see the King's state in its length and breadth?
You blame me now for keeping you aloof
From counsels and the fruit of counsels? Wait
Till I explain this morning's business!

CHARLES [*aside*]. No—
Stoop to my father, yes,—D'Ormea, no:
—The King's son, not to the King's counsellor!
I will do something, but at least retain
The credit of my deed. [*Aloud*.] Then it is this
You now expressly come to tell me?

D'ORMEA This
To tell! You apprehend me?

CHARLES Perfectly.
Further, D'Ormea, you have shown yourself,
For the first time these many weeks and months,
Disposed to do my bidding?

D'ORMEA From the heart!

CHARLES Acquaint my father, first, I wait his pleasure:
Next . . . or, I'll tell you at a fitter time.
Acquaint the King!

D'ORMEA [*aside*]. If I 'scape Victor yet!
First, to prevent this stroke at me: if not,—
Then, to avenge it! [*To* CHARLES.] Gracious sir, I go. [*Goes*.]

230| *1842:* up—all <> me! *1863:* up: all *1888:* me. 231| *1842:* Clears up? 'Tis *1868:* Clear *1888:* up! 'Tis 233| *1849:* me, now, for *1868:* me now for 234| *1842:* of counsels?—Wait *1888:* of counsels? Wait 235| *1842:* 'Till I've explained this *1849:* Till *1863:* Till I explain this 236| *1842:* yes,—to D'Ormea, no! *1849:* no; *1863:* yes,—D'Ormea *1888:* no: 237| *1842:* The King's son *1849:* —The King's son 238| *1842:* something,—but *1868:* something, but 239| *1842:* deed! [*Aloud*.] Then, D'Ormea, this *1863: deed!* [*Aloud*.] Then, it is this *1868:* deed! [*Aloud*.] Then it *1888:* deed. [*Aloud* 242| *1842:* And further <> yourself *1849:* yourself, *1863:* Further 243| *1842:* months *1849:* months, 245| *1888:* pleasure § Omission of colon in 1888 and 1889 apparently a printer's error; restored in Ohio edition. § 246| *1842:* or I'll *1849:* or, I'll 248| *1842:* me—if not, *1849:* not,— *1868:* me: if 249| *1842:* Then to *1849:*

CHARLES God, I forbore! Which more offends, that man
Or that man's master? Is it come to this?
Have they supposed (the sharpest insult yet)
I needed e'en his intervention? No!
No—dull am I, conceded,—but so dull,
Scarcely! Their step decides me.
POLYXENA How decides?
CHARLES You would be freed D'Ormea's eye and hers?
—Could fly the court with me and live content?
So, this it is for which the knights assemble!
The whispers and the closeting of late,
The savageness and insolence of old,
—For this!
POLYXENA What mean you?
CHARLES How? You fail to catch
Their clever plot? I missed it, but could you?
These last two months of care to inculcate
How dull I am,—D'Ormea's present visit
To prove that, being dull, I might be worse
Were I a King—as wretched as now dull—
You recognize in it no winding up
Of a long plot?
POLYXENA Why should there be a plot?
CHARLES The crown's secure now; I should shame the crown—
An old complaint; the point is, how to gain
My place for one, more fit in Victor's eyes,
His mistress the Sebastian's child.
POLYXENA In truth?
CHARLES They dare not quite dethrone Sardinia's Prince:
But they may descant on my dulness till
They sting me into even praying them
Grant leave to hide my head, resign my state,

Then, to 250| *1842:* offends—that *1868:* offends, that 252| *1842:* yet!) *1849:* yet) 256| *1842:* free from D'Ormea's *1868:* freed D'Ormea's 258| *1842:* So—this *1868:* So, this 261| *1842:* CHARLES How? you *1868:* CHARLES How? You 262| *1842:* it—but *1868:* it, but 264| *1842:* am,—with D'Ormea's *1863:* am,—D'Ormea's 266| *1842:* king *1868:* King 267| *1842:* recognise <> winding-up *1849:* winding up *1888:* recognize
270–272| *1842:* complaint: the <> to save / My <> for his Sebastian's *1849:* complaint; the <> to gain / My <> for one more fit in Victor's eyes, / His mistress', the Sebastian's *1868:* one, more <> / His mistress the 276| *1842:* For leave *1868:* Grant

And end the coil. Not see now? In a word,
They'd have me tender them myself my rights
As one incapable;—some cause for that,
Since I delayed thus long to see their drift!
I shall apprise the King he may resume
My rights this moment.
POLYXENA Pause! I dare not think
So ill of Victor.
CHARLES Think no ill of him!
POLYXENA —Nor think him, then, so shallow as to suffer
His purpose be divined thus easily.
And yet—you are the last of a great line;
There's a great heritage at stake; new days
Seemed to await this newest of the realms
Of Europe:—Charles, you must withstand this!
CHARLES Ah—
You dare not then renounce the splendid Court
For one whom all the world despises? Speak!
POLYXENA My gentle husband, speak I will, and truth.
Were this as you believe, and I once sure
Your duty lay in so renouncing rule,
I could . . . could? Oh what happiness it were—
To live, my Charles, and die, alone with you!
CHARLES I grieve I asked you. To the presence, then!
By this, D'Ormea acquaints the King, no doubt,
He fears I am too simple for mere hints,
And that no less will serve than Victor's mouth
Demonstrating in council what I am.
I have not breathed, I think, these many years!
POLYXENA Why, it may be!—if he desire to wed
That woman, call legitimate her child.

---

leave 277| *1842:* see that? In *1849:* see now? In 279| *1842:* incapable:—some *1868:* incapable;—some 282| *1842:* POLYXENA Pause—I *1863:* POLYXENA Pause! I 290| *1842:* court *1868:* Court 295| *1842:* could . . could? Oh, what <> were *1849:* were— *1868:* could . . could? Oh what *1888:* could . . . could 296| *1842:* die alone *1863:* die, alone 297| *1842:* Presence *1863:* presence 298| *1842:* D'Ormea <> King by this, no *1863:* By this, D'Ormea <> King, no 301| *1842:* Teaching me in full council *1868:* Demonstrating in council 302| *1842:*—I have *1868:* I have 303| *1842:* Why—it <> desires *1863:* desire *1868:* Why, it 304| *1842:* woman and legitimate her

CHARLES You see as much? Oh, let his will have way!
You'll not repent confiding in me, love?
There's many a brighter spot in Piedmont, far,
Than Rivoli. I'll seek him: or, suppose
You hear first how I mean to speak my mind?
—Loudly and firmly both, this time, be sure!
I yet may see your Rhine-land, who can tell?
Once away, ever then away! I breathe.
POLYXENA And I too breathe.
CHARLES Come, my Polyxena!

---

child— *1868:* woman, call legitimate her child. 306| *1863:* Love? *1868:* love? 307| *1842:* in Piedmont far *1849:* in Piedmont, far, 308| *1842:* him—or *1868:* him: or 310| *1863:* time be *1868:* time, be 311| *1842:* your Rhine-land—who *1868:* your Rhine-land, who 313| *1842:* breathe! ¶ CHARLES <> Polyxena! [*Exeunt.* *1849:* my Polyxena! *1868:* breathe. ¶ CHARLES

KING VICTOR

PART II

Enter KING VICTOR, *bearing the Regalia on a cushion, from his apartment. He calls loudly.*

VICTOR D'Ormea!—for patience fails me, treading thus
Among the obscure trains I have laid,—my knights
Safe in the hall here—in that anteroom,
My son,—D'Ormea, where? Of this, one touch—
[*Laying down the crown.*]
This fireball to these mute black cold trains—then
Outbreak enough!
[*Contemplating it.*] To lose all, after all!
This, glancing o'er my house for ages—shaped,
Brave meteor, like the crown of Cyprus now,
Jerusalem, Spain, England, every change
The braver,—and when I have clutched a prize
My ancestry died wan with watching for,
To lose it!—by a slip, a fault, a trick
Learnt to advantage once and not unlearned
When past the use,—"just this once more" (I thought)
"Use it with Spain and Austria happily,
And then away with trick!" An oversight
I'd have repaired thrice over, any time
These fifty years, must happen now! There's peace

2–4| *1842:* the trains that I <> knights, / My son,—and D'Ormea *1849:* knights, / Safe in the hall here—in that anteroom, / My 2| *1868:* the obscure trains I <> knights 4| *1863:* son,—D'Ormea 5| *1842:* mute, black, cold <> then! *1868:* mute black cold <> then 7| *1842:* This—glancing *1868:* This, glancing 8| *1842:* Crown <> now— *1863:* crown *1868:* now, 9| *1842:* Jerusalem, Spain, England—every *1868:* Jerusalem, Spain, England, every 12| *1842:* slip—a fault—a *1868:* slip, a fault, a 13| *1842:* once, and not unlearnt *1868:* once and not unlearned 16| *1842:* trick!"—An *1863:* trick!" An 17| *1842:* over any *1849:* over, any 18| *1842:* years must *1849:* years,

At length; and I, to make the most of peace,
Ventured my project on our people here,
As needing not their help: which Europe knows,
And means, cold-blooded, to dispose herself
(Apart from plausibilities of war)
To crush the new-made King—who ne'er till now
Feared her. As Duke, I lost each foot of earth
And laughed at her: my name was left, my sword
Left, all was left! But she can take, she knows,
This crown, herself conceded . . . That's to try,
Kind Europe! My career's not closed as yet!
This boy was ever subject to my will,
Timid and tame—the fitter! D'Ormea, too—
What if the sovereign also rid himself
Of thee, his prime of parasites?—I delay!
D'Ormea! [*As* D'ORMEA *enters, the* KING *seats himself.*]
My son, the Prince—attends he?

D'ORMEA Sir,
He does attend. The crown prepared!—it seems
That you persist in your resolve.

VICTOR Who's come?
The chancellor and the chamberlain? My knights?

D'ORMEA The whole Annunziata. If, my liege,
Your fortune had not tottered worse than now . . .

VICTOR Del Borgo has drawn up the schedules? mine—
My son's, too? Excellent! Only, beware
Of the least blunder, or we look but fools.
First, you read the Annulment of the Oaths;
Del Borgo follows . . . no, the Prince shall sign;
Then let Del Borgo read the Instrument:

---

must 19| *1842:* make of peace the most, *1849:* make the most of peace, 21| *1842:* help—which *1868:* help: which 23| *1842:* (Apart the plausibilities *1849:* (Apart from plausibilities 28| *1842:* crown herself conceded . . . ¶ That's *1849:* crown, herself *1888:* conceded . . . That's 30| *1842:* will— *1868:* will, 32| *1842:* the sovereign's also rid of thee *1868:* the sovereign also rid himself 33| *1842:* His <> parasites?—Yet I *1868:* Of thee, his <> parasites?—I 34| *1842:* son the <> Sire, *1849:* son, the *1868:* Sir, 38| *1842:* Annunziata.—If *1888:* Annunziata. If 39| *1842:* fortunes *1868:* fortune 41| *1842:* son's too? Excellent. Only *1849:* too? Excellent! Only *1863:* son's, too 42| *1842:* or but fools we look. *1849:* or we look but fools. 44| *1842:* follows . . no *1888:* follows . . . no 45| *1842:* the Instrument— *1863:*

On which, I enter.
D'ORMEA Sir, this may be truth;
You, sir, may do as you affect—may break
Your engine, me, to pieces: try at least
If not a spring remain worth saving! Take
My counsel as I've counselled many times!
What if the Spaniard and the Austrian threat?
There's England, Holland, Venice—which ally
Select you?
VICTOR Aha! Come, D'Ormea,—"truth"
Was on your lip a minute since. Allies?
I've broken faith with Venice, Holland, England
—As who knows if not you?
D'ORMEA But why with me
Break faith—with one ally, your best, break faith?
VICTOR When first I stumbled on you, Marquis—'twas
At Mondovi—a little lawyer's clerk . . .
D'ORMEA Therefore your soul's ally!—who brought you through
Your quarrel with the Pope, at pains enough—
Who simply echoed you in these affairs—
On whom you cannot therefore visit these
Affairs' ill-fortune—whom you trust to guide
You safe (yes, on my soul) through these affairs!
VICTOR I was about to notice, had you not
Prevented me, that since that great town kept
With its chicane D'Ormea's satchel stuffed

---

the Instrument: 46| *1842:* enter.— ¶ D'ORMEA Sire, <> truth: *1849:* truth; *1863:* enter. ¶ D'ORMEA *1868:* Sir 47| *1842:* sire *1868:* sir 49| *1842:* spring remains worth saving! Bid *1849:* saving! Take *1868:* remain 50| *1842:* Me counsel as *1849:* My counsel as 53| *1842:* VICTOR Aha! Come, my D'Ormea *1863:* VICTOR Aha! Come, D'Ormea 55| *1842:* with Venice, Holland, England. *1868:* with Venice, Holland, England 56| *1842:* D'ORMEA . . . But not with *1849:* D'ORMEA But why with 57| *1842:* Broke faith—with <> best, broke faith. *1849:* Break faith—with <> best, break faith? 58| *1842:* you, Marquis—(at *1849:* you, Marquis—('twas *1863:* you, Marquis—'twas 59| *1842:* Mondovi 'twas,—a <> clerk . . .) *1849:* At Mondovi—a *1863:* lawyer's clerk . . . . *1868:* lawyer's clerk . . .
60| *1842:* . . Therefore *1849:* . . . Therefore *1863:* Therefore
61| *1842:* the Pope at *1849:* the Pope, at 62| *1842:* Who've simply *1863:* Who simply 63| *1849:* cannot, therefore, visit *1868:* cannot therefore visit
64| *1842:* ill fortune—whom you'll trust *1868:* whom you trust *1888:* ill-fortune
65| *1842:* soul) in these *1868:* soul) through these 67| *1842:* since Mondovi kept *1849:* since that great town kept 68| *1842:* chicane my D'Ormea's <>

And D'Ormea's self sufficiently recluse,
He missed a sight,—my naval armament
When I burned Toulon. How the skiff exults
Upon the galliot's wave!—rises its height,
O'ertops it even; but the great wave bursts,
And hell-deep in the horrible profound
Buries itself the galliot: shall the skiff
Think to escape the sea's black trough in turn?
Apply this: you have been my minister
—Next me, above me possibly;—sad post,
Huge care, abundant lack of peace of mind;
Who would desiderate the eminence?
You gave your soul to get it; you'd yet give
Your soul to keep it, as I mean you shall,
D'Ormea! What if the wave ebbed with me?
Whereas it cants you to another crest;
I toss you to my son; ride out your ride!
D'ORMEA Ah, you so much despise me?
VICTOR You, D'Ormea?
Nowise: and I'll inform you why. A king
Must in his time have many ministers,
And I've been rash enough to part with mine
When I thought proper. Of the tribe, not one
(. . . Or wait, did Pianezze?—ah, just the same!)
Not one of them, ere his remonstrance reached
The length of yours, but has assured me (commonly
Standing much as you stand,—or nearer, say,
The door to make his exit on his speech)
—I should repent of what I did. D'Ormea,
Be candid, you approached it when I bade you
Prepare the schedules! But you stopped in time,

---

stuffed, *1863:* chicane D'Ormea's *1868:* stuffed 71| *1842:* burnt *1868:* burned 73| *1842:* bursts— *1868:* bursts, 75| *1842:* galliot:—shall *1868:* galliot: shall 78| *1842:* me—above *1849:*above me, possibly *1868:* me, above me possibly 81| *1842:* it—you'd *1868:* it; you'd 83| *1842:* My D'Ormea *1863:* D'Ormea 84| *1842:* another's crest— *1863:* another *1868:* crest; 86| *1842:* me then? ¶ VICTOR *1868:* me? ¶ VICTOR 91| *1842:* (. . Or <> Pianezze? . . ah *1888:* (. . . Or <> Pianezze?—ah 93| *1849:* commonly, *1868:* commonly 96| *1842:* —"I should <> did:" now, D'Ormea, *1849:* —I should <> did: now *1863:* did: D'Ormea, *1868:* did. D'Ormea, 97| *1842:* (Be candid—you *1863:* Be *1868:* candid, you 98| *1842:* time) *1863:* time *1868:*

You have not so assured me: how should I
Despise you then?

Enter CHARLES.

VICTOR [*changing his tone*]. Are you instructed? Do
My order, point by point! About it, sir!
D'ORMEA You so despise me! [*Aside.*] One last stay remains—
The boy's discretion there.
[*To* CHARLES.] For your sake, Prince,
I pleaded, wholly in your interest,
To save you from this fate!
CHARLES [*aside*]. Must I be told
The Prince was supplicated for—by him?
VICTOR [*to* D'ORMEA]. Apprise Del Borgo, Spava, and the rest,
Our son attends them; then return.
D'ORMEA One word!
CHARLES [*aside*]. A moment's pause and they would drive me hence,
I do believe!
D'ORMEA [*aside*]. Let but the boy be firm!
VICTOR You disobey?
CHARLES [*to* D'ORMEA]. You do not disobey
Me, at least? Did you promise that or no?
D'ORMEA Sir, I am yours: what would you? Yours am I!
CHARLES When I have said what I shall say, 'tis like
Your face will ne'er again disgust me. Go!
Through you, as through a breast of glass, I see.
And for your conduct, from my youth till now,
Take my contempt! You might have spared me much.
Secured me somewhat, nor so harmed yourself:
That's over now. Go, ne'er to come again!
D'ORMEA As son, the father—father as, the son!
My wits! My wits! [*Goes.*]
VICTOR [*seated*]. And you, what meant you, pray,

---

time, 99| *1842:* —You *1868:* You 100| *1842:* you, then *1868:* you then 101| *1842:* order point by *1849:* order, point by 102| *1842:* me? [*Aside* *1863:* me! [*Aside* 104| *1842:* pleaded—wholly <> interest— *1868:* pleaded, wholly <> interest, 108| *1842:* them: then <> word . . . *1849:* them; then <> word. *1863:* word! 112| *1842:* Me, D'Ormea? Did *1863:* Me, at least? Did 113| *1842:* yours—what <> you? Yours am I. *1849:* you? Yours am I! *1868:* yours: what 119| *1842:* yourself— *1868:* yourself: 120| *1842:* now. Go—ne'er *1868:* now. Go, ne'er 123| *1842:* By speaking *1868:* Speaking

Speaking thus to D'Ormea?
CHARLES Let us not
Waste words upon D'Ormea! Those I spent
Have half unsettled what I came to say.
His presence vexes to my very soul.
VICTOR One called to manage a kingdom, Charles, needs heart
To bear up under worse annoyances
Than seems D'Ormea—to me, at least.
CHARLES [*aside*]. Ah, good!
He keeps me to the point. Then be it so.
[*Aloud.*] Last night, sir, brought me certain papers—these—
To be reported on,—your way of late.
Is it last night's result that you demand?
VICTOR For God's sake, what has night brought forth? Pronounce
The . . . what's your word?—result!
CHARLES Sir, that had proved
Quite worthy of your sneer, no doubt:—a few
Lame thoughts, regard for you alone could wring,
Lame as they are, from brains like mine, believe!
As 'tis, sir, I am spared both toil and sneer.
These are the papers.
VICTOR Well, sir? I suppose
You hardly burned them. Now for your result!
CHARLES I never should have done great things of course,
But . . . oh my father, had you loved me more!
VICTOR Loved? [*Aside.*] Has D'Ormea played me false, I wonder?
[*Aloud.*] Why, Charles, a king's love is diffused—yourself
May overlook, perchance, your part in it.
Our monarchy is absolutest now
In Europe, or my trouble's thrown away.

124| *1842:* Weary ourselves with D'Ormea! Those few words *1888:* Waste words upon D'Ormea! Those I spent 127| *1842:* manage kingdoms. *1868:* manage a kingdom. 129| *1842:* Than D'Ormea seems—to *1868:* Than seems D'Ormea—to 130| *1842:* point! Then *1888:* point. Then 131| *1842:* sire *1849:* Sire *1868:* sir 135| *1842:* The . . what's <> Sire *1868:* Sir *1888:* The . . . what's 136| *1842:* sneers *1863:* sneer 137| *1842:* thoughts regard *1849:* thoughts, regard 138| *1842:* brains, like <> believe. *1849:* believe! *1868:* brains like 139| *1842:* sire *1863:* Sire *1868:* sir 140| *1842:* There are *1863:* These are 141| *1842:* result. *1849:* result! 143| *1842:* But . . oh, my *1849:* more . . . *1863:* more! *1868:* oh my *1888:* But . . . oh 144| *1842:* Loved you? [*Aside* *1868:* Loved? [*Aside* 148| *1842:* away:

I love, my mode, that subjects each and all
May have the power of loving, all and each,
Their mode: I doubt not, many have their sons
To trifle with, talk soft to, all day long:
I have that crown, this chair, D'Ormea, Charles!
CHARLES 'Tis well I am a subject then, not you.
VICTOR [*aside*]. D'Ormea has told him everything.
[*Aloud.*] Aha!
I apprehend you: when all's said, you take
Your private station to be prized beyond
My own, for instance?
CHARLES —Do and ever did
So take it: 'tis the method you pursue
That grieves . . .
VICTOR These words! Let me express, my friend,
Your thoughts. You penetrate what I supposed
Secret. D'Ormea plies his trade betimes!
I purpose to resign my crown to you.
CHARLES To me?
VICTOR Now,—in that chamber.
CHARLES You resign
The crown to me?
VICTOR And time enough, Charles, sure?
Confess with me, at four-and-sixty years
A crown's a load. I covet quiet once
Before I die, and summoned you for that.
CHARLES 'Tis I will speak: you ever hated me.
I bore it,—have insulted me, borne too—
Now you insult yourself; and I remember
What I believed you, what you really are,
And cannot bear it. What! My life has passed
Under your eye, tormented as you know,—

1863: away. 151| *1842:* not many *1849:* not, many 152| *1842:* long— *1863:* long: 153| *1842:* chair, and D'Ormea, Charles. *1849:* and D'Ormea, Charles! *1868:* chair, D'Ormea 155| *1868: Aloud.*] Aha, *1888: Aloud.*] Aha! 159–160| *1842:* method that aggrieves . . . / VICTOR These words! these words! Let *1849:* method you pursue / That grieves . . . ¶ VICTOR These words! Let *1868:* grieves. . . . ¶ VICTOR *1888:* grieves . . . ¶ VICTOR 161| *1842:* thought *1868:* thoughts 162| *1842:* A secret *1868:* Secret 164| *1842:* VICTOR Now—in *1868:* VICTOR Now in *1888:* VICTOR Now,—in 169| *1842:* me, *1888:* me.

Your whole sagacities, one after one,
At leisure brought to play on me—to prove me
A fool, I thought and I submitted; now
You'd prove . . . what would you prove me?

VICTOR This to me?
I hardly know you!

CHARLES Know me? Oh indeed
You do not! Wait till I complain next time
Of my simplicity!—for here's a sage
Knows the world well, is not to be deceived,
And his experience and his Macchiavels,
D'Ormeas, teach him—what?—that I this while
Have envied him his crown! He has not smiled,
I warrant,—has not eaten, drunk, nor slept,
For I was plotting with my Princess yonder!
Who knows what we might do or might not do?
Go now, be politic, astound the world!
That sentry in the antechamber—nay,
The varlet who disposed this precious trap
[*Pointing to the crown.*]
That was to take me—ask them if they think
Their own sons envy them their posts!—Know me!

VICTOR But you know me, it seems: so, learn in brief.
My pleasure. This assembly is convened . . .

CHARLES Tell me, that woman put it in your head!
You were not sole contriver of the scheme,
My father!

VICTOR Now observe me, sir! I jest

171| *1842:* yourself, and *1868:* yourself; and 175| *1842:* sagacities one after one *1849:* sagacities, one after one, 176| *1842:* to bear on me—to prove *1849:* to play on me—to prove me 177| *1842:* Me—fool, I thought, and *1849:* A fool *1868:* thought and 179| *1842:* me? Oh, indeed *1868:* me? Oh indeed 181| *1842:* sage— *1868:* sage 182| *1842:* well—is <> deceived— *1868:* well, is <> deceived, 183| *1849:* experience, and *1868:* experience and 184| *1842:* His D'Ormeas <> I, this while, *1863:* D'Ormeas *1868:* that I this while 186| *1842:* drunk, or slept, *1849:* drunk, nor slept, *1868:* drunk nor *1888:* drunk, nor 187| *1842:* princess *1849:* Princess 188| *1849:* do, or *1868:* do or 189| *1842:* now—be politic—astound the world!— *1849:* Go, now *1863:* world! *1868:* Go now, be politic, astound 190| *1842:* antichamber . . nay *1849:* antechamber . . nay, *1863:* antechamber—nay, 194| *1842:* so learn in brief *1863:* so, learn *1868:* brief. 196| *1842:* me Sebastian put <> head— *1849:* me, that woman put

Seldom—on these points, never. Here, I say,
The knights assemble to see me concede,
And you accept, Sardinia's crown.

CHARLES Farewell!
'Twere vain to hope to change this: I can end it.
Not that I cease from being yours, when sunk
Into obscurity: I'll die for you,
But not annoy you with my presence. Sir,
Farewell! Farewell!

Enter D'ORMEA.

D'ORMEA [*aside*]. Ha, sure he's changed again—
Means not to fall into the cunning trap!
Then Victor, I shall yet escape you, Victor!

VICTOR [*suddenly placing the crown upon the head of* CHARLES]. D'Ormea, your King!
[*To* CHARLES.] My son, obey me! Charles,
Your father, clearer-sighted than yourself,
Decides it must be so. 'Faith, this looks real!
My reasons after; reason upon reason
After: but now, obey me! Trust in me!
By this, you save Sardinia, you save me!
Why, the boy swoons! [*To* D'ORMEA.] Come this side!

D'ORMEA [*as* CHARLES *turns from him to* VICTOR].
You persist?

VICTOR Yes, I conceive the gesture's meaning. 'Faith,
He almost seems to hate you: how is that?

1868: head! 199| *1842:* never. Here to witness *1849:* never. Here, I say, 200| *1842:* (I say they are assembled) me *1849:* The Knights assemble to see me *1863:* knights 201| *1842:* accept Sardinia's *1849:* accept, Sardinia's 202| *1842:* this—I *1868:* this: I 203| *1842:* yours when *1849:* yours, when 204| *1842:* obscurity. I'd die *1849:* obscurity. I'll die *1868:* obscurity: I'll 205| *1842:* presence—Sire, *1863:* presence. Sire, *1868:* Sir, 207| *1842:* trap— *1863:* trap! 208| *1842:* Then, Victor, I *1868:* Then Victor, I 212| *1842:* after—reason upon *1868:* after; reason upon 213| *1842:* After—but *1868:* After: but 214| *1842:* save Savoy, my subjects, me! *1849:* save Sardinia, you save me! 215| *1842:* Why the boy swoons. Come *1849:* swoons! [To D'ORMEA] Come *1863:* Why, the 216| *1842:* Yes—I *1868:* Yes, I 217| *1842:* you—how *1868:*

Be re-assured, my Charles! Is't over now?
Then, Marquis, tell the new King what remains
To do! A moment's work. Del Borgo reads
The Act of Abdication out, you sign it,
Then I sign; after that, come back to me.

D'ORMEA Sir, for the last time, pause!

VICTOR Five minutes longer
I am your sovereign, Marquis. Hesitate—
And I'll so turn those minutes to account
That . . . Ay, you recollect me! [*Aside.*] Could I bring
My foolish mind to undergo the reading
That Act of Abdication!

[*As* CHARLES *motions* D'ORMEA *to precede him.*]

Thanks, dear Charles!

[CHARLES *and* D'ORMEA *retire.*]

VICTOR A novel feature in the boy,—indeed
Just what I feared he wanted most. Quite right,
This earnest tone: your truth, now, for effect!
It answers every purpose: with that look,
That voice,—I hear him: "I began no treaty,"
(He speaks to Spain), "nor ever dreamed of this
You show me; this I from my soul regret;
But if my father signed it, bid not me
Dishonour him—who gave me all, beside:"
And, "True," says Spain, "'twere harsh to visit that
Upon the Prince." Then come the nobles trooping:
"I grieve at these exactions—I had cut
This hand off ere impose them; but shall I
Undo my father's deed?"—and they confer:
"Doubtless he was no party, after all;
Give the Prince time!"
Ay, give us time, but time!

---

you: how 218| *1842:* my Charles. Is't *1849:* my Charles! Is't 223| *1842:* Sire *1868:* Sir 226| *1842:* me! ¶ [*Aside* *1863:* me! [*Aside* 230| *1842:* Just that I <> most—quite *1849:* Just what I <> most. Quite 231| *1842:* tone—your *1868:* tone: your 232| *1842:* look— *1849:* look, 234| *1842:* to Spain,) "nor *1888:* to Spain), "nor 237| *1842:* beside." *1863:* beside:" 238| *1842:* truth *1868:* true *1888:* True 239| *1842:* prince *1849:* Prince 241| *1842:* imposed *1849:* impose 242| *1842:* And *1868:* and 244| *1842:* prince time!"— ¶ Ay <> us time—but *1849:* Prince *1863:* time!" ¶ Ay *1868:* us time,

Only, he must not, when the dark day comes,
Refer our friends to me and frustrate all.
We'll have no child's play, no desponding fits,
No Charles at each cross turn entreating Victor
To take his crown again. Guard against that!

Enter D'ORMEA.

Long live King Charles!
No—Charles's counsellor!
Well, is it over, Marquis? Did I jest?
D'ORMEA "King Charles!" What then may you be?
VICTOR Anything!
A country gentleman that, cured of bustle,
Now beats a quick retreat toward Chambery,
Would hunt and hawk and leave you noisy folk
To drive your trade without him. I'm Count Remont—
Count Tende—any little place's Count!
D'ORMEA Then Victor, Captain against Catinat
At Staffarde, where the French beat you; and Duke
At Turin, where you beat the French; King late
Of Savoy, Piedmont, Montferrat, Sardinia,
—Now, "any little place's Count"—
VICTOR Proceed!
D'ORMEA Breaker of vows to God, who crowned you first;
Breaker of vows to man, who kept you since;

---

but 245| *1842:* not when <> comes *1849:* not, when <> comes, 247| *1842:* desponding-fits, *1868:* desponding fits, 249–250| *1842:* that! / Long <> Charles!— [*Enter* D'ORMEA] ¶ King Charles's *1849:* that! [*Enter* D'ORMEA] / Long <> Charles!— ¶ No—Charles's *1863:* live King Charles! ¶ No 252| *1842:* King Charles! What <> Anything. *1849:* "King Charles!" What <> Anything! 253| *1842:* gentleman that's cured of bustle *1849:* bustle, *1868:* gentleman that, cured 254| *1842:* And beats <> towards Chamberri *1849:* toward Chambery *1868:* Now beats <> Chambery, 255| *1842:* To hunt and hawk, and *1868:* Would hunt and hawk and 258| *1842:* Then, Victor *1849:* against Catinat, *1868:* Then Victor <> Catinat 259| *1842:* At Staffarde where <> you, and *1849:* At Staffarde, where <> you; and 260| *1842:* At Turin where <> French—King, late, *1849:* At Turin, where <> French; King *1868:* the French; King late 262| *1842:* —Now, any <> Count . . . ¶ VICTOR Proceed. *1849:* —Now, "any <> Count"— ¶ VICTOR Proceed! 263| *1842:* to God who <> first, *1849:* to God, who <> first; 264| *1842:* to Man who <> since, *1849:* to Man, who <> since;

Most profligate to me who outraged God
And man to serve you, and am made pay crimes
I was but privy to, by passing thus
To your imbecile son—who, well you know,
Must—(when the people here, and nations there,
Clamour for you the main delinquent, slipped
From King to—"Count of any little place")
Must needs surrender me, all in his reach,—
I, sir, forgive you: for I see the end—
See you on your return—(you will return)—
To him you trust, a moment . . .

VICTOR

Trust him? How?
My poor man, merely a prime-minister,
Make me know where my trust errs!

D'ORMEA

In his fear,
His love, his——but discover for yourself
What you are weakest, trusting in!

VICTOR

Aha,
D'Ormea, not a shrewder scheme than this
In your repertory? You know old Victor—
Vain, choleric, inconstant, rash—(I've heard
Talkers who little thought the King so close)
Felicitous now, were't not, to provoke him
To clean forget, one minute afterward,
His solemn act, and call the nobles back
And pray them give again the very power
He has abjured?—for the dear sake of what?

1868: man 265| *1849:* me, who *1868:* me who 266| *1842:* Man *1868:* man 269| *1842:* Must,—when *1849:* Must, (when *1863:* Must—(when 270| *1842:* you, the <> delinquent, slipt *1868:* you the <> delinquent, slipped 271| *1842:* to—Count <> place *1849:* place) *1868:* to—"Count <> place") 272| *1842:* —Surrender me, all left within his *1868:* Must needs surrender me, all in his 274| *1842:* return (you will return) *1863:* return—(you will return)— 275| *1842:* trust in for the moment . . . ¶ VICTOR How? *1868:* trust thus for <> ¶ VICTOR Trust him? How? *1888:* trust, a moment 276–277| *1842:* Trust in him? (merely a prime minister / This D'Ormea!) How trust in him? ¶ D'ORMEA <> fear— *1849:* prime-minister *1863:* him? merely <> / This D'Ormea! How *1868:* My poor man, merely a prime-minister, / Make me know where my trust errs! ¶ D'ORMEA <> fear, 278| *1842:* love,—but pray discover *1868:* love, his—but discover *1888:* his——but 279| *1842:* weakest trusting *1849:* weakest, trusting 280| *1842:* My D'Ormea *1863:* D'Ormea 284| *1842:* Felicitous, now *1868:* Felicitous now 286| *1842:* act—to call *1849:* act, and call 288| *1842:* of—what? *1849:*

Vengeance on you, D'Ormea! No: such am I,
Count Tende or Count anything you please,
—Only, the same that did the things you say,
And, among other things you say not, used
Your finest fibre, meanest muscle,—you
I used, and now, since you will have it so,
Leave to your fate—mere lumber in the midst,
You and your works. Why, what on earth beside
Are you made for, you sort of ministers?
D'ORMEA Not left, though, to my fate! Your witless son
Has more wit than to load himself with lumber:
He foils you that way, and I follow you.
VICTOR Stay with my son—protect the weaker side!
D'ORMEA Ay, to be tossed the people like a rag,
And flung by them for Spain and Austria's sport,
Abolishing the record of your part
In all this perfidy!
VICTOR Prevent, beside,
My own return!
D'ORMEA That's half prevented now!
'Twill go hard but you find a wondrous charm
In exile, to discredit me. The Alps,
Silk-mills to watch, vines asking vigilance—
Hounds open for the stag, your hawk's a-wing—
Brave days that wait the Louis of the South,
Italy's Janus!
VICTOR So, the lawyer's clerk
Won't tell me that I shall repent!
D'ORMEA You give me
Full leave to ask if you repent?
VICTOR Whene'er

---

abjured!—for *1868:* abjured?—for <> of what? 289| *1842:* you! No, D'Ormea: such *1868:* you, D'Ormea! No: such 296| *1842:* works—Why *1863:* works. Why 298| *1842:* —Left, though, at Chamberri? Your *1849:* —Not left, though, to my fate! Your *1868:* Not 302| *1842:* Ay, be tossed to the *1868:* Ay, to be tossed the 303| *1842:* them to Spain and Austria—so *1868:* them for Spain and Austria's sport, 306| *1842:* now. *1849:* now! 307| *1842:* but you'll find *1863:* but you find 308| *1842:* exile to <> Alps— *1849:* exile, to *1868:* me. The Alps, 309| *1842:* watch—vines *1868:* watch, vines 310| *1842:* stag—your *1868:* stag, your 312| *1842:* VICTOR So the *1849:* VICTOR So, the 314| *1849:*

Sufficient time's elapsed for that, you judge!
[*Shouts inside* "KING CHARLES!"]

D'ORMEA Do you repent?
VICTOR [*after a slight pause*]. . . . I've kept them waiting? Yes!
Come in, complete the Abdication, sir! [*They go out.*]

Enter POLYXENA.

POLYXENA A shout! The sycophants are free of Charles!
Oh is not this like Italy? No fruit
Of his or my distempered fancy, this,
But just an ordinary fact! Beside,
Here they've set forms for such proceedings; Victor
Imprisoned his own mother: he should know,
If any, how a son's to be deprived
Of a son's right. Our duty's palpable.
Ne'er was my husband for the wily king
And the unworthy subjects: be it so!
Come you safe out of them, my Charles! Our life
Grows not the broad and dazzling life, I dreamed
Might prove your lot; for strength was shut in you
None guessed but I—strength which, untramelled once,
Had little shamed your vaunted ancestry—
Patience and self-devotion, fortitude,
Simplicity and utter truthfulness
—All which, they shout to lose!
So, now my work
Begins—to save him from regret. Save Charles
Regret?—the noble nature! He's not made
Like these Italians: 'tis a German soul.

CHARLES *enters crowned.*

VICTOR Whene'er, *1868:* VICTOR Whene'er 315| *1842:* judge. *1849:* judge! 316| *1842:* waiting? Yes. *1849:* waiting? Yes! 317| *1842:* in—complete *1868:* in, complete 318| *1842:* shout? The *1868:* shout! The 319| *1842:* Oh, is *1888:* Oh is 320| *1842:* this— *1868:* this, 321| *1842:* fact! Beside *1849:* fact! Beside, 322| *1842:* proceedings—Victor *1868:* proceedings; Victor 323| *1842:* mother—he *1868:* mother: he 327| *1842:* subjects—be it so. *1849:* so! *1868:* subjects: be 329| *1842:* life I *1849:* life, I 330| *1842:* lot—for *1868:* lot; for 331| *1842:* untrammeled *1868:* untramelled 335| *1842:* which they *1849:* which, they 338| *1842:* Like the

Oh, where's the King's heir? Gone!—the Crown Prince? Gone!—
Where's Savoy? Gone!—Sardinia? Gone! But Charles
Is left! And when my Rhine-land bowers arrive,
If he looked almost handsome yester-twilight
As his grey eyes seemed widening into black
Because I praised him, then how will he look?
Farewell, you stripped and whited mulberry-trees
Bound each to each by lazy ropes of vine!
Now I'll teach you my language: I'm not forced
To speak Italian now, Charles?
[*She sees the crown.*] What is this?
Answer me—who has done this? Answer!
CHARLES He!
I am King now.
POLYXENA Oh worst, worst, worst of all!
Tell me! What, Victor? He has made you King?
What's he then? What's to follow this? You, King?
CHARLES Have I done wrong? Yes, for you were not by!
POLYXENA Tell me from first to last.
CHARLES Hush—a new world
Brightens before me; he is moved away
—The dark form that eclipsed it, he subsides
Into a shape supporting me like you,
And I, alone, tend upward, more and more
Tend upward: I am grown Sardinia's King.
POLYXENA Now stop: was not this Victor, Duke of Savoy
At ten years old?
CHARLES He was.
POLYXENA And the Duke spent

Italians *1868:* Like these Italians 339| *1842:* heir? Gone:—the Crown prince? Gone— *1868:* the Crown-prince? Gone:— *1888:* heir? Gone!—the Crown Prince? Gone!— 340| *1842:* Where's Savoy? Gone:—Sardinia? Gone!—But *1863:* Where's Savoy? Gone:—Sardinia? Gone! But *1888:* Where's Savoy? Gone!—Sardinia 345| *1842:* Farewell you *1849:* Farewell, you 347| *1842:* language—I'm *1868:* language: I'm 349| *1842:* CHARLES He: *1849:* CHARLES He! 351| *1842:* me—what *1868:* me! What 353| *1842:* wrong? Yes—for *1868:* wrong? Yes, for 357| *1842:* like yours, *1849:* like you, 358| *1842:* And I alone tend *1849:* And I, alone, tend 360| *1842:* this Victor Duke *1849:* this Victor,

Since then, just four-and-fifty years in toil
To be—what?
CHARLES King.
POLYXENA Then why unking himself?
CHARLES Those years are cause enough.
POLYXENA The only cause?
CHARLES Some new perplexities.
POLYXENA Which you can solve
Although he cannot?
CHARLES He assures me so.
POLYXENA And this he means shall last—how long?
CHARLES How long?
Think you I fear the perils I confront?
He's praising me before the people's face—
My people!
POLYXENA Then he's changed—grown kind, the King?
Where can the trap be?
CHARLES Heart and soul I pledge!
My father, could I guard the crown you gained,
Transmit as I received it,—all good else
Would I surrender!
POLYXENA Ah, it opens then
Before you, all you dreaded formerly?
You are rejoiced to be a king, my Charles?
CHARLES So much to dare? The better;—much to dread?
The better. I'll adventure though alone.
Triumph or die, there's Victor still to witness
Who dies or triumphs—either way, alone!
POLYXENA Once I had found my share in triumph, Charles,
Or death.

Duke 362| *1842:* then just *1849:* then, just 364| *1842:* Those ten and four-and-fifty years. ¶ POLYXENA Those only? *1849:* Those years are cause enough. ¶ POLYXENA The only cause? 365| *1849:* solve, *1868:* solve 371| *1842:* (Where <> be?) ¶ CHARLES <> soul—and soul, *1849:* CHARLES Heart and soul I pledge! *1863:* Where <> be? ¶ CHARLES 372| *1842:* Crown *1863:* crown 373| *1842:* Deliver it as <> all *1849:* Transmit as <> all good else 375| *1842:* you—all *1868:* you, all 378| *1842:* tho' *1863:* though 380| *1842:* alone. *1849:*

CHARLES But you are I! But you I call
To take, Heaven's proxy, vows I tendered Heaven
A moment since. I will deserve the crown!
POLYXENA You will. [*Aside.*] No doubt it were a glorious thing
For any people, if a heart like his
Ruled over it. I would I saw the trap.

Enter VICTOR.

'Tis he must show me.
VICTOR So, the mask falls off
An old man's foolish love at last. Spare thanks!
I know you, and Polyxena I know.
Here's Charles—I am his guest now—does he bid me
Be seated? And my light-haired blue-eyed child
Must not forget the old man far away
At Chambery, who dozes while she reigns.
POLYXENA Most grateful shall we now be, talking least
Of gratitude—indeed of anything
That hinders what yourself must need to say
To Charles.
CHARLES Pray speak, sir!
VICTOR 'Faith, not much to say:
Only what shows itself, you once i' the point
Of sight. You're now the King: you'll comprehend
Much you may oft have wondered at—the shifts,
Dissimulation, wiliness I showed.
For what's our post? Here's Savoy and here's Piedmont,
Here's Montferrat—a breadth here, a space there—
To o'ersweep all these, what's one weapon worth?
I often think of how they fought in Greece:
(Or Rome, which was it? You're the scholar, Charles!)

---

alone! 382| *1842:* are me! But *1849:* are I! But 386| *1842:* people if *1849:* people, if 387| *1842:* trap! *1849:* trap. 388| *1842:* VICTOR So the *1863:* VICTOR So, the 389| *1842:* last! Spare thanks— *1863:* thanks: *1868:* last. Spare thanks! 392| *1842:* light-haired, blue-eyed *1868:* light-haired blue-eyed 394| *1842:* At Chamberri, who <> reigns? *1849:* At Chambery, who <> reigns. 397| *1842:* must have to *1868:* must need to 398| *1842:* sire <> say— *1849:* Sire *1868:* sir <> say: 399| *1842:* itself, once in the *1868:* itself, you once i' the 400| *1842:* sight. You are now *1868:* sight You're now 405| *1842:* To o'er-sweep all these what's *1849:* these, what's *1888:* o'ersweep 406| *1842:* in Greece *1888:* in Greece: 407| *1842:* scholar,

You made a front-thrust? But if your shield too
Were not adroitly planted, some shrewd knave
Reached you behind; and him foiled, straight if thong
And handle of that shield were not cast loose,
And you enabled to outstrip the wind,
Fresh foes assailed you, either side; 'scape these,
And reach your place of refuge—e'en then, odds
If the gate opened unless breath enough
Were left in you to make its lord a speech.
Oh, you will see!

CHARLES No: straight on shall I go,
Truth helping; win with it or die with it.

VICTOR 'Faith, Charles, you're not made Europe's fighting-man!
The barrier-guarder, if you please. You clutch
Hold and consolidate, with envious France
This side, with Austria that, the territory
I held—ay, and will hold . . . which *you* shall hold
Despite the couple! But I've surely earned
Exemption from these weary politics,
—The privilege to prattle with my son
And daughter here, though Europe wait the while.

POLYXENA Nay, sir,—at Chambery, away for ever,
As soon you will be, 'tis farewell we bid you:
Turn these few fleeting moments to account!
'Tis just as though it were a death.

VICTOR Indeed!

Charles) *1849:* scholar, Charles!) 408| *1842:* shield, too, *1868:* shield too 409| *1842:* planted—some *1868:* planted, some 410| *1842:* and, him *1868:* and him 411| *1842:* loose *1849:* loose, 413| *1842:* you either <> these *1842:* you, either <> these, 416| *1842:* Was left <> Lord *1849:* lord *1868:* Were left 419| *1842:* fighting-man *1849:* fighting-man! 420| *1842:* Its barrier-guarder <> You hold, *1868:* The barrier-guarder <> You clutch 421| *1842:* Not take—consolidate <> envious French *1868:* Hold and consolidate <> envious France 422| *1842:* side and Austrians that, these territories *1849:* side, with Austrians *1868:* with Austria that, the territory 423| *1842:* you *1849:* *you* 424–426| *1842:* earned / The *1849:* earned / Exemption from these weary politics, / —The 427| *1842:* daughter tho' the world should wait *1849:* daughter here, tho' Europe waits *1863:* tho' Europe wait the while § Omission of full stop apparently a printer's error. § *1868:* while. *1888:* though 428| *1842:* Nay, sire,—at Chamberri, away *1849:* Nay, Sire,—at Chambery, away *1868:* sir 429| *1842:* soon you'll be, 'tis a farewell <> you! *1868:* soon you will be, 'tis farewell <>

POLYXENA [*aside*]. Is the trap there?
CHARLES Ay, call this parting—death!
The sacreder your memory becomes.
If I misrule Sardinia, how bring back
My father?
VICTOR I mean . . .
POLYXENA [*who watches* VICTOR *narrowly this while*].
Your father does not mean
You should be ruling for your father's sake:
It is your people must concern you wholly
Instead of him. You mean this, sir? (He drops
My hand!)
CHARLES That people is now part of me.
VICTOR About the people! I took certain measures
Some short time since . . . Oh, I know well, you know
But little of my measures! These affect
The nobles; we've resumed some grants, imposed
A tax or two: prepare yourself, in short,
For clamour on that score. Mark me: you yield
No jot of aught entrusted you!
POLYXENA No jot
You yield!
CHARLES My father, when I took the oath,
Although my eye might stray in search of yours,
I heard it, understood it, promised God
What you require. Till from this eminence
He move me, here I keep, nor shall concede
The meanest of my rights.
VICTOR [*aside*]. The boy's a fool!
—Or rather, I'm a fool: for, what's wrong here?

---

you: 435–436| *1842:* father? No—that thought shall ever urge me. / VICTOR I do not mean . . . ¶ POLYXENA <> does not mean / That you are ruling *1868:* father? ¶ VICTOR I mean . . . ¶ POLYXENA <> does not mean / You should be ruling 438| *1842:* sire *1849:* Sire *1863:* sire *1868:* sir 439| *1842:* People *1863:* people 440| *1842:* People *1863:* people 441| *1842:* since . . Oh, I'm aware you *1868:* since . . Oh, I know well, you *1888:* since . . . Oh 442| *1842:* measures—these *1868:* measures! These 443| *1842:* nobles—we've *1868:* nobles; we've 444| *1842:* two; prepare *1868:* two: prepare 445| *1842:* For clamours on <> score: mark *1863:* clamour *1868:* score. Mark 446| *1842:* of what's entrusted *1868:* of aught entrusted 451| *1842:* moves *1868:* move 452| *1842:* fool.

To-day the sweets of reigning: let to-morrow
Be ready with its bitters.

Enter D'ORMEA.

There's beside
Somewhat to press upon your notice first.
CHARLES Then why delay it for an instant, sir?
That Spanish claim perchance? And, now you speak,
—This morning, my opinion was mature,
Which, boy-like, I was bashful in producing
To one I ne'er am like to fear in future!
My thought is formed upon that Spanish claim.
VICTOR Betimes indeed. Not now, Charles! You require
A host of papers on it.
D'ORMEA [*coming forward*]. Here they are.
[*To* CHARLES.] I, sir, was minister and much beside
Of the late monarch; to say little, him
I served: on you I have, to say e'en less,
No claim. This case contains those papers: with them
I tender you my office.
VICTOR [*hastily*] Keep him, Charles!
There's reason for it—many reasons: you
Distrust him, nor are so far wrong there,—but
He's mixed up in this matter—he'll desire
To quit you, for occasions known to me:
Do not accept those reasons: have him stay!
POLYXENA [*aside*]. His minister thrust on us!
CHARLES [*to* D'ORMEA]. Sir, believe,
In justice to myself, you do not need

1849: fool! 454| *1842:* reigning—let *1868:* reigning: let 457| *1842:* sire? *1849:* Sire? *1868:* sir? 458| *1842:* claim, perchance *1868:* claim perchance 459| *1842:* morning my <> mature *1849:* morning, my <> mature— *1863:* mature, 461| *1842:* To you—I *1849:* To one, I <> fear, in *1868:* one I <> fear in 463| *1842:* (Betimes indeed.) Not now, Charles. You *1849:* (Betimes, indeed *1863:* Betimes, indeed! Not *1868:* Betimes indeed. Not now, Charles! You 464| *1842:* it— ¶ D'ORMEA *1863:* it. ¶ D'ORMEA 465| *1842:* I was the minister *1849:* beside— *1868:* beside *1888:* I, sir, was minister 466| *1842:* monarch: to *1863:* monarch; to 467| *1842:* served; on *1863:* served: on 474| *1842:* reasons—have *1868:* reasons: have 475| *1842:* believe *1849:* believe, 476| *1842:* myself you *1849:* myself, you 477| *1842:* commending: whatsoe'er

E'en this commending: howsoe'er might seem
My feelings toward you, as a private man,
They quit me in the vast and untried field
Of action. Though I shall myself (as late
In your own hearing I engaged to do)
Preside o'er my Sardinia, yet your help
Is necessary. Think the past forgotten
And serve me now!

D'ORMEA I did not offer you
My service—would that I could serve you, sir!
As for the Spanish matter . . .

VICTOR But despatch
At least the dead, in my good daughter's phrase,
Before the living! Help to house me safe
Ere with D'Ormea you set the world a-gape!
Here is a paper—will you overlook
What I propose reserving for my needs?
I get as far from you as possible:
Here's what I reckon my expenditure.

CHARLES [*reading*]. A miserable fifty thousand crowns—

VICTOR Oh, quite enough for country gentlemen!
Beside the exchequer happens . . . but find out
All that, yourself!

CHARLES [*still reading*]. "Count Tende"—what means this?

VICTOR Me: you were but an infant when I burst
Through the defile of Tende upon France.
Had only my allies kept true to me!
No matter. Tende's, then, a name I take
Just as . . .

---

might be *1863:* might seem *1868:* commending: howsoe'er might 478| *1842:* towards you as *1849:* toward *1868:* you, as 480| *1849:* shall, myself, (as *1868:* shall myself (as 483| *1842:* forgotten, *1863:* Past *1868:* the past forgotten 485| *1842:* My services—would I <> sire! *1849:* Sire! *1863:* sire! *1868:* My service—would that I <> sir! 486| *1863:* dispatch *1888:* despatch 489| *1842:* Ere you and D'Ormea set *1868:* Ere with D'Ormea you set 492| *1842:* possible. *1868:* possible: 493| *1842:* There's what *1863:* Here's what 494| *1842:* crowns. *1849:* crowns! *1888:* crowns— 495| *1868:* Oh quite *1888:* Oh, quite 497| *1842:* that yourself. ¶ CHARLES <> *reading*] Count Tende—what is this? *1849:* that, yourself! ¶ CHARLES <> *reading*] "Count Tende"—what means this? 501| *1842:* matter. Tende's then a *1849:* matter.

D'ORMEA —The Marchioness Sebastian takes
The name of Spigno.
CHARLES How, sir?
VICTOR [*to* D'ORMEA]. Fool! All that
Was for my own detailing. [*To* CHARLES.] That anon!
CHARLES [*to* D'ORMEA]. Explain what you have said, sir!
D'ORMEA I supposed
The marriage of the King to her I named,
Profoundly kept a secret these few weeks,
Was not to be one, now he's Count.
POLYXENA [*aside*]. With us
The minister—with him the mistress!
CHARLES [*to* VICTOR]. No—
Tell me you have not taken her—that woman
To live with, past recall!
VICTOR And where's the crime . . .
POLYXENA [*to* CHARLES]. True, sir, this is a matter past recall
And past your cognizance. A day before,
And you had been compelled to note this: now,—
Why note it? The King saved his House from shame:
What the Count did, is no concern of yours.
CHARLES [*after a pause*]. The Spanish claim, D'Ormea!
VICTOR Why, my son,
I took some ill-advised . . . one's age, in fact,
Spoils everything: though I was overreached,
A younger brain, we'll trust, may extricate
Sardinia readily. To-morrow, D'Ormea,
Inform the King!
D'ORMEA [*without regarding* VICTOR, *and leisurely*].
Thus stands the case with Spain:
When first the Infant Carlos claimed his proper
Succession to the throne of Tuscany . . .
VICTOR I tell you, that stands over! Let that rest!
There is the policy!

Tende's, then, a 502| *1842:* D'ORMEA The *1849:* D'ORMEA —The 508| *1842:* one now *1849:* one, now 511| *1842:* with past *1849:* with, past 512| *1842:* recall, *1868:* recall 514| *1842:* this—now *1888:* this: now,— 516| *1842:* the Count does is *1849:* does, is *1868:* the Count did, is 517| *1842:* The Spanish business, D'Ormea *1868:* The Spanish claim, D'Ormea 519| *1842:* over-reached, *1888:* overreached, 521| *1842:* To morrow *1868:* To-morrow 525| *1849:* you that stands *1888:* you, that stands 526| *1842:*

CHARLES [*to* D'ORMEA]. Thus much I know,
And more—too much: the remedy?

D'ORMEA Of course!
No glimpse of one.

VICTOR No remedy at all!
It makes the remedy itself—time makes it.

D'ORMEA [*to* CHARLES]. But if . . .

VICTOR [*still more hastily*]. In fine, I shall take care of that:
And, with another project that I have . . .

D'ORMEA [*turning on him*]. Oh, since Count Tende means to take again
King Victor's crown!—

POLYXENA [*throwing herself at* VICTOR'S *feet*]. E'en now retake it, sir!
Oh speak! We are your subjects both, once more!
Say it—a word effects it! You meant not,
Nor do mean now, to take it: but you must!
'Tis in you—in your nature—and the shame's
Not half the shame 'twould grow to afterwards!

CHARLES Polyxena!

POLYXENA A word recalls the knights—
Say it! What's promising and what's the past?
Say you are still King Victor!

D'ORMEA Better say
The Count repents, in brief! [VICTOR *rises.*]

CHARLES With such a crime
I have not charged you, sir!

POLYXENA (Charles turns from me!)

---

policy. ¶ CHARLES *1849:* policy! ¶ CHARLES 528| *1842:* one— ¶ VICTOR *1849:* one. ¶ VICTOR 530| *1842:* that— *1868:* that: 533| *1842:* sire! *1849:* Sire! *1868:* sir! 534| *1842:* Oh, speak <> both once *1849:* both, once *1888:* Oh speak 536| *1842:* it—but *1868:* it: but 538| *1842:* afterward! *1868:* afterwards! 539| *1842:* Knights— *1863:* knights— 540| *1842:* it!—What's promising *1863:* Past? *1868:* past? *1888:* it! What's promising 543| *1842:* sire! ¶ POLYXENA Charles <> me! [*Exeunt singly.* *1849:* Sire <> me! *1868:* sir *1888:* POLYXENA (Charles <> me!)

SECOND YEAR, 1731.—KING CHARLES

PART I

Enter QUEEN POLYXENA *and* D'ORMEA.—*A pause.*

POLYXENA And now, sir, what have you to say?
D'ORMEA Count Tende . . .
POLYXENA Affirm not I betrayed you; you resolve
On uttering this strange intelligence
—Nay, post yourself to find me ere I reach
The capital, because you know King Charles
Tarries a day or two at Evian baths
Behind me:—but take warning,—here and thus
[*Seating herself in the royal seat.*]
I listen, if I listen—not your friend.
Explicitly the statement, if you still
Persist to urge it on me, must proceed:
I am not made for aught else.
D'ORMEA Good! Count Tende . . .
POLYXENA I, who mistrust you, shall acquaint King Charles
Who even more mistrusts you.
D'ORMEA Does he so?
POLYXENA Why should he not?
D'ORMEA Ay, why not? Motives, seek
You virtuous people, motives! Say, I serve
God at the devil's bidding—will that do?
I'm proud: our people have been pacified,
Really I know not how—
POLYXENA By truthfulness.
D'ORMEA Exactly; that shows I had nought to do

1| *1849:* D'ORMEA Count Tende . . *1888:* D'ORMEA Count Tende. . . 11| *1842:* D'ORMEA Good: Count *1849:* D'ORMEA Good! Count 12| *1842:* acquaint King Charles, *1868:* acquaint King Charles 17| *1842:* People <> pacified *1863:* people <> pacified, 18| *1842:* (Really <> how)— ¶ POLYXENA

With pacifying them. Our foreign perils
Also exceed my means to stay: but here
'Tis otherwise, and my pride's piqued. Count Tende
Completes a full year's absence: would you, madam,
Have the old monarch back, his mistress back,
His measures back? I pray you, act upon
My counsel, or they will be.

POLYXENA When?

D'ORMEA Let's think.
Home-matters settled—Victor's coming now;
Let foreign matters settle—Victor's here
Unless I stop him; as I will, this way.

POLYXENA [*reading the papers he presents*]. If this should prove a plot 'twixt you and Victor?
You seek annoyances to give the pretext
For what you say you fear.

D'ORMEA Oh, possibly!
I go for nothing. Only show King Charles
That thus Count Tende purposes return,
And style me his inviter, if you please!

POLYXENA Half of your tale is true; most like, the Count
Seeks to return: but why stay you with us?
To aid in such emergencies.

D'ORMEA Keep safe
Those papers: or, to serve me, leave no proof
I thus have counselled! When the Count returns,
And the King abdicates, 'twill stead me little
To have thus counselled.

POLYXENA The King abdicate!

D'ORMEA He's good, we knew long since—wise, we discover—
Firm, let us hope:—but I'd have gone to work

1863: Really <> how—¶ POLYXENA 20| *1842:* them: our *1863:* them. Our 22–24| *1842:* piqued. Would you, madam, / Have *1849:* piqued. Count Tende / Completes a full year's absence: would you, madam, / Have 25| *1842:* you act *1849:* you, act 28| *1842:* here: *1868:* here 29| *1842:* him, as I will this *1849:* him; as I will, this 31| *1842:* give him pretext *1863:* give pretext *1868:* give the pretext 32| *1842:* fear! D'ORMEA *1888:* fear. D'ORMEA 35| *1842:* inviter if you please. *1849:* inviter, if *1868:* please! 36| *1842:* like the *1849:* like, the 37| *1842:* Would come: but wherefore are you left with *1849:* Seeks to return: but why stay you with 40| *1842:* counselled: when <> returns *1849:* returns,

With him away. Well!
[CHARLES *without.*] In the Council Chamber?
D'ORMEA All's lost!
POLYXENA Oh, surely not King Charles! He's changed—
That's not this year's care-burthened voice and step:
'Tis last year's step, the Prince's voice!
D'ORMEA I know.
[*Enter* CHARLES:—D'ORMEA *retiring a little.*]
CHARLES Now wish me joy, Polyxena! Wish it me
The old way! [*She embraces him.*]
There was too much cause for that!
But I have found myself again. What news
At Turin? Oh, if you but felt the load
I'm free of—free! I said this year would end
Or it, or me—but I am free, thank God!
POLYXENA How, Charles?
CHARLES You do not guess? The day I found
Sardinia's hideous coil, at home, abroad,
And how my father was involved in it,—
Of course, I vowed to rest and smile no more
Until I cleared his name from obloquy.
We did the people right—'twas much to gain
That point, redress our nobles' grievance, too—
But that took place here, was no crying shame:
All must be done abroad,—if I abroad
Appeased the justly-angered Powers, destroyed
The scandal, took down Victor's name at last
From a bad eminence, I then might breathe
And rest! No moment was to lose. Behold

1868: counselled! when *1888:* When 45| *1842:* And he away *1849:* With him away 46| *1842:* lost. ¶ POLYXENA <> changed. *1849:* lost! ¶ POLYXENA <> changed— 47| *1842:* care—burthened *1849:* care-burthened 48| *1842:* step—the *1849:* know! *1868:* step, the <> know. 51| *1842:* again! What's news *1863:* What *1868:* again. What 54| *1842:* it or *1849:* it, or 55| *1842:* guess! The *1849:* guess? The 56| *1842:* abroad— *1849:* abroad, 58| *1842:* course I <> rest or smile *1849:* course, I *1868:* rest and smile 59| *1842:* Until I freed his *1868:* Until I cleared his 61| *1842:* grievance too— *1849:* grievance, too— 64| *1842:* Appease <> Powers *1849:* Appeased <> Powers 65| *1842:* take *1849:* took 66| *1842:* then may breathe *1849:* then might breathe 67| *1842:* lose:

The proud result—a Treaty, Austria, Spain
Agree to—

D'ORMEA [*aside*]. I shall merely stipulate
For an experienced headsman.

CHARLES Not a soul
Is compromised: the blotted past's a blank:
Even D'Ormea escapes unquestioned. See!
It reached me from Vienna; I remained
At Evian to despatch the Count his news;
'Tis gone to Chambery a week ago—
And here am I: do I deserve to feel
Your warm white arms around me?

D'ORMEA [*coming forward*]. He knows that?

CHARLES What, in Heaven's name, means this?

D'ORMEA He knows that matters
Are settled at Vienna? Not too late!
Plainly, unless you post this very hour
Some man you trust (say, me) to Chambery
And take precautions I acquaint you with,
Your father will return here.

CHARLES Are you crazed,
D'Ormea? Here? For what? As well return
To take his crown!

D'ORMEA He will return for that.

CHARLES [*to* POLYXENA]. You have not listened to this man?

POLYXENA He spoke
About your safety—and I listened.

[*He disengages himself from her arms.*]

CHARLES [*to* D'ORMEA]. What
Apprised you of the Count's intentions?

D'ORMEA Me?

---

behold *1849:* lose. Behold 68| *1842:* a Treaty Austria *1849:* a Treaty, Austria 71| *1842:* Past's *1868:* past's 72| *1842:* Even D'Ormea will escape *1863:* Even D'Ormea escapes 73| *1842:* This reached *1849:* It reached 74| *1863:* dispatch *1888:* despatch 75| *1842:* Chamberri *1849:* Chambery 81| *1842:* Chamberri, *1849:* Chambery, *1863:* Chambery 82| *1849:* precautions I'll acquaint *1863:* precautions I acquaint 83| *1842:* CHARLES Is he crazed, *1863:* CHARLES Are you crazed, 84| *1842:* This D'Ormea *1863:* D'Ormea 85| *1842:* D'ORMEA He does return *1849:* D'ORMEA He will

His heart, sir; you may not be used to read
Such evidence however; therefore read
[*Pointing to* POLYXENA's *papers.*]
My evidence.
CHARLES [*to* POLYXENA]. Oh, worthy this of you!
And of your speech I never have forgotten,
Though I professed forgetfulness; which haunts me
As if I did not know how false it was;
Which made me toil unconsciously thus long
That there might be no least occasion left
For aught of its prediction coming true!
And now, when there is left no least occasion
To instigate my father to such crime—
When I might venture to forget (I hoped)
That speech and recognize Polyxena—
Oh worthy, to revive, and tenfold worse,
That plague! D'Ormea at your ear, his slanders
Still in your hand! Silent?
POLYXENA As the wronged are.
CHARLES And you, D'Ormea, since when have you presumed
To spy upon my father? I conceive
What that wise paper shows, and easily.
Since when?
D'ORMEA The when and where and how belong
To me. 'Tis sad work, but I deal in such.
You ofttimes serve yourself; I'd serve you here:
Use makes me not so squeamish. In a word,

---

return 89| *1842:* sire *1849:* Sire *1863:* sire *1868:* sir 90| *1842:* evidence, however *1868:* evidence however 92| *1842:* forgotten *1849:* forgotten, 93| *1842:* Tho' <> forgetfulness—which *1849:* forgetfulness; which *1863:* Though 94| *1842:* was— *1849:* was; 95| *1842:* inconsciously *1849:* unconsciously 97| *1842:* For what your speech predicted coming *1849:* For aught of its prediction coming 98| *1842:* now when *1849:* now, when 99| *1849:* crime; *1863:* crime— 100| *1842:* forget, I hoped, *1849:* forget (I hoped, 101| *1842:* recognise *1868:* recognize 102| *1842:* Oh, worthy to revive and <> worse *1849:* worthy, to revive, and <> worse, *1868:* Oh worthy 103| *1842:* plague now! D'Ormea *1868:* plague! D'Ormea 105| *1842:* And, D'Ormea, pray since *1849:* pray, since *1863:* And pray, D'Ormea, since *1868:* And you, D'Ormea 106| *1842:* father? (I *1863:* father? I 107| *1842:* shows and easily.) *1849:* shows, and *1863:* easily. 108| *1842:* D'ORMEA The when, and where, and how, belong *1868:* D'ORMEA The when and where and how belong 109| *1842:* me—'Tis *1849:* me. 'Tis 110| *1842:* yourself—I'd *1868:* yourself; I'd

Since the first hour he went to Chambery,
Of his seven servants, five have I suborned.
CHARLES You hate my father?
D'ORMEA Oh, just as you will!
[*Looking at* POLYXENA.]
A minute since, I loved him—hate him, now!
What matter?—if you ponder just one thing:
Has he that treaty?—he is setting forward
Already. Are your guards here?
CHARLES Well for you
They are not! [*To* POLYXENA]. Him I knew of old, but you—
To hear that pickthank, further his designs! [*To* D'ORMEA].
Guards?—were they here, I'd bid them, for your trouble,
Arrest you.
D'ORMEA Guards you shall not want. I lived
The servant of your choice, not of your need.
You never greatly needed me till now
That you discard me. This is my arrest.
Again I tender you my charge—its duty
Would bid me press you read those documents.
Here, sir! [*Offering his badge of office.*]
CHARLES [*taking it*]. The papers also! Do you think
I dare not read them?
POLYXENA Read them, sir!
CHARLES They prove,
My father, still a month within the year
Since he so solemnly consigned it me,
Means to resume his crown? They shall prove that.
Or my best dungeon . . .
D'ORMEA Even say, Chambery!
'Tis vacant, I surmise, by this.
CHARLES You prove

112| *1842:* Chamberri, *1849:* Chambery, 113| *1842:* servants five *1849:* servants, five 114| *1842:* will. *1849:* will! 115| *1842:* since I <> hate him now! *1849:* since, I <> hate him, now! 116| *1842:* if <> thing. *1849:* matters?—If you'll ponder <> thing: *1863:* matters?—If you ponder *1868:* matter 117| *1842:* Treaty?—He *1868:* treaty?—he
119| *1842:* I have none! [*To* *1849:* They are not! [*To* 121| *1842:* Guards? were <> them for your trouble *1849:* Guards?—were <> them, for your trouble,
128| *1842:* sire *1849:* Sire *1863:* sire *1868:* sir 129| *1842:* prove *1849:* prove, 132| *1842:* that, *1888:* that. 133| *1842:* say Chamberri! *1849:* say,

Your words or pay their forfeit, sir. Go there!
Polyxena, one chance to rend the veil
Thickening and blackening 'twixt us two! Do say,
You'll see the falsehood of the charges proved!
Do say, at least, you wish to see them proved
False charges—my heart's love of other times!

POLYXENA Ah, Charles!

CHARLES [*to* D'ORMEA]. Precede me, sir!

D'ORMEA And I'm at length
A martyr for the truth! No end, they say,
Of miracles. My conscious innocence!

[*As they go out, enter—by the middle door, at which he pauses—* VICTOR.]

VICTOR Sure I heard voices? No. Well, I do best
To make at once for this, the heart o' the place.
The old room! Nothing changed! So near my seat,
D'Ormea? [*Pushing away the stool which is by the* KING's *chair.*]
I want that meeting over first,
I know not why. Tush, he, D'Ormea, slow
To hearten me, the supple knave? That burst
Of spite so eased him! He'll inform me . . .
What?
Why come I hither? All's in rough: let all
Remain rough. There's full time to draw back—nay,
There's nought to draw back from, as yet; whereas,
If reason should be, to arrest a course
Of error—reason good, to interpose
And save, as I have saved so many times,
Our House, admonish my son's giddy youth,
Relieve him of a weight that proves too much—
Now is the time,—or now, or never.
'Faith,

Chambery! 137| *1842:* two. Do say *1849:* two! Do say, 144| *1842:* voices? No! Well *1868:* voices? No. Well 146| *1842:* changed!—So *1868:* changed! So 148| *1842:* why. Tush, D'Ormea won't be slow *1868:* why. Tush, he, D'Ormea, slow 149| *1842:* knave! That *1868:* knave? That 151| *1842:* rough—let *1868:* rough: let 152| *1842:* rough; there's *1868:* rough. There's 153| *1842:* from as yet; whereas *1849:* from, as yet; whereas, 154| *1842:* be to *1849:* be, to 155| *1842:* good to *1849:* good, to 157| *1842:* My House—admonish <> youth— *1849:* Our House, admonish <> youth, 159| *1842:* or now or never.

This kind of step is pitiful, not due
To Charles, this stealing back—hither, because
He's from his capital! Oh Victor! Victor!
But thus it is. The age of crafty men
Is loathsome; youth contrives to carry off
Dissimulation; we may intersperse
Extenuating passages of strength,
Ardour, vivacity, and wit—may turn
E'en guile into a voluntary grace:
But one's old age, when graces drop away
And leave guile the pure staple of our lives—
Ah, loathsome!
                                        Not so—or why pause I? Turin
Is mine to have, were I so minded, for
The asking; all the army's mine—I've witnessed
Each private fight beneath me; all the Court's
Mine too; and, best of all, D'Ormea's still
D'Ormea and mine. There's some grace clinging yet.
Had I decided on this step, ere midnight
I'd take the crown.
                                        No. Just this step to rise
Exhausts me. Here am I arrived: the rest
Must be done for me. Would I could sit here
And let things right themselves, the masque unmasque
Of the old King, crownless, grey hair and hot blood,—
The young King, crowned, but calm before his time,
They say,—the eager mistress with her taunts,—
And the sad earnest wife who motions me

'Faith, *1849:* or now, or *1868:* never. ¶ 'Faith, 160| *1842:* pitiful—not *1868:* pitiful, not 161| *1842:* hither because *1849:* hither, because 162| *1842:* his Capital! Oh, Victor—Victor— *1849:* his Capital! Oh, Victor! Victor! *1863:* capital *1868:* capital! Oh Victor! Victor! 163| *1842:* is: the *1863:* is. The 164| *1842:* loathsome—youth *1849:* loathsome; youth 165| *1842:* Dissimulation—we *1849:* Dissimulation; we 167| *1868:* vivacity and *1888:* vivacity, and 168| *1842:* grace,— *1863:* grace:— *1868:* grace: 173| *1842:* Army's *1863:* army's 174| *1863:* court's *1868:* Court's 175| *1842:* all, my D'Ormea's *1868:* all, D'Ormea's 176| *1842:* His D'Ormea; no! There's *1868:* D'Ormea and mine. There's 178| *1842:* crown— ¶ No! Just *1849:* crown. ¶ No *1868:* crown. ¶ No. Just 179| *1842:* me! Here <> arrived—the *1849:* arrived: the *1868:* me. Here 181| *1842:* themselves—the *1849:* themselves, the 182| *1842:* the King <> grey hairs and *1849:* —Of *1863:* Of the old King *1868:* hair 184| *1842:* eager woman with *1863:* eager mistress with 185| *1842:* who beckons

Away—ay, there she knelt to me! E'en yet
I can return and sleep at Chambery
A dream out.
Rather shake if off at Turin,
King Victor! Say: to Turin—yes, or no?
'Tis this relentless noonday-lighted chamber,
Lighted like life but silent as the grave,
That disconcerts me. That's the change must strike.
No silence last year! Some one flung doors wide
(Those two great doors which scrutinize me now)
And out I went 'mid crowds of men—men talking,
Men watching if my lip fell or brow knit,
Men saw me safe forth, put me on my road:
That makes the misery of this return.
Oh had a battle done it! Had I dropped,
Haling some battle, three entire days old,
Hither and thither by the forehead—dropped
In Spain, in Austria, best of all, in France—
Spurned on its horns or underneath its hooves,
When the spent monster went upon its knees
To pad and pash the prostrate wretch—I, Victor,
Sole to have stood up against France, beat down
By inches, brayed to pieces finally
In some vast unimaginable charge,
A flying hell of horse and foot and guns

---

me *1849:* who motions me 187| *1842:* Chamberri *1849:* Chambery 188| *1842:* out. Rather *1868:* out. ¶ Rather 189| *1842:* King Victor! Is't to <> yes or *1849:* yes, or *1868:* King Victor! Say: to 190–193| *1842:* § no ¶ § 'Tis <> chamber / That disconcerts me. Some <> wide *1849:* chamber, / Lighted like life, but silent as the grave, / That <> me! There must be the change— / No silence last year: some *1863:* me! There the change must strike! / No <> year! some *1868:* § ¶ § 'Tis <> / <> life but <> / <> me. That's the <> strike. / No <> Some 194| *1842:* doors that scrutinise *1849:* doors which scrutinise *1863:* scrutinize 195| *1842:* mid *1849:* 'mid 196| *1842:* brow changed; *1863:* brow knit; *1868:* knit, 197| *1842:* forth—put *1868:* forth, put 198| *1842:* return! *1868:* return. 199| *1842:* Oh, had a <> dropped *1863:* dropped, *1868:* Oh had a 200| *1842:* —Haling some battle three <> old *1849:* battle, three <> old, *1863:* Haling 201| *1842:* forehead—sunk *1849:* forehead—dropped 202| *1842:* all in *1849:* all, in 203| *1842:* hooves *1849:* hooves, 204| *1842:* monster goes upon *1863:* monster went upon 206| *1842:* against France—beat *1863:* against France, beat 208| *1842:* By some <> charge— *1849:* charge, *1863:* In some

Over me, and all's lost, for ever lost,
There's no more Victor when the world wakes up!
Then silence, as of a raw battle-field,
Throughout the world. Then after (as whole days
After, you catch at intervals faint noise
Through the stiff crust of frozen blood)—there creeps
A rumour forth, so faint, no noise at all,
That a strange old man, with face outworn for wounds
Is stumbling on from frontier town to town,
Begging a pittance that may help him find
His Turin out; what scorn and laughter follow
The coin you fling into his cap! And last,
Some bright morn, how men crowd about the midst
O' the market-place, where takes the old king breath
Ere with his crutch he strike the palace-gate
Wide ope!
To Turin, yes or no—or no?

Re-enter CHARLES *with papers.*

CHARLES Just as I thought! A miserable falsehood
Of hirelings discontented with their pay
And longing for enfranchisement! A few
Testy expressions of old age that thinks
To keep alive its dignity o'er slaves
By means that suit their natures!
[*Tearing them.*] Thus they shake
My faith in Victor!

[*Turning, he discovers* VICTOR.]

VICTOR [*after a pause*]. Not at Evian, Charles?
What's this? Why do you run to close the doors?
No welcome for your father?
CHARLES [*aside*]. Not his voice!
What would I give for one imperious tone

210| *1842:* ever lost— *1849:* ever lost, 213| *1842:* whole weeks *1849:* whole days 215| *1842:* Thro' <> blood)—to creep *1849:* blood)—there creeps *1863:* Through 217| *1842:* man, face <> wounds, *1849:* man, with face *1888:* wounds 220| *1842:* out; laughter and scorn to follow *1849:* out; what scorn and laughter follow 221| *1842:* cap: and *1849:* cap! and *1863:* And 222| *1842:* morn, to see crowds about *1849:* morn, how men crowd about 223| *1842:* Of the market-place where <> old man breath *1849:* market-place, where <> old king

Of the old sort! That's gone for ever.

VICTOR Must

I ask once more . . .

CHARLES No—I concede it, sir!

You are returned for . . . true, your health declines;

True, Chambery's a bleak unkindly spot;

You'd choose one fitter for your final lodge—

Veneria, or Moncaglier—ay, that's close

And I concede it.

VICTOR I received advices

Of the conclusion of the Spanish matter,

Dated from Evian Baths . . .

CHARLES And you forbore

To visit me at Evian, satisfied

The work I had to do would fully task

The little wit I have, and that your presence

Would only disconcert me—

VICTOR Charles?

CHARLES —Me, set

For ever in a foreign course to yours,

And . . .

Sir, this way of wile were good to catch,

But I have not the sleight of it. The truth!

Though I sink under it! What brings you here?

VICTOR Not hope of this reception, certainly,

From one who'd scarce assume a stranger mode

Of speech, did I return to bring about

Some awfulest calamity!

CHARLES —You mean,

Did you require your crown again! Oh yes,

I should speak otherwise! But turn not that

To jesting! Sir, the truth! Your health declines?

Is aught deficient in your equipage?

Wisely you seek myself to make complaint,

---

breath *1868:* O' 238| *1842:* declines— *1868:* declines; 239| *1842:* Chamberri's <> spot— *1849:* Chambery's <> spot; 241| *1842:* Veneria—or <> close, *1849:* Veneria, or <> close 243| *1842:* matter *1868:* matter, 244| *1842:* baths.—¶ CHARLES *1849:* baths . . . ¶ CHARLES *1868:* Baths 248| *1842:* CHARLES —Me—set *1868:* CHARLES —Me, set 255| *1842:* speech did *1849:* speech, did 256| *1842:* calamity. ¶ CHARLES *1849:* calamity! ¶ CHARLES 257| *1842:* again: Oh *1849:* again! Oh

And foil the malice of the world which laughs
At petty discontents; but I shall care
That not a soul knows of this visit. Speak!
VICTOR [*aside*]. Here is the grateful much-professing son
Prepared to worship me, for whose sole sake
I think to waive my plans of public good!
[*Aloud.*] Nay, Charles, if I did seek to take once more
My crown, were so disposed to plague myself,
What would be warrant for this bitterness?
I gave it—grant I would resume it—well?
CHARLES I should say simply—leaving out the why
And how—you made me swear to keep that crown:
And as you then intended . . .
VICTOR   Fool! What way
Could I intend or not intend? As man,
With a man's will, when I say "I intend,"
I can intend up to a certain point,
No farther. I intended to preserve
The crown of Savoy and Sardinia whole:
And if events arise demonstrating
The way, I hoped should guard it, rather like
To lose it . . .
CHARLES   Keep within your sphere and mine!
It is God's province we usurp on, else.
Here, blindfold through the maze of things we walk
By a slight clue of false, true, right and wrong;
All else is rambling and presumption. I
Have sworn to keep this kingdom: there's my truth.
VICTOR Truth, boy, is here, within my breast; and in
Your recognition of it, truth is, too;

262| *1842:* which seizes *1849:* which laughs 263| *1842:* On petty *1849:* At petty 265| *1842:* grateful, much-professing *1868:* grateful much-professing 266| *1842:* Who was to <> me, and for whose sake *1863:* Prepared to <> me, for whose sole sake 267| *1842:* I near had waived *1849:* I think to waive 269| *1842:* crown, and were disposed <> myself— *1849:* crown, were so disposed *1868:* myself, 271| *1849:* grant, I *1868:* grant I 276| *1842:* man's life, when *1863:* man's will, when 278| *1842:* further *1888:* farther 279| *1842:* Crown *1863:* crown 280| *1842:* arise to demonstrate *1849:* arise demonstrating 281| *1842:* way I took to keep it, rather's like *1863:* way, I hoped should guard it, rather like 283| *1842:* on else. *1849:* on, else. 284| *1842:* thro' *1863:* through 285| *1842:* slight thread of *1863:* slight clue of 288| *1842:* here—within *1868:* here, within 289| *1842:* is too; *1849:* is,

And in the effect of all this tortuous dealing
With falsehood, used to carry out the truth,
—In its success, this falsehood turns, again,
Truth for the world. But you are right: these themes
Are over-subtle. I should rather say
In such a case, frankly,—it fails, my scheme:
I hoped to see you bring about, yourself,
What I must bring about. I interpose
On your behalf—with my son's good in sight—
To hold what he is nearly letting go,
Confirm his title, add a grace perhaps.
There's Sicily, for instance,—granted me
And taken back, some years since: till I give
That island with the rest, my work's half done.
For his sake, therefore, as of those he rules . . .
CHARLES Our sakes are one; and that, you could not say,
Because my answer would present itself
Forthwith:—a year has wrought an age's change.
This people's not the people now, you once
Could benefit; nor is my policy
Your policy.
VICTOR [*with an outburst*]. I know it! You undo
All I have done—my life of toil and care!
I left you this the absolutest rule
In Europe: do you think I sit and smile,
Bid you throw power to the populace—
See my Sardinia, that has kept apart,
Join in the mad and democratic whirl

---

too; 292| *1842:* falsehood is again *1849:* falsehood turns, again, 293| *1842:* world! But *1888:* world. But 297| *1842:* about: I *1868:* about. I 299| *1842:* go— *1868:* go, 300| *1842:* title—add a grace, perhaps— *1863:* perhaps. *1868:* title, add a grace perhaps. 302| *1842:* since—till *1868:* since: till 305| *1842:* one—and that you *1849:* that, you *1868:* one; and 307| *1842:* Forthwith;—a <> change: *1868:* Forthwith:—a <> change. 308| *1842:* now you *1849:* now, you 309| *1842:* benefit, nor *1849:* benefi ; nor 313| *1842:* In Europe—do <> I will sit still *1868:* In Europe: do *1888:* think I sit and smile, 314| *1842:* And see you throw all power to the people— *1849:* power off to *1868:* throw power to the populace— *1888:* Bid you 315| *1842:* has stood apart, *1849:* has kept apart, 316| *1849:* whirl, *1863:*

Whereto I see all Europe haste full tide?
England casts off her kings; France mimics England:
This realm I hoped was safe. Yet here I talk,
When I can save it, not by force alone,
But bidding plagues, which follow sons like you,
Fasten upon my disobedient . . .
[*Recollecting himself.*] Surely
I could say this—if minded so—my son?
CHARLES You could not. Bitterer curses than your curse
Have I long since denounced upon myself
If I misused my power. In fear of these
I entered on those measures—will abide
By them: so, I should say, Count Tende . . .
VICTOR No!
But no! But if, my Charles, your—more than old—
Half-foolish father urged these arguments,
And then confessed them futile, but said plainly
That he forgot his promise, found his strength
Fail him, had thought at savage Chambery
Too much of brilliant Turin, Rivoli here,
And Susa, and Veneria, and Superga—
Pined for the pleasant places he had built
When he was fortunate and young—
CHARLES My father!
VICTOR Stay yet!—and if he said he could not die
Deprived of baubles he had put aside,
He deemed, for ever—of the Crown that binds
Your brain up, whole, sound and impregnable,
Creating kingliness—the Sceptre too,
Whose mere wind, should you wave it, back would beat
Invaders—and the golden Ball which throbs
As if you grasped the palpitating heart

---

whirl 317| *1842:* full-tide? *1868:* full tide? 318| *1842:* kings—France <> England— *1863:* kings; France <> England: 319| *1842:* safe! Yet *1888:* safe. Yet 321| *1842:* plagues which <> you *1849:* plagues, which <> you, 324| *1842:* not! Bitterer *1868:* not. Bitterer 328| *1842:* so I <> Tende—¶ VICTOR *1849:* so, I <> Tende . . . ¶ VICTOR 333| *1842:* Chamberri *1849:* Chambery 338| *1842:* yet—and *1868:* yet!—and 339| *1842:* aside *1849:* aside, 340| *1842:* deemed for *1849:* deemed, for 341| *1842:* sound, and *1868:* sound and 342| *1842:* the Sceptre, too, *1868:* the Sceptre too,

Indeed o' the realm, to mould as choose you may!
—If I must totter up and down the streets
My sires built, where myself have introduced
And fostered laws and letters, sciences,
The civil and the military arts!
Stay, Charles! I see you letting me pretend
To live my former self once more—King Victor,
The venturous yet politic: they style me
Again, the Father of the Prince: friends wink
Good-humouredly at the delusion you
So sedulously guard from all rough truths
That else would break upon my dotage!—You—
Whom now I see preventing my old shame—
I tell not, point by cruel point, my tale—
For is't not in your breast my brow is hid?
Is not your hand extended? Say you not . . .

Enter D'ORMEA *leading in* POLYXENA.

POLYXENA [*advancing and withdrawing* CHARLES—*to* VICTOR].
In this conjuncture even, he would say
(Though with a moistened eye and quivering lip)
The suppliant is my father. I must save
A great man from himself, nor see him fling
His well-earned fame away: there must not follow
Ruin so utter, a break-down of worth
So absolute: no enemy shall learn,
He thrust his child 'twixt danger and himself,
And, when that child somehow stood danger out,
Stole back with serpent wiles to ruin Charles
—Body, that's much,—and soul, that's more—and realm,

346| *1849:* as you may choose! *1888:* as choose you may! 350| *1842:* arts— *1863:* arts! 351| *1842:* Stay, Charles—I *1868:* Stay, Charles! I 352| *1842:* more—King Victor *1849:* more—King Victor, 353| *1842:* politic—they *1868:* politic: they 354| *1842:* Again the Father <> Prince—friends winking *1849:* Again, the Father <> friends wink *1868:* of the Prince: friends 355| *1842:* delusion you're *1849:* delusion you 356| *1842:* So sedulous in guarding from sad truth, *1849:* So sedulously guard from all rough truths 357| *1842:* upon the dotage!—You *1849:* dotage!—You— *1868:* upon my dotage 362| *1842:* conjuncture, even *1849:* say— *1868:* conjuncture even <> say 363| *1842:* (Tho' *1849:* (Though 364| *1842:* father—I *1868:* father. I 368| *1842:*

That's most of all! No enemy shall say . . .
D'ORMEA Do you repent, sir?
VICTOR [*resuming himself*]. D'Ormea? This is well!
Worthily done, King Charles, craftily done!
Judicously you post these, to o'erhear
The little your importunate father thrusts
Himself on you to say!—Ah, they'll correct
The amiable blind facility
You show in answering his peevish suit.
What can he need to sue for? Thanks, D'Ormea!
You have fulfilled your office: but for you,
The old Count might have drawn some few more livres
To swell his income! Had you, lady, missed
The moment, a permission might be granted
To buttress up my ruinous old pile!
But you remember properly the list
Of wise precautions I took when I gave
Nearly as much away—to reap the fruits
I should have looked for!
CHARLES Thanks, sir: degrade me,
So you remain yourself! Adieu!
VICTOR I'll not
Forget it for the future, nor presume
Next time to slight such mediators! Nay—
Had I first moved them both to intercede,
I might secure a chamber in Moncaglier
—Who knows?
CHARLES Adieu!
VICTOR You bid me this adieu
With the old spirit?

---

learn *1849:* learn, 376| *1842:* these to *1849:* these, to 378| *1842:* say! Ay they'll *1868:* say!—Ah, they'll 380| *1842:* showed <> suit: *1863:* suit. *1868:* show 381| *1842:* for? Bravely, D'Ormea, *1888:* for? Thanks, D'Ormea! 382| *1842:* Have you fulfilled *1888:* You have fulfilled 384| *1842:* Lady *1868:* lady 385| *1842:* permission had been granted *1863:* permission would be granted *1888:* permission might be 386| *1842:* To build afresh my <> pile— *1863:* pile! *1868:* To buttress up my 387| *1842:* remembered *1868:* remember 388| *1863:* *I* took *1868:* I took 390| *1842:* I ever looked *1863:* I might have looked *1888:* I should have 391| *1842:* yourself. Adieu *1868:* yourself! Adieu 393| *1842:* such potent mediators! *1863:* such mediators! Nay— 395| *1842:* might have had a *1863:* might secure a 397| *1842:*

CHARLES Adieu!

VICTOR Charles—Charles!

CHARLES Adieu!

[VICTOR *goes.*]

CHARLES You were mistaken, Marquis, as you hear.
'Twas for another purpose the Count came.
The Count desires Moncaglier. Give the order!

D'ORMEA [*leisurely*]. Your minister has lost your confidence,
Asserting late, for his own purposes,
Count Tende would . . .

CHARLES [*flinging his badge back*]. Be still the minister!
And give a loose to your insulting joy;
It irks me more thus stifled than expressed:
Loose it!

D'ORMEA There's none to loose, alas! I see
I never am to die a martyr.

POLYXENA Charles!

CHARLES No praise, at least, Polyxena—no praise!

VICTOR Charles—Charles—¶ CHARLES *1863:* VICTOR Charles—Charles! ¶ CHARLES 398| *1842:* hear! *1888:* hear. 403| *1842:* still our minister! *1863:* still the minister *1868:* minister! 404| *1842:* joy— *1868:* joy; 405| *1842:* expressed. *1868:* expressed: 406| *1842:* alas!—I *1888:* alas! I 407| *1842:* martyr! ¶ POLYXENA *1863:* martyr. ¶ POLYXENA 408| *1842:* least, Polyxena—no praise! [*Exeunt omnes.* *1849:* least, Polyxena—no praise!

KING CHARLES

PART II

D'ORMEA, *seated, folding papers he has been examining.*

This at the last effects it: now, King Charles
Or else King Victor—that's a balance: but now,
D'Ormea the arch-culprit, either turn
O' the scale,—that's sure enough. A point to solve,
My masters, moralists, whate'er your style!
When you discover why I push myself
Into a pitfall you'd pass safely by,
Impart to me among the rest! No matter.
Prompt are the righteous ever with their rede
To us the wrongful; lesson them this once!
For safe among the wicked are you set,
D'Ormea! We lament life's brevity,
Yet quarter e'en the threescore years and ten,
Nor stick to call the quarter roundly "life."
D'Ormea was wicked, say, some twenty years;
A tree so long was stunted; afterward,
What if it grew, continued growing, till
No fellow of the forest equalled it?
'Twas a stump then; a stump it still must be:
While forward saplings, at the outset checked,

---

§ Stage direction: § *1842:* Night.—D'ORMEA *1863:* D'ORMEA 2| *1842:* balance: now *1863:* balance: but now *1868:* now, 3| *1842:* For D'Ormea *1868:* D'Ormea 4| *1842:* scale, that's *1849:* scale,—that's 5| *1842:* masters—moralists—whate'er's your *1863:* whate'er *1868:* masters, moralists, whate'er 10| *1842:* the wicked—lesson *1868:* the wrongful: lesson *1888:* wrongful; lesson 12| *1842:* Old D'Ormea. We *1863:* D'Ormea *1868:* D'Ormea! We 15| *1842:* years— *1849:* years; 16| *1842:* stunted—afterward *1849:* stunted; afterward, 19| *1842:* a shrub then—a shrub

In virtue of that first sprout keep their style
Amid the forest's green fraternity.
Thus I shoot up to surely get lopped down
And bound up for the burning. Now for it!

Enter CHARLES *and* POLYXENA *with* ATTENDANTS.

D'ORMEA [*rises*]. Sir, in the due discharge of this my office—
This enforced summons of yourself from Turin,
And the disclosure I am bound to make
To-night,—there must already be, I feel,
So much that wounds . . .
CHARLES Well, sir?
D'ORMEA —That I, perchance,
May utter also what, another time,
Would irk much,—it may prove less irksome now.
CHARLES What would you utter?
D'ORMEA That I from my soul
Grieve at to-night's event: for you I grieve,
E'en grieve for . . .
CHARLES Tush, another time for talk!
My kingdom is in imminent danger?
D'ORMEA Let
The Count communicate with France—its King,
His grandson, will have Fleury's aid for this,
Though for no other war.
CHARLES First for the levies:
What forces can I muster presently?
[D'ORMEA *delivers papers which* CHARLES *inspects.*]
CHARLES Good—very good. Montorio . . . how is this?
—Equips me double the old complement
Of soldiers?
D'ORMEA Since his land has been relieved

---

it *1868:* a stump then; a stump it 23| *1842:* up—to <> down, *1868:* up to <> down 25| *1842:* Sire *1868:* Sir 28| *1842:* To-night, there *1849:* To night,—there *1863:* To-night 30| *1842:* what another time *1849:* utter, also, what, another time *1868:* utter also what another 33| *1842:* you I grieve— *1868:* you I grieve, 34–35| *1842:* talk! / I've some intelligence, and more expect. / My *1849:* talk! / My 36| *1842:* its King *1849:* its King, 37| *1842:* grandson will <> this *1849:* grandson, will <> this, 38| *1842:* levies. *1849:* levies: 40| *1842:* very good. Montorio . . how *1863:* very good. Montorio . . . how

From double imposts, this he manages:
But under the late monarch . . .

CHARLES Peace! I know.
Count Spava has omitted mentioning
What proxy is to head these troops of his.

D'ORMEA Count Spava means to head his troops himself.
Something to fight for now; "Whereas," says he,
"Under the sovereign's father" . . .

CHARLES It would seem
That all my people love me.

D'ORMEA Yes.

[*To* POLYXENA *while* CHARLES *continues to inspect the papers.*]

A temper
Like Victor's may avail to keep a state;
He terrifies men and they fall not off;
Good to restrain: best, if restraint were all.
But, with the silent circle round him, ends
Such sway: our King's begins precisely there.
For to suggest, impel and set at work,
Is quite another function. Men may slight,
In time of peace, the King who brought them peace:
In war,—his voice, his eyes, help more than fear.
They love you, sir!

CHARLES [*to* ATTENDANTS]. Bring the regalia forth!
Quit the room! And now, Marquis, answer me!
Why should the King of France invade my realm?

D'ORMEA Why? Did I not acquaint your Majesty
An hour ago?

CHARLES I choose to hear again

43| *1842:* double impost this *1849:* impost, this *1868:* imposts 44| *1842:* monarch . . ¶ CHARLES Peace. I *1863:* monarch . . . ¶ CHARLES *1868:* CHARLES Peace! I 48| *1842:* Something's <> now; "whereas *1863:* Something *1868:* Whereas 49| *1842:* Sovereign's *1868:* sovereign's 51| *1842:* state— *1849:* state; 52| *1842:* off— *1849:* off; 53| *1842:* restrain; best <> all: *1868:* restrain: best <> all. 54| *1842:* But with <> him ends *1849:* But, with <> him, ends 55| *1842:* sway. Our *1868:* sway: our 56| *1842:* impel, and *1868:* impel and 57| *1842:* slight *1849:* slight, 58| *1842:* peace the King who brings them *1849:* peace, the King who brought them 60| *1842:* sire <> Regalia *1849:* Sire *1863:* sire! <> regalia *1868:* sir! <> forth!
61| *1842:* room. And <> me—

What then I heard.
D'ORMEA Because, sir, as I said,
Your father is resolved to have his crown
At any risk; and, as I judge, calls in
The foreigner to aid him.
CHARLES And your reason
For saying this?
D'ORMEA [*aside*]. Ay, just his father's way!
[*To* CHARLES.] The Count wrote yesterday to your forces' Chief,
Rhebinder—made demand of help—
CHARLES To try
Rhebinder—he's of alien blood: aught else?
D'ORMEA Receiving a refusal,—some hours after,
The Count called on Del Borgo to deliver
The Act of Abdication: he refusing,
Or hesitating, rather—
CHARLES What ensued?
D'ORMEA At midnight, only two hours since, at Turin,
He rode in person to the citadel
With one attendant, to Soccorso gate,
And bade the governor, San Remi, open—
Admit him.
CHARLES For a purpose I divine.
These three were faithful, then?
D'ORMEA They told it me.
And I—
CHARLES Most faithful—
D'ORMEA Tell it you—with this
Moreover of my own: if, an hour hence,
You have not interposed, the Count will be
O' the road to France for succour.

1868: room! And <> me! 65| *1842:* sire *1849:* Sire *1863:* sire *1868:* sir 66| *1842:* have the crown *1863:* have his crown 67| *1842:* risk, and *1849:* risk; and 68| *1842:* These foreigners *1863:* The foreigner 70| *1842:* your Forces' Chief *1849:* your Forces' Chief, *1863:* forces' 71| *1842:* Rhebinder,—made *1863:* Rhebinder—made 75| *1842:* refused, *1849:* refusing, 76| *1842:* hesitated *1849:* hesitating 79| *1849:* to the Soccorso *1888:* to Soccorso 80| *1842:* governor San Remi open— *1849:* governor, San Remi, open— 82| *1842:* me: *1888:* me. 83| *1849:* this, *1868:* this 84| *1849:* Moreover, of *1868:* Moreover of 86| *1842:* Upon his road <> ¶ CHARLES Good! *1868:* On his <> ¶ CHARLES Very good! *1888:* O' the road

CHARLES Very good!
You do your duty now to me your monarch
Fully, I warrant?—have, that is, your project
For saving both of us disgrace, no doubt?
D'ORMEA I give my counsel,—and the only one.
A month since, I besought you to employ
Restraints which had prevented many a pang:
But now the harsher course must be pursued.
These papers, made for the emergency,
Will pain you to subscribe: this is a list
Of those suspected merely—men to watch;
This—of the few of the Count's very household
You must, however reluctantly, arrest;
While here's a method of remonstrance—sure
Not stronger than the case demands—to take
With the Count's self.
CHARLES Deliver those three papers.
POLYXENA [*while* CHARLES *inspects them—to* D'ORMEA].
You measures are not over-harsh, sir: France
Will hardly be deterred from her intents
By these.
D'ORMEA If who proposes might dispose,
I could soon satisfy you. Even these,
Hear what he'll say at my presenting!
CHARLES [*who has signed them*]. There!
About the warrants! You've my signature.
What turns you pale? I do my duty by you
In acting boldly thus on your advice.
D'ORMEA [*reading them separately*]. Arrest the people I suspected merely?

87| *1842:* duty, now, to *1868:* duty now to 89| *1842:* disgrace, past doubt? *1868:* disgrace, no doubt? 90| *1842:* I have my counsel, which is the *1849:* counsel,—and the *1863:* I give my 93| *1842:* must have its way. *1849:* must be pursued. 97| *1849:* household. *1868:* household 99| *1842:* remonstrance (sure *1863:* remonstrance—sure 100| *1842:* demands) to *1863:* demands—to 103| *1842:* from coming hither *1868:* from her intents 104| *1842:* D'ORMEA What good of my proposing measures *1868:* D'ORMEA If who proposes might dispose, 105| *1842:* Without a chance of their success? E'en these *1849:* these, *1868:* I could soon satisfy you. Even these 106| *1842:* presenting. ¶ CHARLES *1868:* presenting! ¶

CHARLES Did you suspect them?
D'ORMEA Doubtless: but—but—sir,
This Forquieri's governor of Turin,
And Rivarol and he have influence over
Half of the capital! Rabella, too?
Why, sir—
CHARLES Oh, leave the fear to me!
D'ORMEA [*still reading*]. You bid me
Incarcerate the people on this list?
Sir—
CHARLES But you never bade arrest those men,
So close related to my father too,
On trifling grounds?
D'ORMEA Oh, as for that, St. George,
President of Chambrey's senators,
Is hatching treason! still—
[*More troubled.*] Sir, Count Cumiane
Is brother to your father's wife! What's here?
Arrest the wife herself?
CHARLES You seem to think
A venial crime this plot against me. Well?
D'ORMEA [*who has read the last paper*]. Wherefore am I thus ruined?
Why not take
My life at once? This poor formality
Is, let me say, unworthy you! Prevent it
You, madam! I have served you, am prepared
For all disgraces: only, let disgrace
Be plain, be proper—proper for the world
To pass its judgment on 'twixt you and me!
Take back your warrant, I will none of it!
CHARLES Here is a man to talk of fickleness!

CHARLES 111| *1842:* sire, *1849:* Sire, *1863:* sire, *1868:* sir, 112| *1842:* of Turin; *1868:* of Turin, 114| *1842:* capital.—Rabella *1868:* capital! Rabella 115| *1842:* sire <> me. ¶ D'ORMEA *1849:* Sire *1863:* sire <> me! ¶ D'ORMEA *1868:* sir 117| *1842:* Sire— ¶ CHARLES Why, you *1868:* Sir— ¶ CHARLES But you 120| *1842:* Chamberri's *1849:* Chambery's 121| *1842:* treason—but— ¶ [*Still more troubled.*] Sire *1863:* treason! but *1868:* treason! still— ¶ [*More troubled.*] Sir 123| *1849:* think it *1868:* think 124| *1842:* It venial crime to plot *1849:* A venial *1868:* crime this plot 127| *1842:* it, *1868:* it 128| *1842:* served you—am *1849:* served you, am 129| *1842:* disgraces—only *1868:* disgraces: only 132| *1842:*

He stakes his life upon my father's falsehood;
I bid him . . .
D'ORMEA Not you! Were he trebly false,
You do not bid me . . .
CHARLES Is't not written there?
I thought so: give—I'll set it right.
D'ORMEA Is it there?
Oh yes, and plain—arrest him now—drag here
Your father! And were all six times as plain,
Do you suppose I trust it?
CHARLES Just one word!
You bring him, taken in the act of flight,
Or else your life is forfeit.
D'ORMEA Ay, to Turin
I bring him, and to-morrow?
CHARLES Here and now!
The whole thing is a lie, a hateful lie,
As I believed and as my father said.
I knew it from the first, but was compelled
To circumvent you; and the great D'Ormea,
That baffled Alberoni and tricked Coscia,
The miserable sower of such discord
'Twixt sire and son, is in the toils at last.
Oh I see! you arrive—this plan of yours,
Weak as it is, torments sufficiently
A sick old peevish man—wrings hasty speech,
An ill-considered threat from him; that's noted;
Then out you ferret papers, his amusement
In lonely hours of lassitude—examine

warrant—I <> it. *1868:* warrant, I <> it! 134| *1842:* falsehood, *1849:* falsehood; 135| *1842:* him—¶ D'ORMEA *1863:* him . . . ¶ D'ORMEA 136| *1842:* me—¶ CHARLES *1863:* me . . . ¶ CHARLES 138| *1842:* Oh, yes—and <> him—now *1868:* Oh yes, and <> him now 140| *1842:* suppose I'd trust *1863:* suppose I trust 143| *1842:* him? And *1849:* to morrow *1863:* to-morrow *1868:* him, and 144| *1842:* lie—a <> lie— *1868:* lie, a <> lie, 147| *1842:* the crafty D'Ormea, *1868:* the great D'Ormea, 149| *1842:* of the discord *1849:* of such discord 150| *1842:* last! *1868:* last. 151| *1842:* Oh, I see—you *1849:* see! you *1868:* Oh I 153| *1842:* sick, old, peevish <> speech *1868:* sick old peevish <> speech, 154| *1842:* And ill-considered threats *1868:* An ill-considered

The day-by-day report of your paid spies—
And back you come: all was not ripe, you find,
And, as you hope, may keep from ripening yet,
But you were in bare time! Only, 'twere best
I never saw my father—these old men
Are potent in excuses: and meanwhile,
D'Ormea's the man I cannot do without!
POLYXENA Charles—
CHARLES Ah, no question! You against me too!
You'd have me eat and drink and sleep, live, die
With this lie coiled about me, choking me!
No, no, D'Ormea! You venture life, you say,
Upon my father's perfidy: and I
Have, on the whole, no right to disregard
The chains of testimony you thus wind
About me; though I do—do from my soul
Discredit them: still I must authorize
These measures, and I will. Perugia!
[*Many* OFFICERS *enter.*] Count—
You and Solar, with all the force you have,
Stand at the Marquis' orders: what he bids,
Implicitly perform! You are to bring
A traitor here; the man that's likest one
At present, fronts me; you are at his beck
For a full hour! he undertakes to show
A fouler than himself,—but, failing that,
Return with him, and, as my father lives,
He dies this night! The clemency you blame

---

threat 157| *1842:* paid creatures— *1868:* paid spies— 158| *1842:* come—all *1868:* come: all 159| *1842:* And as you hope may <> yet— *1849:* And, as you hope, may *1868:* yet, 162| *1842:* excuses—and, meantime, *1863:* and, meanwhile, *1868:* excuses: and meanwhile, 163| *1849:* without. *1863:* without! 164| *1842:* question! You're for D'Ormea too! *1868:* question! You against me too! 165| *1842:* drink, and sleep, and die *1849:* sleep, live, die *1868:* drink and sleep 166| *1842:* coil'd *1863:* coiled 167| *1842:* No, no—he's caught. [*To D'Ormea.*] You venture *1849:* caught! [*to D'Ormea* *1868:* No, no, D'Ormea! You venture 168| *1842:* perfidy; and *1868:* perfidy: and 170| *1842:* you have wound *1849:* you thus wind 172| *1842:* authorise *1863:* authorize 173| *1842:* measures—and I do. Perugia! *1849:* and I will. Perugia! *1868:* measures, and 175| *1842:* Are at *1868:* Stand at 179| *1842:* hour; he <> show you *1868:* hour! he <> show 182| *1842:* clemency you've blamed

So oft, shall be revoked—rights exercised,
Too long abjured.
[*To* D'ORMEA.] Now sir, about the work!
To save your king and country! Take the warrant!
D'ORMEA You hear the sovereign's mandate, Count Perugia?
Obey me! As your diligence, expect
Reward! All follow to Moncaglier!
CHARLES [*in great anguish*]. D'Ormea! [D'ORMEA *goes.*]
He goes, lit up with that appalling smile!
[*To* POLYXENA, *after a pause.*]
At least you understand all this?
POLYXENA These means
Of our defence—these measures of precaution?
CHARLES It must be the best way; I should have else
Withered beneath his scorn.
POLYXENA What would you say?
CHARLES Why, do you think I mean to keep the crown,
Polyxena?
POLYXENA You then believe the story
In spite of all—that Victor comes?
CHARLES Believe it?
I know that he is coming—feel the strength
That has upheld me leave me at his coming!
'Twas mine, and now he takes his own again.
Some kinds of strength are well enough to have;
But who's to have that strength? Let my crown go!
I meant to keep it; but I cannot—cannot!
Only, he shall not taunt me—he, the first . .
See if he would not be the first to taunt me

1863: clemency you blame 183| *1842:* exercised *1868:* exercised, 184| *1842:* That I've abjured ¶ <> Sir *1863:* sir *1868:* Too long abjured ¶ <> Now sir 186| *1842:* D'ORMEA [*boldly to* PERUGIA.] You <> the Sovereign's mandate *1863:* D'ORMEA You *1868:* sovereign's 188| *1842:* Reward. All <> to Montcaglier ¶ <> D'Ormea! [*Exit* D'ORMEA, *cum suis.* *1849:* Reward! All ¶ <> D'Ormea! [D'ORMEA *goes.* *1888:* Moncaglier 189| *1842:* goes lit *1849:* goes, lit 192| *1842:* way. I *1868:* way: I *1888:* way; I 194| *1842:* Why, you don't think *1888:* Why, do you think 196| *1842:* all—That Victor's coming? ¶ CHARLES Coming? *1849:* CHARLES Believe it? *1863:* all—that *1888:* that Victor comes? CHARLES 197| *1842:* I feel that *1849:* I know that 202| *1842:* it—but *1868:* it; but 203| *1842:* Only he shall <> me—he the first— *1849:* Only, he shall <> me—he, the *1863:* first . . . *1888:* first . . § Incomplete ellipsis in 1888 and 1889 apparently a printer's error;

With having left his kingdom at a word.
With letting it be conquered without stroke,
With . . . no—no—'tis no worse than when he left!
I've just to bid him take it, and, that over,
We'll fly away—fly, for I loathe this Turin,
This Rivoli, all titles loathe, all state.
We'd best go to your country—unless God
Send I die now!

POLYXENA Charles, hear me!

CHARLES And again
Shall you be my Polyxena—you'll take me
Out of this woe! Yes, do speak, and keep speaking!
I would not let you speak just now, for fear
You'd counsel me against him: but talk, now,
As we two used to talk in blessed times:
Bid me endure all his caprices; take me
From this mad post above him!

POLYXENA I believe
We are undone, but from a different cause.
All your resources, down to the least guard,
Are at D'Ormea's beck. What if, the while,
He act in concert with your father? We
Indeed were lost. This lonely Rivoli—
Where find a better place for them?

CHARLES [*pacing the room*]. And why
Does Victor come? To undo all that's done,
Restore the past, prevent the future! Seat
His mistress in your seat, and place in mine

---

restored in Ohio edition. § 205| *1842:* kingdom all exposed— *1849:* kingdom at a word— *1868:* word. 206| *1842:* stroke— *1868:* stroke, 207| *1842:* With . . no—no <> left it, *1868:* With . . . no—no <> left! 209| *1842:* We fly away—fly—for *1849:* We'll fly away *1868:* away—fly, for 210| *1842:* This Rivoli, and titles loathe, and state. *1849:* This Rivoli, all titles *1868:* loathe, all state. 212| *1842:* now. ¶ POLYXENA <> ¶ CHARLES—And *1849:* now! ¶ POLYXENA *1868:* CHARLES And 214| *1842:* woe. Yes, do speak—and *1849:* woe! Yes *1868:* speak, and 215| *1842:* now for *1849:* now, for 216| *1842:* him—but *1849:* him: but 217| *1842:* times— *1849:* times: 218| *1842:* caprices—take *1849:* caprices; take me 219| *1842:* Me from this post *1849:* From this mad post 220| *1842:* cause: *1849:* cause. 222| *1842:* Are now at <> beck: what if this while *1849:* beck. What if, this while, *1863:* if, the while, *1868:* Are at 223| *1842:* acts *1863:* act 226| *1842:* done! *1868:* done, 227| *1842:* past—prevent *1863:* the Past prevent the Future *1868:* past, prevent the future 228| *1842:* Sebastian in your seat and *1849:* His mistress in your seat, and

. . . . Oh, my own people, whom will you find there,
To ask of, to consult with, to care for,
To hold up with your hands? Whom? One that's false—
False—from the head's crown to the foot's sole, false!
The best is, that I knew it in my heart
From the beginning, and expected this,
And hated you, Polyxena, because
You saw thro' him, though I too saw thro' him,
Saw that he meant this while he crowned me, while
He prayed for me,—nay, while he kissed my brow,
I saw——

POLYXENA But if your measures take effect,
D'Ormea true to you?

CHARLES Then worst of all!
I shall have loosed that callous wretch on him!
Well may the woman taunt him with his child—
I, eating here his bread, clothed in his clothes,
Seated upon his seat, let slip D'Ormea
To outrage him! We talk—perchance he tears
My father from his bed; the old hands feel
For one who is not, but who should be there,
He finds D'Ormea! D'Ormea too finds him!
The crowded chamber when the lights go out—
Closed doors—the horrid scuffle in the dark—
The accursed prompting of the minute! My guards!
To horse—and after, with me—and prevent!

POLYXENA [*seizing his hand*]. King Charles! Pause here upon this strip of time
Allotted you out of eternity!
Crowns are from God: you in his name hold yours.

229| *1842:* there *1849:* there, 233| *1842:* is that *1849:* is, that 239| *1842:* saw—¶ POLYXENA *1888:* saw——¶ POLYXENA 240| *1842:* And D'Ormea's true *1868:* D'Ormea true 244| *1842:* seat, give D'Ormea leave *1868:* seat, let slip D'Ormea 245| *1842:* perchance they tear *1868:* perchance he tears
246| *1842:* bed—the *1868:* bed; the 247| *1842:* there— *1868:* there,
248| *1842:* And he finds D'Ormea! D'Ormea, too, finds *1868:* He finds D'Ormea! D'Ormea too finds 249| *1842:*—The crowded *1863:* The crowded 251| *1842:* Th' accursed promptings *1849:* The *1868:* prompting 253| *1842: hand*]. King Charles! Pause you upon *1849: hand*]. King Charles! Pause here upon 255| *1842:* from God—in his name you hold *1863:* His *1868:* from God: in his *1888:* from

Your life's no least thing, were it fit your life
Should be abjured along with rule; but now,
Keep both! Your duty is to live and rule—
You, who would vulgarly look fine enough
In the world's eye, deserting your soul's charge,—
Ay, you would have men's praise, this Rivoli
Would be illumined! While, as 'tis, no doubt,
Something of stain will ever rest on you;
No one will rightly know why you refused
To abdicate; they'll talk of deeds you could
Have done, no doubt,—nor do I much expect
Future achievement will blot out the past,
Envelope it in haze—nor shall we two
Live happy any more. 'Twill be, I feel,
Only in moments that the duty's seen
As palpably as now: the months, the years
Of painful indistinctness are to come,
While daily must we tread these palace-rooms
Pregnant with memories of the past: your eye
May turn to mine and find no comfort there,
Through fancies that beset me, as yourself,
Of other courses, with far other issues,
We might have taken this great night: such bear,
As I will bear! What matters happiness?
Duty! There's man's one moment: this is yours!

[*Putting the crown on his head, and the sceptre in his hand, she places him on his seat: a long pause and silence.*]

Enter D'ORMEA *and* VICTOR, *with* GUARDS.

God: you in his name hold 260| *1842:* eye deserting *1849:* eye, deserting 261| *1842:* men's tongues—this *1849:* men's praise—this *1868:* praise, this 262| *1842:* illumined—while *1849:* illumined: while *1863:* illumined! while *1868:* While 263| *1842:* you— *1849:* you; 265| *1842:* abdicate—they'll *1849:* abdicate; they'll 267| *1842:* achievements *1863:* Past, *1868:* achievement <> past, 268| *1842:* Envelop *1863:* Envelope 269| *1842:* Be happy any more; 'twill *1863:* more. 'Twill *1868:* Live happy 271| *1842:* now—the months *1888:* now: the months 272| *1842:* come— *1849:* come, 273| *1842:* tread the palace rooms *1849:* tread these palace *1863:* palace-rooms 274| *1842:* past—your *1849:* past: your *1863:* Past *1868:* past 275| *1842:* there *1849:* there, 276| *1842:* me as yourself— *1849:* me, as yourself, 277| *1842:* courses with <> issues *1849:* courses, with <> issues, 278| *1842:* night—such bear *1849:* bear, *1868:* night: such 280| *1842:* moment—this <> / ¶ <> D'ORMEA, *cum suis, and* VICTOR. *1849:* D'ORMEA *and* *1868:* moment: this *1888:*

VICTOR At last I speak; but once—that once, to you!
'Tis you I ask, not these your varletry,
Who's King of us?
CHARLES [*from his seat.*] Count Tende . . .
VICTOR – What your spies
Assert I ponder in my soul, I say—
Here to your face, amid your guards! I choose
To take again the crown whose shadow I gave—
For still its potency surrounds the weak
White locks their felon hands have discomposed.
Or I'll not ask who's King, but simply, who
Withholds the crown I claim? Deliver it!
I have no friend in the wide world: nor France
Nor England cares for me: you see the sum
Of what I can avail. Deliver it!
CHARLES Take it, my father!
And now say in turn,
Was it done well, my father—sure not well,
To try me thus! I might have seen much cause
For keeping it—too easily seen cause!
But, from that moment, e'en more woefully
My life had pined away, than pine it will.
Already you have much to answer for.
My life to pine is nothing,—her sunk eyes
Were happy once! No doubt, my people think
I am their King still . . . but I cannot strive!
Take it!
VICTOR [*one hand on the crown* CHARLES *offers, the other on his neck*]. So few years give it quietly,
My son! It will drop from me. See you not?
A crown's unlike a sword to give away—
That, let a strong hand to a weak hand give!
But crowns should slip from palsied brows to heads

VICTOR, *with* Guards. 281| *1842:* that once to you. *1849:* that once, to you! 283| *1842: seat*]. Count Tende . . ¶ VICTOR *1888: seat.*] Count Tende . . . ¶ VICTOR 285| *1842:* guards. I *1849:* guards! I 286| *1842:* crown I gave—its shade, *1849:* crown whose shadow I gave— 289| *1842:* Or, I'll *1868:* Or I'll 290| *1842:* crown he claims? Deliver *1849:* crown I claim? Deliver 291| *1842:* world—nor *1849:* world: nor 292| *1842:* me—you *1849:* me: you 295| *1842:* not well *1849:* not well, 298| *1842:* But from that moment e'en *1849:* But, from that moment, e'en 303| *1842:* That I'm their King still—but *1849:* still . . . but *1868:*

Young as this head: yet mine is weak enough,
E'en weaker than I knew. I seek for phrases
To vindicate my right. 'Tis of a piece!
All is alike gone by with me—who beat
Once D'Orleans in his lines—his very lines!
To have been Eugene's comrade, Louis's rival,
And now . . .

CHARLES [*putting the crown on him, to the rest*]. The King speaks, yet none kneels, I think!

VICTOR I am then King! As I became a King
Despite the nations, kept myself a King,
So I die King, with Kingship dying too
Around me. I have lasted Europe's time.
What wants my story of completion? Where
Must needs the damning break show? Who mistrusts
My children here—tell they of any break
'Twixt my day's sunrise and its fiery fall?
And who were by me when I died but they?
D'Ormea there!

CHARLES What means he?

VICTOR Ever there!
Charles—how to save your story! Mine must go.
Say—say that you refused the crown to me!
Charles, yours shall be my story! You immured
Me, say, at Rivoli. A single year
I spend without a sight of you, then die.
That will serve every purpose—tell that tale
The world!

CHARLES Mistrust me? Help!

VICTOR Past help, past reach!
'Tis in the heart—you cannot reach the heart:
This broke mine, that I did believe, you, Charles,
Would have denied me and disgraced me.

POLYXENA Charles

I am their 309| *1842:* head—yet *1863:* head: yet 314| *1842:* Louis' *1888:* Louis's 315| *1842: him*] The *1849: him, to the rest*] The 317| *1842:* nations—kept <> King— *1849:* nations, kept <> King, 319| *1842:* me! I <> time! *1888:* me. I <> time. 321| *1849:* show! Who *1868:* show? Who 325| *1842:* Who?—D'Ormea *1868:* D'Ormea 326| *1842:* story? Mine must go! *1888:* story! Mine must go. 327| *1842:* me— *1868:* me! 330| *1842:* you and die— *1849:* you, then die— *1888:* die. 334| *1842:* believe you *1849:* believe, you 335| *1842:* denied and so disgraced *1888:* denied me and disgraced

Has never ceased to be your subject, sir!
He reigned at first through setting up yourself
As pattern: if he e'er seemed harsh to you,
'Twas from a too intense appreciation
Of your own character: he acted you—
Ne'er for an instant did I think it real,
Nor look for any other than this end.
I hold him worlds the worse on that account;
But so it was.

CHARLES [*to* POLYXENA]. I love you now indeed.
[*to* VICTOR.] You never knew me.

VICTOR Hardly till this moment,
When I seem learning many other things
Because the time for using them is past.
If 'twere to do again! That's idly wished.
Truthfulness might prove policy as good
As guile. Is this my daughter's forehead? Yes:
I've made it fitter now to be a queen's
Than formerly: I've ploughed the deep lines there
Which keep too well a crown from slipping off.
No matter. Guile has made me King again.
Louis—'twas in King Victor's time:—long since,
When Louis reigned and, also, Victor reigned.
How the world talks already of us two!
God of eclipse and each discoloured star,
Why do I linger then?
Ha! Where lurks he?
D'Ormea! Nearer to your King! Now stand!
[*Collecting his strength as* D'ORMEA *approaches.*]
You lied, D'Ormea! I do not repent. [*Dies.*]

336| *1842:* sire— *1849:* Sire! *1863:* sire! *1868:* sir! 342| *1842:* Or look *1863:* Nor look 344| *1842:* CHARLES I love you, now, indeed! *1849:* CHARLES [*to* POLYXENA] I *1868:* you now indeed! *1888:* indeed. 345| *1842:* me! ¶ VICTOR *1888:* me. ¶ VICTOR 346| *1842:* things, *1868:* things 350| *1842:* forehead? Yes— *1868:* forehead? Yes: 351| *1842:* Queen's *1863:* queen's 352| *1842:* formerly—I've *1868:* formerly: I've 353| *1842:* That keep <> off! *1849:* Which keep *1868:* off. 355| *1842:* Louis—'twas in King Victor's time—long since, *1849: Louis—'twas in King Victor's time—long since, 1868: time:—long* 356| *1842:* When Louis reign'd—and, also, Victor reign'd— *1849: When Louis reign'd—and, also, Victor reign'd— 1863: reigned <> reigned— 1868: reigned and <> reigned.* 358| *1842:* discolour'd *1863:* discoloured 360| *1842:* D'Ormea! Come nearer to *1868:* D'Ormea! Nearer to 361| *1842:* But you <> repent. [*Dies.*] / § centered § THE END. *1849:* repent. [*Dies.* *1868:* You

BY THE SAME AUTHOR

I.

PARACELSUS. A POEM.

Price 6s. boards.

II.

SORDELLO. A POEM.

Price 6s. 6d. boards.

III.

BELLS AND POMEGRANATES.

No. 1.—PIPPA PASSES

Price 6d. sewed.

ESSAY ON CHATTERTON

Edited by Donald Smalley

ESSAY ON CHATTERTON

1842

Conjectures and Researches concerning the Love Madness and Imprisonment of Torquato Tasso. By RICHARD HENRY WILDE. 2 vols. New York. 1842.

Upon the minuteness and obscurity of our attainable evidences with regard to a single important portion of a great poet's history—the Love and Madness of Tasso—great light is thrown by these clever volumes. And further additions to a very meagre stock are not, it seems, to be absolutely despaired of. The Medicean Records may be laid under more liberal contributions, and the Archives of Este cease to remain impenetrable. What even if a ray of light should straggle over the unsunned hoards of sumless wealth in the Vatican? "If windows were in heaven, might this thing be."

But in our days the poorest loophole will have to be broken, we suspect, with far different instruments from those it is the fashion to employ just now in Italy. It is enough at present if the oily instances of this or the other Minister-Residentiary operate so happily upon the ruffled apprehensiveness of this or the other Chamberlain-Omnipotentiary, as to allow a minute's glimpse of the Fortunate Isles through the incessant breakers that girdle them. The rude sea now and then grows civil, indeed; but a positive current setting landwards is the thing wanted, and likely to remain so. Ever and anon we seem on the point of a discovery. A scrap of letter turns up, or a bundle of notices drop out, and the Head Librarian for the time being considers the curiosity of some Dilettante Ambassador for the place being, and, provided the interest of the whole civilized world is kept out of sight with sufficient adroitness, becomes communicative.

"The anger of the Grand Duke arises from his being informed that I had revealed to the Duke of Ferrara . . . . . ! I cannot write all freely, but this is the gospel." So writes Tasso to "the one friend he now believes in, Scipio Gonzaga." And "this blank," sorrowfully subjoins Mr. Wilde, "is found in the first copy of the letter furnished for publication by the learned and candid Muratori, then librarian to the Duke of Modena." It contained an expression, says he, which it would be indecorous to repeat! Thus at every step, where there is the slightest prospect of a clue to the truth, are we mortified by its destruction through reserve or timidity. And if things were so in the green-tree time of the Muratoris, what shall be done in the dry stump of modern Lombardy or Tuscany?

Of certain important manuscripts recently discovered at Rome, and now in the course of publication, we regret to learn that the authenticity is considered too questionable to allow of their being brought forward to any useful purpose: so that, for the present, this result of Mr. Wilde's labour, now before us, must be regarded as conclusive: and fortunately our last, proves also our best, news. It is pleasant to find that the popular notion (we might say instinct) concerning this particular point of Tasso's career, grown up, uncertain how, from biographical gleanings here and gatherings there,—somewhat shaken, as it was sure to be, by subsequent representations,—seems again confirmed by these latest discoveries.

A couplet in a canzone, a paragraph in an epistle, had thus been sufficient to begin with. "Tasso was punished in a living hell by angels, because he unburthened his bosom to his lyre." "He would fain be released from this prison of Saint Anna without being troubled for those things which from frenzy he has done and written in matters of love." After these, and a few other like notices, Professors might search, and Abbates research; the single Leonora become "three lady-loves at once;" and the dim torture at Ferrara a merciful effect of Duke Alfonso's consideration for "Signor Tasso, the noted poet's, deplorable madness;"—but the world, satisfied with its own suspicion, remained deaf to it all.

> "If we suppose," sums up Mr. Wilde, "that his imprisonment was occasioned by the accidental or treacherous disclosure of amatory poetry suspected to be addressed to the princess, every thing becomes intelligible—his mistress's early injunctions of silence—his directions to Rondinelli—the dearer mysteries of his heart half-hinted to Gonzaga—the reference to her who corresponded so little to his love—his heavy sin of temerity—Madalò's more important treasons—the attempt to extort confession—the bitter rigour and unwonted arts—the words and acts that might increase Alfonso's ire—the order to feign insanity—the sacrifice of Abraham—the command that he must aspire to no fame of letters—the prohibition to write—the anger of the princesses—the allusions to his fond faults—to his Proserpine—to Ixion, and to the angels that punished him. By this supposition, also, Leonora's voluntary celibacy, notwithstanding the most advantageous offers of marriage, and Tasso's constant devotion to the duke, in spite of the rigour of his chastisement, are sufficiently accounted for."[1]

[1]Vol. II., p. 166.

How much that establishes old convictions, and how little that is even supplementary to them, have we here!

Such as it is, however, in what Mr. Wilde has done, he has gone the right way to work and done it well. He has steadily restricted himself to the single point in question. It is that point in the poet's history, indeed, from which those to whom sonnets and madrigals, the Rinaldo and the Aminta, are all but unknown, will take warrant for some belief in their reported truth and beauty. It is undoubtedly that to which every student of Italian verse must refer the touching glimmer, as an outbreak through prison-bars, that colours every page of the Giurusalemme. Still it is but a point; and Mr. Wilde has not perhaps done less gracefully and wisely in leaving the rest untouched, than in accomplishing so thoroughly the task he took in hand. He relies upon his subject; is sure of the service he can render by an efficacious treatment of thus much of it; nor entertains any fear lest the bringing in a Before and After, with which he has no immediate concern, should be thought necessary to give interest to the At Present on which he feels he can labour to advantage. We suspect that if we would make any material progress in knowledge of this description, such works must be so undertaken. If, for example, the materials for a complete biography of Tasso are far from exhausted, let some other traveller from the west be now busied in the land of Columbus and Vespucci with the investigation,—say, of the circumstances of the wondrous youth of Tasso; the orations at Naples and the Theses at Padua,—and in the end we should more than probably have two spots of sunshine to find our way by, instead of one such breadth of dubious twilight, as, in a hazy book written on the old principle of doing a little for every part of a subject, and more than a little for none, rarely fails to perplex the more.

Thinking thus, and grieving over what must be admitted to be the scantiness of the piece of sunshine here, and the narrow and not very novel track it would alone serve to lead us into,—a book[2] was sent to us on a subject not very different from Mr. Wilde's, but on which the service he has sought to render to the memory of Tasso has not hitherto been attempted for a memory more foully outraged. We make no apology for a proposed effort to render some such service. It is no very abrupt desertion of the misfortunes of Tasso, to turn to the misfortunes of Chatterton. All these disputed questions in the lives of men of genius—all these so-called calamities of authors—have a common relation-

[2]"The Poetical Works of Thomas Chatterton, with Notices of his Life, a History of the Rowley Controversy, a Selection of his Letters, and Notes Critical and Explanatory." Cambridge. 1842.

ship, a connexion so close and inalienable, that they seldom fail to throw important light upon each other.

To the precocity of genius in the Neapolitan boy at seven years old—the verse and prose from the College of the Jesuits—no parallel can be found in modern times, till we arrive at the verses of Chatterton, to whom Campbell has very properly said "Tasso alone may be compared as a juvenile prodigy." But the parallel will, in other respects, admit of application. The book before us, for example, on the love and madness of the Italian, is in itself a direct text from which to speak of what concerns us most in the disputed character of our own countryman. As the whole of Mr. Wilde's argument may be said to include itself in his commentary upon the opening couplet of the first Sonnet of the collection of *Rime*,

> "True were the loves and transports which I sung,"

so let us say of the Englishman, that his were far from that untruth, that absence of reality, so constantly charged against them. In a word, poor Chatterton's life was not the Lie it is so universally supposed to have been; nor did he "perish in the pride" of refusing to surrender Falsehood and enter on the ways of Truth. We can show, we think, and by some such process as Mr. Wilde adopts in regard to Tasso, that he had already entered on those ways when he was left, without a helping hand, to sink and starve as he might. And to this single point we shall as far as possible restrict ourselves.

Mr. Wilde remarks of the great Italian, that though there are indeed passages in Tasso's life and letters, scarcely reconcilable with the strict regard for truth which Manso, his friend and contemporary, ascribes to him,

> "yet that to whatever dissimulation he may have been driven, upon some memorable occasions—by a hard and, if you will, a criminal, but still almost irresistible necessity—there is no reason to believe him habitually insincere: and that, avoiding every subtle refinement, it cannot be too much to assume that he was like other men, who in the absence of all inducement, were not supposed deliberately to utter falsehood."[3]

It shall be our endeavour, by extending the application of this text from Tasso to Chatterton, to throw a new light upon a not dissimilar portion

[3]Vol. I., p. 12.

of the latter poet's career, and in some degree soften those imputations of habitual insincerity with which the most sympathizing of Chatterton's critics have found themselves compelled to replace the "great veracity" attributed to him by his earliest and most partial biographer.

For Tasso, a few words will say how his first false step was an indiscretion; how, having published love-poetry under a false name, and suffered himself to be suspected its author, he, to avoid the ill-consequences, feigned at the Duke's suggestion, Madness; and how his protracted agony at Saint Anna was but an unremitting attempt to free himself from the effect of this false step without being compelled to reveal the truth, and disavow his whole proceedings since the time of that sad starting-aside from the right way. But before we speak of the corresponding passage in Chatterton's story, something should be premised respecting the characteristic shape his first error took, as induced by the liabilities of that peculiar development of genius of which he was the subject.

Genius almost invariably begins to develop itself by imitation. It has, in the short-sightedness of infancy, faith in the world: and its object is to compete with, or prove superior to, the world's already recognised idols, at their own performances and by their own methods. This done, there grows up a faith in itself: and, no longer taking the performance or method of another for granted, it supersedes these by processes of its own. It creates, and imitates no longer. Seeing cause for faith in something external and better, and having attained to a moral end and aim, it next discovers in itself the only remaining antagonist worthy of its ambition, and in the subduing what at first had seemed its most enviable powers, arrives at the more or less complete fulfilment of its earthly mission. This first instinct of Imitation, which with the mediocre takes the corresponding mediocre form of an implied rather than expressed appropriation of some other man's products, assumed perforce with Chatterton, whose capabilities were of the highest class, a proportionably bolder and broader shape in the direction his genius had chosen to take. And this consideration should have checked the too severe judgment of what followed. For, in simple truth, the startling character of Chatterton's presentment, with all its strange and elaborately got up accompaniments, was in no more than strict keeping with that of the thing he presented. For one whose boy's essay was "Rowley" (a Man, a Time, a Language, all at once) the simultaneous essay of inventing the details of muniment-room treasures and yellow-roll discoveries, by no means exceeded in relative hardihood the mildest possible annexing—whatever the modern author's name may be—to the current poetry or prose of the time. But, alas! for the mere complacent forbearance of the world in the one case, must come sharp and importunate questionings in the other; and, at every advance in such a career, the impossibility of continuing in the spirit of the outset grows more and more apparent. To begin with the step of a giant is one thing, suddenly for another's satisfaction to increase to a colossal stride is a very different. To the falsehood of the mediocre, truth may easily be superinduced, and true works, with them, silently take the place of false works: but before one like Chatterton could extricate himself from the worse than St. Anna dungeon which every hour was building up more surely between him and the common earth and skies, so much was to be dared and done! That the attempt was courageously made in Chatterton's case, there are many reasons for believing. But to understand his true position, we must remove much of the colouring which subsequent occurrences imparted to the dim beginnings of his course of deception. He is to the present day viewed as a kind of Psalmanazar or Macpherson, producing deliberately his fabrications to the world and challenging its attention to them. A view far from the truth. Poor Chatterton never had that chance. Before the world could be appealed to, a few untoward circumstances seem to have effectually determined and given stability to what else had not impossibly proved a mere boy's fancy, destined to go as lightly as it came and leave no trace, save in a fresh exertion of the old means to a new and more commensurate end.

In September, 1768, a New Bridge at Bristol was completed, and early in the next month the principal newspaper of the city contained a prose "description of the Fryar's (Mayor's) first passing over the Old Bridge, taken from an old manuscript." The attention of—what are called in the accounts we have seen—"the literati of Bristol," was excited. Application was made to the publisher for a sight of the surprising and interesting original. No such thing was forthcoming; but the curiosity of Literati must be appeased; and the bearer of the newspaper marvel, one Thomas Chatterton,—a youth of sixteen, educated at Colston's Charity-school where reading, writing and arithmetic only were taught, and, since, a clerk to an attorney of the place,—was recognised on his next appearance at the printing-office with another contribution, and questioned whence he obtained that first-named paper. He was questioned "with threatenings in the first instance, to which he refused any answer, and next with milder usage and promises of patronage," —which extorted from him at last the confession, that the manuscript was one of many his father (parish clerk, usher, or sexton) had taken from a coffer in the church of St. Mary, Redcliff.

It was his own composition; and being the first of what are called the Rowleian forgeries, suggests a remark upon literary forgery in general, and that of Chatterton in particular.[4]

[4]That there should have been a controversy for ten minutes about the genuineness of any ten verses of "Rowley" is a real disgrace to the scholarship of the age in which such a thing took place: we shall not touch on it here, certainly. Conceive the entering on such a discussion at all, when the poor charity-boy had himself already furnished samples of Rowley in the different stages of partial completeness, from the rough draught in the English of the day, ungarnished by a single obsolete word, to the finished piece with its strange incrustation of antiquity! There is never theft for theft's sake with Chatterton. One short poem only, *The Romaunt of the Cnyghte*, is in part a tacking together of old lines from old poets, out of rhyme and time, yet at the same time not so utterly unlike an approximation to the genuine ware. And why? Because the Mr. Burgum, to one of whose ancestors it is attributed, and whose taste solely it was intended to suit, happened to be *hopelessly incapable of understanding any composition of the mixed sort which Chatterton had determined upon producing; and which, retaining what he supposed the ancient garb should also include every modern refinement.* The expedient which would alone serve with the good Mr. Burgum, was to ply him with something entirely unintelligible, so begetting a reverence; and after that with another thing perfectly comprehensible, so ministering to his pleasure. Accordingly, Chatterton, for that once, attempted to write thorough old verse, because he could, as he did, accompany it by thorough new verse too: a modern paraphrase to wit.

But though we will not touch the general and most needless question, it happens that, by a curious piece of fortune, we have been enabled, since taking up the subject of this article, to bring home to Chatterton one, and by no means the least ingenious of his "forgeries," which has hitherto escaped detection. Rowley's *Sermon on the Holy Spirit*, with its orthodoxy and scripture citations, its Latin from St. Cyprian, and its Greek from St. Gregory, is triumphantly referred to by the learned and laborious Jacob Bryant (who wrote one folio to disprove the Tale of Troy and another to prove the Tale of Rowley), as a flight clearly above Chatterton's reach. Now this aforesaid Greek quotation was the single paragraph which struck our eye some two or three days since, in looking hastily through a series of sermons on the Nature of the Holy Spirit, by the Rev. John Hurrion, originally printed, it should seem, in 1732; on a reference to which we found Rowley's discourse to be a mere cento from their pages, artfully enough compiled. For example, thus saith ROWLEY: "Seyncte Paulle prayethe the Holye Spryte toe assyste hys flocke ynn these wordes, The Holye Spryte's communyonn bee wythe you. Lette us dhere desyerr of hymm to ayde us . . . lette us saye wythe Seyncte Cyprian, '*Adesto, Sancte Spiritus, et paraclesin tuam expectantibus illabere cœlitus; sanctifica templum corporis nostri et consecra inhabitaculum tuum.*' Seyncte Paulle sayethe yee are the temple of Godde; for the Spryte of Godde dwellethe ynn you. Gyff yee are the temple of Godde alleyne bie the dwellynge of the Spryte, wote yee notte that the Spryte ys Godde? . . . The Spryte or dyvyne will of Godde moovedd uponn the waterrs att the Creatyonn of the worlde; thys meaneth the Deeitie. . . . Gyff the Spryte bee notte Godde, howe bee ytt the posessynge of the Spryte dothe make a manne sayedd toe be borne of Godde? Itt requyreth the powerr of Godde toe make a manne a new creatyonn, yette such dothe the Spryte. Thus sayethe Seyncte Gregorie Naz. of the Spryte and hys wurchys: **Γενâται Χριστος˙ προτρέχει. Βαπτιζεταί μαρτυρεî. Πειραζέται˙ αναγεî. Δυναμεις ἐπιτελεî˙ ξυμπαραμαρτεî. Ανέρχεται.**" And now let us listen to HURRION, *Serm.* 1. "As therefore the apostle prayed on the behalf of the Corinthians . . . . in these words: 'The communion of the Holy Ghost be with you,' it is very proper to apply to him for his gracious aid and assistance. An example of this we have in Cyprian. 'O Holy Spirit be thou present,' &c.—*Cyp. de Spir. S.* p. 484. [quoted, no doubt, at length, like the other references, in the first edition.] . . . . Now if he that dwells in us as his temple is God, what other conclusion can be drawn from thence but this, that we are the temple of God? &c. &c. [The rest of the verse, with the authority of St. Paul being the text of the Sermon.] . . . . which is also God—as when it is said 'the Spirit of God moved upon the waters, in the creation of the world. *Sermon* 4. Believers are born of the Spirit . . this is a new creation, and requires the same Almighty power to effect as the first creation did . . if the Spirit is not God by nature . . how are they said to be born of God who are regenerated by the Spirit? '*Christ,*' says one of the ancients, '*is born—the Spirit is his forerunner,*' &c." And in a foot-note the Greek text and proper authority are subjoined.

It is, perhaps, worth a remark in concluding this note, that Chatterton, a lawyer's clerk, takes care to find no law-papers in Canning's Coffer, of which tradition had declared it to be full. That way detection was to be feared. But the pieces on devotional subjects, to which his earlier taste inclined, came so profusely from the "Godlie preeste Rowlie," that Chatterton thinks it advisable, from the time of his discoveries, to forget his paraphrases of Job and Isaiah, and to disclaim for himself a belief in Christianity on every and no occasion at all!

Is it worth while to mention, that the very notion of obtaining a free way for impulses that can find vent in no other channel (and consequently of a liberty conceded to an individual, and denied to the world at large), is implied in all literary production? By this fact is explained, not only the popular reverence for, and interest in even the personal history of, the acknowledged and indisputable possessors of this power—as so many men who have leave to do what the rest of their fellows cannot—but also the as popular jealousy of allowing this privilege to the first claimant. And so instinctively does the Young Poet feel that his desire for this kind of self-enfranchisement will be resisted as a matter of course, that we will venture to say, in nine cases out of ten his first assumption of the licence will be made in a borrowed name. The first communication, to even the family circle or the trusted associate, is sure to be "the work of a friend;" if not, "something extracted from a magazine," or "Englished from the German." So is the way gracefully facilitated for Reader and Hearer finding themselves in a new position with respect to each other.

Now unluckily, in Chatterton's case, this communication's whole value, in the eyes of the Bristolians, consisted in its antiquity. Apart from that, there was to them no picturesqueness in "Master Mayor, mounted on a white horse, dight with sable trappings wrought about by the nuns of St. Kenna;" no "most goodly show in the priests and freres all in white albs." Give that up, and all was given; and poor Chatterton could not give all up. He could only determine for the future to produce Ellas and Godwyns, and other "beauteous pieces;" wherein "the plot should be clear, the language spirited; and the songs interspersed in it, flowing, poetical, and elegantly simple; the similes judiciously applied; and though written in the reign of Henry VI., not inferior to many of the present age." Had there but been any merit of this kind, palpable even to Bristol Literati, to fall back upon in the first instance, if the true authorship were confessed! But that was otherwise; and so the false course, as we have said, was unforeseeingly entered upon. Yet still, from the first, he was singularly disposed to become communicative of his projects and contrivances for carrying them into effect. There was, after all, no such elaborate deception about any of them. Indeed, had there only happened to be a single individual of ordinary intelligence among his intimates, the event must assuredly have fallen out differently. But as it was, one companion would be present at the whole process of "antiquating," as Chatterton styled it, his productions (the pounding of ochre and crumpling of parchments); another would hear him carelessly avow himself master of a power "to copy, by the help of books he could name, the style of our elder poets so exactly, that they should escape the detection of Mr. Walpole himself;"—and yet both these persons remain utterly incapable of perceiving that such circumstances had in the slightest degree a bearing upon after events at Bristol! It is to be recollected, too, that really in Bristol itself there was not any thing like a general interest excited in the matter. And when at last, yielding to the pertinacity of inquirers, these and similar facts came lingeringly forth, as the details of so many natural appearances with which unconscious rustics might furnish the philosopher anxious to report and reason upon them—Chatterton was dead.

Of several of his most characteristic compositions, he confessed, at various times, on the least solicitation, the authorship. He had found and versified the argument of the Bristowe Tragedy—he had written the Lines on our Ladye's Church. But these confidences were only to his mother and sister. Why? Because mother and sister were all who cared for him rather than for Rowley, and would look at his connexion with any verses as a point in their favour. As for his two patrons, Barrett and Catcott, they took great interest in the yellow streaks, and verse written like prose without stops; less interest in the poetry; and in Chatterton least, or none at all! And a prophet's fate in his own country was never more amusingly exemplified than when grave Deans and Doctors, writing to inquire after Chatterton's abilities of his old companions, got the answers on record. "Not having any taste myself for ancient poetry," writes Mr. Cary, "I do not recollect Chatterton's ever having shown such writings to me, *but* he often mentioned them, *when*, great as his capacity was, I am convinced that he was incapable of writing them!" "He had intimated," remarks Mr. Smith, "very frequently both a desire to learn, and a design to teach himself—Latin; but I always dissuaded him from it, *as being in itself impracticable*. But I advised him by all means *to try* at French. As to Latin, *depend upon it you will find it too hard for you*. Try at French, if you please: of *that* you may acquire *some* knowledge *without much difficulty*, and it will be of real service to you." "And, sir," winds up Mr. Clayfield, "*take my word for it*, the poems were no more his composition than *mine*!" With such as these there was no fellowship possible for Chatterton. We soon discover him, therefore, looking beyond. From the time of his communication of the Rowley poems, "his ambition," writes Mrs. Newton, his sister, "increased daily. When in spirits he would enjoy his rising fame; confident of advancement, he would promise that my mother and I should be partakers of his success." As a transcriber, we suppose! We find Sir Herbert Croft, to whom this very letter was addressed, declaring "that he will not be sure that the writer and her mother might not have easily been made to believe that injured justice demanded their lives at Tyburn, for being the relatives of him who forged the poems of Rowley." Thus only, in this sideway at the best, could the truth steal out.

Meanwhile the sorry reception given to the so-called falsehood produced its natural effects. On the one hand there is a kind of ambition on being introduced to Mr. Barrett and Mr. Catcott, which increases daily; but on the other we are told that his spirits became at the same time "rather uneven—sometimes so *gloomed*,[5] that for some days together he would say very little, and that by constraint." No doubt, and no wonder! For there was the sense of his being the author of the transcendent chorus to Freedom, or the delicious roundelay in Ella; ever at fierce variance with the pitiful claim he was entitled to make in the character of their mere transcriber.

[5]The only word in Chatterton's communication to the genuineness of which Walpole seems to have objected. "The modern gloomy," says Chatterton, in reply to some critical exception taken against poems he had sent, "seems but a refinement of the old word Glomming, in Anglo-Saxon the twilight." And in a note to a line of the Ballad of Charity, "Look in his *glommed* face" &c., he observes, " 'Glommed' clouded, dejected. A person of some note in the literary world is of opinion that 'glum' and 'glom' are modern cant words, and from this circumstance doubts the authenticity of Rowley MSS. 'Glummong,' in the Saxon signifies twilight, a dark or dubious light and the modern word gloomy is derived from the Saxon 'glum.' " It is to be added that Chatterton, throughout, only objects to men's doubting the genuineness of Rowley on the insufficient grounds they give—and is in the right there.

We shall not pursue this painful part of the question. Day followed day, and found him only more and more deeply involved. What we have restricted our inquiry to, is the justice or injustice of the common charge that henceforth the whole nature of Chatterton became no other than one headstrong spirit of Falsehood, in the midst of which, and by which, he perished at the last. And we think its injustice will be shown without much difficulty, in showing that he really made the most gallant and manly effort of which his circumstances allowed to break through the sorry meshes that entangled him. We purposely forbear, with any view to this, taking for granted the mere instigation of that Moral Sense which it is the worst want of charity to deny to him, and with direct and strong evidences of which his earliest poetry abounded. We will simply inquire what, in the circumstances referred to, would have been the proper course to pursue, had the writer of the "Bristowe Tragedy" chanced to adopt on a single occasion the practice of its hero, "who summed the actions of the day each night before he slept." Confessions at the market-cross avail nothing, and most injure those to whom they are unavoidably made. Should he not have resolutely left Bristol, at least? and, disengaging himself from the still increasing trammels of his daily life of enforced deceit, begun elsewhere a wiser and happier course? That he did so may in our opinion be shown. It is our firm belief that on this, and no other account, he determined to go to London.

"A few months before he left Bristol," mentions his sister, "he wrote letters to several booksellers in London—I believe to learn if there was any probability of his getting an employment there." He had some time previously applied to Dodsley, the noted publisher, for his assistance in printing the tragedy of *Ella*; on the strength of a submitted specimen, which the great man of the Mall did not vouchsafe, it seems, to glance over. He was led, therefore, to make a final experiment on the taste and apprehensiveness of Horace Walpole: not, as in Dodsley's case, by enclosing the despised poetical samples, but by sending a piece of antiquarian ware in which his presumed patron was understood to especially delight. Of nothing are we so thoroughly persuaded as that these attempts were the predetermined last acts of a course of dissimulation he would fain discard for ever—on their success. The Rowleian compositions were all he could immediately refer to, as a proof of the ability he was desirous of employing in almost any other direction. He grounded no claim on his possession of these MSS.; he was not soliciting an opportunity of putting off to advantage the stock in hand, or increasing it; and when Walpole subsequently avowed his regret at having omitted to transcribe before returning, the manuscript thus received, what has been cited as a singular piece of unprincipled effrontery, appears to us perfectly justifiable. For even after the arrival of a discouraging letter, Chatterton's words are, that "if Mr. Walpole wishes to publish them himself, they are at his service." Nay—Mr. Barrett, or "the Town and Country Magazine, to which copies may be sent," or indeed "the world, which it would be the greatest injustice to deprive of so invaluable a curiosity"—may have them and welcome. And Chatterton's anxiety to recover them afterwards is only intelligible on the supposition that his originals were in jeopardy. To the very conceited question Walpole himself has asked—"Did Chatterton impute to me anything but distrust of his MSS.?"—we should answer, Every thing but that. Let the young poet's own verses, indeed, answer.

Walpole, I thought not I should ever see
So mean a heart as thine has proved to be:
Thou, who in luxury nursed, behold'st with scorn
The boy who friendless, fatherless, forlorn,
Asks thy high favour. *Thou mayst call me cheat—*
Say didst thou never practise such deceit?
Who wrote Otranto?—but I will not chide.
Scorn I'll repay with scorn, and pride with pride.
Had I the gifts of wealth and luxury shared—
Not poor and mean—Walpole! thou hadst not dared
Thus to insult. But I shall live and stand
By Rowley's side, when thou art dead and damned.

In this unhappy correspondence with Walpole,—it never seems to have been admitted, yet it cannot be said too often,—there is no new "falsehood" discernible: there is nothing but an unavailing and most affecting effort, to get somehow free from the old. He makes no asseveration of the fact of his discoveries; affirms nothing the denial of which hereafter would be essentially disgraceful to him; commits himself by only a few ambiguous words which at any time a little plain speaking (and blushes, if we will) would explain away. Let it be observed, above all, that there is no attempt to forge, and produce, and insist on the genuineness of the MSS.; though this was a step by which he could have lost nothing and might have gained every thing, since Walpole's recognition of their extraordinary merit was before him. In the course the correspondence took, alas! that very recognition was fatal. If Walpole could suspect a boy of sixteen had written thus, and yet see nothing in a scrivener's office and its duties which such an one had any title to withdraw from, all was over with Chatterton's hopes. At this point, accordingly, he simply replied that, "he is not able to dispute with a person of his literary character: he has transcribed Rowley's poems from a transcript in the possession of a gentleman who is assured of their authenticity," (poor Catcott!) "and he will go a little beyond Walpole's advice, by destroying *all his useless lumber of literature and never urging his pen again but in the law*." Is this any very close or deliberate keeping of Rowley's secret! In a word, he felt that Walpole should have said, "Because I firmly believe you, Chatterton, wrote or forged these verses of Rowley, I will do what you require." [6] And so we all feel now.

[6]Walpole's share in the matter may be told in a few words. Indifferent antiquary as he was, at best—in these matters, at worst, his ignorance was complete. "The admirable reasoning in Bryant's work" could "stagger him," he confesses. On receiving Chatterton's first letter and specimens, as his belief in them was implicit, so his mortification on Gray and Mason's setting him right was proportionable. "They both pronounced the poems to be modern forgeries, and recommended the returning them without any further notice,"—stepping a little out of their province in that, certainly; *but they might have felt Chatterton safer at Bristol than nearer home*. Walpole himself did no more in the refusal he gave, than avail himself of Chatterton's own statement that his communications were "taken from a transcript in the possession of a gentleman who was assured of their authenticity." This unknown personage had clearly the first claim to the good things of the Clerk of the Pipe and Usher of the Receipt, and to the unknown they were left therefore, without more heed. Who can object? Truth to say, he of Strawberry Hill was at all times less disposed to expend his doit on a living beggar than on a dead Indian; and, in his way, cowlsfull of Ellas and Godwyns were nothing to a spurious cardinal's hat, empty enough. Beside, what was there to him in the least pressing in the application of a mere transcriber ("who had not quitted his master, nor was necessitous, nor otherwise poorer than attorney's clerks are"), to "emerge from a dull profession and obtain a place that would enable him to follow his propensities." Therefore is it more a pity that ten years after, when he had partly forgotten the matter (this must be allowed, since, with respect to two points which strengthen his case materially, he professes uncertainty), Walpole should have made, on compulsion, a statement of its main circumstances, and leisurely put himself in what he conceived the handsomest of positions,—which turns out to be not quite so handsome. Never for an instant, forsooth, was he deceived by Rowley. "Chatterton had not commenced their intercourse in a manner to dazzle his judgment, or give him a high idea of Chatterton's own." "Somebody, he at first supposed, desired to laugh at him, not very ingeniously, he thought." Little imagining all this while that his letters were in existence, and forthcoming! and that every piece of encouragement to further forgeries, by the expression of belief in those before him, which he professes would have been the height of baseness in him to make, *he had already made*! Indeed the whole statement is modelled on Benedick's *Old Tale*: "If this were so, so were it uttered—but it is not so, nor 'twas not so—but, indeed, God forbid it should be so!" One while, he "does not believe there ever existed so masterly a genius as Chatterton." And another while, he has regard to the "sad situation of the world, if every muse-struck lad who is bound to an attorney were to have his fetters struck off." Wanting is the excellent Horace Walpole, in short, through all these unhappy matters, in that good memory which Swift has pronounced indispensable to a certain class of statement-makers.

And here would enough seem to have been said on the subject, did not one vile paragraph in the Walpole Explanations leer at us—the news to wit, that "all of the house of forgery are relations, and that Chatterton's ingenuity in counterfeiting styles, and it is believed, hands, might easily have led him to those more facile imitations of prose, promissory notes." House of forgery!—from one not only enabled by his first preface to Otranto to march in at its hall-door, but qualified, by a trait noted in "Walpoliana," to sneak in through its area-wicket! *Exempli gratiâ*. "The compiler having learned that the celebrated epistle to Sir William Chambers was supposed to be written by Mason, very innocently expressed to Mr. Walpole his surprise that Mason, the general characteristic of whose poesy is feeble delicacy, but united with a pleasing neatness, should be capable of composing so spirited a satire. Mr. Walpole, *with an arch and peculiar smile, answered, that it would indeed be surprising*. An instantaneous and unaccountable impression arose that he was himself the author, but delicacy prevented the direct question," &c. &c.

And what was it the poor baffled youth required? To ascertain this will in a manner satisfy our whole inquiry—so let us try to ascertain it. His immediate application to Walpole, on his succeeding in forcing his notice, and seemingly engaging his interest, was for some place in a government-office. Did he want to be richer? who had from his earliest boyhood been accustomed to live upon bread and water, and who would refuse to partake of his mother's occasional luxury of a hot meal,—remarking that "he was about a great work, and must make himself no stupider than God had made him." Did he want to obtain leisure, then, for this work—in other words, for the carrying on of his old deceptions? "He had," says his sister, "little of his master's business to do—sometimes not two hours in a day, which gave him an opportunity to pursue his genius." Mr. Palmer states, that "Chatterton was much alone in his office, and much disliked being disturbed in the daytime." We should like to know what kind of government-office would have allowed greater facility for the pursuit of poetical studies and "forgeries" than he was already in possession of; since what advantages, in a literary life, government-office-labour can have over law-business, we are far from guessing. It may be said that the pure disgust and weariness of that law business had formed motive sufficient. But our sympathy with Chatterton's struggles—were nothing to be escaped from worse than this "servitude" as he styles it—would seriously diminish, we confess. Relieve Henry Jones from the bricklayer's hod, and Stephen Duck from the thrasher's flail, if needs must: but Chatterton, from two hours a day's copying precedents!—Ay, but "he was obliged to sleep in the same room with the footboy, and take his meals with the servants—which degradation, to one possessing such pride as Chatterton, must have been mortifying in the highest degree!" Now, Chatterton taking his stand on the inherent qualities of his own mind, shall part company with an Emperor, if he so please, and have our approbation; but let him waive that prerogative, and condescend to the little rules of little men, and we shall not sufficiently understand this right—in a blue-coat charity-boy, apprenticed out with ten pounds of the school-fund, and looking for patronage to pipe-makers and pewterers—to cherish this sensitiveness of contamination. There are more degrading things than eating with footboys, we imagine. "The desire," for example, "of proving oneself worthy the correspondence of Mr. Stephens (leather breeches-maker of Salisbury), by tracing his family from Fitz Stephen, son of Stephen, Earl of Aumerle, in 1095, son of Od, Earl of Bloys, and Lord of Holderness." In a word, Chatterton was very proud, and such crotchets never yet entered the head of a truly proud man. Another motive remains. Had he any dislike to Bristol or its inhabitants generally? "His company pleased universally," he says: "he believed he had promised to write to some hundreds of his acquaintance." And for the place itself,—while at London, nothing out of the Gothic takes his taste, except St. Paul's and Greenwich-hospital: he is never tired of talking in his letters about Bristol, its Cathedral, its street improvements: he even inserts hints to the projectors of these last, in a local paper: nay, he will forestall his mother's intended visit to him at London, and return to Bristol by Christmas: and when somebody suggested, just before his departure, that his professed hatred for the city was connected with ill-treatment received there, he returns, indignantly, "He who without a more sufficient reason than *commonplace scurrility* can look with disgust on his native place, is a villain, and a villain not fit to live. I am obliged to you for supposing *me* such a villain!" Why then, without this hatred or disgust, does he leave Bristol? Whence arises the utmost distress of mind in which the mad "Will," whereby he announced his intention of committing suicide, is written? On being questioned concerning it "he acknowledged that he wanted for nothing, and denied any distress on that account." "The distress was occasioned," says Dr. Gregory, "by the refusal of a gentleman whom he had complimented in his poems, to accommodate him with a supply of money." Here are his own reasons. "In regard to my motives for the supposed rashness, I shall observe that I keep no worse company than myself: I never drink to excess, and have, without vanity, too much sense to be attached to the mercenary retailers of iniquity. No: it is my PRIDE, my damned, native, unconquerable pride, that plunges me into distraction. You must know that nineteen-twentieth of my composition is Pride. I must either live a Slave, a Servant; to have no Will of my own, no Sentiments of my own, which I may freely declare as such; or DIE. Perplexing alternative! But it distracts me to think of it—I will endeavour to learn Humility—but it cannot be HERE."

That is, at Bristol. It is needless for us here to interpose that our whole argument goes, not upon what Chatterton said, but what he did: it is part of our proof to show that all his distress arose out of the impossibility of his saying any thing to the real purpose. But is there no approximation to the truth in what has just been quoted? Had he *not* reduced himself to the alternative of living, as Rowley's transcriber, "a slave, with no sentiment of his own which he might freely declare as such," or "dying?" And did not the proud man—who, when he felt somewhat later that he had failed, would not bring his poverty to accept the offer of a meal to escape "dying"—solicit and receive, while earlier there was yet the hope of succeeding, his old companions' "subscription of a guinea apiece," to enable himself to break through the "slavery?" This, then, is our solution. For this and no other motive—to break through his slavery—at any sacrifice to get back to truth—he came up to London.

It will, of course, be objected, that Chatterton gave the very reasons for his desire to obtain a release from Bristol that we have rejected. But he was forced to say something, and what came more plausibly? To Walpole the cause assigned was, "that he wished to cease from being dependant on his mother;"—while, by a reference to his indenture of apprenticeship, we find him to have been supplied with "meat, drink, clothing, and lodging" by his master. To others the mercantile character of Bristol is made an insuperable objection;—and he straightway leaves it for Holborn. As who, to avoid the smell of hemlock, should sail to Anticyra! It may also yet be urged—as it has been too often—that Chatterton gave to the very last, occasional symptoms that the fabricating, falsifying spirit was far from extinct in him. "He would turn Methodist preacher, found a new sect," &c. Now no one can suppose, and we are far from asserting, that at word of command, Chatterton wholly put aside the old habit of imposing upon people—if that is to be the phrase. But this "imposing upon people" has not always that basest meaning. It is old as the world itself, the tendency of certain spirits to subdue each man by perceiving what will master him, by straightway supplying it from their own resources, and so obtaining, as tokens of success, his admiration, or fear, or wonder. It has been said even that classes of men are immediately ruled in no other way. Poor Chatterton's freedom from some such tendency we do not claim. He is indeed superior to it when alone, in the lumber-closet on Redcliff Hill, or the lath-walled garret at Shoreditch; but in company with the Thistlethwaites and Burgums, he must often have felt a certain power he had, lying dormant there, of turning their natures to his own account. He, "knowing that a great genius can effect any thing, endeavoured in the foregoing poems to represent an Enthusiastic Methodist, and intended to send it to Romaine, and impose it on the infatuated world as a reality;"—but Now, no sooner is the intellectual effort made than the moral one succeeds, and destroying these poems he determined to kill himself. Every way unsuccessful, every way discouraged, the last scene had come. When he killed himself, his room was found "strewn thick over with torn papers."

To the Rowley forgeries he had recurred but in one instance, the acknowledgment of which by a magazine only appeared after his death. He had come to London to produce works of his own; writings he had hoped to get some hearing for. "At the Walmsleys," says Sir Herbert Croft, "he used frequently to say he had many writings by him, which would produce a great deal of money, if they were printed. To this it was once or twice observed, that they lay in a small compass, for that he had not much luggage. But he said he had them, nevertheless. When he talked of writing something which should procure him money to get some clothes—to paper the room in which he lodged; and to send some more things to his sister, mother, and grandmother—he was asked why he did not enable himself to do all this by means of those writings which were 'worth their weight in gold.' His answer was, that 'they were not written with a design to buy old clothes, or to paper rooms; and that if the world did not behave well, it should never see a line of them.' "

It behaves indifferently, we think, in being so sure these were simply fresh books of the "Battle of Hastings," or remodellings of "the Apostate." Look back a little, and see to what drudgery he had submitted in this London, that he could but get the means at last of going on his own ground. "A History of England"—"a voluminous history of London; to appear in numbers the beginning of next week"—"necessitates him to go to Oxford, Cambridge, Lincoln, Coventry, and every collegiate church near."—*Any thing but Rowley!* And when the hopes he had entertained of engaging in such projects fail him, he cheerfully betakes himself to the lowest of all literary labour. He writes any thing and every thing for the magazines. Projects the Moderator; supports the Town and Country; "writes, for a whim, for the Gospel Magazine;" contributes to the London, Middlesex Freeholders', Court and City;—and Registers and Museums get all they ask from him. Thus, we say, with these ultimate views, was he constantly at work in this London pilgrimage; at work, heart and soul; living on a halfpenny roll, or a penny tart, and a glass of water a day, with now and then a sheep's tongue; writing all the while brave letters about his happiness and success to his grandmother, mother, and sister at Bristol, the only creatures he loved as they loved him; and managing, in as miraculous a way as any of his old exercises of power, to buy them china, and fans, and gowns, and so forth, out of his (we cannot calculate how few) pence a day;—being, as such a genius could not but be, the noblest-hearted of mortals. To be sure he had better have swept a crossing in the streets than adopted such a method of getting bread and water; but he had tried to find another outlet till he was sick to the soul, and in this he had been driven to he resolved to stay. If he could, he would have got, for instance, his livelihood as a surgeon. "Before he left Bristol, Mr. Barrett," says his sister, "lent him many books on surgery, and I believe he bought many more, as I remember to have packed them up to send to him in London;" and almost the only intelligible phrase in a mad letter of gibberish, addressed to a friend about the same time, is to the effect that "he is resolved to forsake the Parnassian mount, and would advise that friend to do so too, and attain the mystery of composing *smegma*"—*ointment* we suppose. But nobody would help him, and this way he was helping himself, though never so little.

Sufficient for the Magazine price and Magazine purpose was the piece contributed. "Maria Friendless" and the "Hunter of Oddities" may be a medley of Johnson and Steele;—the few shillings they brought, fully were they worth, though only meant to-give a minute's pleasure. As well expect to find, at this time of day, the sheep's tongues on which he lived unwasted, and the halfpenny loaves no way diminished, as find his poor "Oratorio" (the price of a gown for his sister), or bundle of words for tunes that procured these viands, as pleasant as ever. "Great profligacy and tergiversation in his political writings!" is muttered now, and was solemnly outspoken once, as if he were not in some sort still a scrivener—writing out in plain text-hand the wants of all kinds of men of all kinds of parties. Such sought utterance, and had a right to find it—there was an end. There might be plenty of falsehood in this new course, as he would soon have found; but it seemed as truth itself, compared with the old expedients he had escaped from. The point is, *No more Rowley*. His connexion with the Magazines had commenced with Rowley—they had readily inserted portions of his poems—and we cannot conceive a more favourable field of enterprise than London would have afforded, had he been disposed to go on with the fabrication. No prying intimates, nor familiar townsmen, in Mrs. Angel's quiet lodging! He had the ear, too, of many booksellers. Now would have been indeed the white minute for discoveries and forgeries. He was often pressed for matter; had to solicit all his Bristol acquaintance for contributions (some of such go under his own name now, possibly); but with the one exception we have alluded to (affecting for a passage in which his own destitute condition is too expressly described to admit of mistake)—the Ballad of Charity—*Rowley was done with*.

We shall go no farther—the little we proposed to attempt, having here its completion—though the plastic and co-ordinating spirit which distinguishes Chatterton so remarkably, seems perhaps stronger than ever in these few last days of his existence. We must not stay to speak of it. But ever in Chatterton did his acquisitions, varied and abundant as they were, do duty so as to seem but a little out of more in reserve. If only a foreign word clung to his memory, he was sure to reproduce it as if a whole language lay close behind—setting sometimes to work with the poorest materials; like any painter a fathom below ground in the Inquisition, who in his penury of colour turns the weather-stains on his dungeon wall into effects of light and shade, or outlines of objects, and makes the single sputter of red paint in his possession go far indeed! Not that we consider the mere fabrication of old poetry so difficult a matter. For what *is* poetry, whether old or new, will have its full flow in such a scheme; and any difficulty or uncouthness of phrase that elsewhere would stop its course at once, here not only passes with it, but confers the advantage of authenticity on what, in other circumstances, it deforms: the uncouthness will be set down to our time, and whatever significancy may lurk in it will expand to an original meaning of unlimited magnitude. But there is fine, the finest poetry in Chatterton. And surely, when such an Adventurer so perishes in the Desert, we do not limit his discoveries to the last authenticated spot of ground he pitched tent upon, dug intrenchments round, and wrote good tidings home from—but rather give him the benefit of the very last heap of ashes we can trace him to have kindled, and call by his name the extreme point to which we can track his torn garments and abandoned treasures.

Thus much has been suggested by Mr. Wilde's method with Tasso. As by balancing conflicting statements, interpreting doubtful passages, and reconciling discrepant utterances, he has examined whether Tasso was true or false, loved or did not love the Princess of Este, was or was not beloved by her,—so have we sought, from similar evidences, if Chatterton was towards the end of his life hardening himself in deception or striving to cast it off. Let others apply in like manner our inquiry to other great spirits partially obscured, and they will but use us—we hope more effectually—as we have used these able and interesting volumes.

BELLS AND POMEGRANATES. NUMBER III.

DRAMATIC LYRICS.

Edited by John Hulsman

DRAMATIC LYRICS.

1842: BELLS AND POMEGRANATES. / N°. III.—DRAMATIC LYRICS. / BY ROBERT BROWNING, / AUTHOR OF "PARACELSUS." *1849:* DRAMATIC ROMANCES AND LYRICS. *1863:* Lyrics, Romances, Men and Women. / Lyrics. *1868:* DRAMATIC LYRICS.

NSCRIBED

ΓO

OHN KENYON, ESQ.

N THE HOPE THAT A RECOLLECTION OF HIS OWN SUCCESSFUL

RHYMED PLEA FOR TOLERANCE"

AAY INDUCE HIM TO ADMIT GOOD-NATUREDLY THIS HUMBLER PROSE

)F ONE OF HIS VERY GRATEFUL AND AFFECTIONATE FRIENDS,

R. B.

---

§ First appeared in *Dramatic Romances and Lyrics*, 1845; repeated in 1849; omitted thereafter §

In this Volume are collected and redistributed the pieces first published in 1842, 1845, and 1855, respectively, under the titles of "Dramatic Lyrics," "Dramatic Romances," and "Men and Women."

Part of these were inscribed to my dear friend John Kenyon: I hope the whole may obtain the honor of an association with his memory.

R. B.

1863: § appeared facing first page of text § *1868:* In a late edition were collected <> Women." It is not worth while to disturb this arrangement. ¶ Part of the Poems were <> Kenyon; I *1888:* § omitted §

Tables of Contents

1845: § DRAMATIC ROMANCES AND LYRICS §

1849: § DRAMATIC ROMANCES AND LYRICS §

1855: § MEN AND WOMEN §

1863: § LYRICS, ROMANCES, MEN, AND WOMEN §

LYRICS.

DRAMATIC LYRICS

1842

CAVALIER TUNES[1]

I MARCHING ALONG

I

Kentish Sir Byng stood for his King,
Bidding the crop-headed Parliament swing:
And, pressing a troop unable to stoop
And see the rogues flourish and honest folk droop,
Marched them along, fifty-score strong,
Great-hearted gentlemen, singing this song.

II

God for King Charles! Pym and such carles
To the Devil that prompts 'em their treasonous parles!
Cavaliers, up! Lips from the cup,
Hands from the pasty, nor bite take nor sup
Till you're—
CHORUS—*Marching along, fifty-score strong,*
Great-hearted gentlemen, singing this song.

[1] Such Poems as the majority in this volume might also come properly enough, I suppose, under the head of "Dramatic Pieces"; being, though often Lyric in expression, always Dramatic in principle, and so many utterances of so many imaginary persons, not mine.—*R. B.*

---

§ Ed. 1842, 1849, 1863, 1868, 1888, 1889. No ms. known § MARCHING ALONG.
5| *1868:* fifty score *1888:* fifty-score 11| *1842:* you're 1| *1842:* § appeared on page preceding text § the following come <> though for the most part Lyric <> mine. R. B. *1849:* § appeared as footnote to title at bottom of first page of text § mine. *1863:* the majority in this volume might also come <> though often Lyric <> mine.—R. B.

III

Hampden to hell, and his obsequies' knell
Serve Hazelrig, Fiennes, and young Harry as well!
England, good cheer! Rupert is near!
Kentish and loyalists, keep we not here
        CHORUS—*Marching along, fifty-score strong,*
                Great-hearted gentlemen, singing this song?

IV

Then, God for King Charles! Pym and his snarls
To the Devil that pricks on such pestilent carles!
Hold by the right, you double your might;
So, onward to Nottingham, fresh for the fight,
        CHORUS—*March we along, fifty-score strong,*
                Great-hearted gentlemen, singing this song!

CHORUS *1863:* you're—¶ CHORUS 13| *1842:* Hell *1868:* hell <> knell. *1888:* knell 14| *1842:* Serve Rudyard, and Fiennes *1849:* Serve Hazelrig, Fiennes 23| *1888:* *fifty score*

II GIVE A ROUSE

I

King Charles, and who'll do him right now?
King Charles, and who's ripe for fight now?
Give a rouse: here's, in hell's despite now,
King Charles!

II

Who gave me the goods that went since?
Who raised me the house that sank once?
Who helped me to gold I spent since?
Who found me in wine you drank once?
Chorus—*King Charles, and who'll do him right now?*
King Charles, and who's ripe for fight now?
Give a rouse: here's, in hell's despite now,
King Charles!

III

To whom used my boy George quaff else,
By the old fool's side that begot him?
For whom did he cheer and laugh else,
While Noll's damned troopers shot him?
Chorus—*King Charles, and who'll do him right now?*
King Charles, and who's ripe for fight now?
Give a rouse: here's, in hell's despite now,
King Charles!

II GIVE A ROUSE 3| *1842:* Hell's *1868:* hell's 10| *1868: now! 1888: now?* 11| *1842: Hell's 1868: hell's* 19| *1842: Hell's 1868: hell's*

III BOOT AND SADDLE

I

Boot, saddle, to horse, and away!
Rescue my castle before the hot day
Brightens to blue from its silvery grey,
  CHORUS—*Boot, saddle, to horse, and away!*

II

Ride past the suburbs, asleep as you'd say;
Many's the friend there, will listen and pray
"God's luck to gallants that strike up the lay—
  CHORUS—*Boot, saddle, to horse, and away!"*

III

Forty miles off, like a roebuck at bay,
Flouts Castle Brancepeth the Roundheads' array:
Who laughs, "Good fellows ere this, by my fay,
  CHORUS—*Boot, saddle, to horse, and away!"*

IV

Who? My wife Gertrude; that, honest and gay,
Laughs when you talk of surrendering, "Nay!
I've better counsellors; what counsel they?
  CHORUS—*Boot, saddle, to horse, and away!"*

Title/ *1842:* III MY WIFE GERTRUDE *1849:* III BOOT AND SADDLE 2| *1842:* my Castle, before *1868:* castle before 3| *1842:* gray, *1863:* grey, 7| *1842:* lay, *1863:* lay— 12| *1842: away?" 1888: away!"*

MY LAST DUCHESS

FERRARA

That's my last Duchess painted on the wall,
Looking as if she were alive. I call
That piece a wonder, now: Frà Pandolf's hands
Worked busily a day, and there she stands.
Will't please you sit and look at her? I said
"Frà Pandolf" by design, for never read
Strangers like you that pictured countenance,
The depth and passion of its earnest glance,
But to myself they turned (since none puts by
The curtain I have drawn for you, but I)
And seemed as they would ask me, if they durst,
How such a glance came there; so, not the first
Are you to turn and ask thus. Sir, 'twas not
Her husband's presence only, called that spot
Of joy into the Duchess' cheek: perhaps
Frà Pandolf chanced to say "Her mantle laps
Over my lady's wrist too much," or "Paint
Must never hope to reproduce the faint
Half-flush that dies along her throat:" such stuff
Was courtesy, she thought, and cause enough
For calling up that spot of joy. She had
A heart—how shall I say?—too soon made glad,
Too easily impressed; she liked whate'er
She looked on, and her looks went everywhere.

MY LAST DUCHESS § Subsequent placement: 1849: *DRL*; 1863: *DR*. In 1842 this and the following poem were grouped together under the title ITALY AND FRANCE § Title / *1842:* I—ITALY / That's *1849:* MY LAST DUCHESS. / FERRARA. / That's 2| *1842:* alive; I *1868:* alive. I 12| *1842:* so not *1849:* so, not 17| *1842:* Lady's *1868:* lady's 19| *1842:* throat;" such *1868:* throat:" such 22| *1842:* heart . . how <> say? . . too *1863:* heart . . . how <> say? . . . too *1868:* heart—how <>

Sir, 'twas all one! My favour at her breast,
The dropping of the daylight in the West,
The bough of cherries some officious fool
Broke in the orchard for her, the white mule
She rode with round the terrace—all and each
Would draw from her alike the approving speech,
Or blush, at least. She thanked men,—good! but thanked
Somehow—I know not how—as if she ranked
My gift of a nine-hundred-year-old name
With anybody's gift. Who'd stoop to blame
This sort of trifling? Even had you skill
In speech—(which I have not)—to make your will
Quite clear to such an one, and say, "Just this
Or that in you disgusts me; here you miss,
Or there exceed the mark"—and if she let
Herself be lessoned so, nor plainly set
Her wits to yours, forsooth, and made excuse,
—E'en then would be some stooping; and I choose
Never to stoop. Oh sir, she smiled, no doubt,
Whene'er I passed her; but who passed without
Much the same smile? This grew; I gave commands;
Then all smiles stopped together. There she stands
As if alive. Will't please you rise? We'll meet
The company below, then. I repeat,
The Count your master's known munificence
Is ample warrant that no just pretence
Of mine for dowry will be disallowed;
Though his fair daughter's self, as I avowed
At starting, is my object. Nay, we'll go
Together down, sir. Notice Neptune, though,
Taming a sea-horse, thought a rarity,
Which Claus of Innsbruck cast in bronze for me!

---

say?—too   25| *1842:* favor *1863:* favour   30| *1842:* the forward speech *1849:* the approving speech   31| *1842:* good; but *1868:* good! but   32| *1842:* Somehow . . I <> how . . as *1863:* Somehow . . . I <> how . . . as *1868:* Somehow—I <> how—as   33| *1842:* nine hundred years old *1863:* nine-hundred-years-old   36| *1842:* not)—could make *1849:* not)—to make   37| *1842:* say "Just *1868:* say, "Just   42| *1842:* stooping, and I chuse *1868:* stooping; and I choose   43| *1842:* Oh, Sir *1868:* Oh sir   48| *1842:* below then *1849:* below, then   54| *1842:* down, Sir! Notice Neptune, tho' *1863:* though *1868:* sir. Notice   56| *1842:* me. *1868:* me!

COUNT GISMOND

AIX IN PROVENCE

I

Christ God who savest man, save most
Of men Count Gismond who saved me!
Count Gauthier, when he chose his post,
Chose time and place and company
To suit it; when he struck at length
My honour, 'twas with all his strength.

II

And doubtlessly ere he could draw
All points to one, he must have schemed!
That miserable morning saw
Few half so happy as I seemed,
While being dressed in queen's array
To give our tourney prize away.

III

I thought they loved me, did me grace
To please themselves; 'twas all their deed;
God makes, or fair or foul, our face;
If showing mine so caused to bleed
My cousins' hearts, they should have dropped
A word, and straight the play had stopped.

COUNT GISMOND § Subsequent placement: 1849: *DRL*; 1863: *DR* § Title / *1842:* II—FRANCE / Christ *1849:* COUNT GISMOND / *Aix in Provence* / Christ [1]| *1842:* Christ God, who *1849:* men *1863:* man *1868:* Christ God who [6]| *1842:* My honor's face 'twas with full strength. *1849:* My honor 'twas with all his strength. *1863:* honour *1868:* honour, 'twas [11]| *1842:* Queen's *1868:* queen's [12]| *1842:* Tourney *1868:* tourney [13]| *1842:* thought all loved *1849:* thought they loved [17]| *1842:* Cousins' *1849:* cousins' *1863:* Cousins' *1868:* cousins' [18]| *1842:* and

IV

They, too, so beauteous! Each a queen
By virtue of her brow and breast;
Not needing to be crowned, I mean,
As I do. E'en when I was dressed,
Had either of them spoke, instead
Of glancing sideways with still head!

V

But no: they let me laugh, and sing
My birthday song quite through, adjust
The last rose in my garland, fling
A last look on the mirror, trust
My arms to each an arm of theirs,
And so descend the castle-stairs—

VI

And come out on the morning-troop
Of merry friends who kissed my cheek,
And called me queen, and made me stoop
Under the canopy—(a streak
That pierced it, of the outside sun,
Powdered with gold its gloom's soft dun)—

VII

And they could let me take my state
And foolish throne amid applause
Of all come there to celebrate
My queen's-day—Oh I think the cause
Of much was, they forgot no crowd
Makes up for parents in their shroud!

---

all the *1849:* and straight the 26| *1842:* through; adjust *1849:* through, adjust *1863:* birthday-song *1868:* birthday song 31| *1842:* morning troop *1863:* morning-troop 33| *1842:* Queen *1868:* queen 40| *1842:* My Queen's

VIII

However that be, all eyes were bent
Upon me, when my cousins cast
Theirs down; 'twas time I should present
The victor's crown, but . . . there, 'twill last
No long time . . . the old mist again
Blinds me as then it did. How vain!

IX

See! Gismond's at the gate, in talk
With his two boys: I can proceed.
Well, at that moment, who should stalk
Forth boldly—to my face, indeed—
But Gauthier, and he thundered "Stay!"
And all stayed. "Bring no crowns, I say!

X

"Bring torches! Wind the penance-sheet
About her! Let her shun the chaste,
Or lay herself before their feet!
Shall she whose body I embraced
A night long, queen it in the day?
For honour's sake no crowns, I say!"

XI

I? What I answered? As I live,
I never fancied such a thing
As answer possible to give.
What says the body when they spring
Some monstrous torture-engine's whole
Strength on it? No more says the soul.

---

day—Oh, I *1863:* Queen's-day *1868:* queen's-day—Oh I 43| *1842:* Howe'er that be, when eyes *1849:* be, all eyes *1868:* However 44| *1842:* me, both my Cousins *1849:* me, when my cousins 46| *1842:* victor with his . . . there *1849:* victor's crown, but . . . there 47| *1842:* time . . the *1849:* time . . . the 48| *1842:* me . . but the true mist was rain. *1849:* me as then it did. How vain! 52| *1842:* Forth calmly (to <> indeed) *1849:* Forth boldly (to *1868:* boldly—to <> indeed— 54| *1842:* all did stay. "No <> say!" *1849:* all stayed. "Bring no *1863:* say! 58| *1842:* she, whose *1868:* she whose 60| *1842:* Honor's *1863:* Honour's *1868:* honour's 62| *1842:* never thought there was such thing *1849:*

XII

Till out strode Gismond; then I knew
That I was saved. I never met
His face before, but, at first view,
I felt quite sure that God had set
Himself to Satan; who would spend
A minute's mistrust on the end?

XIII

He strode to Gauthier, in his throat
Gave him the lie, then struck his mouth
With one back-handed blow that wrote
In blood men's verdict there. North, South,
East, West, I looked. The lie was dead,
And damned, and truth stood up instead.

XIV

This glads me most, that I enjoyed
The heart of joy, with my content
In watching Gismond unalloyed
By any doubt of the event:
God took that on him—I was bid
Watch Gismond for my part: I did.

XV

Did I not watch him while he let
His armourer just brace his greaves,
Rivet his hauberk, on the fret
The while! His foot . . . my memory leaves
No least stamp out, nor how anon
He pulled his ringing gauntlets on.

---

never fancied such a thing 70| *1863:* hath *1868:* had 80| *1842:* joy, nor my *1849:* joy, with my 81| *1842:* watching Gismond was alloyed *1849:* watching Gismond unalloyed 83| *1842:* him—me he bid *1849:* him—I was bid *1863:* Him *1868:* him 88| *1842:* foot . . my *1863:* foot . . . my 92| *1842:* finished

XVI

And e'en before the trumpet's sound
Was finished, prone lay the false knight,
Prone as he lie, upon the ground:
Gismond flew at him, used no sleight
O' the sword, but open-breasted drove,
Cleaving till out the truth he clove.

XVII

Which done, he dragged him to my feet
And said "Here die, but end thy breath
In full confession, lest thou fleet
From my first, to God's second death!
Say, hast thou lied?" And, "I have lied
To God and her," he said, and died.

XVIII

Then Gismond, kneeling to me, asked
—What safe my heart holds, though no word
Could I repeat now, if I tasked
My powers for ever, to a third
Dear even as you are. Pass the rest
Until I sank upon his breast.

XIX

Over my head his arm he flung
Against the world; and scarce I felt
His sword (that dripped by me and swung)
A little shifted in its belt:
For he began to say the while
How South our home lay many a mile.

---

there lay prone the Knight, *1849:* finished, prone lay the false Knight, *1868:* knight, 94| *1842:* My Knight flew *1849:* Gismond flew 95| *1842:* Of *1868:* O' 104| *1842:* holds tho' no *1849:* holds, though no 111| *1842:* sword, that<> swung, *1863:* sword (that<> swung) *1888:* swung). 112| *1842:*

XX

So 'mid the shouting multitude
We two walked forth to never more
Return. My cousins have pursued
Their life, untroubled as before
I vexed them. Gauthier's dwelling-place
God lighten! May his soul find grace!

XXI

Our elder boy has got the clear
Great brow; tho' when his brother's black
Full eye shows scorn, it . . . Gismond here?
And have you brought my tercel back?
I just was telling Adela
How many birds it struck since May.

---

belt, *1849:* belt,— *1863:* belt: 116| *1842:* We too walked *1849:* We two walked 117| *1842:* Cousins *1849:* cousins *1863:* Cousins *1868:* cousins 118| *1842:* life untroubled *1849:* life, untroubled

INCIDENT OF THE FRENCH CAMP

I

You know, we French stormed Ratisbon:
　　A mile or so away,
On a little mound, Napoleon
　　Stood on our storming-day;
With neck out-thrust, you fancy how,
　　Legs wide, arms locked behind,
As if to balance the prone brow
　　Oppressive with its mind.

II

Just as perhaps he mused "My plans
　　That soar, to earth may fall,
Let once my army-leader Lannes
　　Waver at yonder wall,"—
Out 'twixt the battery-smokes there flew
　　A rider, bound on bound
Full-galloping; nor bridle drew
　　Until he reached the mound.

III

Then off there flung in smiling joy,
　　And held himself erect
By just his horse's mane, a boy:
　　You hardly could suspect—
(So tight he kept his lips compressed,
　　Scarce any blood came through)
You looked twice ere you saw his breast
　　Was all but shot in two.

INCIDENT OF THE FRENCH CAMP § Subsequent placement: 1863: *DR* In 1842 this and the following poem were grouped together under the title CAMP AND CLOISTER § Title / *1842:* I.—CAMP. *(French.)* *1849:* INCIDENT OF THE FRENCH CAMP 1| *1842:* know we *1849:* know, we 2| *1842:* away *1888:* away, 3| *1842:* Napoléon *1863:* Napoleon 10| *1842:* fall *1849:* fall, 12| *1842:* wall," *1849:* wall,"— 21| *1842:* compressed *1849:* compressed, 22| *1842:* thro')

IV

"Well," cried he, "Emperor, by God's grace
We've got you Ratisbon!
The Marshal's in the market-place,
And you'll be there anon
To see your flag-bird flap his vans
Where I, to heart's desire,
"Perched him!" The chief's eye flashed; his plans
Soared up again like fire.

V

The chief's eye flashed; but presently
Softened itself, as sheathes
A film the mother-eagle's eye
When her bruised eaglet breathes;
"You're wounded!" "Nay," the soldier's pride
Touched to the quick, he said:
"I'm killed, Sire!" And his chief beside
Smiling the boy fell dead.

1863: through) 31| *1842:* Chief's *1868:* chief's 33| *1842:* Chief's *1868:* chief's 35| *1842:* mother eagle's *1863:* mother-eagles's 36| *1842:* breathes: *1868:* breathes; 37| *1842:* wounded!" "Nay," his soldier's *1868:* wounded!" "Nay," the soldier's 39| *1842:* his Chief beside, *1868:* chief *1888:* beside

SOLILOQUY OF THE SPANISH CLOISTER

I

Gr-r-r—there go, my heart's abhorrence!
        Water your damned flower-pots, do!
If hate killed men, Brother Lawrence,
        God's blood, would not mine kill you!
What? your myrtle-bush wants trimming?
        Oh, that rose has prior claims—
Needs its leaden vase filled brimming?
        Hell dry you up with its flames!

II

At the meal we sit together:
        Salve tibi! I must hear
Wise talk of the kind of weather,
        Sort of season, time of year:
Not a plenteous cork-crop: scarcely
        Dare we hope oak-galls, I doubt:
What's the Latin name for "parsley"?
        What's the Greek name for Swine's Snout?

III

Whew! We'll have our platter burnished,
        Laid with care on our own shelf!
With a fire-new spoon we're furnished,
        And a goblet for ourself,
Rinsed like something sacrificial
        E're 'tis fit to touch our chaps—
Marked with L. for our initial!
        (He-he! There his lily snaps!)

SOLILOQUY OF THE SPANISH CLOISTER Title / *1842:* II.—CLOISTER. *(Spanish.)* *1849:* SOLILOQUY OF THE SPANISH CLOISTER 15| *1868: parsley?"* *1888: parsley"?* 17| *1842:* Phew *1849:* Whew 24| *1842:* (He, he *1863:*

IV

Saint, forsooth! While brown Dolores
Squats outside the Convent bank
With Sanchicha, telling stories,
Steeping tresses in the tank,
Blue-black, lustrous, thick like horsehairs,
—Can't I see his dead eye glow,
Bright as 'twere a Barbary corsair's?
(That is, if he'd let it show!)

V

When he finishes refection,
Knife and fork he never lays
Cross-wise, to my recollection,
As do I, in Jesu's praise.
I the Trinity illustrate,
Drinking watered orange-pulp—
In three sips the Arian frustrate;
While he drains his at one gulp.

VI

Oh, those melons? If he's able
We're to have a feast! so nice!
One goes to the Abbot's table,
All of us get each a slice.
How go on your flowers? None double?
Not one fruit-sort can you spy?
Strange!—And I, too, at such trouble,
Keep them close-nipped on the sly!

(He-he 26| *1842:* bank, *1868:* bank 30| *1842:* eye grow *1849:* eye glow *1863:* glow, 31| *1842:* Bright, as *1863:* Bright as 32| *1842:* that <> show. *1849:* (That <> show!) 34| *1842:* fork across he lays *1849:* fork he never lays 35| *1842:* Never, to *1849:* Cross-wise, to 37| *1842:* I, the *1868:* I the 38| *1842:* orange-pulp; *1849:* orange-pulp— 40| *1842:* gulp! *1868:* gulp. 41| *1842:* melons! If *1868:* melons? If 42| *1842:* feast; so *1868:* feast! so 47| *1868:* trouble *1888:* trouble, 48| *1842:* 'em *1863:*

VII

There's a great text in Galatians,
Once you trip on it, entails
Twenty-nine distinct damnations,
One sure, if another fails:
If I trip him just a-dying,
Sure of heaven as sure can be,
Spin him round and send him flying
Off to hell, a Manichee?

VIII

Or, my scrofulous French novel
On grey paper with blunt type!
Simply glance at it, you grovel
Hand and foot in Belial's gripe:
If I double down its pages
At the woeful sixteenth print,
When he gathers his greengages,
Ope a sieve and slip it in't?

IX

Or, there's Satan!—one might venture
Pledge one's soul to him, yet leave
Such a flaw in the indenture
As he'd miss till, past retrieve,
Blasted lay that rose-acacia
We're so proud of! *Hy, Zy, Hine . . .*
'St, there's Vespers! *Plena gratiâ*
Ave, Virgo! Gr-r-r—you swine!

---

them 50| *1842:* entails *1888:* entails, 52| *1842:* fails. *1868:* fails: 54| *1842:* Heaven *1868:* heaven 56| *1842:* to Hell a *1849:* to Hell, a *1868:* hell 57| *1842:* novel, *1868:* novel 60| *1842:* gripe. *1849:* gripe: 65| *1842:* Or, the Devil!—one *1849:* Or, there's Satan!—one 66| *1842:* soul yet slily leave *1849:* soul to him, yet leave 71| *1842:* St *1849:* 'St

IN A GONDOLA

HE SINGS

I send my heart up to thee, all my heart
    In this my singing.
For the stars help me, and the sea bears part;
    The very night is clinging
Closer to Venice' streets to leave one space
    Above me, whence thy face
May light my joyous heart to thee its dwelling-
  place.

SHE SPEAKS

Say after me, and try to say
My very words, as if each word
Came from you of your own accord,
In your own voice, in your own way:
"This woman's heart and soul and brain
Are mine as much as this gold chain
She bids me wear; which" (say again)
"I choose to make by cherishing
A precious thing, or choose to fling
Over the boat-side, ring by ring."
And yet once more say . . . no word more!
Since words are only words. Give o'er!

IN A GONDOLA § Subsequent placement: 1863: *DR* § *1842:* § I. used instead of speech designation § *1849:* § Speech designation § *He sings.* 2| *1842:* singing! *1863:* singing *1868:* singing. 7–8| *1842:* § II. used instead of speech designation § *1849:* § speech designation § *She speaks.* 9| *1842:* My words as *1849:* My very words, as 12–17| *1842:* § lines italicized, except for parenthesis in l. 14; 1849, lines in quotation marks, except for parenthesis in l. 14. § 12| *1842: heart, and soul, and* *1863:* heart and soul and 14| *1842: which* (say *1849:* which" (say 15| *1842: I* *1849:* "I 17| *1842: by ring;* *1849:* by ring." 19–20| *1842:* § no space;

Unless you call me, all the same,
Familiarly by my pet name,
Which if the Three should hear you call,
And me reply to, would proclaim
At once our secret to them all.
Ask of me, too, command me, blame—
Do, break down the partition-wall
'Twixt us, the daylight world beholds
Curtained in dusk and splendid folds!
What's left but—all of me to take?
I am the Three's: prevent them, slake
Your thirst! 'Tis said, the Arab sage,
In practising with gems, can loose
Their subtle spirit in his cruce
And leave but ashes: so, sweet mage,
Leave them my ashes when thy use
Sucks out my soul, thy heritage!

HE SINGS

I

Past we glide, and past, and past!
 What's that poor Agnese doing
Where they make the shutters fast?
 Grey Zanobi's just a-wooing
To his couch the purchased bride:
 Past we glide!

1868, space § 21| *1842:* pet-name *1868:* pet name, 22| *1842:* call *1849:* call, 24| *1842:* all, *1849:* all: *1863:* all. 26| *1842:* Do break *1863:* Do, break 27| *1842:* us the *1849:* us, the 28| *1842:* folds. *1868:* folds! 28–29| *1842:* III. *1849:* § numerical division eliminated and space between lines closed § 30| *1842:* the Three's, prevent *1849:* the Three's; prevent *1863:* the Three's: prevent 31| *1842:* said the Arab sage *1849:* said, the *1888:* sage, 32| *1842:* gems can *1888:* gems, can 36–37| *1842:* § IV. used instead of speech

II

Past we glide, and past, and past!
    Why's the Pucci Palace flaring
Like a beacon to the blast?
    Guests by hundreds, not one caring
If the dear host's neck were wried:
    Past we glide!

SHE SINGS

I

The moth's kiss, first!
Kiss me as if you made believe
You were not sure, this eve,
How my face, your flower, had pursed
Its petals up; so, here and there
You brush it, till I grow aware
Who wants me, and wide ope I burst.

II

The bee's kiss, now!
Kiss me as if you entered gay
My heart at some noonday,
A bud that dares not disallow
The claim, so all is rendered up,
And passively its shattered cup
Over your head to sleep I bow.

---

designation § *1849:* § speech designation § *He sings.* 46| *1842:* hundreds—not *1863:* hundreds, not 48–49| *1842:* § V. used instead of speech designation § *1849:* § speech designation § *She sings.* 49| *1842:* Moth's *1868:* moth's 51| *1842:* sure this *1849:* sure, this 53| *1842:* so, here *1849:* so here 54| *1842:* Brush *1849:* You brush 55| *1849:* wide open burst. *1868:* wide ope I burst. 56| *1842:* Bee's *1868:* bee's 62–63| *1842:* § VI. used instead of speech

HE SINGS

I

What are we two?
I am a Jew,
And carry thee, farther than friends can pursue,
To a feast of our tribe;
Where they need thee to bribe
The devil that blasts them unless he imbibe
Thy . . . Scatter the vision for ever! And now,
As of old, I am I, thou art thou!

II

Say again, what we are?
The sprite of a star,
I lure thee above where the destinies bar
My plumes their full play
Till a ruddier ray
Than my pale one announce there is withering away
Some . . Scatter the vision for ever! And now.
As of old, I am I, thou art thou!

HE MUSES

Oh, which were best, to roam or rest?
The land's lap or the water's breast?
To sleep on yellow millet-sheaves,
Or swim in lucid shallows just
Eluding water-lily leaves,
An inch from Death's black fingers, thrust
To lock you, whom release he must;
Which life were best on Summer eves?

---

designation § *1849:* § speech designation § *He sings.* 66| *1842:* tribe, *1863:* tribe; 69| *1842:* Thy . . . Shatter the *1863:* Thy . . . Scatter the 70| *1842:* am I, Thou art Thou! *1868:* thou art thou! 71| *1842:* But again *1849:* Say again 73| *1842:* Destinies *1863:* destinies 77| *1842:* now, *1849:* Some . . . Shatter the *1863:* Some . . . Scatter the *1868:* now. 78| *1842:* am I, Thou art Thou! *1868:* thou art thou! 78–79| *1842:* § VII. used instead of speech designation § *1849:* § speech designation § *He muses.* 82| *1842:* shallows, just *1868:* shallows just 86–87| *1842:* § VIII. used instead of speech designation § *1849:*

HE SPEAKS, MUSING

Lie back; could thought of mine improve you?
From this shoulder let there spring
A wing; from this, another wing;
Wings, not legs and feet, shall move you!
Snow-white must they spring, to blend
With your flesh, but I intend
They shall deepen to the end,
Broader, into burning gold,
Till both wings crescent-wise enfold
Your perfect self, from 'neath your feet
To o'er your head, where, lo, they meet
As if a million sword-blades hurled
Defiance from you to the world!

Rescue me thou, the only real!
And scare away this mad ideal
That came, nor motions to depart!
Thanks! Now, stay ever as thou art!

STILL HE MUSES

I

What if the Three should catch at last
Thy serenader? While there's cast
Paul's cloak about my head, and fast
Gian pinions me, Himself has past
His stylet thro' my back; I reel;
And . . . is it thou I feel?

---

§ speech designation § *He speaks, musing.* 87| *1842:* could I improve *1849:* could thought of mine improve 100| *1863:* Thou *1868:* thou 101| *1842:* Ideal *1868:* ideal 103–104| *1842:* § IX. used instead of speech designation § *1849:* § speech designation § *Still he muses.* 104| *1842:* He and the Couple catch *1849:* What if the Three should catch 105| *1842:* serenader; while *1849:* serenader? While 109| *1842:* it Thee I *1849:* it Thou I *1868:* thou 110| *1842:* me, do

II

They trail me, these three godless knaves,
Past every church that saints and saves,
Nor stop till, where the cold sea raves
By Lido's wet accursed graves,
They scoop mine, roll me to its brink,
And . . . on thy breast I sink!

SHE REPLIES, MUSING

Dip your arm o'er the boat-side, elbow-deep,
As I do: thus: were death so unlike sleep,
Caught this way? Death's to fear from flame or steel,
Or poison doubtless; but from water—feel!

Go find the bottom! Would you stay me? There!
Now pluck a great blade of that ribbon-grass
To plait in where the foolish jewel was,
I flung away: since you have praised my hair,
'Tis proper to be choice in what I wear.

---

these godless *1849:* me, these three godless 111| *1842:* that sains and *1868:* that saints and 115| *1842:* Thy *1868:* thy 115–116| *1842:* § X. used instead of speech designation § *1849:* § speech designation § *She replies, musing.* 116| *1842:* boat-side elbow-deep *1849:* boat-side, elbow-deep, 117| *1842:* were Death so unlike Sleep *1849:* unlike Sleep, *1863:* death <> sleep, 118| *1842:* steel *1849:* flame, or steel, *1868:* flame or 119| *1842:* doubtless, but *1849:* doubtless; but 123| *1842:* hair *1849:* hair, 124–125| *1842:* § XI. used instead of speech

Row home? must we row home? Too surely
Know I where its front's demurely
Over the Giudecca piled;
Window just with window mating,
Door on door exactly waiting,
All's the set face of a child:
But behind it, where's a trace
Of the staidness and reserve,
And formal lines without a curve,
In the samechild's playing-face?
No two windows look one way
O'er the small sea-water thread
Below them. Ah, the autumn day
I, passing, saw you overhead!
First, out a cloud of curtain blew,
Then a sweet cry, and last came you—
To catch your lory that must needs
Escape just then, of all times then,
To peck a tall plant's fleecy seeds,
And make me happiest of men.
I scarce could breathe to see you reach
So far back o'er the balcony
To catch him ere he climbed too high
Above you in the Smyrna peach
That quick the round smooth cord of gold,
This coiled hair on your head, unrolled,
Fell down you like a gorgeous snake
The Roman girls were wont, of old,
When Rome there was, for coolness' sake
To let lie curling o'er their bosoms.

---

designation § *1849:* § speech designation § *He speaks.* 125| *1842:* Must we, must we *Home?* Too *1849:* Row home? must we row home? Too 133| *1842:* Formal *1849:* And formal 139| *1842:* First out *1849:* First, out 140| *1842:* Then, a *1849:* last, came *1868:* Then a <> last came 141| *1842:* loory *1868:* lory 146| *1842:* balcony, *1868:* balcony 147| *1849:* (To *1868:* To 148| *1842:* peach, *1849:* peach) *1868:* peach 152| *1842:* old *1849:* old, 154| *1842:*

Dear lory, may his beak retain
Ever its delicate rose stain
As if the wounded lotus-blossoms
Had marked their thief to know again!

Stay longer yet, for others' sake
Than mine! What should your chamber do?
—With all its rarities that ache
In silence while day lasts, but wake
At night-time and their life renew,
Suspended just to pleasure you
Who brought against their will together
These objects, and, while day lasts, weave
Around them such a magic tether
That dumb they look: your harp, believe,
With all the sensitive tight strings
Which dare not speak, now to itself
Breathes slumberously, as if some elf
Went in and out the chords, his wings
Make murmur wheresoe'er they graze,
As an angel may, between the maze
Of midnight palace-pillars, on
And on, to sow God's plagues, have gone
Through guilty glorious Babylon.
And while such murmurs flow, the nymph
Bends o'er the harp-top from her shell
As the dry limpet for the lymph
Come with a tune he knows so well.
And how your statues' hearts must swell!

To place within their *1849:* To let lie curling o'er their 155| *1842:* loory *1868:* lory 158| *1842:* Marked *1849:* Had marked 158–159| *1842:* XII. *1849:* § numerical division eliminated; space between lines retained § 160| *1842:* what *1868:* What 165| *1842:* That brought reluctantly together *1849:* —That brought against their will together *1863:* That *1868:* Who brought 166| *1842:* objects and *1849:* objects, and 167| *1842:* Round them *1849:* Around them 168| *1849:* That they look dumb: your *1868:* That dumb they look: your 170| *1842:* That dare *1868:* Which dare 171| *1842:* slumbrously as *1863:* slumberously *1868:* slumberously, as 172| *1842:* out tall chords his *1849:* out the chords, his 173| *1842:* Get murmurs from whene'er they *1849:* Make murmur wheresoe'er they 174| *1842:* As may an angel thro' the *1849:* As an angel may, between the 175–177| *1842:* Of pillars on God's quest have gone / At guilty *1849:* Of midnight palace-pillars, on / And on, to sow God's plagues have gone / Through guilty 176| *1868:* plagues, have 179| *1842:* shell, *1863:* shell 182| *1842:* how the Statues' *1849:* how your statues' 183| *1842:* how the pictures

And how your pictures must descend
To see each other, friend with friend!
Oh, could you take them by surprise,
You'd find Schidone's eager Duke
Doing the quaintest courtesies
To that prim saint by Haste-thee-Luke!
And, deeper into her rock den,
Bold Castelfranco's Magdalen
You'd find retreated from the ken
Of that robed counsel-keeping Ser—
As if the Tizian thinks of her,
And is not, rather, gravely bent
On seeing for himself what toys
Are these, his progeny invent,
What litter now the board employs
Whereon he signed a document
That got him murdered! Each enjoys
Its night so well, you cannot break
The sport up, so, indeed must make
More stay with me, for others' sake.

SHE SPEAKS

I

To-morrow, if a harp-string, say,
Is used to tie the jasmine back
That overfloods my room with sweets,
Contrive your Zorzi somehow meets
My Zanze! If the ribbon's black,
The Three are watching: keep away!

1849: how your pictures 188| *1842:* prim Saint by Haste-thee-Luke: *1863:* by Haste-thee-Luke! *1868:* saint 189| *1842:* And deeper <> den *1849:* And, deeper <> den, 193| *1842:* her! *1849:* her, 194| *1842:* As if he is not rather bent *1849:* And is not, rather, gravely bent 195| *1842:* On trying for *1849:* On seeing for 196| *1842:* these his *1849:* these, his 201| *1842:* so, for others' sake *1849:* so, indeed must make 202| *1842:* Than mine, your stay must longer make! *1849:* More stay with me, for others' sake. 202–203| *1842:* § XIII. used instead of speech designation § *1849:* § speech designation § *She speaks.*
206| *1842:* Be sure that Zorzi *1849:* Contrive your Zorzi 207| *1842:* My Zanze: if <> black *1849:* black, *1868:* My Zanze! If 208| *1842:* I use, they're watching;

II

Your gondola—let Zorzi wreathe
A mesh of water-weeds about
Its prow, as if he unaware
Had struck some quay or bridge-foot stair!
That I may throw a paper out
As you and he go underneath.

There's Zanze's vigilant taper; safe are we.
Only one minute more to-night with me?
Resume your past self of a month ago!
Be you the bashful gallant, I will be
The lady with the colder breast than snow.
Now bow you, as becomes, nor touch my hand
More than I touch yours when I step to land,
And say, "All thanks, Siora!"—
                                        Heart to heart
And lips to lips! Yet once more, ere we part,
Clasp me and make me thine, as mine thou art!
                                                [*He is surprised, and stabbed.*]
It was ordained to be so, sweet!—and best
Come now, beneath thine eyes, upon thy breast.
Still kiss me! Care not for the cowards! Care
Only to put aside thy beauteous hair
My blood will hurt! The Three, I do not scorn
To death, because they never lived: but I
Have lived indeed, and so—(yet one more kiss)—can die!

---

keep away. *1849:* The Three are watching *1868:* watching: keep away!
212| *1842:* stair; *1868:* stair! 214–215| *1842:* XIV. *1849:* § numerical division eliminated; space between lines retained § 215| *1842:* we! *1868:* we. 219| *1842:* snow: *1868:* snow. 222| *1842:* say, All <> Siora . . . ¶ Heart to heart, *1849:* thank, Siora!— ¶ Heart to heart, *1863:* say, "All *1868:* to heart 223| *1842:* to lips! Once, ere *1849:* to lips! Yet once more, ere 224| *1842:* Make me thine as *1849:* Clasp me, and make me thine, as *1868:* me and 224–225| *1842:* XV. *1849:* § numerical division eliminated; replaced by stage direction § 225| *1842:* It was to be so, Sweet, and *1849:* It was ordained to <> Sweet,—and *1868:* sweet!—and 226| *1842:* Comes 'neath thine eyes, and on thy *1849:* Comes now, beneath thine *1868:* eyes, upon thy 229| *1842:* hurt. The Three I *1849:* hurt! The Three, I 231| *1842:* die. *1849:* die!

ARTEMIS PROLOGIZES

I am a goddess of the ambrosial courts,
And save by Here, Queen of Pride, surpassed
By none whose temples whiten this the world.
Through heaven I roll my lucid moon along;
I shed in hell o'er my pale people peace;
On earth I, caring for the creatures, guard
Each pregnant yellow wolf and fox-bitch sleek,
And every feathered mother's callow brood,
And all that love green haunts and loneliness.
Of men, the chaste adore me, hanging crowns
Of poppies red to blackness, bell and stem,
Upon my image at Athenai here;
And this dead Youth, Asclepios bends above,
Was dearest to me. He, my buskined step
To follow through the wild-wood leafy ways,
And chase the panting stag, or swift with darts
Stop the swift ounce, or lay the leopard low,
Neglected homage to another god:
Whence Aphrodite, by no midnight smoke
Of tapers lulled, in jealousy despatched
A noisome lust that, as the gadbee stings,
Possessed his stepdame Phaidra for himself
The son of Theseus her great absent spouse.
Hippolutos exclaiming in his rage
Against the fury of the Queen, she judged
Life insupportable; and, pricked at heart
An Amazonian stranger's race should dare

ARTEMIS PROLOGIZES § Subsequent placement: 1849: *DRL;* 1863: *MW* § Title / *1842:* PROLOGUIZES *1863:* PROLOGIZES 1| *1842:* Goddess *1868:* goddess 4| *1842:* Thro' Heaven I roll its lucid *1849:* roll my lucid *1863:* Through *1868:* heaven 5| *1842:* In Hades shed o'er *1849:* I shed in Hell o'er *1868:* hell 6| *1842:* On Earth, I *1863:* On Earth I *1868:* earth 13| *1842:* Of such this Youth *1849:* And this dead Youth 14| *1842:* me, and my *1849:* me. He my *1863:* me. He, my 15| *1842:* thro' *1863:* through 18| *1842:* He paid not homage to another God: *1849:* Neglected homage *1868:* god: 20| *1849:* dispatched *1868:* despatched 22| *1842:* for the child *1849:* for himself 23| *1842:* Of Theseus her great husband then afar. *1849:* The son of Theseus her great absent spouse. 24| *1842:* But when Hippolutos exclaimed with rage *1849:* Hippolutos exclaiming in his rage 25| *1842:* the miserable Queen *1863:* the fury of the Queen 26| *1842:* Intolerable life, and *1849:* Life insupportable, and *1863:* insupportable; and 27| *1842:* race had right *1849:* race should dare

To scorn her, perished by the murderous cord:
Yet, ere she perished, blasted in a scroll
The fame of him her swerving made not swerve.
And Theseus, read, returning, and believed,
And exiled, in the blindness of his wrath,
The man without a crime who, last as first,
Loyal, divulged not to his sire the truth.
Now Theseus from Poseidon had obtained
That of his wishes should be granted three,
And one he imprecated straight—"Alive
May ne'er Hippolutos reach other lands!"
Poseidon heard, ai ai! And scarce the prince
Had stepped into the fixed boots of the car
That give the feet a stay against the strength
Of the Henetian horses, and around
His body flung the rein, and urged their speed
Along the rocks and shingles of the shore,
When from the gaping wave a monster flung
His obscene body in the coursers' path.
These, mad with terror, as the sea-bull sprawled
Wallowing about their feet, lost care of him
That reared them; and the master-chariot-pole
Snapping beneath their plunges like a reed,
Hippolutos, whose feet were trammelled fast,
Was yet dragged forward by the circling rein
Which either hand directed; nor they quenched
The frenzy of their flight before each trace,
Wheel-spoke and splinter of the woeful car,
Each boulder-stone, sharp stub and spiny shell,
Huge fish-bone wrecked and wreathed amid the sands
On that detested beach, was bright with blood
And morsels of his flesh: then fell the steeds

30| *1842:* swerve, *1863:* swerve. 31| *1842:* Which Theseus saw, returning *1849:* Which Theseus read, returning 32| *1842:* So, in <> wrath exiled *1849:* So, exiled in <> wrath, *1863:* And exiled, in 33| *1842:* crime, who *1863:* crime who 35| *1842:* But Theseus *1849:* Now Theseus 36| *1842:* Three, *1868:* three, 37| *1842:* And this one imprecated now—alive *1849:* this he imprecated straight—alive *1863:* And one he *1868:* straight—"Alive 38| *1842:* lands! *1868:* lands!" 40| *1842:* car, *1863:* car 43| *1842:* reins *1868:* rein 46| *1842:* path: *1849:* path! *1863:* path. 47| *1842:* terror as *1863:* terror, as 51| *1842:* trammeled sure, *1849:* trammeled fast, *1868:* trammelled 53| *1842:* nor they quenched *1849:* nor was quenched *1863:* nor they quenched 56| *1842:* stub, and *1863:* stub and 61| *1842:* horror fixed. *1849:*

Head-foremost, crashing in their mooned fronts,
Shivering with sweat, each white eye horror-fixed.
His people, who had witnessed all afar,
Bore back the ruins of Hippolutos.
But when his sire, too swoln with pride, rejoiced
(Indomitable as a man foredoomed)
That vast Poseidon had fulfilled his prayer,
I, in a flood of glory visible,
Stood o'er my dying votary and, deed
By deed, revealed, as all took place, the truth.
Then Theseus lay the woefullest of men,
And worthily; but ere the death-veils hid
His face, the murdered prince full pardon breathed
To his rash sire. Whereat Athenai wails.

So I, who ne'er forsake my votaries,
Lest in the cross-way none the honey-cake
Should tender, nor pour out the dog's hot life;
Lest at my fane the priests disconsolate
Should dress my image with some faded poor
Few crowns, made favours of, nor dare object
Such slackness to my worshippers who turn
Elsewhere the trusting heart and loaded hand,
As they had climbed Olumpos to report
Of Artemis and nowhere found her throne—
I interposed: and, this eventful night,—
(While round the funeral pyre the populace
Stood with fierce light on their black robes which bound
Each sobbing head, while yet their hair they clipped
O'er the dead body of their withered prince,
And, in his palace, Theseus prostrated

---

horror-fixed. 64| *1842:* rejoiced, *1863:* rejoiced 65| *1842:* Indomitable <> foredoomed, *1849:* (Indomitable <> foredoomed) 68| *1842:* votary, and deed *1863:* votary and, deed 69| *1842:* deed revealed *1863:* deed, revealed 73| *1842:* sire. Whence now Athenai *1849:* sire. Whereat Athenai 73–74| *1842:* § no space § *1868:* § space § 74| *1842:* But I *1849:* So I *1868:* ¶ So 77| *1842:* fane disconsolate the priests *1849:* fane the priests disconsolate 79| *1842:* favors *1849:* favours 81| *1849:* The trusting <> hand elsewhere, *1868:* Elsewhere the <> hand, 84| *1842:* night, *1868:* night,— 85| *1842:* While *1868:* (While 86| *1842:* Stand <> robes that blind *1849:* Stood *1863:* robes to blind *1868:* robes which bound 87| *1842:* clip *1849:*

On the cold hearth, his brow cold as the slab
'Twas bruised on, groaned away the heavy grief—
As the pyre fell, and down the cross logs crashed
Sending a crowd of sparkles through the night,
And the gay fire, elate with mastery,
Towered like a serpent o'er the clotted jars
Of wine, dissolving oils and frankincense,
And splendid gums like gold),—my potency
Conveyed the perished man to my retreat
In the thrice-venerable forest here.
And this white-bearded sage who squeezes now
The berried plant, is Phoibos' son of fame,
Asclepios, whom my radiant brother taught
The doctrine of each herb and flower and root,
To know their secret'st virtue and express
The saving soul of all: who so has soothed
With lavers the torn brow and murdered cheeks,
Composed the hair and brought its gloss again,
And called the red bloom to the pale skin back,
And laid the strips and jagged ends of flesh
Even once more, and slacked the sinew's knot
Of every tortured limb—that now he lies
As if mere sleep possessed him underneath
These interwoven oaks and pines. Oh cheer,
Divine presenter of the healing rod,
Thy snake, with ardent throat and lulling eye,
Twines his lithe spires around! I say, much cheer!
Proceed thou with thy wisest pharmacies!
And ye, white crowd of woodland sister-nymphs,
Ply, as the sage directs, these buds and leaves
That strew the turf around the twain! While I
Await, in fitting silence, the event.

---

clipped 91| *1842:* 'Tis <> groans *1849:* 'Twas <> groaned 92| *1842:* crashed, *1863:* crashed 93| *1842:* thro' *1863:* through 97| *1842:* gold,—my *1868:* gold,)—my 99| *1842:* thrice venerable *1863:* thrice-venerable 100| *1842:* Sage *1863:* sage 101| *1842:* plant is *1849:* plant, is 105| *1842:* all-who *1863:* all: who 113| *1842:* pines. Oh, cheer, *1868:* pines. Oh cheer, 114| *1842:* rod *1863:* rod, 119| *1842:* Sage *1863:* sage 120| *1842:* Twain *1863:* twain 121| *1842:* In fitting silence the event await. *1849:* Await, in fitting silence, the event.

WARING

I

I

What's become of Waring
Since he gave us all the slip,
Chose land-travel or seafaring,
Boots and chest or staff and scrip,
Rather than pace up and down
Any longer London town?

II

Who'd have guessed it from his lip
Or his brow's accustomed bearing,
On the night he thus took ship
Or started landward?—little caring
For us, it seems, who supped together
(Friends of his too, I remember)
And walked home thro' the merry weather,
The snowiest in all December.
I left his arm that night myself
For what's-his-name's, the new prose-poet
Who wrote the book there, on the shelf—
How, forsooth, was I to know it
If Waring meant to glide away
Like a ghost at break of day?
Never looked he half so gay!

WARING § Subsequent placement: 1849: *DRL;* 1863: *DR* § 4| *1842:* chest, or *1863:* chest or 6| *1842:* London-town? *1868:* London town? 7| *1842:* lip, *1863:* lip 9| *1842:* ship, *1868:* ship 10| *1842:* landward, little *1849:* landward?—little 11| *1842:* together, *1863:* together 14| *1842:* Snowiest <> December; *1849:* The snowiest *1863:* all December. 16| *1842:* prose-poet, *1863:* prose-poet 17| *1842:* That wrote *1868:* Who wrote

III

He was prouder than the devil:
How he must have cursed our revel!
Ay and many other meetings,
Indoor visits, outdoor greetings,
As up and down he paced this London,
With no work done, but great works undone,
Where scarce twenty knew his name.
Why not, then, have earlier spoken,
Written, bustled? Who's to blame
If your silence kept unbroken?
"True, but there were sundry jottings,
Stray-leaves, fragments, blurrs and blottings,
Certain first steps were achieved
Already which"—(is that your meaning?)
"Had well borne out whoe'er believed
In more to come!" But who goes gleaning
Hedgeside chance-blades, while full-sheaved
Stand cornfields by him? Pride, o'erweening
Pride alone, puts forth such claims
O'er the day's distinguished names.

IV

Meantime, how much I loved him,
I find out now I've lost him.
I who cared not if I moved him,
Who could so carelessly accost him,
Henceforth never shall get free
Of his ghostly company,
His eyes that just a little wink
As deep I go into the merit
Of this and that distinguished spirit—
His cheeks' raised colour, soon to sink,

22| *1842:* Devil: *1868:* devil: 24| *1842:* Ay, and *1868:* Ay and 32| *1842:* True *1849:* "True 35| *1842:* which—(is *1849:* which"—(is 36| *1842:* Had *1849:* "Had 37| *1842:* come: but *1849:* come!" But 38| *1842:* Hedge-side *1888:* Hedgeside 43| *1842:* him: *1868:* him. 44| *1842:* I, who *1868:* I who 45| *1842:* —Could *1849:* Who could 46| *1842:* Never *1849:* Henceforth never 48| *1842:* And eyes *1849:* His eyes 53| *1842:*

As long I dwell on some stupendous
And tremendous (Heaven defend us!)
Monstr'-inform'-ingens-horrend-ous
Demoniaco-seraphic
Penman's latest piece of graphic.
Nay, my very wrist grows warm
With his dragging weight of arm.
E'en so, swimmingly appears,
Through one's after-supper musings,
Some lost lady of old years
With her beauteous vain endeavour
And goodness unrepaid as ever;
The face, accustomed to refusings,
We, puppies that we were . . . Oh never
Surely, nice of conscience, scrupled
Being aught like false, forsooth, to?
Telling aught but honest truth to?
What a sin, had we centupled
Its possessor's grace and sweetness!
No! she heard in its completeness
Truth, for truth's a weighty matter,
And truth, at issue, we can't flatter!
Well, 'tis done with; she's exempt
From damning us thro' such a sally;
And so she glides, as down a valley,
Taking up with her contempt,
Past our reach; and in, the flowers
Shut her unregarded hours.

---

tremendous (God defend *1849:* tremendous (Heaven defend 58| *1842:* arm! *1868:* arm. 60| *1842:* Thro' *1863:* Through 61| *1842:* lost Lady of <> years, *1863:* years *1868:* lady 62| *1842:* endeavour, *1863:* endeavour 69| *1842:* sin had *1849:* sin, had 73| *1842:* And, truth *1863:* And truth 74| *1842:* with: she's *1863:* with; she's 84| *1842:* bent! *1868:* bent.

V

Oh, could I have him back once more,
This Waring, but one half-day more!
Back, with the quiet face of yore,
So hungry for acknowledgment
Like mine! I'd fool him to his bent.
Feed, should not he, to heart's content?
I'd say, " to only have conceived,
Planned your great works, apart from progress,
Surpasses little works achieved!"
I'd lie so, I should be believed.
I'd make such havoc of the claims
Of the day's distinguished names
To feast him with, as feasts an ogress
Her feverish sharp-toothed gold-crowned child!
Or as one feasts a creature rarely
Captured here, unreconciled
To capture; and completely gives
Its pettish humours license, barely
Requiring that it lives.

VI

Ichabod, Ichabod,
The glory is departed!
Travels Waring East away?
Who, of knowledge, by hearsay,
Reports a man upstarted
Somewhere as a god,
Hordes grown European-hearted,
Millions of the wild made tame
On a sudden at his fame?
In Vishnu-land what Avatar?
Or who in Moscow, toward the Czar,

86| *1842:* conceived *1868:* conceived, 87| *1842:* Your great works, tho' they never progress, *1849:* they ne'er make progress, *1868:* Planned your great works, apart from progress, 88| *1842:* Surpasses all we've yet achieved!" *1868:* Surpasses little works achieved!" 93| *1842:* Her sharp-toothed golden-crowned *1868:* Her feverish sharp-toothed gold-crowned 94| *1842:* Or, as *1868:* Or as 104| *1842:* God *1868:* god 109| *1842:* Or, North in *1849:* Or who, in *1868:* who in

With the demurest of footfalls
Over the Kremlin's pavement bright
With serpentine and syenite,
Steps, with five other Generals
That simultaneously take snuff,
For each to have pretext enough
And kerchiefwise unfold his sash
Which, softness' self, is yet the stuff
To hold fast where a steel chain snaps,
And leave the grand white neck no gash?
Waring in Moscow, to those rough
Cold northern natures born perhaps,
Like the lambwhite maiden dear
From the circle of mute kings
Unable to repress the tear,
Each as his sceptre down he flings,
To Dian's fane at Taurica,
Where now a captive priestess, she alway
Mingles her tender grave Hellenic speech
With theirs, tuned to the hailstone-beaten beach
As pours some pigeon, from the myrrhy lands
Rapt by the whirlblast to fierce Scythian strands
Where breed the swallows, her melodious cry
Amid their barbarous twitter!
In Russia? Never! Spain were fitter!
Ay, most likely 'tis in Spain
That we and Waring meet again
Now, while he turns down that cool narrow lane
Into the blackness, out of grave Madrid
All fire and shine, abrupt as when there's slid
Its stiff gold blazing pall

110| *1842:* Who, with the gentlest of *1849:* With the demurest of 111| *1842:* pavement, bright *1868:* pavement bright 112| *1842:* siennite, *1849:* syenite, 113| *1842:* other Generals, *1863:* other Generals 114| *1842:* Who simultaneously *1849:* That simultaneously 115| *1842:* That each may have *1849:* For each to have 116| *1842:* kerchiefwise unfurl his *1863:* kerchiefwise unfold his 120| *1842:* In Moscow, Waring, to *1849:* Waring, in Moscow, to *1868:* Waring in 121| *1842:* Cold natures borne, perhaps, *1849:* Cold northern natures borne *1868:* born 122| *1842:* maiden, (clear *1849:* maiden dear 123| *1842:* Thro' the <> kings, *1849:* From the *1863:* kings 125| *1842:* flings), *1849:* flings, 126| *1842:* To the Dome at *1849:* To Dian's fane at 127| *1842:* a priestess *1849:* a captive priestess 129| *1842:* beach, *1868:* beach 136| *1842:* again— *1863:* again 139| *1842:* shine—abrupt *1863:*

From some black coffin-lid.
Or, best of all,
I love to think
The leaving us was just a feint;
Back here to London did he slink,
And now works on without a wink
Of sleep, and we are on the brink
Of something great in fresco-paint:
Some garret's ceiling, walls and floor,
Up and down and o'er and o'er
He splashes, as none splashed before
Since great Caldara Polidore.
Or Music means this land of ours
Some favour yet, to pity won
By Purcell from his Rosy Bowers,—
"Give me my so-long promised son,
Let Waring end what I begun!"
Then down he creeps and out he steals
Only when the night conceals
His face; in Kent 'tis cherry-time,
Or hops are picking: or at prime
Of March he wanders as, too happy,
Years ago when he was young,
Some mild eve when woods grew sappy
And the early moths had sprung
To life from many a trembling sheath
Woven the warm boughs beneath;
While small birds said to themselves
What should soon be actual song,
And young gnats, by tens and twelves,
Made as if they were the throng
That crowd around and carry aloft
The sound they have nursed, so sweet and pure,
Out of a myriad noises soft,
Into a tone that can endure

---

shine, abrupt 145| *1842:* slink; *1863:* slink, 152–158| *1842:* great Caldara Polidore: / Then *1849:* § adds 153–157 § 152| *1842:* great Caldara Polidore: *1863:* great Caldara Polidore. 154| *1849:* favor *1863:* favour 156| *1849:* so long *1863:* so-long 160| *1842:* face—in *1863:* face; in 161| *1842:* Or, hops are picking; or, at *1863:* picking: or *1868:* Or hops <> or at 162| *1842:* Of March, he steals as when, too *1849:* he wanders as, too *1868:* Of March he 164| *1842:* woods were sappy, *1849:* woods grew sappy, *1863:* sappy

Amid the noise of a July noon
When all God's creatures crave their boon,
All at once and all in tune,
And get it, happy as Waring then,
Having first within his ken
What a man might do with men:
And far too glad, in the even-glow,
To mix with the world he meant to take
Into his hand, he told you, so—
And out of it his world to make,
To contract and to expand
As he shut or oped his hand.
Oh Waring, what's to really be?
A clear stage and a crowd to see!
Some Garrick, say, out shall not he
The heart of Hamlet's mystery pluck?
Or, where most unclean beasts are rife,
Some Junius—am I right?—shall tuck
His sleeve, and forth with flaying-knife!
Some Chatterton shall have the luck
Of calling Rowley into life!
Some one shall somehow run a muck
With this old world for want of strife
Sound asleep. Contrive, contrive
To rouse us, Waring! Who's alive?
Our men scarce seem in earnest now.
Distinguished names!—but 'tis, somehow,
As if they played at being names
Still more distinguished, like the games
Of children. Turn our sport to earnest
With a visage of the sternest!
Bring the real times back, confessed
Still better than our very best!

176| *1842:* noon, *1863:* noon 181| *1842:* men, *1868:* men: 188| *1842:* Oh, Waring *1868:* Oh Waring 190| *1842:* Some Garrick—say—out *1868:* Some Garrick, say, out 194| *1842:* and out with *1863:* and forth with 198| *1842:* world, for *1868:* world for 199| *1842:* asleep: contrive *1863:* asleep. Contrive 201| *1842:* now: *1863:* now. 202| *1842:* names, but *1849:* names!—but 208| *1842:* than the very *1849:* than our very 210| *1842:*

II

I

"When I last saw Waring . . ."
(How all turned to him who spoke!
You saw Waring? Truth or joke?
In land-travel or sea-faring?)

II

"We were sailing by Triest
Where a day or two we harboured:
A sunset was in the West,
When, looking over the vessel's side,
One of our company espied
A sudden speck to larboard.
And as a sea-duck flies and swims
At once, so came the light craft up,
With its sole lateen sail that trims
And turns (the water round its rims
Dancing, as round a sinking cup)
And by us like a fish it curled,
And drew itself up close beside,
Its great sail on the instant furled,
And o'er its thwarts a shrill voice cried,
(A neck as bronzed as a Lascar's)
'Buy wine of us, you English Brig?
Or fruit, tobacco and cigars?
A pilot for you to Triest?
Without one, look you ne'er so big,
They'll never let you up the bay!
We natives should know best.'
I turned, and 'just those fellows' way,'
Our captain said, 'The 'long-shore thieves
Are laughing at us in their sleeves.'

---

spoke— *1868:* spoke! 212| *1842:* land-travel, or *1868:* land-travel or 213| *1842:* by Triest, *1868:* by Triest 219| *1842:* And, as *1868:* And as 223| *1842:* Dancing as *1849:* Dancing, as 227| *1842:* its planks, a *1868:* its thwarts a 231| *1842:* Pilot *1868:* pilot 241| *1842:* hat, and *1863:* hat

III

"In truth, the boy leaned laughing back;
And one, half-hidden by his side
Under the furled sail, soon I spied,
With great grass hat and kerchief black,
Who looked up with his kingly throat,
Said somewhat, while the other shook
His hair back from his eyes to look
Their longest at us; then the boat,
I know not how, turned sharply round,
Laying her whole side on the sea
As a leaping fish does; from the lee
Into the weather, cut somehow
Her sparkling path beneath our bow
And so went off, as with a bound,
Into the rosy and golden half
O' the sky, to overtake the sun
And reach the shore, like the sea-calf
Its singing cave; yet I caught one
Glance ere away the boat quite passed,
And neither time nor toil could mar
Those features: so I saw the last
Of Waring!"—You? Oh, never star
Was lost here but it rose afar!
Look East, where whole new thousands are!
In Vishnu-land what Avatar?

---

and 242| *1842:* up, with *1863:* up with 243| *1842:* somewhat while *1849:* somewhat, while 245| *1842:* us; and the *1849:* us; then the 248| *1863:* lee, *1868:* lee 249| *1842:* weather cut *1849:* weather, cut 250| *1842:* bow; *1868:* bow 252| *1842:* the rose and *1863:* the rosy and 253| *1842:* Of <> sun, *1863:* sun *1868:* O' 254| *1842:* shore like *1849:* shore, like 260| *1842:* here, but *1868:* here but

RUDEL TO THE LADY OF TRIPOLI

I

I know a Mount, the gracious Sun perceives
First, when he visits, last, too, when he leaves
The world; and, vainly favoured, it repays
The day-long glory of his steadfast gaze
By no change of its large calm front of snow.
And underneath the Mount, a Flower I know,
He cannot have perceived, that changes ever
At his approach; and, in the lost endeavour
To live his life, has parted, one by one,
With all a flower's true graces, for the grace
Of being but a foolish mimic sun,
With ray-like florets round a disk like face.
Men nobly call by many a name the Mount
As over many a land of theirs its large
Calm front of snow like a triumphal targe
Is reared, and still with old names, fresh names vie,
Each to its proper praise and own account:
Men call the Flower the Sunflower, sportively.

II

Oh, Angel of the East, one, one gold look
Across the waters to this twilight nook,
—The far sad waters, Angel, to this nook!

RUDEL TO THE LADY OF TRIPOLI § Subsequent placement: 1849: *DRL;* 1863: *MW;* In 1842 this and the following poem were grouped together under the title *Queen-Worship* § Title/ *1842:* I.—RUDEL AND THE *1849:* RUDEL TO THE 1| *1842:* a Mount the Sun *1849:* a Mount, the gracious Sun 2| *1842:* First when he visits *1868:* First, when he visits 3| *1842:* and it *1849:* and, vainly favored, it *1863:* favoured 4| *1842:* his gaze *1849:* his steadfast gaze 5| *1842:* calm steadfast front *1849:* calm front 6| *1842:* A *1849:* And underneath the Mount, a 8| *1842:* approach, and in *1849:* approach; and, in 9| *1842:* life has *1849:* life, has 13| *1842:* the Mount, *1863:* the Mount 15| *1842:* Calm steadfast front like *1849:* Calm front of snow like 16| *1842:* fresh ones vie, *1868:* fresh names vie, 18| *1842:* the Flower, the *1888:* the Flower the 23| *1842:* Go! Saying

III

Dear Pilgrim, art thou for the East indeed?
Go!—saying ever as thou dost proceed,
That I, French Rudel, choose for my device
A sunflower outspread like a sacrifice
Before its idol. See! These inexpert
And hurried fingers could not fail to hurt
The woven picture; 'tis a woman's skill
Indeed; but nothing baffled me, so, ill
Or well, the work is finished. Say, men feed
On songs I sing, and therefore bask the bees
On my flower's breast as on a platform broad:
But, as the flower's concern is not for these
But solely for the sun, so men applaud
In vain this Rudel, he not looking here
But to the East—the East! Go, say this, Pilgrim dear!

1868: Go!—saying   26| *1842:* idol: see   *1849:* idol. See   32| *1842:* On the flower's   *1849:* On my flower's

CRISTINA

I

She should never have looked at me
    If she meant I should not love her!
There are plenty . . . men, you call such
    I suppose . . . she may discover
All her soul to, if she pleases,
    And yet leave much as she found them:
But I'm not so, and she knew it
    When she fixed me, glancing round them.

II

What? To fix me thus meant nothing?
    But I can't tell (there's my weakness)
What her look said!—no vile cant, sure,
    About "need to strew the bleakness
Of some lone shore with its pearl-seed,
    That the sea feels"—no "strange yearning
That such souls have, most to lavish
    Where there's chance of least returning."

CRISTINA § Subsequent placement: 1849: *DRL;* 1863: *DL* § Title/ *1842:* II.—CRISTINA *1849:* CRISTINA 1| *1842:* should not have <> me, *1849:* should never have *1863:* me 2| *1842:* her: *1849:* her! 3| *1842:* There's plenty . . men *1849:* There are plenty *1888:* plenty . . . men 4| *1842:* suppose . . she *1888:* suppose . . . she 6| *1842:* them. *1849:* them: 10| *1842:* tell . . . there's my weakness . . *1863:* tell (there's my weakness) 11| *1842:* said: no *1849:* said!—no 14| *1842:* Sea *1863:* sea 21| *1842:* Stand plain out from *1849:*

III

Oh, we're sunk enough here, God knows!
 But not quite so sunk that moments,
Sure tho' seldom, are denied us,
 When the spirit's true endowments
Stand out plainly from its false ones,
 And apprise it if pursuing
Or the right way or the wrong way,
 To its triumph or undoing.

IV

There are flashes struck from midnights,
 There are fire-flames noondays kindle,
Whereby piled-up honours perish,
 Whereby swollen ambitions dwindle,
While just this or that poor impulse,
 Which for once had play unstifled,
Seems the sole work of a life-time
 That away the rest have trifled.

V

Doubt you if, in some such moment,
 As she fixed me, she felt clearly,
Ages past the soul existed,
 Here an age 'tis resting merely,
And hence fleets again for ages,
 While the true end, sole and single,
It stops here for is, this love-way,
 With some other soul to mingle?

Stand out plainly from 23| *1849:* The right *1849:* Or the right 27| *1842:* honors *1863:* honours 28| *1842:* swoln *1868:* swollen 29| *1842:* While this *1849:* While just this 30| *1863:* unstifled *1888:* unstifled, 32| *1842:* Away *1849:* That away 37| *1842:* Hence, fleets <> ages: *1849:* And hence *1863:* hence fleets <> ages, 38| *1842:* And

VI

Else it loses what it lived for,
And eternally must lose it;
Better ends may be in prospect,
Deeper blisses (if you choose it),
But this life's end and this love-bliss
Have been lost here. Doubt you whether
This she felt as, looking at me,
Mine and her souls rushed together?

VII

Oh, observe! Of course, next moment,
The world's honours, in derision,
Trampled out the light for ever:
Never fear but there's provision
Of the devil's to quench knowledge
Lest we walk the earth in rapture!
—Making those who catch God's secret
Just so much more prize their capture!

VIII

Such am I: the secret's mine now!
She has lost me, I have gained her;
Her soul's mine: and thus, grown perfect,
I shall pass my life's remainder.
Life will just hold out the proving
Both our powers, alone and blended:
And then, come next life quickly!
This world's use will have been ended.

---

the *1849:* While the 41| *1842:* for *1868:* for, 44| *1842:* blisses, if <> it, *1863:* blisses (if <>it) *1868:* it), 47| *1842:* felt, as *1863:* felt as 48| *1842:* together. *1868:* together? 50| *1842:* honors *1863:* honours 53| *1842:* Devil's *1868:* devil's 55| *1842:* Making <> catch the secret *1849:* —Making <> catch God's secret 56| *1842:* capture. *1863:* capture! 58| *1842:* me—I <> her! *1863:* me, I <> her; 59| *1842:* mine: And, thus *1863:* mine. And thus 60| *1842:* remainder, *1863:* remainder. 61| *1842:* That just holds out *1849:* Life will just hold out 62| *1842:* Our <> blended— *1849:* Both our *1863:* blended; *1868:* blended: 63| *1842:* quickly, *1849:* quickly! 64| *1842:* This life will <> ended! *1849:* This world's use will <> ended.

JOHANNES AGRICOLA IN MEDITATION

There's heaven above, and night by night
I look right through its gorgeous roof;
No suns and moons through e'er so bright
Avail to stop me; splendour-proof
I keep the broods of stars aloof:
For I intend to get to God,
For 'tis to God I speed so fast,
For in God's breast, my own abode,
Those shoals of dazzling glory, passed,
I lay my spirit down at last.
I lie where I have always lain,
God smiles as he has always smiled;
Ere suns and moons could wax and wane,
Ere stars were thundergirt, or piled
The heavens, God thought on me his child;
Ordained a life for me, arrayed

JOHANNES AGRICOLA IN MEDITATION § First published January, 1836 in the *Monthly Repository*, where it was signed "Z." Subsequent placement: 1863: *DR;* 1868: *MW*. In 1842 this and the following poem were grouped together under the title MADHOUSE CELLS § Title / *1836:* JOHANNES AGRICOLA. *1842:* I. *1849:* I.—MADHOUSE CELL. JOHANNES AGRICOLA IN MEDITATION Headnote / § appeared only in 1836 § "Antinomians, so denominated for rejecting the Law as a thing of no use under the Gospel dispensation: they say, that good works do not further, nor evil works hinder salvation; that the child of God cannot sin, that God never chastiseth him, that murder, drunkenness, &c. are sins in the wicked but not in him, that the child of grace being once assured of salvation, afterwards never doubteth ...... that God doth not love any man for his holiness, that sanctification is no evidence of justification, &c. Pontanus, in his Catalogue of Heresies, says John Agricola was the author of this sect, A.D. 1535."—*Dictionary of all Religions,* 1704 1–60| *1836:* § every fifth line not indented § *1868:* § every fifth line indented § 1| *1836:* There's Heaven above: and *1842:* above, and *1849:* by night, *1863:* heaven *1868:* by night 2| *1836:* roof— *1842:* roof; 4| *1836:* me:—splendor-proof *1842:* me; splendor-proof *1888:* splendour-proof 6| *1836:* to God . . . *1842:* to God, 7| *1836:* fast! *1842:* fast, 9| *1836:* glory past, *1863:* glory, past, *1868:* passed, 11| *1836:* lie—where *1842:* lie where 12| *1836:* smiles—as <> smiled;— *1842:* smiles as <> smiled; *1863:* He *1868:* he 15| *1836:* heavens . . . God *1842:* The Heavens, God *1863:* heavens <> His *1868:* his 16| *1836:* me—arrayed *1842:* me, arrayed

Its circumstances every one
To the minutest; ay, God said
This head this hand should rest upon
Thus, ere he fashioned star or sun.
And having thus created me,
Thus rooted me, he bade me grow,
Guiltless for ever, like a tree
That buds and blooms, nor seeks to know
The law by which it prospers so:
But sure that thought and word and deed
All go to swell his love for me,
Me, made because that love had need
Of something irreversibly
Pledged solely its content to be.
Yes, yes, a tree which must ascend,
No poison-gourd foredoomed to stoop.
I have God's warrant, could I blend
All hideous sins, as in a cup,
To drink the mingled venoms up;
Secure my nature will convert
The draught to blossoming gladness fast:
While sweet dews turn to the gourd's hurt,
And bloat, and while they bloat it, blast,
As from the first its lot was cast.
For as I lie, smiled on, full-fed
By unexhausted power to bless,
I gaze below on hell's fierce bed,
And those its waves of flame oppress,
Swarming in ghastly wretchedness;
Whose life on earth aspired to be

17| *1836:* circumstances, every *1868:* circumstances every 18| *1836:* minutest . . . ay *1842:* minutest; ay 20| *1836:* Thus,—ere <> sun! *1842:* Thus, ere <> sun. *1863:* He *1868:* he 22| *1836:* grow— *1842:* grow, 25| *1836:* A law *1849:* The law 27| *1836:* me— *1842:* me, *1863:* His *1868:* his 28| *1836:* Me—made *1842:* Me made *1849:* Me, made 29| *1836:* something irrevocably *1868:* something irreversibly 31| *1836:* yes,—a <> ascend— *1842:* yes, a <> ascend, *1849:* ascend,— *1863:* ascend, 32| *1836:* stoop: *1842:* stoop! *1888:* stoop. 34| *1836:* cup,— *1842:* cup, 35| *1836:* up, *1868:* up; 37| *1836:* fast: *1842:* fast, *1868:* fast: 39| *1836:* blast— *1842:* blast, 41| *1836:* full fed *1868:* full-fed 42| *1836:* With unexhausted blessedness,— *1842:* By unexhausted power to bless, 43| *1836:* Hell's *1868:* hell's 45| *1836:* wretchedness, *1849:* wretchedness; 46| *1836:* whose like

One altar-smoke, so pure!—to win
If not love like God's love for me,
At least to keep his anger in;
And all their striving turned to sin.
Priest, doctor, hermit, monk grown white
With prayer, the broken-hearted nun,
The martyr, the wan acolyte,
The incense-swinging child,—undone
Before God fashioned star or sun!
God, whom I praise; how could I praise,
If such as I might understand,
Make out and reckon on his ways,
And bargain for his love, and stand,
Paying a price, at his right hand?

---

on *1842:* whose life on 47| *1836:* altar-smoke,—so *1842:* altar-smoke, so 48| *1836:* like God's love to me, *1868:* like God's love for me, 49| *1836:* in . . . *1842:* in, *1863:* keep His anger in; *1868:* his 50| *1836:* sin! *1863:* sin. 51| *1836:* § line indented § *1868:* § line not indented § 52| *1836:* § line not indented § prayer: the broken hearted nun, *1842:* prayer, the broken-hearted nun, *1868:* § line indented § 53| *1836:* § line indented § *1868:* § line not indented § 54| *1836:* § line not indented § child . . . undone *1842:* child,—undone *1868:* § line indented § 56| *1836:* God—whom I praise . . . how <> praise *1842:* God, whom I praise; how *1849:* could I praise, 58| *1836:* out, and *1842:* on, his *1863:* out and <> on His *1868:* his 59| *1842:* His *1868:* his

PORPHYRIA'S LOVER

The rain set early in to-night,
The sullen wind was soon awake,
It tore the elm-tops down for spite,
And did its worst to vex the lake:
I listened with heart fit to break.
When glided in Porphyria; straight
She shut the cold out and the storm,
And kneeled and made the cheerless grate
Blaze up, and all the cottage warm;
Which done, she rose, and from her form
Withdrew the dripping cloak and shawl,
And laid her soiled gloves by, untied
Her hat and let the damp hair fall,
And, last, she sat down by my side
And called me. When no voice replied,
She put my arm about her waist,
And made her smooth white shoulder bare,
And all her yellow hair displaced,
And, stooping, made my cheek lie there,
And spread, o'er all, her yellow hair,
Murmuring how she loved me—she
Too weak, for all her heart's endeavour,
To set its struggling passion free
From pride, and vainer ties dissever,
And give herself to me for ever.
But passion sometimes would prevail,
Nor could to-night's gay feast restrain
A sudden thought of one so pale

PORPHYRIA'S LOVER § First published January, 1836 in the *Monthly Repository,* where it was signed "Z." Subsequent placement: 1863: *DR* § Title / *1836:* PORPHYRIA. *1842:* II. *1849:* II.—MADHOUSE CELL. / PORPHYRIA'S LOVER *1863:* PORPHYRIA'S LOVER 1–60| *1842:* § every fifth line not indented § *1888:* § every fifth line indented § 1| *1836:* to-night: *1842:* to-night, 2| *1836:* awake— *1842:* awake, 4| *1842:* lake, *1888:* lake: 5| *1836:* listened, with <> break, *1842:* listened with *1849:* break; *1863:* break. 6| *1842:* in Porphyria: straight *1863:* in Porphyria; straight 12| *1836:* by; untied *1842:* by, untied 14| *1836:* sate *1863:* sat 19| *1836:* there *1842:* there, 20| *1836:* spread o'er all her *1868:* spread, o'er all, her 21| *1842:* me; she *1863:* me—she 25| *1836:* ever: *1863:* ever. 29| *1836:* her—and <> vain; *1842:* her, and

For love of her, and all in vain:
So, she was come through wind and rain.
Be sure I looked up at her eyes
Happy and proud; at last I knew
Porphyria worshipped me; surprise
Made my heart swell, and still it grew
While I debated what to do.
That moment she was mine, mine, fair,
Perfectly pure and good: I found
A thing to do, and all her hair
In one long yellow string I wound
Three times her little throat around,
And strangled her. No pain felt she;
I am quite sure she felt no pain.
As a shut bud that holds a bee,
I warily oped her lids: again
Laughed the blue eyes without a stain.
And I untightened next the tress
About her neck; her cheek once more
Blushed bright beneath my burning kiss:
I propped her head up as before,
Only, this time my shoulder bore
Her head, which droops upon it still:
The smiling rosy little head,
So glad it has its utmost will,
That all it scorned at once is fled,
And I, its love, am gained instead!
Porphyria's love: she guessed not how
Her darling one wish would be heard.
And thus we sit together now,
And all night long we have not stirred,
And yet God has not said a word!

1868: vain: 30| *1836:* And she *1849:* So, she 32| *1836:* Proud—very proud—at *1842:* Proud, very proud; at *1863:* Happy and proud 33| *1836:* me: surprise *1842:* me; surprise 36| *1836:* mine,—mine, fair *1842:* mine, mine, fair, 40| *1836:* around *1842:* around, 41| *1836:* she— *1842:* she: *1849:* she; 43| *1836:* bee *1863:* bee, 44| *1836:* lids—again *1842:* lids; again *1868:* lids: again 47| *1836:* neck—her *1842:* neck; her 50| *1836: my* *1842:* my *1849: my* *1868:* my 51| *1836:* head—which *1842:* head, which 52| *1836:* head! *1842:* head, 53| *1836:* will; *1842:* will, 55| *1836:* instead, *1842:* instead! 57| *1836:* darling, one *1842:* darling one 58| *1836:* now: *1842:* now, 59| *1836:* stirred,— *1842:* stirred,

THROUGH THE METIDJA TO ABD-EL-KADR

I

As I ride, as I ride,
With a full heart for my guide,
So its tide rocks my side,
As I ride, as I ride,
That, as I were double-eyed,
He, in whom our Tribes confide,
Is descried, ways untried
As I ride, as I ride.

II

As I ride, as I ride
To our Chief and his Allied,
Who dares chide my heart's pride
As I ride, as I ride?
Or are witnesses denied—
Through the desert waste and wide
Do I glide unespied
As I ride, as I ride?

III

As I ride, as I ride,
When an inner voice has cried,
The sands slide, nor abide
(As I ride, as I ride)
O'er each visioned homicide
That came vaunting (has he lied?)
To reside—where he died,
As I ride, as I ride.

THROUGH THE METIDJA TO ABD-EL-KADR § Subsequent placement: 1849: *DRL;* 1863: *DL* § 21| *1842:* Homicide *1863:* homicide 23| *1842:* To abide—where he

IV

As I ride, as I ride,
Ne'er has spur my swift horse plied,
Yet his hide, streaked and pied,
As I ride, as I ride,
Shows where sweat has sprung and dried,
—Zebra-footed, ostrich-thighed—
How has vied stride with stride
As I ride, as I ride!

V

As I ride, as I ride,
Could I loose what Fate has tied,
Ere I pried, she should hide
(As I ride, as I ride)
All that's meant me—satisfied
When the Prophet and the Bride
Stop veins I'd have subside
As I ride, as I ride!

---

died *1849:* To reside—where he died, 36| *1842:* As I ride, as I ride, *1863:* (As I ride, as I ride) 37| *1842:* me: satisfied *1863:* me—satisfied

THE PIED PIPER OF HAMELIN;

A CHILD'S STORY

(WRITTEN FOR, AND INSCRIBED TO, W. M. THE YOUNGER.)

I

Hamelin Town's in Brunswick,
By famous Hanover city;
The river Weser, deep and wide,
Washes its wall on the southern side;
A pleasanter spot you never spied;
But, when begins my ditty,
Almost five hundred years ago,
To see the townsfolk suffer so
From vermin, was a pity.

II

Rats!
They fought the dogs and killed the cats,
And bit the babies in the cradles,
And ate the cheeses out of the vats,
And licked the soup from the cooks' own ladles,
Split open the kegs of salted sprats,
Made nests inside men's Sunday hats,
And even spoiled the women's chats
By drowning their speaking
With shrieking and squeaking
In fifty different sharps and flats

THE PIED PIPER OF HAMELIN / A CHILD'S STORY § Subsequent placement: 1849: *DRL;* 1863: *DR* § 6| *1842:* ditty. *1849:* ditty, 11| *1842:* dogs, and *1868:* dogs and 13| *1842:* eat *1849:* ate 17| *1842:* chats, *1888:* chats 23| *1842:*

III

At last the people in a body
To the Town Hall came flocking:
"'Tis clear," cried they, "our Mayor's a noddy;
And as for our Corporation—shocking
To think we buy gowns lined with ermine
For dolts that can't or won't determine
What's best to rid us of our vermin!
You hope, because you're old and obese,
To find in the furry civic robe ease?
Rouse up, sirs! Give your brains a racking
To find the remedy we're lacking,
Or, sure as fate, we'll snd you packing!"
At this the Mayor and Corporation
Quaked with a mighty consternation.

IV

An hour they sat in council,
At length the Mayor broke silence:
"For a guilder I'd my ermine gown sell,
I wish I were a mile hence!
It's easy to bid one rack one's brain—
I'm sure my poor head aches again,
I've scratched it so, and all in vain.
Oh for a trap, a trap, a trap!"
Just as he said this, what should hap
At the chamber door but a gentle tap?
"Bless us," cried the Mayor, "what's that?"
(With the Corporation as he sat,
Looking little though wondrous fat;

'Tis clear, cried they, our *1849:* " 'Tis clear," cried they, "our 27| *1842:* What's like to *1849:* What's best to 27–30| *1842:* vermin! / Rouse *1849:* vermin! / You hope, because you're old and obese, / To find in the furry civic robe ease? / Rouse 30| *1842:* Sirs *1868:* sirs 32| *1842:* packing! *1849:* packing!" 33–34| *1842:* § lines not indented § *1849:* § lines indented § 35| *1842:* sate *1868:* sat 37| *1842:* For <> sell; *1849:* "For *1868:* sell, 40| *1842:* again *1868:* again, 42| *1842:* for a trap, a trap, a trap! *1849:* for a trap, a trap, a trap!" 45| *1842:* Bless us, cried the Mayor, what's that? *1849:* "Bless us," cried the Mayor, "what's that?" 46| *1842:* sate, *1849:* sat, 47–52| *1842:* fat) / Only *1849:*

Nor brighter was his eye, nor moister
Than a too-long-opened oyster,
Save when at noon his paunch grew mutinous
For a plate of turtle green and glutinous)
"Only a scraping of shoes on the mat?
Anything like the sound of a rat
Makes my heart go pit-a-pat!"

V

"Come in!"—the Mayor cried, looking bigger:
And in did come the strangest figure!
His queer long coat from heel to head
Was half of yellow and half of red,
And he himself was tall and thin,
With sharp blue eyes, each like a pin,
And light loose hair, yet swarthy skin,
No tuft on cheek nor beard on chin,
But lips where smiles went out and in;
There was no guessing his kith and kin:
And nobody could enough admire
The tall man and his quaint attire.
Quoth one: "It's as my great-grandsire,
Starting up at the Trump of Doom's tone,
Had walked this way from his painted tomb stone!"

VI

He advanced to the council-table:
And, "Please your honours," said he, "I'm able,
By means of a secret charm, to draw
All creatures living beneath the sun,
That creep or swim or fly or run,

---

§ 48–51 added § fat; //// "Only 53| *1842:* Any thing *1849:* Anything 54| *1842:* pit-a-pat! *1849:* pit-a-pat!" 55| *1842:* Come in!—the *1849:* "Come in!"—the 58| *1842:* red; *1868:* red, 61| *1888:* skin 63| *1842:* in— *1868:* in; 64| *1842:* kin! *1868:* kin: 66| *1842:* attire: *1868:* attire. 67| *1842:* one: It's *1849:* one: "It's 69| *1842:* tomb-stone! *1849:* tomb-stone!" 71| *1842:* And, Please your honours, said he, I'm *1849:* And, "Please your honours," said he, "I'm 72| *1863:* charm to *1868:* charm, to 73| *1842:* § line not indented § *1888:* § line indented § 74| *1842:* § line not

After me so as you never saw!
And I chiefly use my charm
On creatures that do people harm,
The mole and toad and newt and viper;
And people call me the Pied Piper."
(And here they noticed round his neck
A scarf of red and yellow stripe,
To match with his coat of the self-same cheque;
And at the scarf's end hung a pipe;
And his fingers, they noticed, were ever straying
As if impatient to be playing
Upon this pipe, as low it dangled
Over his vesture so old-fangled.)
"Yet," said he, "poor piper as I am,
In Tartary I freed the Cham,
Last June, from his huge swarms of gnats;
I eased in Asia the Nizam
Of a monstrous brood of vampyre-bats:
And as for what your brain bewilders,
If I can rid your town of rats
Will you give me a thousand guilders?"
"One? fifty thousand!"—was the exclamation
Of the astonished Mayor and Corporation.

VII

Into the street the Piper stept,
Smiling first a little smile,
As if he knew what magic slept
In his quiet pipe the while;
Then, like a musical adept,
To blow the pipe his lips he wrinkled,
And green and blue his sharp eyes twinkled,
Like a candle-flame where salt is sprinkled;

---

indented § creep, or swim, or fly, or *1863:* creep or swim or fly or *1888:* § line indented § 78| *1842:* mole, and toad, and newt, and *1863:* mole and toad and newt and 79| *1842:* the Pied Piper. *1849:* the Pied Piper." 81| *1842:* § line not indented § *1888:* § line indented § 93| *1842:* And, as *1863:* And as 94| *1842:* § line not indented § *1888:* § line indented § 95| *1842:* guilders? *1849:* guilders?" 96| *1842:* One <> thousand!—was *1849:* "One <> thousand!"—was 104| *1842:* twinkled *1868:* twinkled, 105| *1842:* candle

And ere three shrill notes the pipe uttered,
You heard as if an army muttered;
And the muttering grew to a grumbling;
And the grumbling grew to a mighty rumbling;
And out of the houses the rats came tumbling.
Great rats, small rats, lean rats, brawny rats,
Brown rats, black rats, grey rats, tawny rats,
Grave old plodders, gay young friskers,
    Fathers, mothers, uncles, cousins,
Cocking tails and pricking whiskers,
    Families by tens and dozens,
Brothers, sisters, husbands, wives—
Followed the Piper for their lives.
From street to street he piped advancing,
And step for step they followed dancing,
Until they came to the river Weser,
    Wherein all plunged and perished!
—Save one who, stout as Julius Cæsar,
Swam across and lived to carry
    (As he, the manuscript he cherished)
To Rat-land home his commentary:
Which was, "At the first shrill notes of the pipe,
I heard a sound as of scraping tripe,
And putting apples, wondrous ripe,
Into a cider-press's gripe:
And a moving away of pickle-tub-boards,
And a leaving ajar of conserve-cupboards,
And a drawing the corks of train-oil-flasks,
And a breaking the hoops of butter-casks:
And it seemed as if a voice
    (Sweeter far than bý harp or bý psaltery
Is breathed) called out, 'Oh rats, rejoice!
    The world is grown to one vast drysaltery!

---

flame *1863:* candle-flame 121| *1842:* river Weser *1888:* river Weser, 122| *1842:* § line not indented § perished *1863:* perished! *1888:* § line indented § 125| *1842:* § line not indented § he the *1863:* he, the *1888:* § line indented § 126| *1842:* commentary, *1863:* commentary: 127| *1842:* was, At *1849:* was, "At 134| *1842:* butter-casks; *1868:* butter-casks: 136| *1842:* § line not indented § Sweeter than by harp or by *1849:* Sweeter far than <> or bý *1868:* bý harp *1888:* § line indented § 137| *1842:* out, Oh *1868:* out, 'Oh 138| *1842:* § line not indented § grown one *1849:* grown to one *1888:* § line

So munch on, crunch on, take your nuncheon,
Breakfast, supper, dinner, luncheon!'
And just as a bulky sugar-puncheon,
All ready staved, like a great sun shone
Glorious scarce an inch before me,
Just as methought it said, 'Come, bore me!'
—I found the Weser rolling o'er me."

VIII

You should have heard the Hamelin people
Ringing the bells till they rocked the steeple.
"Go," cried the Mayor, "and get long poles,
Poke out the nests and block up the holes!
Consult with carpenters and builders,
And leave in our town not even a trace
Of the rats!"—when suddenly, up the face
Of the Piper perked in the market-place,
With a, "First, if you please, my thousand guilders!"

IX

A thousand guilders! The Mayor looked blue;
So did the Corporation too.
For council dinners made rare havoc
With Claret, Moselle, Vin-de-Grave, Hock;
And half the money would replenish
Their cellar's biggest butt with Rhenish.
To pay this sum to a wandering fellow
With a gipsy coat of red and yellow!
"Beside," quoth the Mayor with a knowing wink,
"Our business was done at the river's brink;

---

indented § 139| *1863:* So, munch *1868:* So munch 140| *1842:* luncheon! *1868:* luncheon!' 141| *1842:* as one bulky sugar puncheon, *1849:* as a bulky sugar-puncheon, 142| *1842:* Ready *1849:* All ready 144| *1842:* said, Come, bore me! *1868:* said, 'Come, bore me!' 145| *1842:* me. *1849:* me." 147| *1842:* steeple; *1863:* steeple. 148| *1842:* Go, cried the Mayor, and <> poles! *1849:* "Go," cried the Mayor, "and *1868:* poles, 152| *1842:* rat!—when suddenly up *1849:* rat!"—when *1863:* suddenly, up 154| *1842:* a, First <> guilders! *1849:* a, "First <> guilders!" 157| *1842:* havock *1863:* havoc 163| *1842:* Beside, quoth *1849:* "Beside," quoth 170| *1842:* But, as *1863:* But

We saw with our eyes the vermin sink,
And what's dead can't come to life, I think.
So, friend, we're not the folks to shrink
From the duty of giving you something for drink,
And a matter of money to put in your poke;
But as for the guilders, what we spoke
Of them, as you very well know, was in joke.
Beside, our losses have made us thrifty.
A thousand guilders! Come, take fifty!"

X

The Piper's face fell, and he cried
"No trifling! I can't wait, beside!
I've promised to visit by dinnertime
Bagdat, and accept the prime
Of the Head-Cook's pottage, all he's rich in,
For having left, in the Caliph's kitchen,
Of a nest of scorpions no survivor:
With him I proved no bargain-driver,
With you, don't think I'll bate a stiver!
And folks who put me in a passion
May find me pipe after another fashion."

XI

"How?" cried the Mayor, "d'ye think brook
Being worse treated than a Cook?
Insulted by a lazy ribald
With idle pipe and vesture piebald?
You threaten us, fellow? Do your worst,
Blow your pipe there till you burst!"

---

as 172| *1842:* thrifty; *1863:* thrifty. 173| *1842:* fifty! *1849:* fifty!" 174| *1842:* cried, *1849:* piper's *1868:* Piper's <> cried 175| *1842:* No *1849:* "No 176| *1842:* dinner time *1868:* dinnertime 178| *1842:* Head Cook's *1863:* Head-Cook's 180| *1842:* survivor— *1868:* survivor: 184| *1842:* fashion. *1849:* fashion." 185| *1842:* How? cried the Mayor, d'ye *1849:* "How?" cried the Mayor, "d'ye 190| *1842:* burst! *1849:* burst!" 191| *1842:*

XII

Once more he stept into the street
And to his lips again
Laid his long pipe of smooth straight cane;
And ere he blew three notes (such sweet
Soft notes as yet musician's cunning
Never gave the enraptured air)
There was a rustling that seemed like a bustling
Of merry crowds justling at pitching and hustling,
Small feet were pattering, wooden shoes clattering,
Little hands clapping and little tongues chattering,
And, like fowls in a farm-yard when barley is scattering,
Out came the children running.
All the little boys and girls,
With rosy cheeks and flaxen curls,
And sparkling eyes and teeth like pearls,
Tripping and skipping, ran merrily after
The wonderful music with shouting and laughter.

XIII

The Mayor was dumb, and the Council stood
As if they were changed into blocks of wood,
Unable to move a step, or cry
To the children merrily skipping by,
—Could only follow with the eye
That joyous crowd at the Piper's back.
But how the Mayor was on the rack,
And the wretched Council's bosoms beat,
As the Piper turned from the High Street
To where the Weser rolled its waters
Right in the way of their sons and daughters!
However he turned from South to West,
And to Koppelberg Hill his steps addressed,
And after him the children pressed;

---

street; *1868:* street, *1888:* street 193| *1842:* § line not indented § *1888:* § line indented § 194| *1842:* § line indented § *1888:* § line not indented § 196| *1842:* th' *1849:* the 197| *1842:* rustling, that seem'd *1849:* seemed *1868:* rustling that 200| *1842:* clapping, and *1863:* clapping and 211| *1842:* by— *1868:* by, 212| *1842:* Could *1849:* And could *1868:* —Could 220| *1842:* Coppelburg *1849:* Koppelberg 223| *1842:* He *1849:* "He

Great was the joy in every breast.
"He never can cross that mighty top!
He's forced to let the piping drop,
And we shall see our children stop!"
When, lo, as they reached the mountain-side,
A wondrous portal opened wide,
As if a cavern was suddenly hollowed;
And the Piper advanced and the children followed,
And when all were in to the very last,
The door in the mountain-side shut fast.
Did I say, all? No! One was lame,
    And could not dance the whole of the way;
And in after years, if you would blame
    His sadness, he was used to say,—
"It's dull in our town since my playmates left!
I can't forget that I'm bereft
Of all the pleasant sights they see,
Which the Piper also promised me.
For he led us, he said, to a joyous land,
Joining the town and just at hand,
Where waters gushed and fruit-trees grew
And flowers put forth a fairer hue,
And everything was strange and new;
The sparrows were brighter than peacocks here,
And their dogs outran our fallow deer,
And honey-bees had lost their stings,
And horses were born with eagles' wings:
And just as I became assured
My lame foot would be speedily cured,
The music stopped and I stood still,
And found myself outside the hill.
Left alone against my will,
To go now limping as before,
And never hear of that country more!"

225| *1842:* stop! *1849:* stop!" 226| *1842:* mountain's side, *1868:* mountain-side, 229| *1842:* follow'd, *1849:* followed, 231| *1842:* mountain side *1863:* mountain-side 233| *1842:* § line not indented § *1888:* § line indented § 235| *1842:* § line not indented § *1888:* § line indented § 236| *1842:* It's *1849:* "It's 239| *1842:* me; *1863:* me. 242| *1842:* grew, *1888:* grew 244| *1842:* every thing *1849:* everything 248| *1842:* wings; *1863:* wings: 252| *1842:* Hill, *1868:* hill, 255| *1842:* more! *1849:*

XIV

Alas, alas for Hamelin!
There came into many a burgher's pate
A text which says that heaven's gate
Opes to the rich at as easy rate
As the needle's eye takes a camel in!
The mayor sent East, West, North and South,
To offer the Piper, by word of mouth,
Wherever it was men's lot to find him,
Silver and gold to his heart's content,
If he'd only return the way he went,
And bring the children behind him.
But when they saw 'twas a lost endeavour,
And Piper and dancers were gone for ever,
They made a decree that lawyers never
Should think their records dated duly
If, after the day of the month and year,
These words did not as well appear,
"And so long after what happened here
"On the Twenty-second of July,
"Thirteen hundred and seventy-six:"
And the better in memory to fix
The place of the children's last retreat,
They called it, the Pied Piper's Street—
Where any one playing on pipe or tabor
Was sure for the future to lose his labour.
Nor suffered they hostelry or tavern
To shock with mirth a street so solemn;
But opposite the place of the cavern
They wrote the story on a column,
And on the great church-window painted
The same, to make the world acquainted

---

more!" 258| *1842:* says, that Heaven's Gate *1868:* says that heaven's gate 259| *1842:* Rich <> easy a rate *1849:* easy rate *1868:* rich 261| *1842:* Mayor <> South *1863:* and South, *1868:* mayor 262| *1842:* the Piper by *1863:* the Piper, by 274| *1849:* Júly, *1868:* July, 277| *1842:* Children's *1863:* children's 278| *1842:* The *1849:* the 281| *1842:* Hostelry or Tavern *1863:* hostelry or tavern 285| *1842:* Great Church Window *1863:* great Church-Window *1868:* church-window

How their children were stolen away,
And there it stands to this very day.
And I must not omit to say
That in Transylvania there's a tribe
Of alien people who ascribe
The outlandish ways and dress
On which their neighbours lay such stress,
To their fathers and mothers having risen
Out of some subterraneous prison
Into which they were trepanned
Long time ago in a mighty band
Out of Hamelin town in Brunswick land,
But how or why, they don't understand.

XV

So, Willy, let me and you be wipers
Of scores out with all men—especially pipers!
And, whether they pipe us free fróm rats or fróm mice,
If we've promised them aught, let us keep our promise!

287| *1842:* away; *1868:* away, 291| *1842:* people that ascribe *1888:* people who ascribe 293| *1842:* stress *1849:* stress, 299| *1842:* why they *1849:* why, they 300| *1842:* let you and me be *1863:* let me and you be 301| *1842:* pipers: *1868:* pipers! 302| *1842:* And, whether they rid us from rats or from mice, *1849:* they pipe us free, from <> or fróm mice, *1868:* free fróm rats 303| *1842:* promise. *1868:* promise!

BY THE SAME AUTHOR.

I.

PARACELSUS. A POEM.

Price 6s. boards.

II.

SORDELLO. A POEM.

Price 6s. 6d. boards.

III.

BELLS AND POMEGRANATES.

No. I—PIPPA PASSES.

Price 6d. sewed.

IV.

BELLS AND POMEGRANATES.

No. II.—KING VICTOR AND KING CHARLES.

Price 1s. sewed.

BELLS AND POMEGRANATES. NUMBER IV

THE RETURN OF THE DRUSES

Edited by Morse Peckham

THE RETURN OF THE DRUSES:

A TRAGEDY.

1843: BELLS AND POMEGRANATES. / N°. IV.—THE RETURN OF THE DRUSES. / *A TRAGEDY.* / IN FIVE ACTS. / BY ROBERT BROWNING. / AUTHOR OF "PARACELSUS." *1849:* THE / RETURN OF THE DRUSES. / A TRAGEDY. *1863:* § at top of first page of text § TRAGEDY. / 1843. *1868:* § on page preceding first page of text § *1888:* TRAGEDY

THE RETURN OF THE DRUSES

A TRAGEDY

PERSONS.

The Grand-Master's Prefect.

The Patriarch's Nuncio.

The Republic's Admiral.

Loys de Dreux, *Knight-Novice.*

Initiated Druses—Djabal, Khalil, Anael, Maani, Karshook, Raghib, Ayoob, *and others.*

Uninitiated Druses.

Prefect's Guard.

Nuncio's Attendants.

Admiral's Force.

Time, 14—

Place.—*An Islet of the Southern Sporades, colonized by Druses of Lebanon, and garrisoned by the Knights-Hospitallers of Rhodes.*

Scene.—A Hall in the Prefect's Palace.

1849: § at top of first page of text § *1868:* § on page preceding first page of text §

THE RETURN OF THE DRUSES

1843

ACT I

Enter stealthily KARSHOOK, RAGHIB, AYOOB *and other initiated* Druses, *each as he enters casting off a robe that conceals his distinctive black vest and white turban; then, as giving a loose to exultation,—*

KARSHOOK The moon is carried off in purple fire:
Day breaks at last! Break glory, with the day,
On Djabal's dread incarnate mystery
Now ready to resume its pristine shape
Of Hakeem, as the Khalif vanished erst
In what seemed death to uninstructed eyes,
On red Mokattam's verge—our Founder's flesh,
As he resumes our Founder's function!
RAGHIB —Death
Sweep to the Christian Prefect that enslaved
So long us sad Druse exiles o'er the sea!
AYOOB Most joy be thine, O Mother-mount! Thy brood
Returns to thee, no outcasts as we left,
But thus—but thus! Behind, our Prefect's corse;
Before, a presence like the morning—thine,

§ ED. 1843, 1849, 1863, 1868, 1888, 1889; no MS known § 2–4| *1843:* the day / On Djabal, ready to resume his shape *1849:* the day, / On Djabal's dread incarnate mystery / Now ready to resume its pristine shape 5–7| *1843:* erst / On red Mokattam's brow—our *1849:* erst / In what seemed death to uninstructed eyes, / On red Mokattam's verge—our 8| *1843:* RAGHIB Death *1849:* RAGHIB —Death 11| *1849:* —Most *1888:* Most 15| *1843:* late, and Hakeem *1849:* late,—God

Absolute Djabal late,—God Hakeem now
That day breaks!
KARSHOOK Off then, with disguise at last!
As from our forms this hateful garb we strip,
Lose every tongue its glozing accent too,
Discard each limb the ignoble gesture! Cry,
'Tis the Druse Nation, warders on our Mount
Of the world's secret, since the birth of time,
—No kindred slips, no offsets from thy stock,
No spawn of Christians are we, Prefect, we
Who rise . . .
AYOOB Who shout . .
RAGHIB Who seize, a first-fruits, ha—
Spoil of the spoiler! Brave!

[*They begin to tear down, and to dispute for, the decorations of the hall.*]

KARSHOOK Hold!
AYOOB —Mine, I say;
And mine shall it continue!
KARSHOOK Just this fringe!
Take anything beside! Lo, spire on spire,
Curl serpentwise wreathed columns to the top
O' the roof, and hide themselves mysteriously
Among the twinkling lights and darks that haunt
Yon cornice! Where the huge veil, they suspend
Before the Prefect's chamber of delight,
Floats wide, then falls again as if its slave,
The scented air, took heart now, and anon
Lost heart to buoy its breadths of gorgeousness
Above the gloom they droop in—all the porch
Is jewelled o'er with frostwork charactery;
And, see, yon eight-point cross of white flame, winking
Hoar-silvery like some fresh-broke marble stone:

Hakeem 20| *1843:* mount *1888:* our Mount 26| *1843:* KARSHOOK Just that fringe! *1849:* KARSHOOK Just this fringe! 29| *1843:* Of *1888:* O' 31| *1843:* cornice,—where <> veil they *1849:* cornice! Where <> veil, they 32| *1843:* the Prefect's Chamber of delight *1849:* delight, *1863:* chamber 33| *1843:* again, as *1849:* again (as *1863:* again as 35| *1843:* heart, to *1868:* heart to 36| *1843:* in,—all *1849:* in)—all *1863:* in—all 37| *1843:* frosted charactery, *1849:* frost-work charactery; *1863:* frostwork 38| *1843:* A Rhodian eight-point *1849:* And see yon eight-point *1888:* And, see, yon 39| *1843:* Hoar-silvered <>

Raze out the Rhodian cross there, so thou leav'st me
This single fringe!

AYOOB Ha, wouldst thou, dog-fox? Help!
—Three hand-breadths of gold fringe, my son was set
To twist, the night he died!

KARSHOOK Nay, hear the knave!
And I could witness my one daughter borne,
A week since, to the Prefect's couch, yet fold
These arms, be mute, lest word of mine should mar
Our Master's work, delay the Prefect here
A day, prevent his sailing hence for Rhodes—
How know I else?—Hear me denied my right
By such a knave!

RAGHIB [*interposing*]. Each ravage for himself!
Booty enough! On, Druses! Be there found
Blood and a heap behind us; with us, Djabal
Turned Hakeem; and before us, Lebanon!
Yields the porch? Spare not! There his minions dragged
Thy daughter, Karshook, to the Prefect's couch!
Ayoob! Thy son, to soothe the Prefect's pride,
Bent o'er that task, the death-sweat on his brow,
Carving the spice-tree's heart in scroll-work there!
Onward in Djabal's name!

As the tumult is at height, enter KHALIL. *A pause and silence.*

KHALIL Was it for this,
Djabal hath summoned you? Deserve you thus
A portion in to-day's event? What, here—
When most behoves your feet fall soft, your eyes
Sink low, your tongues lie still,—at Djabal's side,
Close in his very hearing, who, perchance,

---

marble-stone: *1849:* Hoar-silvery *1888:* marble stone: 40| *1843:* the Prefect's Cross *1849:* the Rhodian's Cross *1863:* the Rhodian cross 41| *1843:* That single *1849:* This single 42| *1843:* handbreadths <> fringe my *1849:* fringe, my *1868:* hand-breadths 43| *1843:* twist the *1849:* twist, the 44| *1843:* borne *1849:* borne, 45| *1843:* since to *1849:* since, to 46| *1843:* mute lest *1849:* mute, lest 47| *1843:* master's *1849:* Our Master's 51| *1843:* enough! On Druses *1849:* enough! On, Druses 53| *1843:* us Lebanon! *1849:* us, Lebanon! 55| *1841:* couch: *1849:* couch! 56| *1843:* Ayoob, thy *1849:* Ayoob! Thy 58| *1843:* there: *1849:* there! 59| *1843:* this *1849:*

Assumes e'en now God Hakeem's dreaded shape,—
Dispute you for these gauds?

AYOOB How say'st thou, Khalil?
Doubtless our Master prompts thee! Take the fringe,
Old Karshook! I supposed it was a day . . .

KHALIL For pillage?

KARSHOOK Hearken, Khalil! Never spoke
A boy so like a song-bird; we avouch thee
Prettiest of all our Master's instruments
Except thy bright twin-sister; thou and Anael
Challenge his prime regard: but we may crave
(Such nothings as we be) a portion too
Of Djabal's favour; in him we believed,
His bound ourselves, him moon by moon obeyed,
Kept silence till this daybreak—so, may claim
Reward: who grudges me my claim?

AYOOB To-day
Is not as yesterday!

RAGHIB Stand off!

KHALIL Rebel you?
Must I, the delegate of Djabal, draw
His wrath on you, the day of our Return?

OTHER DRUSES Wrench from their grasp the fringe!
Hounds! must the earth
Vomit her plagues on us thro' thee?—and thee?
Plague me not, Khalil, for their fault!

KHALIL Oh, shame!
Thus breaks to-day on you, the mystic tribe
Who, flying the approach of Osman, bore
Our faith, a merest spark, from Syria's ridge
Its birthplace, hither! "Let the sea divide
These hunters from their prey," you said; "and safe
In this dim islet's virgin solitude
Tend we our faith, the spark, till happier time

---

this, 65| *1843:* now lost Hakeem's *1849:* now God Hakeem's 72| *1843:* twin-sister—thou *1868:* twin-sister; thou 75| *1843:* favor *1863:* favour 77| *1843:* so may *1863:* so, may 80| *1843:* of Hakeem, draw *1849:* of Djabal, draw 82| *1843:* from his grasp <> Hound *1849:* from their grasp *1888:* fringe! Hounds 86| *1843:* That, flying *1849:* Who, flying 87| *1843:* from Syria's Ridge *1863:* ridge 88| *1843:* birth-place, hither: let *1849:* hither! Let *1863:* birthplace *1868:* hither! "Let 89| *1843:* prey, you said, and *1868:* prey," you

Fan it to fire; till Hakeem rise again,
According to his word that, in the flesh
Which faded on Mokattam ages since,
He, at our extreme need, would interpose,
And, reinstating all in power and bliss,
Lead us himself to Lebanon once more."
Was't not thus you departed years ago,
Ere I was born?

DRUSES 'Twas even thus, years ago.

KHALIL And did you call—(according to old laws
Which bid us, lest the sacred grow profane,
Assimilate ourselves in outward rites
With strangers fortune makes our lords, and live
As Christian with the Christian, Jew with Jew,
Druse only with the Druses)—did you call
Or no, to stand 'twixt you and Osman's rage
(Mad to pursue e'en hither thro' the sea
The remnant of our tribe), a race self-vowed
To endless warfare with his hordes and him,
The White-cross Knights of the adjacent Isle?

KARSHOOK And why else rend we down, wrench up, rase out?
These Knights of Rhodes we thus solicited
For help, bestowed on us a fiercer pest
Than aught we fled—their Prefect; who began
His promised mere paternal governance
By a prompt massacre of all our Sheikhs
Able to thwart the Order in its scheme
Of crushing, with our nation's memory,
Each chance of our return, and taming us
Bondslaves to Rhodes for ever—all, he thinks
To end by this day's treason.

KHALIL Say I not?

---

said; "and 92| *1843:* fire; again till Hakeem rise *1849:* fire; till Hakeem rise again, 97| *1843:* more. *1868:* more." 100| *1843:* you not—(according *1849:* you call—(according 101| *1843:* the Sacred grow Prophane, *1863:* sacred grow profane, 106| *1849:* rage, *1888:* rage 108| *1843:* of your tribe) a *1868:* of our tribe *1888:* tribe), a 111| *1843:* raze *1868:* rase 112| *1843:* The Knights *1849:* These Knights 114–119| *1843:* began / By massacre, who thinks to end to-day / By treachery, a scheme of theirs for crushing / Each *1843:* began / His promised mere paternal governance, / By a prompt massacre of all our Sheikhs / Able to thwart the Order in its scheme / Of crushing, with our nationalities, / Each 118| *1868:* our nation's memory *1888:* memory, 120–121| *1843:* Bond slaves <>

You, fitted to the Order's purposes,
Your Sheikhs cut off, your rites, your garb proscribed,
Must yet receive one degradation more;
The Knights at last throw off the mask—transfer,
As tributary now and appanage,
This islet they are but protectors of,
To their own ever-craving liege, the Church,
Who licenses all crimes that pay her thus.
You, from their Prefect, were to be consigned
(Pursuant of I know not what vile pact)
To the Knights' Patriarch, ardent to outvie
His predecessor in all wickedness.
When suddenly rose Djabal in the midst,
Djabal, the man in semblance, but our God
Confessed by signs and portents. Ye saw fire
Bicker round Djabal, heard strange music flit
Bird-like about his brow?

DRUSES We saw—we heard!
Djabal is Hakeem, the incarnate Dread,
The phantasm Khalif, King of Prodigies!

KHALIL And as he said has not our Khalif done,
And so disposed events (from land to land
Passing invisibly) that when, this morn,
The pact of villany complete, there comes
This Patriarch's Nuncio with this Master's Prefect
Their treason to consummate,—each will face
For a crouching handful, an uplifted nation:

---

ever. KHALIL *1843:* ever—all, he thinks / To end by this day's treason. KHALIL 123| *1843:* off, your very garb *1888:* off, your rites, your garb 124–130| *1843:* more; / You 125–129| § added 1849, variants from 1889 § 126| *1849:* now, and *1868:* now and 128| *1843:* ever-craving lord, the *1868:* ever-craving liege, the 129| *1843:* Which licenses <> pay it thus— *1863:* thus. *1868:* Who licenses <> pay her thus. 130–132| *1843:* consigned / To the *1849:* consigned / Pursuant to I know not what vile pact, / To the *1863:* (Pursuant <> pact) 133| *1843:* wickedness; *1863:* wickedness. 134| *1843:* rose Hakeem in *1849:* rose Djabal in 135| *1843:* man, in <> our Khalif *1849:* our God *1868:* man in 138–141| *1843:* heard. / And <> hath <> done? *1843:* heard! / Djabal is Hakeem, the incarnate Dread, / The phantasm Khalif, King of Prodigies! / And <> done, 141| *1888:* has 142| *1843:* —Not so *1849:* And so 143| *1843:* Going invisibly *1849:* Passing invisibly 146| *1843:* To consummate their treason, each *1849:* Their treason to consummate,—each 147| *1843:* nation; *1888:*

For simulated Christians, confessed Druses:
And, for slaves past hope of the Mother-mount,
Freedmen returning there 'neath Venice' flag;
That Venice which, the Hospitallers' foe,
Grants us from Candia escort home at price
Of our relinquished isle, Rhodes counts her own—
Venice, whose promised argosies should stand
Toward harbour: is it now that you, and you,
And you, selected from the rest to bear
The burthen of the Khalif's secret, further
To-day's event, entitled by your wrongs,
And witness in the Prefect's hall his fate—
That you dare clutch these gauds? Ay, drop them!

KARSHOOK

True,
Most true, all this; and yet, may one dare hint,
Thou art the youngest of us?—though employed
Abundantly as Djabal's confidant,
Transmitter of his mandates, even now.
Much less, whene'er beside him Anael graces
The cedar throne, his queen-bride, art thou like
To occupy its lowest step that day!
Now, Khalil, wert thou checked as thou aspirest,
Forbidden such or such an honour,—say,
Would silence serve so amply?

KHALIL

Karshook thinks
I covet honours? Well, nor idly thinks.
Honours? I have demanded of them all
The greatest.

KARSHOOK

I supposed so.

KHALIL

Judge, yourselves!

---

nation: 148| *1843:* confessed Druses; *1888:* confessed Druses: 151| *1843:* —Venice, which, these proud Hospitallers' *1849:* That Venice, which, the Hospitallers' *1863:* That Venice which 153| *1843:* relinquished islet—Venice, brothers, *1849:* relinquished isle—Rhodes counts her own— *1863:* isle, Rhodes 154| *1843:* Whose promised <> stand by this *1849:* Venice, whose <> stand 155| *1843:* Towards the harbour <> that you, *1849:* Toward the harbour <> that you, and you, *1888:* Toward harbour 156| *1843:* to carry *1849:* to bear 162| *1843:* tho' *1863:* though 164| *1843:* now: *1863:* now. 165| *1843:* less whene'er *1849:* less, whene'er 166| *1843:* his Queen-bride *1868:* queen-bride 168| *1843:* And, Khalil *1849:* Now, Khalil 169| *1843:* honor *1863:* honour 171| *1843:* honors <> thinks! *1863:* honours *1888:* thinks. 172| *1843:* Honors *1863:* Honours 173| *1843:* greatest! <> Judge yourselves! *1888:* greatest. <> Judge,

Turn, thus: 'tis in the alcove at the back
Of yonder columned porch, whose entrance now
The veil hides, that our Prefect holds his state,
Receives the Nuncio, when the one, from Rhodes,
The other lands from Syria; there they meet.
Now, I have sued with earnest prayers . . .

KARSHOOK For what
Shall the Bride's brother vainly sue?

KHALIL That mine—
Avenging in one blow a myriad wrongs
—Might be the hand to slay the Prefect there!
Djabal reserves that office for himself. [*A silence.*]
Thus far, as youngest of you all, I speak
—Scarce more enlightened than yourselves; since, near
As I approach him, nearer as I trust
Soon to approach our Master, he reveals
Only the God's power, not the glory yet.
Therefore I reasoned with you: now, as servant
To Djabal, bearing his authority,
Hear me appoint your several posts! Till noon
None see him save myself and Anael: once
The deed achieved, our Khalif, casting off
The embodied Awe's tremendous mystery,
The weakness of the flesh disguise, resumes
His proper glory, ne'er to fade again.

Enter a DRUSE.

THE DRUSE Our Prefect lands from Rhodes!—without a sign
That he suspects aught since he left our Isle;
Nor in his train a single guard beyond

---

yourselves! 174| *1843:* Turn—thus *1868:* Turn, thus 176| *1843:* state; *1868:* state, 177| *1843:* the Nuncio when *1849:* the Nuncio, when 181| *1843:* wrongs, *1863:* wrongs 182| *1843:* hand that slays *1849:* hand to slay 184| *1843:* spoke *1849:* speak 185| *1843:* yourselves: since *1868:* yourselves; since 188| *1843:* the Khalif's power, not glory yet: *1849:* the God's power, not the glory *1863:* yet. 192| *1843:* sees <> Anael—once *1863:* see *1868:* and Anael: once 193–196| *1843:* our Khalif will appear. / *Enter* *1849:* our Khalif, casting off / The embodied Awe's tremendous mystery, / The weakness of the flesh disguise, resumes / His proper glory, ne'er to fade again. / *Enter* 197| *1843:* from Rhodes!—

The few he sailed with hence: so have we learned
From Loys.
KARSHOOK Loys? Is not Loys gone
For ever?
AYOOB Loys, the Frank Knight, returned?
THE DRUSE Loys, the boy, stood on the leading prow
Conspicuous in his gay attire, and leapt
Into the surf the foremost. Since daydawn
I kept watch to the Northward; take but note
Of my poor vigilance to Djabal!
KHALIL Peace!
Thou, Karshook, with thy company, receive
The Prefect as appointed: see, all keep
The wonted show of servitude: announce
His entry here by the accustomed peal
Of trumpets, then await the further pleasure
Of Djabal! (Loys back, whom Djabal sent
To Rhodes that we might spare the single Knight
Worth sparing!)

Enter a second DRUSE.

THE DRUSE I espied it first! Say, I
First spied the Nuncio's galley from the South!
Said'st thou a Crossed-keys' flag would flap the mast?
It nears apace! One galley and no more.
If Djabal chance to ask who spied the flag,
Forget not, I it was!
KHALIL Thou, Ayoob, bring
The Nuncio and his followers hither! Break
One rule prescribed, ye wither in your blood,
Die at your fault!

Enter a third DRUSE.

Without *1868:* without 200| *1843:* hence—so *1849:* hence: so 201| *1843:* From Loÿs *1849:* From Loys § 1843 Loÿs throughout § 204| *1843:* attire—has leapt *1849:* attire,—and leapt *1868:* attire, and 205| *1843:* surf already: since *1849:* surf the foremost: since *1863:* foremost. Since 209| *1843:* see all *1849:* see, all 215| *1843:* espied him first *1849:* espied it first 217| *1843:* Saidst <> Flag *1863:* flag *1868:* Said'st 218| *1843:* more— *1868:* more. 220| *1843:*

THE DRUSE I shall see home, see home!
—Shall banquet in the sombre groves again!
Hail to thee, Khalil! Venice looms afar;
The argosies of Venice, like a cloud,
Bear up from Candia in the distance!
KHALIL Joy!
Summon our people, Raghib! Bid all forth!
Tell them the long-kept secret, old and young!
Set free the captive, let the trampled raise
Their faces from the dust, because at length
The cycle is complete, God Hakeem's reign
Begins anew! Say, Venice for our guard,
Ere night we steer for Syria! Hear you, Druses?
Hear you this crowning witness to the claims
Of Djabal? Oh, I spoke of hope and fear,
Reward and punishment, because he bade
Who has the right; for me, what should I say
But, mar not those imperial lineaments,
No majesty of all that rapt regard
Vex by the least omission! Let him rise
Without a check from you!
DRUSES Let Djabal rise!

Enter LOYS.—*The* DRUSES *are silent.*

LOYS Who speaks of Djabal?—for I seek him, friends!
[*Aside.*] *Tu Dieu!* 'Tis as our Isle broke out in song
For joy, its Prefect-incubus drops off
To-day, and I succeed him in his rule!
But no—they cannot dream of their good fortune!
[*Aloud.*] Peace to you, Druses! I have tidings for you
But first for Djabal: where's your tall bewitcher,
With that small Arab thin-lipped silver-mouth?
KHALIL [*aside to* KARSHOOK]. Loys, in truth! Yet Djabal cannot err!
KARSHOOK [*to* KHALIL]. And who takes charge of Loys? That's forgotten,

---

not I *1849:* not, I 224| *1843:* again. *1849:* again! 225| *1843:* afar— *1849:* afar; 230| *1843:* captives, have the *1849:* captives, let the 232| *1843:* complete, and Hakeem's *1849:* complete, God Hakeem's 236| *1843:* Of Djabal! Oh *1849:* Of Djabal? Oh 245| *1843:* joy its *1849:* joy, its 248| *1843:* for you, *1888:* for you 250| *1843:* silver mouth? *1863:* silver-mouth?

Despite thy wariness! Will Loys stand
And see his comrades slaughtered?
LOYS [*aside*]. How they shrink
And whisper, with those rapid faces! What?
The sight of me in their oppressors' garb
Strikes terror to the simple tribe? God's shame
On those that bring our Order ill repute!
But all's at end now; better days begin
For these mild mountaineers from over-sea:
The timidest shall have in me no Prefect
To cower at thus! [*Aloud.*] I asked for Djabal—
KARSHOOK [*aside*]. Better
One lured him, ere he can suspect, inside
The corridor; 'twere easy to despatch
A youngster. [*To* LOYS.] Djabal passed some minutes since
Thro' yonder porch, and . . .
KHALIL [*aside*]. Hold! What, him despatch?
The only Christian of them all we charge
No tyranny upon? Who,—noblest Knight
Of all that learned from time to time their trade
Of lust and cruelty among us,—heir
To Europe's pomp, a truest child of pride,—
Yet stood between the Prefect and ourselves
From the beginning? Loys, Djabal makes
Account of, and precisely sent to Rhodes
For safety? I take charge of him!
[*To* LOYS.] Sir Loys,—
LOYS There, cousins! Does Sir Loys strike you dead?
KHALIL [*advancing*]. Djabal has intercourse with few or none
Till noontide: but, your pleasure?
LOYS "Intercourse
With few or none?"—(Ah, Khalil, when you spoke
I saw not your smooth face! All health!—and health
To Anael! How fares Anael?)—"Intercourse

254| *1843:* comrade *1868:* comrades 255| *1843:* faces! What! *1849:* faces! What? 257| *1843:* tribe! God's *1849:* tribe? God's 260| *1843:* over-sea; *1863:* over-sea: 262| *1843:* for Djabal. KARSHOOK *1849:* for Djabal— KARSHOOK 264| *1843:* easy then despatch *1849:* easy to despatch *1863:* dispatch *1888:* despatch 266| *1843:* and . . . KHALIL *1888:* and . . KHALIL 271| 1843: pomps *1868:* pomp 275| *1843:* safety?—I have charge *1849:* safety?—I take charge *1888:* safety? I 279| *1868:* none?"—(Ah Khalil *1888:*

With few or none?" Forget you, I've been friendly
With Djabal long ere you or any Druse?
—Enough of him at Rennes, I think, beneath
The Duke my father's roof! He'd tell by the hour,
With fixed white eyes beneath his swarthy brow,
Plausiblest stories . . .

KHALIL Stories, say you?—Ah,
The quaint attire!

LOYS My dress for the last time!
How sad I cannot make you understand,
This ermine, o'er a shield, betokens me
Of Bretagne, ancientest of provinces
And noblest; and, what's best and oldest there,
See, Dreux', our house's blazon, which the Nuncio
Tacks to an Hospitaller's vest to-day!

KHALIL The Nuncio we await? What brings you back
From Rhodes, Sir Loys?

LOYS How you island-tribe
Forget the world's awake while here you drowse!
What brings me back? What should not bring me, rather!
Our Patriarch's Nuncio visits you to-day—
Is not my year's probation out? I come
To take the knightly vows.

KHALIL What's that you wear?

LOYS This Rhodian cross? The cross your Prefect wore.
You should have seen, as I saw, the full Chapter
Rise, to a man, while they transferred this cross
From that unworthy Prefect's neck to . . . (fool—
My secret will escape me!) In a word,
My year's probation passed, a Knight ere eve
Am I; bound, like the rest, to yield my wealth
To the common stock, to live in chastity,
(We Knights espouse alone our Order's fame)
—Change this gay weed for the black white-crossed gown,

---

none?"—(Ah, Khalil 282| *1843:* you I've *1849:* you, I've 288| *1843:* time. *1849:* time! 296| *1843:* island tribe *1863:* island-tribe 297| *1849:* Forget, the *1868:* Forget the world *1888:* world's 298–300| *1843:* rather? / Is *1849:* rather? / Our Patriarch's Nuncio visits you to-day— / Is 298| *1888:* rather! 304| *1843:* Rise to a man while *1849:* Rise, to a man, while 307| *1843:* probation's passed, and Knight *1863:* probation passed, a Knight 311| *1843:* black *1888:*

And fight to death against the Infidel
—Not, therefore, against you, you Christians with
Such partial difference only as befits
The peacefullest of tribes. But Khalil, prithee,
Is not the Isle brighter than wont to-day?
KHALIL Ah, the new sword!
LOYS See now! You handle sword
As 'twere a camel-staff. Pull! That's my motto,
Annealed "*Pro fide*," on the blade in blue.
KHALIL No curve in it? Surely a blade should curve.
LOYS Straight from the wrist! Loose—it should poise itself!
KHALIL [*waving with irrepressible exultation the sword*]. We are a nation, Loys, of old fame
Among the mountains! Rights have we to keep
With the sword too!
[*Remembering himself.*] But I forget—you bid me
Seek Djabal?
LOYS What! A sword's sight scares you not?
(The People I will make of him and them!
Oh let my Prefect-sway begin at once!)
Bring Djabal—say, indeed, that come he must!
KHALIL At noon seek Djabal in the Prefect's Chamber,
And find . . . [*Aside.*] Nay, 'tis thy cursed race's token,
Frank pride, no special insolence of thine!
[*Aloud.*] Tarry, and I will do your bidding, Loys!
[*To the rest aside.*] Now, forth you! I proceed to Djabal straight.
Leave this poor boy, who knows not what he says!
Oh will it not add joy to even thy joy,
Djabal, that I report all friends were true?
[KHALIL *goes, followed by the* DRUSES.]
LOYS *Tu Dieu!* How happy I shall make these Druses!
Was't not surpassingly contrived of me
To get the long list of their wrongs by heart,

---

back 312| *1843:* the Infidel. *1849:* the Infidel 315| *1843:* tribes! But *1888:* tribes. But 318| *1843:* camel's staff *1849:* camel-staff 319| *1843:* Annealed, "*Pro* *1868:* Annealed "*Pro* 327| *1843:* Oh, let *1868:* Oh let 330| *1843:* find—[*Aside.*] Nay *1863:* find . . . [*Aside.*] Nay 332| *1843:* [*Aloud.*] Tarry and *1863:* [*Aloud.*] Tarry, and 333–335| *1843:* straight. / Oh, adds it not a joy *1849:* straight. / Leave this poor boy, who knows not what he says. / Oh, will it not add joy to *1868:* says! Oh will 336–337| *1843:* [*Exit* KHALIL, *followed* *1849:* [KHALIL *goes,*

Then take the first pretence for stealing off
From these poor islanders, present myself
Sudden at Rhodes before the noble Chapter,
And (as best proof of ardour in its cause
Which ere tonight will have become, too, mine)
Acquaint it with this plague-sore in its body,
This Prefect and his villanous career?
The princely Synod! All I dared request
Was his dismissal; and they graciously
Consigned his very office to myself—
Myself may cure the Isle diseased!
And well
For them, they did so! Since I never felt
How lone a lot, tho' brilliant, I embrace,
Till now that, past retrieval, it is mine.
To live thus, and thus die! Yet, as I leapt
On shore, so home a feeling greeted me
That I could half believe in Djabal's story,
He used to tempt my father with, at Rennes—
And me, too, since the story brought me here—
Of some Count Dreux and ancestor of ours
Who, sick of wandering from Bouillon's war,
Left his old name in Lebanon.
Long days
At least to spend in the Isle! and, my news known
An hour hence, what if Anael turn on me
The great black eyes I must forget?
Why, fool,
Recall them, then? My business is with Djabal,
Not Anael! Djabal tarries: if I seek him?—
The Isle is brighter than its wont to-day.

---

followed 347| *1843:* dared to ask *1849:* dared request 350| *1843:* may heal whate'er's diseased! ¶ And good *1868:* may cure the Isle diseased! ¶ And well 351| *1843:* them they *1849:* them, they 353| *1843:* past retrieve, the lot is mine— *1849:* retrieval, it is *1868:* mine. 356–359| *1843:* story / Of some *1849:* story, / He used to tempt my father with, at Rennes— / And me, too, since the story brought me here— / Of some 363| *1843:* turns *1868:* turn 367| *1843:* to-day! [*Exit.* *1849:* to-day! § stage direction dropped § *1888:* to-day.

ACT II

Enter DJABAL.

DJABAL That a strong man should think himself a God!
I—Hakeem? To have wandered through the world,
Sown falsehood, and thence reaped now scorn, now faith,
For my one chant with many a change, my tale
Of outrage, and my prayer for vengeance—this
Required, forsooth, no mere man's faculty,
Nought less than Hakeem's? The persuading Loys
To pass probation here; the getting access
By Loys to the Prefect; worst of all,
The gaining my tribe's confidence by fraud
That would disgrace the very Frank,—a few
Of Europe's secrets which subdue the flame,
The wave,—to ply a simple tribe with these,
Took Hakeem?
And I feel this first to-day!
Does the day break, is the hour imminent
When one deed, when my whole life's deed, my deed
Must be accomplished? Hakeem? Why the God?
Shout, rather, "Djabal, Youssof's child, thought slain
With his whole race, the Druses' Sheikhs, this Prefect
Endeavoured to extirpate—saved, a child,
Returns from traversing the world, a man,
Able to take revenge, lead back the march
To Lebanon"—so shout, and who gainsays.

1| § added 1849 § 2| *1843:* thro' *1863:* through 5–7| *1843:* vengeance—took / No less than Hakeem *1849:* vengeance—this / Required, forsooth, no mere man's faculty, / Nor less than Hakeem's *1888:* Nought less 11| *1843:* very Franks, a *1849:* very Franks,—a *1868:* very Frank 12| *1843:* secrets that subdue *1868:* secrets which subdue 13| *1843:* these *1849:* these, 17| *1843:* accomplished? Hakeem? What of Hakeem? *1849:* accomplished? Hakeem? Why the God? 19| *1843:* the Druses' Sheikhs this *1849:* the Druses' Sheikhs, this

But now, because delusion mixed itself
Insensibly with this career, all's changed!
Have I brought Venice to afford us convoy?
"True—but my jugglings wrought that!" Put I heart
Into our people where no heart lurked?—"Ah,
What cannot an impostor do!"
Not this!
Not do this which I do! Not bid avaunt
Falsehood! Thou shalt not keep thy hold on me!
—Nor even get a hold on me! 'Tis now—
This day—hour—minute—'tis as here I stand
On the accursed threshold of the Prefect,
That I am found deceiving and deceived!
And now what do I?—hasten to the few
Deceived, ere they deceive the many—shout,
"As I professed, I did believe myself!
Say, Druses, had you seen a butchery—
If Ayoob, Karshook saw——Maani there
Must tell you how I saw my father sink;
My mother's arms twine still about my neck;
I hear my brother shriek, here's yet the scar
Of what was meant for my own death-blow—say,
If you had woke like me, grown year by year
Out of the tumult in a far-off clime,
Would it be wondrous such delusion grew?
I walked the world, asked help at every hand;
Came help or no? Not this and this? Which helps
When I returned with, found the Prefect here,
The Druses here, all here but Hakeem's self,
The Khalif of the thousand prophecies,
Reserved for such a juncture,—could I call
My mission aught but Hakeem's? Promised Hakeem
More than performs the Djabal—you absolve?

27| *1843:* True <> that! Put *1849:* "True <> that!" Put 28| *1843:* lurked?—Ah, *1843:* lurked?—"Ah, 29| *1843:* do! ¶ Not *1849:* do!" ¶ Not 30| *1843:* bid, avaunt *1888:* bid avaunt 32| *1843:* now *1849:* now— 36| *1843:* Hasten *1868:* hasten 38| *1843:* As *1868:* "As 40| *1843:* Maäni *1849:* Maani 43| *1843:* brother's *1868:* brother 47| *1843:* wondrous that delusions *1849:* wondrous such delusion 51–53| *1843:* self, / Reserved *1849:* self, / The Khalif of the thousand prophecies, / Reserved 51| *1868:*

—Me, you will never shame before the crowd
Yet happily ignorant?—Me, both throngs surround,
The few deceived, the many unabused,
—Who, thus surrounded, slay for you and them
The Prefect, lead to Lebanon? No Khalif,
But Sheikh once more! Mere Djabal—not" . . .

Enter KHALIL *hastily.*

KHALIL —God Hakeem!
'Tis told! The whole Druse nation knows thee, Hakeem,
As we! and mothers lift on high their babes
Who seem aware, so glisten their great eyes,
Thou hast not failed us; ancient brows are proud;
Our elders could not earlier die, it seems,
Than at thy coming! The Druse heart is thine!
Take it! my lord and theirs, be thou adored!

DJABAL [*aside*]. Adored!—but I renounce it utterly!

KHALIL Already are they instituting choirs
And dances to the Khalif, as of old
'Tis chronicled thou bad'st them.

DJABAL [*aside*]. I abjure it!
'Tis not mine—not for me!

KHALIL Why pour they wine
Flavoured like honey and bruised mountain-herbs,
Or wear those strings of sun-dried cedar-fruit?
Oh, let me tell thee—Esaad, we supposed
Doting, is carried forth, eager to see
The last sun rise on the Isle: he can see now!
The shamed Druse women never wept before:
They can look up when we reach home, they say.
Smell!—sweet cane, saved in Lilith's breast thus long—

---

here, but *1888:* here but 57–59| *1843:* ignorant?—Me both <> surround! / —Who *1849:* ignorant?—Me, both <> surround / The few deceived, the many unabused, / —Who 57| *1888:* surround, 61| *1843:* more! Djabal—no longer . . . KHALIL —Hakeem! *1849:* more! Mere Djabal—not . . . KHALIL —God Hakeem! *1868:* not" . . KHALIL —God *1888:* not" . . . KHALIL —God 65| *1843:* proud! *1888:* proud; 66| *1843:* our Elders *1868:* elders 68| *1843:* my Lord *1868:* lord 72| *1843:* you bade *1849:* thou bad'st 74| *1843:* mountain herbs? *1868:* mountain-herbs, 76| *1843:* Oh—let <> you *1849:* thee *1868:* Oh, let 78| *1843:* The sun <> Isle—he *1849:* The last sun *1868:* the Isle: he 81| *1843:* Smell!

Sweet!—it grows wild in Lebanon. And I
Alone do nothing for thee! 'Tis my office
Just to announce what well thou know'st—but thus
Thou bidst me. At this self-same moment tend
The Prefect, Nuncio and the Admiral
Hither by their three sea-paths: nor forget
Who were the trusty watchers!—thou forget?
Like me, who do forget that Anael bade . . .
DJABAL [*aside*]. Ay, Anael, Anael—is that said at last?
Louder than all, that would be said, I knew!
What does abjuring mean, confessing mean,
To the people? Till that woman crossed my path,
On went I, solely for my people's sake:
I saw her, and I then first saw myself,
And slackened pace: "if I should prove indeed
Hakeem—with Anael by!"
KHALIL [*aside*]. Ah, he is rapt!
Dare I at such a moment break on him
Even to do my sister's bidding? Yes:
The eyes are Djabal's and not Hakeem's yet,
Though but till I have spoken this, perchance.
DJABAL [*aside*]. To yearn to tell her, and yet have no one
Great heart's word that will tell her! I could gasp
Doubtless one such word out, and die.
[*Aloud.*] You said
That Anael . . .
KHALIL . . . Fain would see thee, speak with thee
Before thou change, discard this Djabal's shape
She knows, for Hakeem's shape she is to know.

Sweet *1868:* Smell!—sweet 83| *1843:* you *1849:* thee 84| *1843:* you know; but *1849:* thou know'st—but 85| *1843:* You bid <> selfsame *1849:* Thou bidst *1868:* self-same 86| *1843:* The Prefect, Nuncio, and *1868:* The Prefect, Nuncio and 87| *1843:* Hither, by <> sea-paths—nor *1863:* sea-paths: nor *1868:* Hither by 88| *1843:* You *1849:* Thou *1863:* thou 94| *1843:* went I solely *1849:* went I, solely 95| *1843:* and myself too saw I first, *1849:* and I first saw too myself, *1868:* and I then first saw myself, 97| *1843:* with Anael here!" KHALIL (Ah <> rapt!) *1849:* with Anael by!" KHALIL [*aside*] Ah <> rapt! 98| *1843:* on you *1849:* on him 99| *1843:* bidding? Yes! *1868:* bidding? Yes: 100| *1843:* are Djabal's, and <> yet! *1868:* are Djabal's and <> yet, 103| *1843:* heart's-word *1863:* heart's word 104| *1843:* die! / [*Aloud.*] *1868:* die. / [*Aloud.*] 105| *1843:* you <> you, *1849:* thee <> thee, 106| *1843:* you *1849:* thou 107| *1843:* to know: *1863:* to know. 108| *1843:* Something's

Something to say that will not from her mind!
I know not what—"Let him but come!" she said.
DJABAL [*half-apart*]. My nation—all my Druses—how fare they?
Those I must save, and suffer thus to save,
Hold they their posts? Wait they their Khalif too?
KHALIL All at the signal pant to flock around
That banner of a brow!
DJABAL [*aside*]. And when they flock,
Confess them this: and after, for reward,
Be chased with howlings to her feet perchance!
—Have the poor outraged Druses, deaf and blind,
Precede me there, forestall my story there,
Tell it in mocks and jeers!
I lose myself.
Who needs a Hakeem to direct him now?
I need the veriest child—why not this child?
[*Turning abruptly to* KHALIL.]
You are a Druse too, Khalil; you were nourished
Like Anael with our mysteries: if she
Could vow, so nourished, to love only one
Who should avenge the Druses, whence proceeds
Your silence? Wherefore made you no essay,
Who thus implicitly can execute
My bidding? What have I done, you could not?
Who, knowing more than Anael the prostration
Of our once lofty tribe, the daily life
Of this detested . . .
Does he come, you say,
This Prefect? All's in readiness?
KHALIL The sword,
The sacred robe, the Khalif's mystic tiar,
Laid up so long, are all disposed beside
The Prefect's chamber.

<> mind: *1868:* Something <> mind! 109| *1843:* not how—"Let *1849:* not what—"Let 115| *1843:* Confess to them, and *1849:* Confess them this—and *1868:* this: and 116| *1843:* perchance? *1888:* perchance! 118| *1843:* there—forestall my story, there— *1863:* forestal *1868:* there, forestall my story there, 119| *1843:* jeers— / I <> myself! *1863:* jeers! / I *1888:* myself. 129| *1843:* And, knowing *1849:* Who, knowing 131| *1843:* detested . . . / (Does *1849:* detested . . . / Does 135| *1843:* chamber.) DJABAL *1849:* chamber.

DJABAL —Why did you despair?
KHALIL I know our nation's state? Too surely know,
As thou who speak'st to prove me! Wrongs like ours
Should wake revenge: but when I sought the wronged
And spoke,—"The Prefect stabbed your son—arise!
Your daughter, while you starve, eats shameless bread
In his pavilion—then arise!"—my speech
Fell idly: 'twas, "Be silent, or worse fare!
Endure till time's slow cycle prove complete!
Who mayst thou be that takest on thee to thrust
Into this peril—art thou Hakeem?" No!
Only a mission like thy mission renders
All these obedient at a breath, subdues
Their private passions, brings their wills to one.
DJABAL You think so?
KHALIL Even now—when they have witnessed
Thy miracles—had I not threatened all
With Hakeem's vengeance, they would mar the work,
And couch ere this, each with his special prize,
Safe in his dwelling, leaving our main hope
To perish. No! When these have kissed thy feet
At Lebanon, the past purged off, the present
Clear,—for the future, even Hakeem's mission
May end, and I perchance, or any youth,
Shall rule them thus renewed.—I tutor thee!
DJABAL And wisely. (He is Anael's brother, pure
As Anael's self.) Go say, I come to her.
Haste! I will follow you. [KHALIL *goes.*]
Oh, not confess

DJABAL 136| *1843:* our Nation's state. Too *1849:* state? Too *1863:* nation's 137| *1843:* you, who speak <> like theirs *1849:* thou <> speak'st <> like ours *1868:* thou who 141| *1843:* then, arise *1868:* then arise 142| *1843:* idly—'twas *1888:* idly: 'twas 143| *1843:* Endure, till *1868:* Endure till <> complete; *1888:* complete! 144| *1843:* may'st <> tak'st *1849:* takest *1888:* mayst 146| *1843:* your *1849:* thy 148| *1843:* one! *1888:* one. 150| *1843:* Your miracles <> threatened them *1849:* Thy *1868:* threatened all 151| *1843:* the whole, *1868:* the work, 152| *1843:* And lie ere *1863:* And couch ere 154| *1843:* perish! No *1888:* perish. No 155| *1843:* the Past <> the Present *1868:* past <> present 156| *1843:* Clear, for the Future even *1849:* Clear,—for the Future, even *1868:* future 157| *1843:* any child, *1849:* any youth, 158| *1843:* Could rule <> renewed.—I talk to thee! *1849:* Can *1868:* Shall rule *1888:* renewed.—I tutor thee! 159| *1863:* wisely. He *1888:* wisely. (He 160| *1863:* self! Go *1888:* self.) Go 161| *1843:* you. [*Exit* KHALIL.¶ Oh *1849:* you. [KHALIL goes. ¶ Oh

To these, the blinded multitude—confess,
Before at least the fortune of my deed
Half-authorize its means! Only to her
Let me confess my fault, who in my path
Curled up like incense from a Mage-king's tomb
When he would have the wayfarer descend
Through the earth's rift and bear hid treasure forth!
How should child's-carelessness prove manhood's crime
Till now that I, whose lone youth hurried past,
Letting each joy 'scape for the Druses' sake,
At length recover in one Druse all joy?
Were her brow brighter, her eyes richer, still
Would I confess. On the gulf's verge I pause.
How could I slay the Prefect, thus and thus?
Anael, be mine to guard me, not destroy! [*Goes.*]

Enter ANAEL, *and* MAANI *who is assisting to array her in the ancient dress of the Druses.*

ANAEL Those saffron vestures of the tabret-girls!
Comes Djabal, think you?
MAANI Doubtless Djabal comes.
ANAEL Dost thou snow-swathe thee kinglier, Lebanon,
Than in my dreams?—Nay all the tresses off
My forehead! Look I lovely so? He says
That I am lovely.
MAANI Lovely: nay, that hangs

162| *1843:* these—the *1868:* these, the 164| *1843:* Half authorize *1888:* Half-authorize 166| *1843:* mage-king's *1888:* a Mage-king's 168| *1843:* Thro' <> and take hid treasure up. *1863:* Through *1868:* and bear hid treasure forth! 169| *1843:* When should my first child's-carelessness have stopped *1888:* How should child's-carelessness prove manhood's crime 170| *1843:* If not when I <> past *1888:* Till now that I <> past, 172–173| *1843:* length recovered in <> joys? / § space § / Were *1849:* joys? / Were *1868:* joy? *1888:* recover 174| *1843:* confess! On *1888:* confess. On 176–177| *1843:* Be thou my guardian, not destroyer, Anael! [*Exit.* / <> MAANI, who <> / <> saffron-vestures *1849:* Anael, be mine to guard me, not destroy! [*Goes. 1863:* saffron vestures *1868:* MAANI who 180| *1843:* dreams?—Nay, all *1888:* dreams?—Nay all 181| *1843:* forehead—look *1863:* forehead! look *1868:* forehead! Look 182| *1843:* MAANI Lovely! nay *1863:* MAANI Lovely:

Awry.
ANAEL You tell me how a khandjar hangs?
The sharp side, thus, along the heart, see, marks
The maiden of our class. Are you content
For Djabal as for me?
MAANI Content, my child.
ANAEL Oh mother, tell me more of him! He comes
Even now—tell more, fill up my soul with him!
MAANI And did I not . . . yes, surely . . . tell you all?
ANAEL What will be changed in Djabal when the Change
Arrives? Which feature? Not his eyes!
MAANI 'Tis writ
Our Hakeem's eyes rolled fire and clove the dark
Superbly.
ANAEL Not his eyes! His voice perhaps?
Yet that's no change; for a grave current lived
—Grandly beneath the surface ever lived,
That, scattering, broke as in live silver spray
While . . ah, the bliss . . he would discourse to me
In that enforced still fashion, word on word!
'Tis the old current which must swell thro' that,
For what least tone, Maani, could I lose?
'Tis surely not his voice will change!
—If Hakeem
Only stood by! If Djabal, somehow, passed
Out of the radiance as from out a robe;
Possessed, but was not it!
He lived with you?
Well—and that morning Djabal saw me first
And heard me vow never to wed but one
Who saved my People—on that day . . . proceed!
MAANI Once more, then: from the time of his return
In secret, changed so since he left the Isle
That I, who screened our Emir's last of sons,

---

nay 183| *1843:* kandjar *1849:* khandjar 187| *1843:* Oh, mother <> him. He *1863:* him! He *1868:* Oh mother 191| *1843:* writ, *1868:* writ 192| *1843:* Our Khalif's eyes *1849:* Our Hakeem's eyes 197| *1843:* While . . . ah, the bliss . . . he *1888:* While . . ah, the bliss . . he 198| *1843:* enforced, still *1868:* enforced still 199| *1843:* current that must *1849:* current which must 200| *1843:* tone, Maäni *1849:* Maani 206| *1843:* heard my vow *1868:* heard me vow 207| *1843:* my People first—that *1849:* my People—on that 208| *1843:*

This Djabal, from the Prefect's massacre
—Who bade him ne'er forget the child he was,
—Who dreamed so long the youth he might become—
I knew not in the man that child; the man
Who spoke alone of hope to save our tribe,
How he had gone from land to land to save
Our tribe—allies were sure, nor foes to dread.
And much he mused, days, nights, alone he mused:
But never till that day when, pale and worn
As by a persevering woe, he cried
"Is there not one Druse left me?"—and I showed
The way to Khalil's and your hiding-place
From the abhorred eye of the Prefect here,
So that he saw you, heard you speak—till then,
Never did he announce—(how the moon seemed
To ope and shut, the while, above us both!)
—His mission was the mission promised us;
The cycle had revolved; all things renewing,
He was lost Hakeem clothed in flesh to lead
His children home anon, now veiled to work
Great purposes: the Druses now would change!
ANAEL And they have changed! And obstacles did sink,
And furtherances rose! And round his form
Played fire, and music beat her angel wings!
My people, let me more rejoice, oh more
For you than for myself! Did I but watch
Afar the pageant, feel our Khalif pass,
One of the throng, how proud were I—tho' ne'er
Singled by Djabal's glance! But to be chosen
His own from all, the most his own of all,
To be exalted with him, side by side,
Lead the exulting Druses, meet . . . ah, how
Worthily meet the maidens who await

---

more then *1849:* more, then 213| *1843:* he had become— *1849:* he might become— 215| *1843:* hopes *1868:* hope 217| *1843:* dread; *1888:* dread. 218| *1843:* alone he mused; *1863:* alone he mused: 221| *1843:* me?"—And *1863:* and 226| *1843:* shut the while above *1849:* shut, the while, above 227| *1843:* us— *1868:* us; 228| *1843:* revolved—all *1868:* revolved; all 231| *1843:* purposes—the *1868:* purposes: the 235| *1843:* oh, more *1868:* oh more 237| *1843:* feel the Khalif *1849:* feel our Khalif 241| *1843:* by side. *1888:* by side, 243| *1843:* who have watched *1849:* who await

Ever beneath the cedars—how deserve
This honour, in their eyes? So bright are they
Who saffron-vested sound the tabret there,
The girls who throng there in my dream! One hour
And all is over: how shall I do aught
That may deserve next hour's exalting?—How?—

[*Suddenly to* MAANI.]

Mother, I am not worthy him! I read it
Still in his eyes! He stands as if to tell me
I am not, yet forbears. Why else revert
To one theme ever?—how mere human gifts
Suffice him in myself—whose worship fades,
Whose awe goes ever off at his approach,
As now, who when he comes . . .
[DJABAL *enters.*] Oh why is it
I cannot kneel to you?

DJABAL Rather, 'tis I
Should kneel to you, my Anael!

ANAEL Even so!
For never seem you—shall I speak the truth?—
Never a God to me! 'Tis the Man's hand,
Eye, voice! Oh do you veil these to our people,
Or but to me? To them, I think, to them!
And brightness is their veil, shadow—my truth!
You mean that I should never kneel to you
—So, thus I kneel!

DJABAL [*preventing her*]. No—no!

[*Feeling the khandjar as he raises her.*]

Ha, have you chosen . . .

ANAEL The khandjar with our ancient garb. But, Djabal,
Change not, be not exalted yet! Give time

245| *1843:* honor in *1849:* honor, in *1888:* honour 246| *1843:* That saffron-vestured sound <> there— *1868:* Who saffron-vested sound <> there, 247| *1843:* dreams *1868:* dream 250| *1849:* worthy of him *1868:* worthy him 255| *1843:* goes off ever at *1849:* goes ever off at 256| *1843:* now,.that as he *1849:* that when he *1868:* now, who when 257| *1843:* DJABAL Rather 'tis *1849:* DJABAL Rather, 'tis 259| *1843:* you . . . shall <> truth? . . . *1849:* you—shall <> truth?— 261| *1843:* voice! Oh, do *1868:* voice! Oh do 262| *1843:* me? Them, let me think *1849:* me? To them, I think 265| *1843:*—So I will kneel! DJABAL *1888:*—So, thus I kneel! DJABAL 267| *1843:* yet—give *1849:* yet! give *1868:* yet! Give

That I may plan more, perfect more! My blood
Beats, beats!
[*Aside.*] Oh must I then—since Loys leaves us
Never to come again, renew in me
These doubts so near effaced already—must
I needs confess them now to Djabal?—own
That when I saw that stranger, heard his voice,
My faith fell, and the woeful thought flashed first
That each effect of Djabal's presence, taken
For proof of more than human attributes
In him, by me whose heart at his approach
Beat fast, whose brain while he was by swam round,
Whose soul at his departure died away,
—That every such effect might have been wrought
In other frames, tho' not in mine, by Loys
Or any merely mortal presence? Doubt
Is fading fast; shall I reveal it now?
How shall I meet the rapture presently,
With doubt unexpiated, undisclosed?
DJABAL [*aside*]. Avow the truth? I cannot! In what words
Avow that all she loved in me was false?
—Which yet has served that flower-like love of hers
To climb by, like the clinging gourd, and clasp
With its divinest wealth of leaf and bloom.
Could I take down the prop-work, in itself
So vile, yet interlaced and overlaid
With painted cups and fruitage—might these still
Bask in the sun, unconscious their own strength
Of matted stalk and tendril had replaced
The old support thus silently withdrawn!
But no; the beauteous fabric crushes too.
'Tis not for my sake but for Anael's sake
I leave her soul this Hakeem where it leans.

268| *1843:* perfect more. My *1868:* perfect more! My 269| *1843:* Beats—beats! / [*Aside.*] O must *1863:* [*Aside.*] Oh *1868:* Beats, beats! / [*Aside.*] Oh 271| *1843:* Those *1863:* These 272| *1843:* to Djabal?—Own *1868:* own 273| *1843:* when I Loys saw and Loys heard, *1849:* when I saw that stranger—heard his voice, *1868:* stranger, heard 277| *1843:* him by *1849:* him, by 281| *1843:* others' *1868:* other 285| *1843:* And yet to be rewarded presently *1849:* How can I be <> presently, *1868:* How shall I meet the rapture presently, 285| *1843:* undisclosed! *1849:* undisclosed? 287| *1843:* loves <> is *1868:* loved <> was 290| *1843:* bloom: *1849:* bloom. 299–301| *1843:* leans! / And *1849:*

Oh could I vanish from her, quit the Isle!
And yet—a thought comes: here my work is done
At every point; the Druses must return—
Have convoy to their birth-place back, whoe'er
The leader be, myself or any Druse—
Venice is pledged to that: 'tis for myself,
For my own vengeance in the Prefect's death,
I stay now, not for them: to slay or spare
The Prefect, whom imports it save myself?
He cannot bar their passage from the Isle;
What would his death be but my own reward?
Then, mine I will forego. It is foregone!
Let him escape with all my House's blood!
Ere he can reach land, Djabal disappears,
And Hakeem, Anael loved, shall, fresh as first,
Live in her memory, keeping her sublime
Above the world. She cannot touch that world
By ever knowing what I truly am,
Since Loys,—of mankind the only one
Able to link my present with my past,
My life in Europe with my Island life,
Thence, able to unmask me,—I've disposed
Safely at last at Rhodes, and . . .

Enter KHALIL.

KHALIL Loys greets thee!
DJABAL Loys? To drag me back? It cannot be!
ANAEL [*aside*]. Loys! Ah, doubt may not be stifled so!
KHALIL Can I have erred that thou so gazest? Yes,

---

leans! / Oh, could I vanish from them—quit the Isle! / And *1868:* Oh could <> from her—quit *1888:* her, quit 302–305| *1843:* return— // Venice *1849:* return— / Have convoy to their birth-place back, whoe'er / The leader be, myself or any Druse— / Venice 305–307| *1843:* myself / I <> them—to *1849:* myself, / For my own vengeance in the Prefect's death, / I *1868:* them: to 308–310| *1843:* The Prefect whom <> myself? / What *1849:* The Prefect, whom <> myself? / He cannot bar their passage from the Isle; / What 313| *1843:* can land I will have disappeared, *1849:* can reach land, Djabal disappears, 319| *1863:* my Present <> my Past, *1868:* present <> past, 320| *1843:* That life in <> with this Island *1849:* My life in <> with my Island 321| *1843:* Thence able *1849:* Thence, able 322| *1843:* you! *1849:* thee! 324–325| *1843:* so! / Doubt must be quite destroyed or quite confirmed, / Must find day somehow, live or dead. 'Tis well! / Can <> that you so gaze on

I told thee not in the glad press of tidings
Of higher import, Loys is returned
Before the Prefect, with, if possible,
Twice the light-heartedness of old. As though
On some inauguration he expects,
Today, the world's fate hung!

DJABAL —And asks for me?
KHALIL Thou knowest all things. Thee in chief he greets,
But every Druse of us is to be happy
At his arrival, he declares: were Loys
Thou, Master, he could have no wider soul
To take us in with. How I love that Loys!
DJABAL [*aside*]. Shame winds me with her tether round and round.
ANAEL [*aside*]. Loys? I take the trial! it is meet,
The little I can do, be done; that faith,
All I can offer, want no perfecting
Which my own act may compass. Ay, this way
All may go well, nor that ignoble doubt
Be chased by other aid than mine. Advance
Close to my fear, weigh Loys with my Lord,
The mortal with the more than mortal gifts!
DJABAL [*aside*]. Before, there were so few deceived! and now
There's doubtless not one least Druse in the Isle
But, having learned my superhuman claims,
And calling me his Khalif-God, will clash
The whole truth out from Loys at first word!
While Loys, for his part, will hold me up,
With a Frank's unimaginable scorn
Of such imposture, to my people's eyes!

---

me? *1849:* so! / Can <> that thou so gazest? Yes, 326| *1843:* True, I forgot, in *1849:* I told thee not, in *1868:* not in 329| *1843:* old. You'd think *1849:* old. As though 330| *1843:* expects *1849:* expects, 331| *1843:* hung. DJABAL *1849:* hung! DJABAL 332| *1843:* Ah, you know all things! You in *1849:* Thou knowest all <> Thee *1888:* things. Thee 333| *1843:* every body else is *1849:* every Druse of us is 335| *1843:* Thou, Khalif, he *1849:* Thou, Master, he 337| *1843:* DJABAL Shame *1849:* DJABAL [*aside*] Shame <> and round! *1888:* round. 338| *1843:* trial: meet it is *1849:* trial! it is meet, 339| *1843:* do be *1849:* do, be 341| *1843:* compass. Aye *1868:* compass. Ay 342| *1843:* well nor <> ignoble spot *1849:* well, nor <> ignoble doubt 343| *1843:* mine. Best go *1849:* mine. Advance 345| *1843:* mortal's <> mortal's *1868:* mortal <> mortal 346| *1843:* deceived, and *1849:* deceived! and 348| *1843:* But (having *1863:* But, having 349| *1843:* his Khalif now) will *1849:* his Khalif-God) will *1863:* his Khalif-God, will 351| *1843:* And Loys *1849:* While Loys 353–354| *1843:* Of this

Could I but keep him longer yet awhile
From them, amuse him here until I plan
How he and I at once may leave the Isle!
Khalil I cannot part with from my side—
My only help in this emergency:
There's Anael!

ANAEL Please you?

DJABAL Anael—none but she!

[*To* ANAEL.] I pass some minutes in the chamber there,
Ere I see Loys: you shall speak with him
Until I join you. Khalil follows me.

ANAEL [*aside*]. As I divined: he bids me save myself,
Offers me a probation—I accept.
Let me see Loys!

LOYS [*without*]. Djabal!

ANAEL [*aside*]. 'Tis his voice.
The smooth Frank trifler with our people's wrongs,
The self-complacent boy-inquirer, loud
On this and that inflicted tyranny,
—Aught serving to parade an ignorance
Of how wrong feels, inflicted! Let me close
With what I viewed at distance: let myself
Probe this delusion to the core!

DJABAL He comes.
Khalil, along with me! while Anael waits
Till I return once more—and but once more.

---

imposture <> eyes, / To Khalil's eyes, to Anael's eyes! Oh, how / —How hold him longer yet a little while *1849:* Of such imposture <> eyes! / Could I but hold him longer yet awhile *1863:* but keep him 356–359| *1843:* the Isle? / There's <> DJABAL (Anael only!) Anael, *1849:* the Isle? / Khalil I cannot part with from my side— / My only help in this emergency: / There's <> DJABAL (Anael—none but she!) 356| *1868:* the Isle! 359| *1863:* DJABAL Anael <> she! 360| *1843:* I would pass some few minutes here within *1849:* [*To* ANAEL.] I pass some minutes in the chamber there, 362| *1843:* you and declare the end. *1849:* you. Khalil follows me. 363| *1843:* myself, *1888:* myself 364| *1843:* Allows me the probation—I accept! *1849:* Offers me a probation *1888:* accept. 371| *1843:* distance, and, myself, *1849:* distance; let myself *1863:* distance! let *1868:* distance: let 372| *1843:* comes! *1868:* comes. 373| *1863:* me; while *1868:* me! while 374| *1843:* more! / [*Exeunt* DJABAL *and* KHALIL. *Manet* ANAEL. *1849:* more! § stage direction dropped § *1888:* more.

ACT III

ANAEL *and* LOYS.

ANAEL Here leave me! Here I wait another. 'Twas
For no mad protestation of a love
Like this you say possesses you, I came.
LOYS Love? how protest a love I dare not feel?
Mad words may doubtless have escaped me: you
Are here—I only feel you here!
ANAEL No more!
LOYS But once again, whom could you love? I dare,
Alas, say nothing of myself, who am
A Knight now, for when Knighthood we embrace,
Love we abjure: so, speak on safely: speak,
Lest I speak, and betray my faith! And yet
To say your breathing passes through me, changes
My blood to spirit, and my spirit to you,
As Heaven the sacrificer's wine to it—
This is not to protest my love! You said
You could love one . . .
ANAEL One only! We are bent
To earth—who raises up my tribe, I love;
The Prefect bows us—who removes him; we
Have ancient rights—who gives them back to us,
I love. Forbear me! Let my hand go!
LOYS Him
You could love only? Where is Djabal? Stay!

4| *1849:* Love—how *1868:* Love? how 5| *1843:* me—you *1868:* me: you 7| *1843:* Say but again *1849:* But once again 9| *1843:* now, and when *1849:* now, for when 10| *1843:* so speak on safely—speak, *1863:* so, speak *1868:* safely: speak, 11| *1843:* speak and <> faith so? Sure *1849:* speak, and <> so! Sure *1863:* faith. And yet *1868:* faith! And 12| *1843:* thro' *1863:* through 15| *1843:* love? You *1863:* love! You 17| *1843:* To the earth *1849:* To earth 18| *1843:* The Prefect bends us *1849:* The Prefect bows us 20| *1843:* love.—Forbear *1863:* love. Forbear 22| *1843:* Yet *1849:* [*Aside.*] Yet

[*Aside.*] Yet wherefore stay? Who does this but myself?
Had I apprised her that I come to do
Just this, what more could she acknowledge? No,
She sees into my heart's core! What is it
Feeds either cheek with red, as June some rose?
Why turns she from me? Ah fool, over-fond
To dream I could call up . . .
. . . What never dream
Yet feigned! 'Tis love! Oh Anael speak to me!
Djabal—
ANAEL Seek Djabal by the Prefect's chamber
At noon! [*She paces the room.*]
LOYS [*aside*]. And am I not the Prefect now?
Is it my fate to be the only one
Able to win her love, the only one
Unable to accept her love? The past
Breaks up beneath my footing: came I here
This morn as to a slave, to set her free
And take her thanks, and then spend day by day
Content beside her in the Isle? What works
This knowledge in me now? Her eye has broken
The faint disguise away: for Anael's sake
I left the Isle, for her espoused the cause
Of the Druses, all for her I thought, till now,
To live without!
—As I must live! To-day
Ordains me Knight, forbids me . . . never shall
Forbid me to profess myself, heart, arm,
Thy soldier!
ANAEL Djabal you demanded, comes.

23| *1843:* apprized *1863:* apprised 25| *1843:* core: what *1863:* core! What 26| *1843:* red as *1849:* red, as 28| *1843:* up . . / . . What *1868:* up . . . / . . . What 29| *1843:* love! Oh Anael, speak *1868:* love! Oh Anael speak 30| *1843:* Djabal! ANAEL *1868:* Djabal—ANAEL 31| *1843:* LOYS And *1849:* LOYS [*aside*] And 34| *1843:* love? The Past *1868:* past 35| *1843:* footing—came *1849:* footing: came 38| *1843:* Beside her in the Isle content? What *1849:* Content beside her in the Isle? What 39| *1843:* now! Her *1868:* now? Her 40| *1843:* away—for *1849:* away; for *1863:* away: for 41| *1843:* isle *1849:* Isle 43| *1843:* without! ¶ As <> live: to-day *1849:* without! ¶—As <> live! To-day 44| *1843:* me—never *1863:* me . . . never 45| *1843:* arm *1849:* arm, 46| *1843:* you awaited, comes! *1849:* you

LOYS [*aside*]. What wouldst thou, Loys? See him? Nought beside
Is wanting: I have felt his voice a spell
From first to last. He brought me here, made known
The Druses to me, drove me hence to seek
Redress for them; and shall I meet him now,
When nought is wanting but a word of his,
To—what?—induce me to spurn hope, faith, pride,
Honour away,—to cast my lot among
His tribe, become a proverb in men's mouths,
Breaking my high pact of companionship
With those who graciously bestowed on me
The very opportunities I turn
Against them! Let me not see Djabal now!
ANAEL The Prefect also comes.
LOYS [*aside*]. Him let me see,
Not Djabal! Him, degraded at a word,
To soothe me,—to attest belief in me—
And after, Djabal! Yes, ere I return
To her, the Nuncio's vow shall have destroyed
This heart's rebellion, and coerced this will
For ever.
Anael, not before the vows
Irrevocably fix me . . .
Let me fly!
The Prefect, or I lose myself for ever! [*Goes.*]
ANAEL Yes, I am calm now; just one way remains—
One, to attest my faith in him: for, see,
I were quite lost else: Loys, Djabal, stand
On either side—two men! I balance looks
And words, give Djabal a man's preference,

---

demanded, comes! *1888:* comes. 47| *1843:* LOYS What *1849:* LOYS [*aside*] What 48| *1843:* wanting—I *1849:* wanting: I 51| *1843:* now *1849:* now, 52| *1843:* his *1849:* his, 54| *1843:* Honor *1863:* Honour 59–60| *1843:* them. Loys, they procured thee, think, / What now procures her love! Not Djabal <> / The <> LOYS Him *1849:* them. / Let me not see Djabal <> / The <> LOYS [*aside*] Him *1863:* them! Let 62| *1843:* To please me,—to *1863:* To soothe me,—to 63| *1843:* And, after *1868:* And after 65| *1843:* coërced *1863:* coerced 66| *1843:* not until the *1849:* not before the 67| *1843:* me leave her! *1849:* me fly! 68| *1843:* ever. [*Exit.* *1849:* ever! [*Goes.* 69| *1843:* now—just *1849:* now; just 70| *1843:* So I attest *1849:* One, to attest 71| *1843:* I am quite lost now: Loys and Djabal stand *1849:* I were quite lost else: Loys,

No more. In Djabal, Hakeem is absorbed!
And for a love like this, the God who saves
My race, selects me for his bride? One way!

Enter DJABAL.

DJABAL [*to himself*]. No moment is to waste then; 'tis resolved.
If Khalil may be trusted to lead back
My Druses, and if Loys can be lured
Out of the Isle—if I procure his silence,
Or promise never to return at least,—
All's over. Even now my bark awaits:
I reach the next wild islet and the next,
And lose myself beneath the sun for ever.
And now, to Anael!
ANAEL Djabal, I am thine!
DJABAL Mine? Djabal's?—As if Hakeem had not been?
ANAEL Not Djabal's? Say first, do you read my thought?
Why need I speak, if you can read my thought?
DJABAL I do not, I have said a thousand times.
ANAEL (My secret's safe, I shall surprise him yet!)
Djabal, I knew your secret from the first:
Djabal, when first I saw you . . . (by our porch
You leant, and pressed the tinkling veil away,
And one fringe fell behind your neck—I see!)
. . . I knew you were not human, for I said
"This dim secluded house where the sea beats
Is heaven to me—my people's huts are hell
To them; this august form will follow me,

Djabal, stand 74| *1843:* more. The Khalif is absorbed in Djabal! *1849:* more. In Djabal, Hakeem is absorbed! 75| *1843:* Is it for <> this that he who *1849:* And for <> this, the God who 76| *1843:* way!— *1888:* way! 77| *1843:* to spare then *1849:* to waste, then 79| *1843:* The Druses *1868:* My Druses 80| *1843:* the Isle—can I <> silence *1849:* the Isle—if I <> silence, 82| *1843:* bark is ready; *1849:* bark awaits— *1868:* awaits: 84| *1843:* myself thus in the <> ever! *1849:* myself beneath the *1868:* ever. 85| *1843:* Anael remains now.—Think! She loved in me / But Hakeem—Hakeem's vanished; and on Djabal / Had never glanced— ANAEL <> thine own! *1849:* And now, to Anael! ANAEL <> thine! 87| *1843:* thoughts? *1868:* thought? 88| *1843:* thoughts? *1868:* thought? 91| *1843:* first— *1868:* first: 93| *1843:* leant and *1849:* leant, and 95| *1843:* I knew *1849:* . . . I knew 97| *1843:* Is Heaven <> are Hell

Mix with the waves his voice will,—I have him;
And they, the Prefect! Oh, my happiness
Rounds to the full whether I choose or no!
His eyes met mine, he was about to speak,
His hand grew damp—surely he meant to say
He let me love him: in that moment's bliss
I shall forget my people pine for home—
They pass and they repass with pallid eyes!"
I vowed at once a certain vow; this vow—
Not to embrace you till my tribe was saved.
Embrace me!
DJABAL [*apart*]. And she loved me! Nought remained
But that! Nay, Anael, is the Prefect dead?
ANAEL Ah, you reproach me! True, his death crowns all,
I know—or should know: and I would do much,
Believe! but, death! Oh, you, who have known death,
Would never doom the Prefect, were death fearful
As we report!
Death!—a fire curls within us
From the foot's palm, and fills up to the brain,
Up, out, then shatters the whole bubble-shell
Of flesh, perchance!
Death!—witness, I would die,
Whate'er death be, would venture now to die
For Khalil, for Maani—what for thee?
Nay but embrace me, Djabal, in assurance
My vow will not be broken, for I must
Do something to attest my faith in you,
Be worthy you!
DJABAL [*avoiding her*]. I come for that—to say
Such an occasion is at hand: 'tis like

1868: heaven <> hell 99| *1843:* will, him have I *1849:* will,—I have him; 100| *1843:* they the Prefect; Oh *1869:* they, the *1888:* the Prefect! Oh 104| *1843:* him—in *1849:* him: in 105| *1843:* people, pine *1849:* people pine 107| *1843:* vow—this *1849:* vow; this 108| *1843:* saved— *1849:* saved. 109| *1843:* me! DJABAL [*shrinking*] And *1849:* me! DJABAL [*apart*] And 112| *1843:* know—I should know—and *1849:* know—or should *1863:* should know: and 113| *1843:* Believe—but, death—Oh *1849:* Believe! but *1868:* death! Oh 118| *1843:* flesh perchance </> witness I *1849:* flesh, perchance </> witness, I 120| *1843:* For Maäni—for Khalil—but, for him?— *1849:* For Khalil—for Maani—what for thee? *1868:* For Khalil, for Maani 124| *1849:* worthy of you *1868:* worthy you 125| *1843:* hand—'tis *1849:* hand: 'tis

I leave you—that we part, my Anael,—part
For ever!

ANAEL We part? Just so! I have succumbed,—
I am, he thinks, unworthy—and nought less
Will serve than such approval of my faith.
Then, we part not! Remains there no way short
Of that? Oh not that!

Death!—yet a hurt bird
Died in my hands; its eyes filmed—"Nay, it sleeps,"
I said, "will wake to-morrow well:" 'twas dead.

DJABAL I stand here and time fleets. Anael—I come
To bid a last farewell to you: perhaps
We never meet again. But, ere the Prefect
Arrive . . .

Enter KHALIL, *breathlessly.*

KHALIL He's here! The Prefect! Twenty guards,
No more: no sign he dreams of danger. All
Awaits thee only. Ayoob, Karshook, keep
Their posts—wait but the deed's accomplishment
To join us with thy Druses to a man.
Still holds his course the Nuncio—near and near
The fleet from Candia steering.

DJABAL [*aside*]. All is lost!
—Or won?

KHALIL And I have laid the sacred robe,
The sword, the head-tiar, at the porch—the place
Commanded. Thou wilt hear the Prefect's trumpet.

127| *1843:* succumbed, he thinks, *1849:* succumbed,— 129| *1843:* faith! *1868:* faith. 130| *1843:* not! Yet remains *1849:* not! Remains 131| *1843:* that? Oh, not *1868:* that? Oh not 132| *1843:* my arms—its <> Nay it sleeps" *1849:* my hands—its *1863:* Nay, it sleeps," *1868:* hands: its *1888:* hands; its 133| *1843:* well"—'twas dead! *1868:* well:" 'twas dead. 134| *1843:* fleets—Anael *1849:* fleets. Anael 135| *1843:* you—we never *1849:* you: perhaps 136| *1843:* Perhaps shall meet again—but *1849:* We never meet *1863:* again. But 137| *1843:* Arrives *1849:* Arrive 138| *1843:* more—no <> danger—all *1863:* danger. All *1888:* more: no 139| *1843:* Awaits you only—Ayoob *1849:* thee *1868:* only. Ayoob 141| *1843:* your Druses <> man! *1849:* thy *1888:* man.
143| *1843:* from Candia's *1863:* Candia 144| *1843:* robes, *1868:* robe,
145| *1843:* porch as 'twas *1849:* porch—the place 146| *1843:* Commanded—You

DJABAL Then I keep Anael,—him then, past recall,
I slay—'tis forced on me. As I began
I must conclude—so be it!
KHALIL For the rest,
Save Loys, our foe's solitary sword,
All is so safe that . . . I will ne'er entreat
Thy post again of thee: tho' danger none,
There must be glory only meet for thee
In slaying the Prefect.
ANAEL [*aside*]. And 'tis now that Djabal
Would leave me!—in the glory meet for him!
DJABAL As glory, I would yield the deed to you
Or any Druse; what peril there may be,
I keep. [*Aside.*] All things conspire to hound me on.
Not now, my soul, draw back, at least! Not now!
The course is plain, howe'er obscure all else.
Once offer this tremendous sacrifice,
Prevent what else will be irreparable,
Secure these transcendental helps, regain
The Cedars—then let all dark clear itself!
I slay him!
KHALIL Anael, and no part for us!
[*To* DJABAL.] Hast thou possessed her with . . .
DJABAL [*to* ANAEL]. Whom speak you to?
What is it you behold there? Nay, this smile
Turns stranger. Shudder you? The man must die,
As thousands of our race have died thro' him.
One blow, and I discharge his weary soul
From the flesh that pollutes it! Let him fill

---

will *1849:* Commanded—Thou wilt *1863:* Commanded. Thou 147| *1843:* Anael, I keep them, him then, past retrieve, *1849:* Then I keep Anael,—him then, past recal, *1863:* recall, 148| *1843:* me! As *1888:* me. As 149| *1843:* rest *1863:* rest, 150| *1843:* (Save Loys, but a solitary sword) *1849:* (Save Loys, our foe's solitary *1863:* Save <> sword, 151| *1843:* that—I *1849:* that . . . I 152| *1843:* Your post <> of you—tho' danger's *1849:* Thy post <> of thee *1863:* thee: tho' danger 153| *1843:* you *1849:* thee 154| *1843:* the Prefect! ANAEL And *1849:* ANAEL [*aside*] And *1888:* the Prefect. ANAEL 156| *1843:* glory I <> you, *1849:* glory, I *1868:* you 157| *1843:* any one; what <> be *1849:* be, *1863:* any Druse; what 158| *1843:* keep. All <> on! *1869:* keep. [*Aside*] All *1888:* on. 160| *1843:* else— *1868:* else. 164| *1843:* all this clear *1849:* all dark clear 168| *1843:* stranger—shudder *1849:* stranger. Shudder 170| *1843:* A blow *1849:* One blow 171| *1843:* The body that pollutes it—let

Straight some new expiatory form, of earth
Or sea, the reptile or some aëry thing:
What is there in his death?
ANAEL My brother said,
Is there no part in it for us?
DJABAL For Khalil,—
The trumpet will announce the Nuncio's entry;
Here, I shall find the Prefect hastening
In the Pavilion to receive him—here
I slay the Prefect; meanwhile Ayoob leads
The Nuncio with his guards within: once these
Secured in the outer hall, bid Ayoob bar
Entry or egress till I give the sign
Which waits the landing of the argosies
You will announce to me: this double sign
That justice is performed and help arrived,
When Ayoob shall receive, but not before,
Let him throw ope the palace doors, admit
The Druses to behold their tyrant, ere
We leave for ever this detested spot.
Go, Khalil, hurry all! No pause, no pause!
Whirl on the dream, secure to wake anon!
KHALIL What sign? and who the bearer?
DJABAL Who shall show
My ring, admit to Ayoob. How she stands!
Have I not . . . I must have some task for her.
Anael, not that way! 'Tis the Prefect's chamber!
Anael, keep you the ring—give you the sign!

1849: From the flesh that *1863:* it; let *1868:* it! Let 172| *1843:* Some new <> form of earth, *1849:* Straight some <> form, of earth 173| *1843:* reptile, or <> thing— *1863:* thing: *1868:* reptile or 174| *1843:* said *1849:* said, 177| *1843:* Here I *1849:* Here, I 178| *1849:* here, *1868:* here 180| *1843:* within—once he *1849:* once these *1863:* within: once 184–187| *1843:* Yourself announce: when he receives my sign / Let *1849:* You will announce to me; this double sign / That justice is performed and help arrived, / When Ayoob shall receive, but not before, / Let 185| *1863:* me: this 188| *1843:* tyrant ere *1849:* tyrant, ere 190| *1843:* all—no pause—no *1863:* all! no pause, no *1868:* all! No pause, no 192| *1843:* sign? DJABAL Whoe'er shall show my ring admit *1849:* sign? and who the bearer? DJABAL Who shall show 193| *1843:* To Ayoob and the Nuncio. How *1849:* My ring, admit to Ayoob—How *1863:* to Ayoob. How 194| *1843:* not—I *1849:* not . . . I 195| *1843:* way! That's the <> chamber. *1849:* way!

(It holds her safe amid the stir.) You will
Be faithful?

ANAEL [*taking the ring*]. I would fain be worthy. Hark!

[*Trumpet without.*]

KHALIL He comes.

DJABAL And I too come.

ANAEL One word, but one!
Say, shall you be exalted at the deed?
Then? On the instant?

DJABAL I exalted? What?
He, there—we, thus—our wrongs revenged, our tribe
Set free? Oh, then shall I, assure yourself,
Shall you, shall each of us, be in his death
Exalted!

KHALIL He is here.

DJABAL Away—away! [*They go.*]

Enter the PREFECT *with* GUARDS, *and* LOYS.

THE PREFECT [*to* GUARDS]. Back, I say, to the galley every guard!
That's my sole care now; see each bench retains
Its complement of rowers; I embark
O' the instant, since this Knight will have it so.
Alas me! Could you have the heart, my Loys!
[*To a* GUARD *who whispers.*] Oh, bring the holy Nuncio here forthwith!

[*The* GUARDS *go.*]

Loys, a rueful sight, confess, to see
The grey discarded Prefect leave his post,
With tears i' the eye! So, you are Prefect now?
You depose me—you succeed me? Ha, ha!

LOYS And dare you laugh, whom laughter less becomes
Than yesterday's forced meekness we beheld . . .

'Tis the <> chamber! *1863:* chamber *1868:* chamber! 197| *1843:* stir)—You *1863:* stir.) You 198| *1843:* worthy you! *1849:* worthy of you! *1888:* worthy. Hark! 199| *1843:* comes! DJABAL <> come! ANAEL *1888:* comes. DJABAL <> come. ANAEL 202| *1843:* He there—we thus <> revenged—our *1849:* He, there—we, thus *1868:* revenged, our 203| *1843:* free—Oh then *1849:* free—Oh, then *1863:* free? Oh 205| *1843:* DJABAL Away—away! [*Exeunt.* *1849:* DJABAL Away—away! [*They go.* *1888:* DJABAL Away—away 207| *1843:* now—see *1849:* now; see 208| *1843:* rowers—I *1849:* rowers; I 211| *1843:* [*Exeunt* Guards. *1849:* [*The* Guards *go.* 214| *1843:* eye! So you

PREFECT —When you so eloquently pleaded, Loys,
For my dismissal from the post? Ah, meek
With cause enough, consult the Nuncio else!
And wish him the like meekness: for so staunch
A servant of the Church can scarce have bought
His share in the Isle, and paid for it, hard pieces!
You've my successor to condole with, Nuncio!
I shall be safe by then i' the galley, Loys!
LOYS You make as you would tell me you rejoice
To leave your scene of . . .
PREFECT Trade in the dear Druses?
Blood and sweat traffic? Spare what yesterday
We heard enough of! Drove I in the Isle
A profitable game? Learn wit, my son,
Which you'll need shortly! Did it never breed
Suspicion in you, all was not pure profit,
When I, the insatiate . . . and so forth—was bent
On having a partaker in my rule?
Why did I yield this Nuncio half the gain,
If not that I might also shift—what on him?
Half of the peril, Loys!
LOYS Peril?
PREFECT Hark you!
I'd love you if you'd let me—this for reason,
You save my life at price of . . . well, say risk
At least, of yours. I came a long time since
To the Isle; our Hospitallers bade me tame
These savage wizards, and reward myself—
LOYS The Knights who so repudiate your crime?
PREFECT Loys, the Knights! we doubtless understood
Each other; as for trusting to reward
From any friend beside myself . . . no, no!

1863: eye! So, you 218| *1843:* . . . When *1863:* —When 221| *1843:* meekness—for *1868:* meekness: for 222| *1843:* church *1888:* Church 229| *1843:* We had enough <> isle *1849:* Isle *1888:* We heard enough 232| *1843:* you all *1849:* you, all 233| *1843:* forth . . . was *1863:* forth—was 234| *1843:* an associate in *1849:* a partaker in 236| *1843:* shift . . . what *1863:* shift—what 241| *1843:* the Isle: our *1849:* the Isle; our 242| *1843:* myself. *1849:* myself— 244| *1843:* the Knights—we <> understand *1849:* the Knights! we <> understood 246| *1843:* myself . . . No, no! *1863:* myself

I clutched mine on the spot, when it was sweet,
And I had taste for it. I felt these wizards
Alive—was sure they were not on me, only
When I was on them: but with age comes caution:
And stinging pleasures please less and sting more.
Year by year, fear by fear! The girls were brighter
Than ever ('faith, there's yet one Anael left,
I set my heart upon—Oh, prithee, let
That brave new sword lie still!)—These joys looked brighter,
But silenter the town, too, as I passed.
With this alcove's delicious memories
Began to mingle visions of gaunt fathers,
Quick-eyed sons, fugitives from the mine, the oar,
Stealing to catch me. Brief, when I began
To quake with fear—(I think I hear the Chapter
Solicited to let me leave, now all
Worth staying for was gained and gone!)—I say,
Just when, for the remainder of my life,
All methods of escape seemed lost—that then
Up should a young hot-headed Loys spring,
Talk very long and loud,—in fine, compel
The Knights to break their whole arrangement, have me
Home for pure shame—from this safehold of mine
Where but ten thousand Druses seek my life,
To my wild place of banishment, San Gines
By Murcia, where my three fat manors lying,
Purchased by gains here and the Nuncio's gold,
Are all I have to guard me,—that such fortune
Should fall to me, I hardly could expect.
Therefore I say, I'd love you.

LOYS
Can it be?
I play into your hands then? Oh no, no!

. . . no, no! 247| *1843:* sweet *1849:* sweet, 252| *1843:* brighter, *1863:* brighter 254| *1843:* upon)—Oh *1849:* upon—Oh 255| *1843:* still!—These joys were brighter, *1849:* still!)—These joys looked brighter, 256| *1843:* town too as *1849:* town, too, as 258| *1843:* Yet to be mingled *1849:* Began to mingle 260| *1843:* me: brief *1888:* me. Brief 263| *1843:* say *1849:* say, 264| *1843:* That when for <> life *1849:* Just when *1888:* when, for <> life, 265| *1843:* lost—just then *1849:* lost—that then 267| *1843:* loud, in *1863:* loud,—in 275| *1843:* me I <> expect! *1849:* me, I *1888:* expect. 276| *1843:* Therefore, I say <> you! LOYS *1868:* Therefore I say *1888:* you. LOYS 277| *1843:* then? Oh,

The Venerable Chapter, the Great Order
Sunk o' the sudden into fiends of the pit?
But I will back—will yet unveil you!
PREFECT Me?
To whom?—perhaps Sir Galeas, who in Chapter
Shook his white head thrice—and some dozen times
My hand next morning shook, for value paid!
To that Italian saint, Sir Cosimo?—
Indignant at my wringing year by year
A thousand bezants from the coral-divers,
As you recounted; felt the saint aggrieved?
Well might he—I allowed for his half-share
Merely one hundred. To Sir . . .
LOYS See! you dare
Inculpate the whole Order; yet should I,
A youth, a sole voice, have the power to change
Their evil way, had they been firm in it?
Answer me!
PREFECT Oh, the son of Bretagne's Duke,
And that son's wealth, the father's influence, too,
And the young arm, we'll even say, my Loys,
—The fear of losing or diverting these
Into another channel, by gainsaying
A novice too abruptly, could not influence
The Order! You might join, for aught they cared,
Their red-cross rivals of the Temple! Well,
I thank you for my part, at all events.
Stay here till they withdraw you! You'll inhabit
My palace—sleep, perchance, in the alcove
Whither I go to meet our holy friend.
Good! and now disbelieve me if you can,—
This is the first time for long years I enter
Thus [*lifts the arras*] without feeling just as if I lifted

---

no, no! *1868:* then? Oh no, no! 283| *1843:* hand this morning shook for <> paid? *1849:* shook, for <> paid *1863:* hand next morning <> paid! 284| *1843:* that Italian Saint Sir *1849:* that Italian Saint, Sir *1868:* saint 287| *1843:* felt he not aggrieved? *1868:* felt the saint aggrieved? 288| *1843:* half share *1849:* half-share 292| *1843:* way had *1849:* way, had 297| *1843:* channel by *1849:* channel, by 301| *1843:* part at <> events! *1849:* part, at *1868:* events. 303–305| *1843:* This palace <> in this alcove; / Good <> can: *1849:* alcove, / Where now I got to meet our holy friend: / Good *1863:* My palace <> in the

The lid up of my tomb.
LOYS They share his crime!
God's punishment will overtake you yet.
PREFECT Thank you it does not! Pardon this last flash:
I bear a sober visage presently
With the disinterested Nuncio here—
His purchase-money safe at Murcia, too!
Let me repeat—for the first time, no draught
Coming as from a sepulchre salutes me.
When we next meet, this folly may have passed,
We'll hope. Ha, ha! [*Goes through the arras.*]
LOYS Assure me but . . . he's gone!
He could not lie. Then what have I escaped,
I, who had so nigh given up happiness
For ever, to be linked with him and them!
Oh, opportunest of discoveries! I
Their Knight? I utterly renounce them all!
Hark! What, he meets by this the Nuncio? Yes,
The same hyæna groan-like laughter! Quick—
To Djabal! I am one of them at last,
These simple hearted Druses—Anael's tribe!
Djabal! She's mine at last. Djabal, I say! [*Goes.*]

---

alcove, *1868:* alcove / Whither I <> friend. / <> can,— 308| *1843:* tomb! LOYS *1868:* tomb. LOYS 309| *1843:* yet! *1868:* yet. 311| *1843:* a graver visage *1849:* a sober visage 313| *1843:* at Murcia too! *1863:* at Murcia, too! 314| *1843:* time no *1849:* time, no 316| *1843:* meet this *1849:* meet, this 317| *1843:* hope—Ha, ha! / [*Exit through* <> but—he's *1849:* hope—Ha, ha! [*Goes through* <> but . . . he's *1868:* hope. Ha, ha! [*Goes* 318| *1843:* lie! Then <> escaped! *1868:* lie. Then <> escaped, 319| *1843:* have *1863:* had 323–325| *1843:* Hark! what <> Nuncio? Quick / To *1849:* Hark! What <> Nuncio? Yes / The same hyæna groan-like laughter! Quick— / To *1863:* hyæna-groan-like *1868:* yes, / <> hyæna groan-like 323| *1888:* Yes 327| *1843:* last—Djabal, I say!— [*Exit.* *1849:* say!— [*Goes* *1863:* say! *1868:* last. Djabal

ACT IV

Enter DJABAL.

DJABAL Let me but slay the Prefect. The end now!
To-morrow will be time enough to pry
Into the means I took: suffice, they served,
Ignoble as they were, to hurl revenge
Ture to its object. [*Seeing the robe, etc. disposed.*]
Mine should never so
Have hurried to accomplishment! Thee, Djabal,
Far other mood befitted! Calm the Robe
Should clothe this doom's awarder!
[*Taking the robe.*] Shall I dare
Assume my nation's Robe? I am at least
A Druse again, chill Europe's policy
Drops from me: I dare take the Robe. Why not
The Tiar? I rule the Druses, and what more
Betokens it than rule?—yet—yet— [*Lays down the tiar.*]
[*Footsteps in the alcove.*] He comes! [*Taking the sword.*]
If the Sword serve, let the Tiar lie! So, feet
Clogged with the blood of twenty years can fall
Thus lightly! Round me, all ye ghosts! He'll lift . . .
Which arm to push the arras wide?—or both?
Stab from the neck down to the heart—there stay!
Near he comes—nearer—the next footstep! Now!
[*As he dashes aside the arras,* ANAEL *is discovered.*]
Ha! Anael! Nay, my Anael, can it be?
Heard you the trumpet? I must slay him here,
And here you ruin all. Why speak you not?

1| *1843:* the Prefect—The *1863:* the Prefect. The 5| *1843:* object. ¶ . . . Mine *1863:* object. ¶ Mine 7| *1843:* moods *1868:* mood 8| *1843:* awarder. / Well, I *1849:* awarder! / Shall I 10| *1843:* again—chill *1849:* again, chill 11| *1843:* me—I <> Robe: why *1849:* the Robe. Why *1868:* me: I 14| *1843:* serves *1849:* sword *1863:* Sword *1868:* serve 16| *1843:* lift . . . *1888:* lift . .

Anael, the Prefect comes! [ANAEL *screams.*] So slow to feel
'Tis not a sight for you to look upon?
A moment's work—but such work! Till you go,
I must be idle—idle, I risk all! [*Pointing to her hair.*]
Those locks are well, and you are beauteous thus,
But with the dagger 'tis, I have to do!

ANAEL With mine!

DJABAL Blood—Anael?

ANAEL Djabal, 'tis thy deed!
It must be! I had hoped to claim it mine—
Be worthy thee—but I must needs confess
'Twas not I, but thyself . . . not I have . . . Djabal!
Speak to me!

DJABAL Oh, my punishment!

ANAEL Speak to me
While I can speak! touch me, despite the blood!
When the command passed from thy soul to mine,
I went, fire leading me, muttering of thee,
And the approaching exaltation,—"make
One sacrifice!" I said,—and he sat there,
Bade me approach; and, as I did approach,
Thy fire with music burst into my brain.
'Twas but a moment's work, thou saidst—perchance
It may have been so! Well, it is thy deed.

DJABAL It is my deed.

ANAEL His blood all this!—this! and . . .
And more! Sustain me, Djabal! Wait not—now
Let flash thy glory! Change thyself and me!
It must be! Ere the Druses flock to us!
At least confirm me! Djabal, blood gushed forth—

23| *1843:* comes! So late to *1868:* comes! So slow to 25| *1843:* go *1849:* go, 28| *1843:* 'tis I *1849:* 'tis, I 29| *1843:* Mine—Look! DJABAL *1849:* With mine! DJABAL 30| *1843:* be—I *1843:* be! I 32| *1843:* thyself . . not I have . . Djabal! *1888:* thyself . . . not I have . . . Djabal! 33| *1843:* ANAEL Speak to me! *1863:* ANAEL Speak to me 34| *1843:* speak—touch me—despite *1863:* speak! touch me, despite 35| *1843:* mine *1849:* mine, 37| *1843:* exaltation,—make *1868:* exaltation,—"make 38| *1843:* sacrifice! I <> sate *1863:* sat *1868:* sacrifice!" I 40| *1843:* brain— *1863:* brain: *1888:* brain. 42| *1843:* so—well *1849:* so! well *1868:* so! Well 43| *1843:* this!—this! And . . *1849:* blood, all *1868:* blood all <> and . . *1888:* and . . . 44| *1843:* more—sustain me, Djabal—wait *1863:* me, Djabal! wait *1868:* more! Sustain me, Djabal! Wait 47| *1843:* me! Djabal—blood *1863:* me! Djabal! blood *1868:* me! Djabal, blood

He was our tyrant—but I looked he'd fall
Prone as asleep—why else is death called sleep?
Sleep? He bent o'er his breast! 'Tis sin, I know,—
Punish me, Djabal, but wilt thou let him?
Be it thou that punishest, not he—who creeps
On his red breast—is here! 'Tis the small groan
Of a child—no worse! Bestow the new life, then!
Too swift it cannot be, too strange, surpassing!
[*Following him as he retreats.*]
Now! Change us both! Change me and change thou!
DJABAL [*sinks on his knees*]. Thus!
Behold my change! You have done nobly. I!—
ANAEL Can Hakeem kneel?
DJABAL No Hakeem, and scarce Djabal!
I have dealt falsely, and this woe is come.
No—hear me ere scorn blast me! Once and ever,
The deed is mine. Oh think upon the past!
ANAEL [*to herself*]. Did I strike once, or twice, or many times?
DJABAL I came to lead my tribe where, bathed in glooms,
Doth Bahumid the Renovator sleep:
Anael, I saw my tribe: I said, "Without
A miracle this cannot be"—I said
"Be there a miracle!"—for I saw you.
ANAEL His head lies south the portal.
DJABAL —Weighed with this

48| *1843:* our Tyrant *1849:* tyrant 49| *1843:* is Death *1863:* death 50| *1843:* his neck—'Tis <> know, *1849:* his breast—'Tis *1863:* breast! 'Tis <> know,— 51| *1843:* me Djabal *1849:* me, Djabal 53| *1843:* here—'tis *1849:* here—'Tis *1863:* here! 'tis *1868:* here! 'Tis 54| *1843:* life then! *1849:* life, then! 55| *1843:* [*Following him up and down.* *1888:* [*Following him as he retreats.* 57| *1843:* nobly! I! *1888:* nobly. I! 58| *1843:* DJABAL No Hakeem, but mere Djabal! *1863:* DJABAL No Hakeem, and scarce Djabal! 59| *1843:* have spoke falsely *1849:* spoken *1888:* have dealt falsely 61| *1843:* mine . . Oh <> Past! *1863:* mine! Oh *1868:* past! *1888:* mine. Oh 62| *1843:* (Did <> times?) *1849:* Did <> times? 63| *1843:* . . I *1863:* I 64| *1843:* sleep— *1863:* sleep: 65| *1843:* Anael—I saw my tribe—I *1849:* Anael, I saw *1863:* tribe: I 67| *1843:* you! *1888:* you. 68–70| *1843:* (His <> portal!) DJABAL —To this end / What was I with my *1849:* His <> portal! DJABAL —Weighed with this / The general good, how could I choose my own, / What matter was my 68| *1888:*

The general good, how could I choose my own?
What matter was my purity of soul?
Little by little I engaged myself—
Heaven would accept me for its instrument,
I hoped: I said Heaven had accepted me.
ANAEL Is it this blood breeds dreams in me? Who said
You were not Hakeem? And your miracles—
The fire that plays innocuous round your form?
[*Again changing her whole manner.*]
Ah, thou wouldst try me—thou art Hakeem still!
DJABAL Woe—woe! As if the Druses of the Mount
(Scarce Arabs, even there, but here, in the Isle,
Beneath their former selves) should comprehend
The subtle lore of Europe! A few secrets
That would not easily affect the meanest
Of the crowd there, could wholly subjugate
The best of our poor tribe. Again that eye?
ANAEL [*after a pause springs to his neck*]. Djabal, in this there can be no deceit!
Why, Djabal, were you human only,—think,
Maani is but human, Khalil human,
Loys is human even—did their words
Haunt me, their looks pursue me? Shame on you
So to have tried me! Rather, shame on me
So to need trying! Could I, with the Prefect
And the blood, there—could I see only you?
—Hang by your neck over this gulf of blood?
Speak, I am saved! Speak, Djabal! Am I saved?
[*As* DJABAL *slowly unclasps her arms, and puts her silently from him,*]
Hakeem would save me. Thou art Djabal. Crouch!
Bow to the dust, thou basest of our kind!

---

portal. 69| *1863:* own? 72| *1843:* instrument *1849:* instrument, 73| *1843:* hoped—I said it had <> me! *1849:* said, Heaven had *1863:* hoped: I *1868:* said Heaven *1888:* me. 74| *1843:* me?—Who *1888:* me? Who 77| *1843:* you would <> you are *1849:* thou wouldst <> thou art 79| *1843:* (Scarce Arabs even there—but *1863:* —Scarce <> there, but *1868:* (Scarce Arabs, even 80| *1863:* selves—should *1868:* selves) should 84| *1843:* tribe! Again *1888:* tribe. Again 87| *1843:* Maäni *1849:* Maani 93| *1843:* gulph *1849:* gulf 95| *1843:* me! Thou art Djabal! Crouch! *1888:* me. Thou art Djabal.

The pile of thee, I reared up to the cloud—
Full, midway, of our fathers' trophied tombs,
Based on the living rock, devoured not by
The unstable desert's jaws of sand,—falls prone.
Fire, music, quenched: and now thou liest there
A ruin, obscene creatures will moan through.
—Let us come, Djabal!

DJABAL Whither come?

ANAEL At once—
Lest so it grow intolerable. Come!
Will I not share it with thee? Best at once!
So, feel less pain! Let them deride,—thy tribe
Now trusting in thee,—Loys shall deride!
Come to them, hand in hand, with me!

DJABAL Where come?

ANAEL Where?—to the Druses thou hast wronged! Confess,
Now that the end is gained—(I love thee now—)
That thou hast so deceived them—(perchance love thee
Better than ever.) Come, receive their doom
Of infamy! O, best of all I love thee!
Shame with the man, no triumph with the God,
Be mine! Come!

DJABAL Never! More shame yet? and why?
Why? You have called this deed mine—it is mine!
And with it I accept its circumstance.
How can I longer strive with fate? The past
Is past: my false life shall henceforth show true.

Crouch! 97| *1843:* thee I *1849:* thee, I 98| *1843:* Fathers' *1863:* fathers' 100| *1843:* prone! *1888:* prone. 102| *1843:* ruin obscene <> thro'! *1849:* ruin, obscene *1863:* through! *1888:* through. 106| *1843:* So feel <> deride—thy *1863:* So, feel *1868:* deride,—thy 109| *1843:* Confess *1849:* Confess, 110| *1843:* gained . . . (I <> now) *1849:* gained—(I *1863:* thee now—) 111| *1843:* them . . (better love *1849:* them—(perchance love 112| *1843:* Perchance than ever:) Come *1849:* Better than ever!) Come *1888:* ever.) Come 113| *1843:* infamy . . . (Oh *1849:* infamy—(Oh *1863:* infamy! Oh *1868:* infamy! O 114| *1843:* the God *1849:* the God, 115| *1843:* mine!) Come! DJABAL Never! more *1863:* mine! Come! DJABAL Never! More 117| *1843:* circumstance— *1849:* circumstance. 118| *1843:* with Fate? The Past *1863:* fate *1868:* past 119| *1843:* past—my <> henceforth come true— *1849:* henceforth show true— *1863:* true. *1868:* past: my *1888:* true 120–122| *1843:* me: the <> this—/ What *1849:* this; / They bear us to fresh scenes and happier skies; / What *1863:*

Hear me! The argosies touch land by this;
They bear us to fresh scenes and happier skies.
What if we reign together?—if we keep
Our secret for the Druses' good?—by means
Of even their superstition, plant in them
New life? I learn from Europe: all who seek
Man's good must awe man, by such means as these.
We two will be divine to them—we are!
All great works in this world spring from the ruins
Of greater projects—ever, on our earth,
Babels men block out, Babylons they build.
I wrest the weapon from your hand! I claim
The deed! Retire! You have my ring—you bar
All access to the Nuncio till the forces
From Venice land.

ANAEL Thou wilt feign Hakeem then?

DJABAL [*putting the Tiara of Hakeem on his head*].
And from this moment that I dare ope wide
Eyes that till now refused to see, begins
My true dominion: for I know myself,
And what am I to personate. No word?

[ANAEL *goes.*]

'Tis come on me at last! His blood on her——
What memories will follow that! Her eye,
Her fierce distorted lip and ploughed black brow!
Ah, fool! Has Europe then so poorly tamed
The Syrian blood from out thee? Thou, presume
To work in this foul earth by means not foul?
Scheme, as for heaven,—but, on the earth, be glad

---

me! the < / > skies: 120| *1868:* me! The 124| *1843:* Of their gross superstition plant *1849:* Of even their superstition, plant 125| *1843:* life? I am from *1849:* life? I learn from 126| *1843:* awe man: by <> these, *1849:* awe man, by <> these. 127–128| *1843:* are! / Let them conceive the rest—and I will keep them / Still safe in ignorance of all the past— / All *1849:* are! / All 130| *1849:* Men block out Babels, to build Babylons. *1863:* Babels men block out, Babylons they build. 134| *1843:* land! ANAEL You will feign *1849:* ANAEL Thou wilt feign *1888:* land. ANAEL 135| *1843:* [*puts* *1849:* [*putting* 136| *1843:* that refused till now to *1849:* that till now refused to 137| *1843:* dominion! for *1868:* dominion: for 138| *1843:* [*Exit* ANAEL. *1849:* [ANAEL *goes.* 140| *1843:* Such memories *1849:* What memories 141| *1843:* And her distorted <> brow—— *1849:* Her fierce distorted *1863:* brow! 143| *1843:* thee? Thou presume *1849:*

If a least ray like heaven's be left thee!
Thus
I shall be calm—in readiness—no way
Surprised. [*A noise without.*]
This should be Khalil and my Druses.
Venice is come then! Thus I grasp thee, sword!
Druses, 'tis Hakeem saves you! In! Behold
Your Prefect!

Enter LOYS. DJABAL *hides the khandjar in his robe.*

LOYS Oh, well found, Djabal!—but no time for words.
You know who waits there? [*Pointing to the alcove.*]
Well!—and that 'tis there
He meets the Nuncio? Well! Now, a surprise—
He there—
DJABAL I know—
LOYS ——is now no mortal's lord,
Is absolutely powerless—call him, dead—
He is no longer Prefect—you are Prefect!
Oh, shrink not! I do nothing in the dark,
Nothing unworthy Breton blood, believe!
I understood at once your urgency
That I should leave this isle for Rhodes; I felt
What you were loath to speak—your need of help.
I have fulfilled the task, that earnestness
Imposed on me: have, face to face, confronted
The Prefect in full Chapter, charged on him
The enormities of his long rule; he stood
Mute, offered no defence, no crime denied.
On which, I spoke of you, and of your tribe,

---

thee? Thou, presume 146| *1843:* If but a ray like Heaven's <> thee! Thus *1849:* If a least ray like <> thee! / Thus *1868:* heaven's 148| *1843:* my Druses! *1888:* my Druses. 151| *1843:* The Prefect! *1849:* Your Prefect! 152| *1843:* well met Djabal!—but he's close at hand, *1849:* well found, Djabal!—but no time for words. 153| *1843:* there? [*Points* <> Well; and *1849:* there? [*Pointing* <> Well!—and 154| *1843:* the Nuncio? Well! now *1849:* the Nuncio? Well! Now *1888:* the Nuncio? Well? Now 155| *1843:* lord. *1868:* lord, 158| *1868:* Oh shrink *1888:* Oh, shrink 161| *1843:* for Rhodes—I *1849:* for Rhodes; I 162| *1843:* help; *1863:* help. 163| *1843:* task that *1849:* task, that 164| *1843:* me; have *1888:* me: have 166| *1843:* What you have told and I have seen; he *1849:* The enormities of his long rule; he *1863:* rule: he *1888:* rule; he 167| *1843:* denied; *1863:* denied. 168| *1843:* which I <> you and of your

Your faith so like our own, and all you urged
Of old to me: I spoke, too, of your goodness,
Your patience—brief, I hold henceforth the Isle
In charge, am nominally lord,—but you,
You are associated in my rule—
Are the true Prefect! Ay, such faith had they
In my assurance of your loyalty
(For who insults an imbecile old man?)
That we assume the Prefecture this hour.
You gaze at me? Hear greater wonders yet—
I cast down all the fabric I have built.
These Knights, I was prepared to worship. . . . but
Of that another time; what's now to say,
Is—I shall never be a Knight! Oh, Djabal,
Here first I throw all prejudice aside,
And call you brother! I am Druse like you:
My wealth, my friends, my power, are wholly yours,
Your people's, which is now my people: for
There is a maiden of your tribe, I love—
She loves me—Khalil's sister——

DJABAL

Anael?

LOYS

Start you?

Seems what I say, unknightly? Thus it chanced:
When first I came, a novice, to the isle . . .

Enter one of the NUNCIO'S GUARDS *from the alcove.*

Druses' *1849:* which, I <> you, and of your tribe, 169| *1843:* Slight difference in faith from us . . all you've urged *1849:* Your faith so like our own, and all *1863:* all you urged 170| *1843:* So oft to me—I <> goodness *1849:* goodness, *1863:* Of old to *1888:* me: I 171| *1843:* And patience *1849:* Your patience 172| *1843:* nominally Prefect, but / *1849:* nominally Prefect,—but you, *1868:* nominally lord,—but 174| *1843:* You are the Prefect *1849:* Are the true Prefect
177| *1843:* hour! *1888:* hour. 178| *1843:* me! a greater wonder *1849:* me! Hear greater wonders 179| *1843:* See me throw down this fabric <> built! *1849:* I throw down all this fabric *1868:* all the fabric *1888:* I cast down <> built.
180| *1843:* worship . . but *1888:* worship. . . . but 181| *1843:* say *1849:* that, another <> say, *1868:* that another 184| *1843:* you! *1888:* you:
186| *1843:* my people—for *1863:* Your People's <> People *1868:* people's <> people: for 187| *1843:* tribe I *1849:* tribe, I 189| *1843:* What I say seems unknightly <> chanced— *1849:* Seems what I say, unknightly <> chanced:
190| *1843:* came a novice to the Isle . . . *1849:* came, a novice, to *1868:* isle . . .

GUARD Oh horrible! Sir Loys! Here is Loys!
And here— [*Others enter from the alcove.*]
[*Pointing to* DJABAL.] Secure him, bind him—this is he!
[*They surround* DJABAL.]
LOYS Madmen—what is't you do? Stand from my friend,
And tell me!
GUARD Thou canst have no part in this—
Surely no part! But slay him not! The Nuncio
Commanded, slay him not!
LOYS Speak, or . . .
GUARD The Prefect
Lies murdered there by him thou dost embrace.
LOYS By Djabal? Miserable fools! How Djabal?
[*A* GUARD *lifts* DJABAL'S *robe*; DJABAL *flings down the khandjar.*]
LOYS [*after a pause*]. Thou hast received some insult worse than all,
Some outrage not to be endured—
[*To the* GUARDS.] Stand back!
He is my friend—more than my friend. Thou hast
Slain him upon that provocation.
GUARD No!
No provocation! 'Tis a long devised
Conspiracy: the whole tribe is involved.
He is their Khalif—'tis on that pretence—
Their mighty Khalif who died long ago,
And now comes back to life and light again!
All is just now revealed, I know not how,
By one of his confederates—who, struck
With horror at this murder, first apprised
The Nuncio. As 'twas said, we find this Djabal
Here where we take him.
DJABAL [*aside*]. Who broke faith with me?

191| *1843:* Oh, horrible *1868:* Oh horrible 192| *1843:* Djabal! / Secure *1849:* And here— / Secure 194| *1843:* GUARDS *1849:* GUARD 195| *1843:* part—but *1868:* part! But 196| *1843:* Slay *1868:* slay 197| *1843:* embrace— *1849:* embrace. 198| *1843:* miserable *1868:* Miserable 199| *1843:* all— *1868:* all, 201| *1843:* than my friend! Thou *1888:* than my friend. Thou 202| *1843:* provocation! GUARDS *1849:* GUARD *1888:* provocation. GUARD 204| *1843:* Conspiracy—the <> involved— *1849:* Conspiracy: the <> involved: *1863:* involved. 205–208| *1843:* pretence— / All *1849:* pretence— / Their mighty Khalif who died long ago, / And now is come to life and light again— / All *1868:* now comes back to *1888:* again! 210| *1843:* murder, has apprized *1849:* murder, first apprized *1863:* apprised 211| *1843:* said we *1849:* said, we 212| *1843:*

LOYS [*to* DJABAL]. Hear'st thou? Speak! Till thou speak, I keep off these,
Or die with thee. Deny this story! Thou
A Khalif, an impostor? Thou, my friend,
Whose tale was of an inoffensive tribe,
With . . . but thou know'st—on that tale's truth I pledged
My faith before the Chapter: what art thou?

DJABAL Loys, I am as thou hast heard. All's true.
No more concealment! As these tell thee, all
Was long since planned. Our Druses are enough
To crush this handful: the Venetians land
Even now in our behalf. Loys, we part.
Thou, serving much, wouldst fain have served me more;
It might not be. I thank thee. As thou hearest,
We are a separated tribe: farewell!

LOYS Oh where will truth be found now? Canst thou so
Belie the Druses? Do they share thy crime?
Those thou professest of our Breton stock,
Are partners with thee? Why, I saw but now
Khalil, my friend: he spoke with me—no word
Of this! and Anael—whom I love, and who
Loves me—she spoke no word of this.

DJABAL Poor boy!
Anael, who loves thee? Khalil, fast thy friend?
We, offsets from a wandering Count of Dreux?
No: older than the oldest, princelier
Than Europe's princeliest race, our tribe: enough
For thine, that on our simple faith we found
A monarchy to shame your monarchies

---

breaks *1863:* broke 213| *1843:* speak I *1849:* speak, I 216| *1843:* inoffensive race. *1863:* race, *1888:* inoffensive tribe, 219| *1843:* true! *1888:* true. 223| *1843:* part here! *1868:* part! *1888:* part. 224| *1843:* Thou hast served much, would'st *1849:* Thou, serving much *1863:* wouldst 225| *1843:* thee—As *1849:* thee. As 227| *1843:* Oh, where *1868:* Oh where 228| *1843:* the Druses?—This not thy sole crime? *1849:* the Druses? Do they share thy crime? 229| *1843:* stock *1849:* thou professedst of <> stock, *1868:* professest 230| *1843:* thee? Why I *1849:* thee? Why, I 231| *1843:* Khalil my friend—he *1849:* Khalil, my *1888:* friend: he 233| *1843:* this! DJABAL Poor Boy! *1868:* boy! *1888:* this. DJABAL 234| *1843:* Anael who <> Khalil fast *1849:* Anael, who <> Khalil, fast 236| *1843:* No—older <> oldest—princelier *1888:* No: older <> oldest, princelier 237| *1843:* princeliest tribe are we.—Enough *1863:* we. Enough *1888:* princeliest race, our tribe: enough 238| *1843:* For thee that *1849:* thee, that

At their own trick and secret of success.
The child of this our tribe shall laugh upon
The palace-step of him whose life ere night
Is forfeit, as that child shall know, and yet
Shall laugh there! What, we Druses wait forsooth
The kind interposition of a boy
—Can only save ourselves if thou concede:
—Khalil admire thee? He is my right-hand,
My delegate!—Anael accept thy love?
She is my bride!
LOYS Thy bride? She one of them?
DJABAL My bride!
LOYS And she retains her glorious eyes!
She, with those eyes, has shared this miscreant's guilt!
Ah—who but she directed me to find
Djabal within the Prefect's chamber? Khalil
Bade me seek Djabal there, too. All is truth.
What spoke the Prefect worse of them than this?
Did the Church ill to institute long since
Perpetual warfare with such serpentry?
And I—have I desired to shift my part,
Evade my share in her design? 'Tis well.
DJABAL Loys, I wronged thee—but unwittingly:
I never thought there was in thee a virtue
That could attach itself to what thou deemest
A race below thine own. I wronged thee, Loys,
But that is over: all is over now,
Save the protection I ensure against
My people's anger. By their Khalif's side,
Thou art secure and mayst depart: so, come!
LOYS Thy side? I take protection at thy hand?

1888: For thine, that 243| *1843:* forfeit—as <> know—and *1849:* forfeit, as <> know, and 245| *1843:* boy? *1863:* boy 246| *1843:* ourselves when thou concedest? *1868:* ourselves if thou concede? 247| *1843:* right hand, *1888:* right-hand, 249| *1843:* my Bride! LOYS Thy Bride *1868:* bride <> bride 250| *1843:* Bride *1868:* bride 254| *1843:* there! Too true it is! *1849:* there, too! All is true! *1868:* is truth! *1888:* too. All is truth. 258| *1843:* serpentry *1863:* serpentry? 259| *1843:* As these? Have *1863:* And I—have 260| *1843:* well! *1888:* well. 261| *1843:* unwittingly. *1849:* unwittingly: 264| *1843:* over. All *1849:* over: all 266| *1843:* anger—by <> side *1849:* side, *1863:* anger. By 267| *1843:* may'st *1888:* mayst 268| *1843:* side?—I *1888:* side?

Enter other GUARDS.

GUARDS Fly with him! Fly, Sir Loys! 'Tis too true:
And only by his side thou mayst escape.
The whole tribe is in full revolt: they flock
About the palace—will be here—on thee—
And there are twenty of us, we the Guards
O' the Nuncio, to withstand them! Even we
Had stayed to meet our death in ignorance,
But that one Druse, a single faithful Druse,
Made known the horror to the Nuncio. Fly!
The Nuncio stands aghast. At least let us
Escape thy wrath, O Hakeem! We are nought
In thy tribe's persecution! [*To* LOYS.] Keep by him!
They hail him Hakeem, their dead Prince returned:
He is their God, they shout, and at his beck
Are life and death!

LOYS [*springing at the khandjar* DJABAL *had thrown down, seizes him by the throat*].
Thus by his side am I!
Thus I resume my knighthood and its warfare,
Thus end thee, miscreant, in thy pride of place!
Thus art thou caught. Without, thy dupes may cluster:
Friends aid thee, foes avoid thee,—thou art Hakeem,
How say they?—God art thou! but also here
Is the least, youngest, meanest the Church calls
Her servant, and his single arm avails
To aid her as she lists. I rise, and thou
Art crushed. Hordes of thy Druses flock without:

I 269| *1843:* him! fly, my Master! 'tis too true! *1849:* him! fly, Sir Loys! 'tis *1868:* him! Fly, Sir Loys! 'Tis *1888:* true: 270| *1843:* may'st escape— *1849:* escape! *1888:* mayst escape. 271| *1843:* revolt—they *1868:* revolt: they 273| *1843:* us, with the *1849:* us, we, the *1868:* we the 274–278| *1843:* Of <> them! Fly—below / The *1849:* them! Even we / Had stayed to meet our death in ignorance, / But that one Druse, a single faithful Druse, / Made known the horror to the Nuncio! Fly! / The 277| *1863:* to the Nuncio. Fly! 274| *1888:* O' 279| *1843:* their *1868:* thy 280–282| *1843:* [*To* LOYS] / Keep by him! / He *1849:* [*To* LOYS] Keep by him! / They hail him Hakeem, their dead Prince, returned— / He 281| *1863:* returned: *1868:* dead Prince returned: 284| *1843:* warfare! *1868:* warfare, 286| *1843:* caught! Without *1868:* caught. Without 287| *1843:* art Khalif, *1849:* art Hakeem, 289| *1843:* least, meanest, youngest the *1868:* least, youngest, meanest the 292| *1843:* crushed! Hordes <> without; *1868:* without: *1888:*

Here thou hast me, who represent the Cross,
Honour and Faith, 'gainst Hell, Mahound and thee.
Die! [DJABAL *remains calm.*] Implore my mercy, Hakeem, that my scorn
May help me! Nay, I cannot ply thy trade;
I am no Druse, no stabber: and thine eye,
Thy form, are too much as they were—my friend
Had such. Speak! Beg for mercy at my foot! [DJABAL *still silent.*]
Heaven could not ask so much of me—not, sure,
So much. I cannot kill him so.
[*After a pause.*] Thou art
Strong in thy cause, then—dost outbrave us, then.
Heardst thou that one of thine accomplices,
Thy very people, has accused thee? Meet
His charge! Thou hast not even slain the Prefect
As thy own vile creed warrants. Meet that Druse!
Come with me and disprove him—be thou tried
By him, nor seek appeal! Promise me this,
Or I will do God's office. What, shalt thou
Boast of assassins at thy beck, yet truth
Want even an executioner? Consent,
Or I will strike—look in my face—I will!
DJABAL Give me again my khandjar, if thou darest! [LOYS *gives it.*]
Let but one Druse accuse me, and I plunge
This home. A Druse betray me? Let us go!
[*Aside.*] Who has betrayed me? [*Shouts without.*]
Hearest thou? I hear
No plainer than long years ago I heard
That shout—but in no dream now. They return!
Wilt thou be leader with me, Loys? Well.

---

crushed. Hordes 293| *1841:* me who *1849:* me, who 294| *1843:* Honor <> Mahound, and *1849:* Honour *1868:* 'gainst Hell, Mahound and 295| *1843:* *calm.*] / Implore my mercy, Khalif, that *1849:* calm.] Implore my mercy, / Hakeem, that 296| *1843:* me! Nay—I <> trade— *1863:* me! Nay, I <> trade; 297| *1843:* no Druse—no stabber—and *1863:* no Druse, no stabber: and 299| *1843:* such! Speak *1888:* such. Speak 300| *1843:* not sure *1849:* not, sure, 301| *1843:* so! / Thou *1888:* so! / [*After a pause.*] Thou 302| *1843:* cause then! Dost *1849:* cause, then *1868:* then!—dost *1888:* then—dost 303| *1843:* Heard'st *1863:* Heardst 306| *1843:* that charge— *1849:* that Druse— *1868:* that Druse! 308| *1843:* appeal—this promise me— *1849:* appeal—promise me this— *1868:* appeal! Promise me this, 309| *1843:* office! What *1888:* office. What 310| *1843:* yet Truth *1868:* truth 313| *1843:* khandjar if *1849:* khandjar, if 318| *1849:* now! They Return! *1888:* return!

ACT V

The Uninitiated DRUSES, *filling the hall tumultuously, and speaking together.*

Here flock we, obeying the summons. Lo, Hakeem hath appeared, and the Prefect is dead, and we return to Lebanon! My manufacture of goats' fleece must, I doubt, soon fall away there. Come, old Nasif—link thine arm in mine—we fight, if needs be. Come, what is a great fight-word?—"Lebanon?" (My daughter—my daughter!)—But is Khalil to have the office of Hamza?—Nay, rather, if he be wise, the monopoly of henna and cloves. Where is Hakeem?—The only prophet I ever saw, prophesied at Cairo once, in my youth: a little black Copht, dressed all in black too, with a great strip of yellow cloth flapping down behind him like the back-fin of a water-serpent. Is this he? Biamrallah! Biamreh! HAKEEM!

Enter the NUNCIO, *with* GUARDS.

NUNCIO [*to his* ATTENDANTS]. Hold both, the sorcerer and this accomplice
Ye talk of, that accuseth him! And tell
Sir Loys he is mine, the Church's hope:
Bid him approve himself our Knight indeed!
Lo, this black disemboguing of the Isle!
[*To the* DRUSES.] Ah children, what a sight for these old eyes
That kept themselves alive this voyage through
To smile their very last on you! I came

Stage directions / *1843: The Uninitiated* Druses, *covering the stage tumultuously* *1868: The Uninitiated* DRUSES, *filling the hall tumultuously* 3| *1843:* there—Come *1863:* there. Come 4| *1843:* be—Come *1863:* be. Come 5| *1843:* fightword? Lebanon? (My *1849:* fight-word? "Lebanon?" (My *1863:* fight-word?—"Lebanon 7| *1843:* cloves—Where *1863:* cloves. Where 8| *1843:* once in my youth—a *1849:* once, in *1863:* youth: a 10| *1843:* water-serpent—Is *1863:* water-serpent. Is 13| *1843:* hope! *1849:* hope: 17| *1843:* Ah, Children *1849:* children *1868:* Ah children 19| *1868:* ye *1888:*

To gather one and all you wandering sheep
Into my fold, as though a father came . . .
As though, in coming, a father should . . .
[*To his* GUARDS.] (Ten, twelve
—Twelve guards of you, and not an outlet? None?
The wizards stop each avenue? Keep close!)
[*To the* DRUSES.] As if one came to a son's house, I say,
So did I come—no guard with me—to find . . .
Alas—alas!

A DRUSE Who is the old man?

ANOTHER Oh, ye are to shout!
Children, he styles you.

DRUSES Ay, the Prefect's slain!
Glory to the Khalif, our Father!

NUNCIO Even so
I find, (ye prompt aright) your father slain.
While most he plotted for your good, that father
(Alas, how kind, ye never knew)—lies slain.
[*Aside.*] (And hell's worm gnaw the glozing knave—with me,
For being duped by his cajoleries!
Are these the Christians? These the docile crew
My bezants went to make me Bishop o'er?)
[*To his* ATTENDANTS, *who whisper.*] What say ye does this wizard style himself?
Hakeem? Biamrallah? The third Fatemite?
What is this jargon? He—the insane Khalif,
Dead near three hundred years ago, come back
In flesh and blood again?

DRUSES He mutters! Hear ye?
He is blaspheming Hakeem. The old man
Is our dead Prefect's friend. Tear him!

NUNCIO Ye dare not.
I stand here with my five-and-seventy years,

---

you 21| *1843:* tho' *1863:* though 22| *1843:* tho' <> twelve, *1863:* though *1888:* twelve 23| *1843:* Twelve *1849:* —Twelve 30| *1843:* find, ye <> aright, your Father slain; *1849:* find, (ye <> aright) your *1868:* father slain! *1888:* slain. 31| *1843:* *1863:* Father *1868:* father 32| *1843:* (Alas! how kind ye <> slain— *1849:* kind, ye <> slain! *1863:* (Alas, how *1888:* slain. 33| *1843:* [*Aside.*] (And Hell's <> me *1849:* me, *1863:* hell's 42| *1843:* blaspheming Hakeem—The *1849:* blaspheming Hakeem. The 43| *1843:* friend! Tear <> not! *1888:* friend. Tear <> not. 44| *1843:* five-and-sixty years, *1849:*

The Patriarch's power behind me, God's above.
Those years have witnessed sin enough; ere now
Misguided men arose against their lords,
And found excuse; but ye, to be enslaved
By sorceries, cheats—alas! the same tricks, tried
On my poor children in this nook o' the earth,
Could triumph, that have been successively
Exploded, laughed to scorn, all nations through:
"*Romaioi, Ioudaioite kai proselutoi,*
Cretes and Arabians"—you are duped the last.
Said I, refrain from tearing me? I pray ye
Tear me! Shall I return to tell the Patriarch
That so much love was wasted—every gift
Rejected, from his benison I brought,
Down to the galley-full of bezants, sunk
An hour since at the harbour's mouth, by that . . .
That . . . never will I speak his hated name!
[*To his* SERVANTS.] What was the name his fellow slipfetter
Called their arch-wizard by? [*They whisper.*] Oh, Djabal was't.

DRUSES But how a sorcerer? false wherein?

NUNCIO (Ay, Djabal!)
How false? Ye know not, Djabal has confessed . . .
Nay, that by tokens found on him we learn . . .
What I sailed hither solely to divulge—
How by his spells the demons were allured
To seize you: not that these be aught save lies
And mere illusions. Is this clear? I say,
By measures such as these, he would have led you
Into a monstrous ruin: follow ye?
Say, shall ye perish for his sake, my sons?

---

five-and-seventy years, 45| *1843:* behind, and God's above me! *1868:* behind me, God's above! 49| *1843:* sorceries—cheats;—alas <> tricks tried *1849:* tricks, tried *1863:* sorceries, cheats *1868:* cheats—alas 50| *1843:* of the earth *1849:* earth, *1888:* o' 51| *1843:* triumph,—that *1868:* triumph, that 52| *1843:* thro'— *1863:* through— *1868:* through: 53| *1843:* "*Romaioi, Ioudaioi te kai* *1863:* "*Romaioi, Ioudaioite kai* 54| *1843:* last! *1888:* last. 58| *1843:* benizon *1849:* benison 59| *1843:* to that galley-full *1849:* to the galley-full 62| *1863: was* *1868:* was 63| *1843: whisper.*] One Djabal *1849: whisper.*] Oh, Djabal 65| *1843:* not Djabal *1849:* not, Djabal 69| *1843:* you—not *1868:* you: not 70| *1843:* illusions—is *1849:* illusions. Is 71| *1843:* these he *1849:* these, he 72| *1843:* ruin—follow *1849:* ruin:

DRUSES Hark ye!

NUNCIO —Be of one privilege amerced?
No! Infinite the Patriarch's mercies are!
No! With the Patriarch's licence, still I bid
Tear him to pieces who misled you! Haste!

DRUSES The old man's beard shakes, and his eyes are white fire! After all, I know nothing of Djabal beyond what Karshook says; he knows but what Khalil says, who knows just what Djabal says himself. Now, the little Copht Prophet, I saw at Cairo in my youth, began by promising each bystander three full measures of wheat . . .

Enter KHALIL *and the initiated* DRUSES.

KHALIL Venice and her deliverance are at hand:
Their fleet stands through the harbour. Hath he slain
The Prefect yet? Is Djabal's change come yet?

NUNCIO [*to* ATTENDANTS]. What's this of Venice? Who's this boy?
[ATTENDANTS *whisper.*] One Khalil?
Djabal's accomplice, Loys called, but now,
The only Druse, save Djabal's self, to fear?
[*To the Druses.*] I cannot hear ye with these aged ears:
Is it so? Ye would have my troops assist?
Doth he abet him in his sorceries?
Down with the cheat, guards, as my children bid!
[*They spring at* KHALIL; *as he beats them back,*]
Stay! No more bloodshed! Spare deluded youth!
Whom seek'st thou? (I will teach him)—whom, my child?
Thou know'st not what these know, what these declare.

---

follow 75| *1843:* mercies be! *1868:* mercies are! 76| *1843:* license *1863:* licence <> bid ye *1868:* Ibid 78| *1843:* white! After *1849:* white fire! After 79| *1843:* says, he *1849:* says; he 80| *1843:* himself—Now the *1849:* says; who <> Now, the *1863:* himself. Now *1868:* says, who 81| *1843:* Prophet I <> youth began *1849:* Prophet, I <> youth, began 82| *1843:* each bystander . . . *1849:* each bystander three full measures of wheat . . . 83| *1843:* hand! *1888:* hand: 84| *1843:* thro' the harbour! Hath *1863:* through *1888:* harbour. Hath 87| *1843:* called but now *1849:* called, but now, 88| *1843:* only Druse save <> self to *1849:* only Druse, save <> self, to 89| *1843:* ears . . . *1849:* ears: 93| *1843:* Stay—no <> bloodshed—spare *1868:* Stay! No <> bloodshed! Spare 94| *1843:* him)—Whom *1868:* whom 95| *1843:* knowest <> know, and just have told. *1849:* these know, have just told me. *1863:* know, what these

I am an old man as thou seest—have done
With life; and what should move me but the truth?
Art thou the only fond one of thy tribe?
'Tis I interpret for thy tribe.

KHALIL   Oh, this
Is the expected Nuncio! Druses, hear—
Endure ye this? Unworthy to partake
The glory Hakeem gains you! While I speak,
The ships touch land: who makes for Lebanon?
They plant the winged lion in these halls!

NUNCIO [*aside*]. If it be true! Venice? Oh, never true!
Yet Venice would so gladly thwart our Knights,
So fain get footing here, stand close by Rhodes!
Oh, to be duped this way!

KHALIL   Ere he appear
And lead you gloriously, repent, I say!

NUNCIO [*aside*]. Nor any way to stretch the arch-wizard stark
Ere the Venetians come? Cut off the head,
The trunk were easily stilled. [*To the* DRUSES.] He? Bring him forth!
Since so you needs will have it, I assent.
You'd judge him, say you, on the spot—confound
The sorcerer in his very circle? Where's
Our short black-bearded sallow friend who swore
He'd earn the Patriarch's guerdon by one stab?
Bring Djabal forth at once!

DRUSES   Ay, bring him forth!
The Patriarch drives a trade in oil and silk,
And we're the Patriarch's children—true men, we!

---

declare. *1868:* thou know'st not 96| *1843:* man, as *1888:* man as 97| *1843:* With earth, and *1863:* earth; and *1868:* With life, and 99| *1843:* tribe! KHALIL *1849:* tribe!— KHALIL *1863:* tribe! KHALIL *1888:* tribe. KHALIL 102| *1843:* you! Why, by this *1849:* you! While I speak, 103| *1843:* land—who *1849:* land: who 104| *1843:* They'll plant *1868:* They plant 105| *1843:* NUNCIO (If <> Venice?—Oh *1849:* NUNCIO [*aside.*] If *1888:* true! Venice? Oh 106| *1843:* Yet, Venice <> thwart the Knights, *1849:* thwart our Knights, *1868:* Yet Venice 107| *1843:* And fain <> here so close *1849:* here, so *1863:* here, stand close *1888:* So fain 108| *1843:* way!) KHALIL <> appears *1849:* way! KHALIL *1868:* appear 109| *1843:* To lead *1868:* And lead 110| *1843:* NUNCIO (Oh, any *1849:* NUNCIO [*aside.*] Oh *1863:* Nor any 111| *1843:* come! Were he cut off *1849:* off, *1863:* come? Be he cut off *1868:* come? Cut off the head, 112| *1843:* The rest were easily tamed.) He *1849:* tamed. [*To the* DRUSES.] He *1868:* The trunk were easily stilled. [*To* 114| *1843:* spot? Confound *1868:* confound *1888:* spot—confound 116| *1843:* who said *1888:* who swore 119| *1843:* silk—

Where is the glory? Show us all the glory!
KHALIL You dare not so insult him! What, not see . .
(I tell thee, Nuncio, these are uninstructed,
Untrusted: they know nothing of our Khalif!)
—Not see that if he lets a doubt arise
'Tis but to give yourselves the chance of seeming
To have some influence in your own Return!
That all may say ye would have trusted him
Without the all-convincing glory—ay,
And did! Embrace the occasion, friends! For, think—
What wonder when his change takes place? But now
For your sakes, he should not reveal himself.
No: could I ask and have, I would not ask
The change yet!

Enter DJABAL *and* LOYS.

Spite of all, reveal thyself!
I had said, pardon them for me—for Anael—
For our sakes pardon these besotted men—
Ay, for thine own—they hurt not thee! Yet now
One thought swells in me and keeps down all else.
This Nuncio couples shame with thee, has called
Imposture thy whole course, all bitter things
Has said: he is but an old fretful man!
Hakeem—nay, I must call thee Hakeem now—
Reveal thyself! See! Where is Anael? See!
LOYS [*to* DJABAL]. Here are thy people. Keep thy word to me!
DJABAL Who of my people hath accused me?
NUNCIO So!
So this is Djabal, Hakeem, and what not?

1863: silk: *1868:* silk, 124| *1843:* Untrusted—they *1888:* Untrusted: they 127| *1843:* return! *1849:* Return! 128| *1843:* say they would *1868:* say ye would 129| *1843:* ay *1849:* ay, 131| *1849:* What merit when <> now, *1863:* now *1868:* What wonder when 132| *1843:* sakes he <> himself! *1849:* sakes, he *1888:* himself. 133| *1843:* No—could <> have. I *1849:* have, I *1888:* No: could 135| *1843:* said pardon *1849:* said, pardon 137| *1843:* Ay—for *1868:* Ay, for 138| *1843:* else! *1863:* else. 141| *1843:* said—he *1868:* said: he 143| *1843:* thyself! See, Druses! (Anel?)—See! *1849:* thyself! See! Where is Anael?—See! *1888:* is Anael? See! 144| *1843:* people! Keep *1863:* Thy People *1868:* people *1888:* people. Keep 145| *1843:* accused his Khalif? *1849:* accused me? ¶ NUNCIO So! *1863:* People *1868:* people 146| *1843:* So, this *1868:*

A fit deed, Loys, for thy first Knight's day!
May it be augury of thy after-life!
Ever prove truncheon of the Church as now
That, Nuncio of the Patriarch, having charge
Of the Isle here, I claim thee [*turning to* DJABAL] as these bid me,
Forfeit for murder done thy lawful prince,
Thou conjurer that peep'st and mutterest!
Why should I hold thee from their hands? (Spells, children?
But hear how I dispose of all his spells!)
Thou art a prophet?—wouldst entice thy tribe
From me?—thou workest miracles? (Attend!
Let him but move me with his spells!) I, Nuncio . . .
DJABAL . . . Which how thou camest to be, I say not now,
Though I have also been at Stamboul, Luke!
Ply thee with spells, forsooth! What need of spells?
If Venice, in her Admiral's person, stoop
To ratify thy compact with her foe,
The Hospitallers, for this Isle—withdraw
Her warrant of the deed which reinstates
My people in their freedom, tricked away
By him I slew,—refuse to convoy us
To Lebanon and keep the Isle we leave—
Then will be time to try what spells can do!
Dost thou dispute the Republic's power?
NUNCIO Lo ye!
He tempts me too, the wily exorcist!
No! The renowned Republic was and is
The Patriarch's friend: 'tis not for courting Venice
That I—that these implore thy blood of me.

So this 148| *1843:* after life! *1863:* after-life! 149| *1843:* Ever be truncheon *1863:* Ever prove truncheon 152–154| *1843:* prince! / Why *1849:* murder on thy <> prince, / Thou conjurer that peep'st and mutterest! / Why 153| *1863:* peepest *1868:* peep'st 156| *1843:* a Prophet?—would'st *1863:* wouldst *1868:* prophet 157| *1843:* Away?—thou *1868:* From me?—thou 159| *1843:* thou cam'st to be I *1849:* be, I *1863:* camest 161| *1843:* —Ply thee, Luke Mystochthydi, with my spells? / *1849:* thee with spells, forsooth! What need of spells? *1888:* Ply 162| *1843:* person, choose *1849:* person, stoop 163| *1849:* foes, *1868:* foe, 166| *1843:* in its freedom *1849:* in their freedom *1863:* People *1868:* people 168| *1843:* Afar to Lebanon at price of the Isle, / *1849:* To Lebanon and keep the Isle we leave— 169| *1843:* —Then time <> what miracles may do! *1849:* —Then will be time <> what spells can do! *1888:* Then 170–172| *1843:* ye! / No *1849:* ye! / He tempts me, too, the wily exorcist! / No *1868:* me too 173| *1843:* friend: 'Tis *1849:* 'tis 174| *1843:* me! *1888:* me.

Lo ye, the subtle miscreant! Ha, so subtle?
Ye, Druses, hear him. Will ye be deceived?
How he evades me! Where's the miracle
He works? I bid him to the proof—fish up
Your galley-full of bezants that he sank!
That were a miracle! One miracle!
Enough of trifling, for it chafes my years.
I am the Nuncio, Druses! I stand forth
To save you from the good Republic's rage
When she shall find her fleet was summoned here
To aid the mummeries of a knave like this.

[*As the* DRUSES *hesitate, his* ATTENDANTS *whisper.*]

Ah, well suggested! Why, we hold the while
One who his close confederate till now,
Confesses Djabal at the last a cheat,
And every miracle a cheat. Who throws me
His head? I make three offers, once I offer,—
And twice . . .

DJABAL Let who moves perish at my foot!

KHALIL Thanks, Hakeem, thanks! Oh, Anael, Maani,
Why tarry they?

DRUSES [*to each other*]. He can! He can! Live fire—
[*To the* NUNCIO.] I say he can, old man! Thou know'st him not.
Live fire like that thou seest now in his eyes,
Plays fawning round him. See! The change begins.
All the brow lightens as he lifts his arm.
Look not at me! It was not I!

DJABAL What Druse
Accused me, as he saith? I bid each bone
Crumble within that Druse! None, Loys, none
Of my own people, as thou said'st, have raised

176| *1843:* him! Will *1888:* him. Will 179| *1843:* sunk! *1863:* galley full *1868:* sank! *1888:* galley-full 181| *1843:* my age— *1863:* my years. 182| *1843:* stand here *1849:* stand forth 183| *1843:* good Republic's wrath *1849:* good Republic's rage 184| *1843:* summoned just *1849:* summoned here 185| *1843:* of this wizard here! *1849:* this crafty knave! *1863:* of a knave like this! *1888:* this. 186| *1843:* hold this while *1863:* hold the while 187| *1843:* One, who *1863:* One who 189| *1843:* cheat! Who *1888:* cheat. Who 191| *1843:* foot? *1849:* foot! 192| *1843:* thanks! Oh, Anael, Maäni *1868:* thanks! Oh, Anael, Maani, 194–196| *1843:* (I <> not.) / —Live fire plays round him—See <> begins? *1849:* not—) / Live fire like that thou seest now in his eyes, / Plays fawning round him—See <> begins! *1863:* I <> not— // <> him. See *1888:* not. // <> begins. 196–198| *1843:* begins? / Look *1849:* begins! / All the brow lightens as he lifts his arm! / Look *1888:* begins. / <> arm. 199| *1843:* Accuseth *1849:*

A voice against me.
NUNCIO [*aside*]. Venice to come! Death!
DJABAL [*continuing*]. Confess and go unscathed, however false!
Seest thou my Druses, Luke? I would submit
To thy pure malice did one Druse confess!
How said I, Loys?
NUNCIO [*to his* ATTENDANTS *who whisper*]. Ah, ye counsel so?
[*Aloud*]. Bring in the witness, then, who, first of all,
Disclosed the treason! Now I have thee, wizard!
Ye hear that? If one speaks, he bids you tear him
Joint after joint: well then, one does speak! One,
Befooled by Djabal, even as yourselves,
But who hath voluntarily proposed
To expiate, by confessing thus, the fault
Of having trusted him. [*They bring in a veiled* DRUSE.]
LOYS Now, Djabal, now!
NUNCIO Friend, Djabal fronts thee! Make a ring, sons. Speak!
Expose this Djabal—what he was, and how:
The wiles he used, the aims he cherished: all,
Explicitly as late 'twas spoken to these
My servants: I absolve and pardon thee.
LOYS Thou hast the dagger ready, Djabal?
DJABAL Speak,
Recreant!
DRUSES Stand back, fool! farther! Suddenly
You shall see some huge serpent glide from under

Accused 201| *1843:* saidst *1868:* said'st 203| *1843:* Now speak and go unscathed, how false soe'er! *1849:* Confess and go unscathed, however false! 205| *1843:* one least Druse speak! *1849:* one Druse confess! 207| *1843:* witness then *1849:* witness, then 208| *1843:* Told this man's treasons! Now <> thee, Djabal! *1849:* Disclosed the treason! Now <> thee, wizard! 210| *1843:* after joint—well *1868:* after joint: well 211| *1843:* Whom I have not as yet e'en spoken with, *1849:* Befooled by Djabal, even as yourselves, 214| *1843:* LOYS Now Djabal *1863:* LOYS Now, Djabal 215| *1843:* fronts you! (Make <> sons!)—Say *1849:* sons!)—Speak *1863:* fronts thee! Make <> sons!—Speak! *1888:* sons. Speak! 216| *1843:* The course of Djabal; what <> how; *1849:* Expose this Djabal *1868:* this Djabal—what *1888:* how: 217/ *1843:* cherished; all *1849:* all, *1888:* cherished: all, 218–220| *1843:* late you spoke to these! / Thou *1849:* these / My servants—I absolve and pardon you. / Thou *1863:* late 'twas spoken <> / servants: I <> pardon

The empty vest, or down will thunder crash!
Back, Khalil!

KHALIL I go back? Thus go I back!
[*To* ANAEL.] Unveil! Nay, thou shalt face the Khalif! Thus!

[*He tears away* ANAEL'S *veil:* DJABAL *folds his arms and bows his head; the* DRUSES *fall back;* LOYS *springs from the side of* DJABAL *and the* NUNCIO.]

LOYS Then she was true—she only of them all!
True to her eyes—may keep those glorious eyes,
And now be mine, once again mine! Oh, Anael!
Dared I think thee a partner in his crime—
That blood could soil that hand? nay, 'tis mine—Anael,
—Not mine?—who offer thee before all these
My heart, my sword, my name—so thou wilt say
That Djabal, who affirms thou art his bride,
Lies—say but that he lies!

DJABAL Thou, Anael?

LOYS Nay, Djabal, nay, one chance for me—the last!
Thou hast had every other; thou hast spoken
Days, nights, what falsehood listed thee—let me
Speak first now; I will speak now!

NUNCIO Loys, pause!
Thou art the Duke's son, Bretagne's choicest stock,
Loys of Dreux, God's sepulchre's first sword:
This wilt thou spit on, this degrade, this trample
To earth?

LOYS [*to* ANAEL]. Who had forseen that one day, Loys
Would stake these gifts against some other good
In the whole world? I give them thee! I would

---

thee. 223| *1843:* vest—or *1863:* vest, or 225| *1843:* Unveil! Nay thou *1849:* Unveil! Nay, thou 227| *1843:* eyes *1849:* eyes, 228| *1843:* again mine! Oh, Anael— *1849:* again mine! Oh, Anael! 229| *1843:* crime? *1849:* crime— 231| *1843:* —Mine now? Who *1849:* —Not mine?—Who 233| *1843:* This Djabal *1849:* That Djabal 234| *1863:* Lies! say *1868:* Lies—say 235| *1868:* Nay Djabal *1888:* Nay, Djabal 236| *1843:* other—thou *1863:* other; thou 238| *1843:* first—I <> speak—Anael!— NUNCIO *1849:* first, now; I <> speak, now!— NUNCIO *1863:* now! NUNCIO *1868:* first now; I 239| *1843:* son, Breton's <> stock— *1863:* stock, *1888:* son, Bretagne's 240| *1843:* Loys de Dreux—God's <> sword— *1849:* Loys of Dreux *1863:* of Dreux, God's <> sword: 241| *1843:* degrade—this *1849:* degrade, this 242| *1843:* earth? LOYS Ah, who had said, "One day this Loys *1849:* earth? LOYS [to ANAEL]. Ah, who had foreseen, "One day, Loys *1868:* to ANAEL] Who had foreseen that one day 243| *1843:* Will *1868:* Would 244| *1843:* world?"—I give *1868:* world? I

My strong will might bestow real shape on them,
That I might see, with my own eyes, thy foot
Tread on their very neck! 'Tis not by gifts
I put aside this Djabal: we will stand—
We do stand, see, two men! Djabal, stand forth!
Who's worth her, I or thou? I—who for Anael
Uprightly, purely kept my way, the long
True way—left thee each by-path, boldly lived
Without the lies and blood,—or thou, or thou?
Me! love me, Anael! Leave the blood and him!
[*To* DJABAL.] Now speak—now, quick on this that I have said,—
Thou with the blood, speak if thou art a man!

DJABAL [*to* ANAEL]. And was it thou betrayedst me? 'Tis well!
I have deserved this of thee, and submit.
Nor 'tis much evil thou inflictest: life
Ends here. The cedars shall not wave for us:
For there was crime, and must be punishment.
See fate! By thee I was seduced, by thee
I perish: yet do I—can I repent?
I with my Arab instinct, thwarted ever
By my Frank policy,—and with, in turn,
My Frank brain, thwarted by my Arab heart—
While these remained in equipoise, I lived
—Nothing; had either been predominant,
As a Frank schemer or an Arab mystic,

---

give 248| *1843:* this Djabal—we <> stand . . . *1849:* stand— *1863:* this Djabal: we 249| *1843:* stand—see—two *1868:* stand, see, two 250| *1843:* her—I or *1863:* her, I or 251| *1843:* Kept tamely, soberly my *1849:* Kept, purely, uprightly my *1863:* Uprightly, purely, kept my *1868:* purely kept 252| *1843:* by-path—kept / *1849:* by-path—boldly lived 254| *1843:* Come out of this blood! Love me, Anael, leave him! *1849:* I! Love me, Anael! Leave the blood and him! *1868:* Me!—love me *1888:* Me! love 255| *1843:* quick upon what I <> said, *1849:* quick on this that I <> said,— 257| *1843:* Ah, was <> me? Then, speak! *1849:* And was <> me? 'Tis well! 258| *1843:* 'Tis well—I have deserved this—I submit— *1849:* I have deserved this of thee, and submit: *1863:* submit.
259| *1843:* inflictest—life *1849:* inflictest: life 260| *1843:* us— *1863:* us:
262| *1843:* seduced—by *1863:* seduced; by *1868:* seduced! by *1888:* seduced, by
263| *1843:* perish—yet do I, can I repent! *1849:* repent? *1863:* perish: yet do I—can 264| *1843:* I, with an Arab instinct thwarted *1849:* with my Arab instinct, thwarted *1868:* I with 265| *1843:* and, in its turn, *1849:* and, within turn, *1863:* and, with, in turn, *1868:* and with 266| *1843:* A Frank brain thwarted *1849:* My Frank brain, thwarted 267| *1843:* equipoise I *1849:* equipoise, I
268| *1843:* Nothing *1849:* —Nothing 269| *1843:* mystic *1849:* mystic,

I had been something;—now, each has destroyed
The other—and behold, from out their crash,
A third and better nature rises up—
My mere man's-nature! And I yield to it:
I love thee, I who did not love before!

ANAEL Djabal!

DJABAL It seemed love, but it was not love:
How could I love while thou adoredst me?
Now thou despisest, art above me so
Immeasurably! Thou, no other, doomest
My death now; this my steel shall execute
Thy judgment; I shall feel thy hand in it.
Oh luxury to worship, to submit,
Transcended, doomed to death by thee!

ANAEL My Djabal!

DJABAL Dost hesitate? I force thee then. Approach,
Druses! for I am out of reach of fate;
No further evil waits me. Speak the doom!
Hear, Druses, and hear, Nuncio, and hear, Loys!

ANAEL HAKEEM! [*She falls dead.*]

[*The* DRUSES *scream, grovelling before him.*]

DRUSES Ah Hakeem!—not on me thy wrath!
Biamrallah, pardon! never doubted I!
Ha, dog, how sayest thou?

[*They surround and seize the* NUNCIO *and his* GUARDS. LOYS *flings himself upon the body of* ANAEL, *on which* DJABAL *continues to gaze as stupefied.*]

NUNCIO Caitiffs! Have ye eyes?
Whips, racks should teach you! What, his fools? his dupes?

271| *1843:* behold from <> crash *1849:* behold, from <> crash, 273| *1843:* mere Man's-nature <> it— *1863:* it: *1868:* man's-nature 274–276| *1843:* thee—I—who <> before! / Djabal— DJABAL . . . How *1849:* before! / Djabal— DJABAL It seemed love, but true love it was not— / How 275| *1863:* Djabal! DJABAL It seemed *1868:* thee, I who <> / <> but it was not love— *1888:* not love: 278| *1843:* Immeasurably—thou *1868:* Immeasurably! Thou 279| *1843:* now—this *1863:* now; this 280| *1843:* judgment—I <> it! *1863:* judgment; I *1888:* it. 281| *1843:* Oh, luxury *1888:* Oh luxury 282| *1843:* To be transcended <> thee! / *1849:* Transcended <> thee! ANAEL My Djabal! 283| *1843:* My Djabal! ¶ DJABAL Dost *1849:* Dost *1863:* thee, then *1868:* thee then 285| *1843:* evil can befall me—Speak! / *1849:* evil waits me—Speak the truth! *1863:* me. Speak *1868:* the doom! 288| *1843:* pardon—never *1863:* pardon! never 289| *1843:* Ah, dog <> *stupefied.*] Caitives *1868:* Ha, dog *1888:* Caitiffs 290| *1843:* racks, should

Leave me! Unhand me!
KHALIL [*approaching* DJABAL *timidly*]. Save her for my sake!
She was already thine; she would have shared
To-day thine exaltation: think, this day
Her hair was plaited thus because of thee!
Yes, feel the soft bright hair—feel!
NUNCIO [*struggling with those who have seized him*].
What, because
His leman dies for him? You think it hard
To die? Oh, would you were at Rhodes, and choice
Of deaths should suit you!
KHALIL [*bending over* ANAEL'S *body*]. Just restore her life!
So little does it! there—the eyelids tremble!
'Twas not my breath that made them: and the lips
Move of themselves. I could restore her life!
Hakeem, we have forgotten—have presumed
On our free converse: we are better taught.
See, I kiss—how I kiss thy garment's hem
For her! She kisses it—Oh, take her deed
In mine! Thou dost believe now, Anael?—See,
She smiles! Were her lips open o'er the teeth
Thus, when I spoke first? She believes in thee!
Go not without her to the cedars, lord!
Or leave us both—I cannot go alone!
I have obeyed thee, if I dare so speak:
Hath Hakeem thus forgot all Djabal knew?
Thou feelest then my tears fall hot and fast
Upon thy hand, and yet thou speakest not?
Ere the Venetian trumpet sound—ere thou

1868: racks should 292| *1843:* thine—she *1863:* thine; she 293| *1843:* exaltation—think! this *1863:* exaltation: think *1868:* think, this 294| *1843:* thee— *1863:* thee. *1868:* thee! 299| *1843:* it—there *1863:* it! there 300| *1843:* them—and *1863:* them: and 301| *1843:* themselves—I *1863:* themselves. I 303| *1843:* converse—we *1863:* converse: we 306| *1843:* mine—Thou *1863:* mine! Thou 307| *1843:* smiles! was her lip ope thus o'er *1849:* smiles! Were her lips open o'er 308| *1843:* When first I spoke? She doth believe *1849:* So, when I spoke first? She believes *1863:* Thus, when 309| *1843:* the Cedars, Hakeem! *1849:* the Cedars, Lord! *1868:* lord! *1888:* cedars 310| *1843:* alone— *1849:* alone! 311| *1843:* if I must say so— *1849:* if I dare say *1863:* if I dare so speak: 314| *1843:* hand—and <> not! *1863:* hand, and

Exalt thyself, O Hakeem! save thou her!

NUNCIO And the accursed Republic will arrive
And find me in their toils—dead, very like,
Under their feet!
What way—not one way yet
To foil them? None? [*Observing* DJABAL'S *face.*]
What ails the Khalif? Ah,
That ghastly face! A way to foil them yet!
[*To the* DRUSES.] Look to your Khalif, Druses! Is that face
God Hakeem's? Where is triumph,—where is . . . what
Said he of exaltation—hath he promised
So much to-day? Why then, exalt thyself!
Cast off that husk, thy form, set free thy soul
In splendour! Now, bear witness! here I stand—
I challenge him exalt himself, and I
Become, for that, a Druse like all of you!

THE DRUSES Exalt thyself! Exalt thyself, O Hakeem!

DJABAL [*advances*]. I can confess now all from first to last.
There is no longer shame for me. I am . . .
[*Here the Venetian trumpet sounds: the* DRUSES *shout,* DJABAL'S *eye catches the expression of those about him, and, as the old dream comes back, he is again confident and inspired.*]
—Am I not Hakeem? And ye would have crawled
But yesterday within these impure courts
Where now ye stand erect! Not grand enough?
—What more could be conceded to such beasts
As all of you, so sunk and base as you,
Than a mere man? A man among such beasts
Was miracle enough: yet him you doubt,
Him you forsake, him fain would you destroy—
With the Venetians at your gate, the Nuncio
Thus—(see the baffled hypocrite!) and, best,

<> not? 316| *1843:* save her—save her! *1863:* save thou her! 321| *1843:* face—a *1868:* face! A 323| *1843:* A Khalif's? Where is triumph—where is *1849:* God Hakeem's? Where is triumph *1868:* triumph,—where 325| *1843:* thyself? *1849:* thyself! 327| *1843:* splendour: now <> witness—here *1849:* splendour! Now *1863:* witness! here 330| *1843:* thyself—exalt thyself—O *1863:* thyself! Exalt thyself, O 332–333| § stage directions § *1843: shout, his eye* *1888: shout,* DJABAL'S *eye* 333| *1843:* . . . Am I *not* *1863:* —Am *1868:* not 335| *1843:* erect!—Not *1888:* erect! Not 338| *1843:* But a <> man?—A *1863:* Than a *1888:* man? A 339| *1843:* enough—yet *1868:* enough: yet 342| *1843:* and

The Prefect there!

DRUSES No, Hakeem, ever thine!

NUNCIO He lies—and twice he lies—and thrice he lies!
Exalt thyself, Mahound! Exalt thyself!

DJABAL Druses! we shall henceforth be far away—
Out of mere mortal ken—above the cedars—
But we shall see ye go, hear ye return,
Repeopling the old solitudes,—through thee,
My Khalil! Thou art full of me: I fill
Thee full—my hands thus fill thee! Yestereve,
—Nay, but this morn, I deemed thee ignorant
Of all to do, requiring word of mine
To teach it: now, thou hast all gifts in one,
With truth and purity go other gifts,
All gifts come clustering to that. Go, lead
My people home whate'er betide!
[*Turning to the* DRUSES.] Ye take
This Khalil for my delegate? To him
Bow as to me? He leads to Lebanon—
Ye follow?

DRUSES We follow! Now exalt thyself!

DJABAL [*raises* LOYS]. Then to thee, Loys! How I wronged thee, Loys!
Yet, wronged, no less thou shalt have full revenge,
Fit for thy noble self, revenge—and thus.
Thou, loaded with such wrongs, the princely soul,
The first sword of Christ's sepulchre—thou shalt
Guard Khalil and my Druses home again!
Justice, no less, God's justice and no more,
For those I leave! To seeking this, devote
Some few days out of thy Knight's brilliant life:
And, this obtained them, leave their Lebanon,
My Druses' blessing in thine ears—(they shall

---

best *1863:* and, best, 346| *1843:* away! *1868:* away— 347| *1843:* Cedars— *1868:* cedars— 348| *1843:* go—hear ye return— *1849:* ye go, here ye return, 349| *1843:* thro' *1863:* through 350| *1843:* me—I *1888:* me: I 351| *1843:* thee! Yester'eve *1863:* thee! Yestereve, 352| *1843:* morn—I *1863:* morn, I 354| *1843:* it—now *1863:* it: now 355| *1843:* gifts! *1868:* gifts, 356| *1843:* that—go lead *1849:* go, lead *1863:* that! Go *1868:* that. Go 357| *1843:* My People *1868:* people 362| *1843:* —Yet *1888:* Yet 363| *1843:* thus: *1863:* thus. 367| *1843:* less—God's *1888:* less, God's 368| *1843:* leave!—to *1888:* leave! To 369| *1843:* life, *1863:* life:

Bless thee with blessing sure to have its way)
—One cedar-blossom in thy ducal cap,
One thought of Anael in thy heart,—perchance,
One thought of him who thus, to bid thee speed,
His last word to the living speaks! This done,
Resume thy course, and, first amidst the first
In Europe, take my heart along with thee!
Go boldly, go serenely, go augustly—
What shall withstand thee then?
[*He bends over* ANAEL.] And last to thee!
Ah, did I dream I was to have, this day,
Exalted thee? A vain dream: hast thou not
Won greater exaltation? What remains
But press to thee, exalt myself to thee?
Thus I exalt myself, set free my soul!

[*He stabs himself. As he falls, supported by* KHALIL *and* LOYS, *the* VENETIANS *enter; the* ADMIRAL *advances.*]

ADMIRAL God and St. Mark for Venice! Plant the Lion!

[*At the clash of the planted standard, the* DRUSES *shout and move tumultuously forward,* LOYS *drawing his sword.*]

DJABAL [*leading them a few steps between* KHALIL *and* LOYS].
On to the Mountain! At the Mountain, Druses!

[*Dies.*]

373| *1843:* thy Ducal *1868:* ducal 374| *1843:* heart—perchance, *1868:* heart,—perchance 377| *1843:* amid *1888:* amidst 381| *1843:* have this day *1863:* have, this day, 382| *1843:* dream—hast *1888:* dream: hast 388| *1843:* to the Mountain. At *1863:* to the Mountain! At

BY THE SAME AUTHOR.

I.

PARACELSUS. A POEM.

Price 6s. boards.

II.

SORDELLO. A POEM.

Price 6s. 6d. boards.

III.

BELLS AND POMEGRANATES.

No. I.—PIPPA PASSES. Price 6d.

No. II.—KING VICTOR AND KING CHARLES. Price 1s.

No. III.—DRAMATIC LYRICS. Price 1s.

EDITORIAL NOTES

PIPPA PASSES

The Manuscript

The only known MS is now in The Miriam Lutcher Stark Library of the University of Texas, which has granted permission to reproduce the variants. The MS consists of six pages. Pages 1–5 contain B's extensive revisions of the Introduction in his hand. Page 6 contains the heading for Part I and the first six lines in MS. These lines are followed by lines 8–36 of the 1889 text of the *Bells and Pomegranates* edition pasted to the page. There are one word change and ten punctuation changes, all of which were incorporated in the 1849 *Poems.* It is evident that the MS is part of B's revision of the 1841 text for republication. The punctuation changes are within the text, though the word change is in the margin and in the text. The Introduction is by far the most extensively revised section of the poem in the 1849 edition; no section, in fact, was so heavily revised in that or in subsequent editions. It seems likely that the missing pages consisted of the *Bells and Pomegranates* text used as copy. This, together with the British Museum's copy of Volumes I to X of the 1888 edition, supports the belief gained from the study of the various editions that B ordinarily used the preceding edition as copy to be corrected for the next edition.

The Text

Series title] *Bells and pomegranates* The title for the series comes from Exodus 25–31, which tells of the Lord's instructions to Moses for the Ark, the Tabernacle, the Veil, the Altar, the Court of the Tabernacle, the priestly garments, the sacrifices, and the installation of Aaron and his sons as priests. The pertinent passages are as follows (words in square brackets are taken from the New English Bible): "And take thou unto thee Aaron thy brother, and his sons with him, from among the children of Israel, that he may minister unto me in the priest's office . . . (28:1). And thou shalt make holy garments for Aaron thy brother for glory and beauty [dignity and grandeur] (28:2). And thou shalt speak unto all that are wise hearted, whom I have filled with the spirit of wisdom, [Tell all the craftsmen whom I have endowed with skill] that they may make Aaron's garments to consecrate him, that he may minister unto me in the priest's office (28:3). And these are the garments which they shall make; a breastplate, and an ephod, and a robe, and a broidered coat, a mitre, and a girdle . . . (28:4). And they shall make the ephod of gold, of blue, and of purple, of scarlet, and fine twined linen, with cunning work (28:6). And thou shalt make the robe [mantle] of the ephod all of blue [violet]. And there shall be an hole in the top of it, in the midst thereof: it shall have a binding of woven work round about the hole of it, as it were the hole of an habergeon [with an oversewn edge], that it be not rent. And beneath upon the hem of it thou shalt make pomegranates of blue, and of purple, and of scarlet [violet, purple, and scarlet stuff], round about the hem thereof; and bells of gold between them round about: a golden bell and a pomegranate, [a golden bell and a pomegranate, upon the hem of the robe round about.] And it shall be upon Aaron to minister [Aaron shall wear it when he ministers]: and his sound [the sound of it] shall be heard when he goeth in unto the holy place before the Lord, and when he cometh out, that he die not (28:31–35)." In a letter of October 17, 1845, Elizabeth Barrett requested an explanation of the series title. Browning responded October 18 with the following: "The Rabbis make Bells & Pomegranates symbolical of Pleasure and Profit, the Gay & the Grave, the Poetry & the Prose, Singing and Sermonizing—such a mixture of effects as in the original hour (that is quarter of an hour) of confidence & creation, I meant the whole should prove at last: well, it *has* succeeded beyond my most adventurous wishes in one respect—'Blessed eyes mine eyes have been, if—' if there was any sweetness in the tongue or flavour in the seeds to *her*" (*The Letters of Robert Browning and Elizabeth Barrett Barrett 1845–1846*, ed. Elvan Kintner [Cambridge, Mass.: Harvard University Press, 1969], 1:241). B published a more extended explanation in *B & P* VIII, on the verso of the title page of *A Soul's Tragedy* (see vol. V of this edition).

Composition and publication] *Pippa Passes* was advertised in *Sordello* (published the first week of March, 1840) as "Nearly Ready." It was probably written between May 26, 1839, when Browning told Macready that *Sordello* was finished, and some time before the date of publication, April, 1841, as Number I of *B & P*. A letter to Eliza Flower, dated only March 9, could have been written in 1841 as well as 1840, and does not necessarily indicate that the work was finished at the time the letter was written (Hood, *Ltrs*, 4).

Title] *Pippa* Diminutive of Felippa, female form of Felipe, or Philip. St. Philip, Apostle, carried the Gospel to Scythia. In art he is often represented as carrying a pilgrim's staff topped with a cross.

Persons] *Foreign Students* In the 1830s Italy was particularly popular with art students from all over Europe, all bent on renewing art. Because of the Nazarene painters, the German contingent was very large. The Nazarenes had come from Vienna to Rome in 1810. They consisted of the painters J. F. Overbeck, Pforr, Peter von Cornelius, and later, Fohr and Schnorr von Carolsfeld. The art-loving Ludwig, Crown Prince of Bavaria (crowned 1825), was a kind of patron, and partly because of his influence several of them executed mural projects in Germany in the 1830s.

Austrian Police From the early 15th cent. to 1797 most of Italy E of the R. Adda (just E of Milan) and N of Cremona and Mantua (a few miles N of the R. Po) was controlled by Venice as the Venetian Republic, which was terminated by Napoleon in 1797. Shortly after in that same year, the area E and N of the Adige was ceded to Austria in return for Lombardy and the rest of the old Venetian Republic. From 1805 to 1813 both Lombardy and the Veneto, together with some of the Papal States, were combined into a Kingdom of Italy, of which Napoleon, Emperor in 1805, was also King. In 1813 the Austrians and Neapolitans drove out the French. In 1815 the Congress of Vienna gave the area from W of Milan and N of the Po to the Austrian Empire, which governed it as the Kingdom of Lombardo–Venetia. In 1804, Franz II, Holy Roman Emperor at the time of its dissolution in 1806, became Emperor of Austria and in 1815 King of Lombardo–Venetia. To the Italians, most of whom were anti-Austrian and many of whom were prorepublicans, the Austrian rule was entirely repressive, and the Austrian police were the instruments of that repression.

Bluphocks The name is said to be a reference to the *Edinburgh Review*, the great and frequently unscrupulous Whig quarterly, which was bound in blue and buff (P-C).

INTRODUCTION

Stage directions] *New Year's Day* January 1 is hard to reconcile with other information about the time at which the play takes place: e.g., the blooming martagon (Intro. 88); Pippa's second song (I, 1, 221), and Luigi's reference to the cuckoo, the traditional harbinger of spring (III, 1, 135). The last reference in particular would be more meaningful if it is assumed that B means the old New Year's Day, March 25, officially abandoned for January 1 in England in 1752 and in Italy in 1582.

Asolo, Trevisan Asolo, a very ancient town of about 4,000 inhabitants, 33 mi. NE of Venice, sits on the ridge of a W spur of Mt. Celato, 300 feet above the plain to the S. It is in the Venetian province of Treviso—of which the chief city is also named Treviso, 25 mi. SE of Asolo. Trevisan is the area traditionally dependent on Treviso and centered in it.

Silk-mills Silk has been cultivated in N Italy since the early Middle Ages. Piedmont, Lombardy, and the Veneto are the principal silk regions.

89] *St. Agnes* A beautiful Roman saint of the third cent., martyred for refusing to marry.

90] *Turk bird's* The turkey.

131] *Possagno* A town nearly 6 mi. to the N and a little W of Asolo. Pippa goes down the steep road north from Asolo, across a valley, and at about 4 mi. enters the Orgagna valley, which runs across a range of hills running E and W. Further N, across another valley, Possagno lies at the foot of the first range of the Alps.

132] *Orcana* Orgagna, see l. 131n.
166] *turret* A tower which is the oldest part of La Roca, a late Roman fortress on the top of the hill of Asolo, above the town. It offers splendid views towards the Alps to the N and across the vast plain to Venice and Padua to the S.
181] *Dome* In It. *Il Duomo* (S. Maria di Breda), the chief church of a town.

PART I [i]

28] *St. Mark's* The most famous church of Venice, originally the chapel of the Palace of the Doges.
29] *Vicenza* A city 40 mi. W of Venice and 26 mi. SW of Asolo.
30] *Padua* A city 20 mi. W of Venice and 26 mi. S of Asolo.
59] *Capuchin* Monk of an austere branch of the Order of St. Francis.
76] *proof-mark* "The sign on the print which shows whether it is among the first impressions from the plate" [P-C]. An indication of rarity and value.
102] *Venus' body* "Corpo di Venere," an Italian oath.

PART I [ii]

Stage directions] *Possagno* The sculptor Jules and the foreign students are at Possagno because it was the birthplace of the neoclassic sculptor Antonio Canova (1775–1822). In later years it was his residence. After his death his half-brother and heir, Monsignor Sartori-Canova, constructed next to the birthplace and home of Canova a Gipsoteca, or museum of plaster casts. This building was built between 1834 and 1836, and in it was placed the bulk of the contents of Canova's Roman studio—sketches in clay, plaster models for the completed marble. Other works, such as paintings, were assembled in the house. In 1853 the house and museum were given to the town. Before his death Canova designed and started to construct in Possagno a splendid neoclassic church, known as Il Tempio di Canova (Canova's Temple), finished in 1834.
11] *Trieste* A city across the Adriatic from Venice, also under Austrian control.
16] *Æsculapius* Legendary Greek god and physician, son of Apollo.
16] *Hebe* Cup-bearer to the Greek gods.
17] *Phœbus* Apollo, Greek god of the sun.
18] *Mercury* Divine messenger of the Greek gods.
22] *et canibus nostris* Virgil *Eclogues* 3. 66–67. Lines spoken by the shepherd Menalcas: "At mihi sese offert ultra, meus, ignis, Amyntas, notior ut iam sit canibus non Delia nostris" [But my flame Amyntas comes to me unsought, so that now Delia is not better known to my dogs].
22] *Delia* Virgilian shepherdess. See also preceding note.
31] *Munich* Capital of the Kingdom of Bavaria, it became an important center for the study of art in the 1820s under the patronage of Ludwig I, who came to the throne in 1825. (See *Persons, Foreign Students.*) To a sculptor

Munich was particularly interesting because when still Crown Prince, Ludwig commissioned the architect Leo von Klenze to build a museum, the Glyptothek, to house his collection of Greek and Roman statues. The most important works were the sculptures from Aegina, an island S of Attica, which were excavated by Haller von Hallerstein and the English architect, C. R. Cockerell, in 1811. Ludwig bought them in 1812 and commissioned Bertel Thorwaldsen (1768–1844) the Danish sculptor to restore them. Thorwaldsen was the principal European rival and successor to Canova; he modelled his style on Greek rather than Roman sculpture. After fourteen years of planning and construction the Glyptothek was opened to the public in 1828. As one of the first European buildings built as a museum, it attracted a great deal of interest. The murals were by Cornelius (see *Persons*).

48] *Canova* See I, 2, *Stage directions.*

74] *Psiche-fanciulla* The statue *Psyche as a Girl* created by Canova in 1789. In 1793 he made a replica of it which eventually was acquired by Napoleon, who gave it to the Queen of Bavaria in 1805. Presumably in the 1830s it could still be seen in Munich. Eventually it ended up in Leningrad. The Possagno Gipsoteca has only a gesso (plaster of paris) head, used as a model for execution in marble.

78] *Pietà The Deposition of Christ* with Mary, the Magdalene, and the dead Christ before the cross. Canova planned this statue to be executed in marble for his Temple (see I, 2, *Stage directions, Possagno*), but died before he finished it. A bronze cast was made in 1828 and placed in the Temple.

90–91] *Malamocco* A fishing village on the island of the same name; it is one of a chain of islands separating the Adriatic from the Lagoon of Venice. Much of the population is of Greek descent.

93] *Alciphron* Greek writer of A.D. c. 200, author of imaginary letters about Athenian life in the 4th cent. B.C.

96] *lire* It. sing. *lira,* basic monetary unit of Italy. In 19th cent. = 0/0/9½ English; $.19 U.S.

98] *Tydeus* Ancient Greek hero, brother-in-law of Polynices and one of the leaders in the latter's attack on Thebes.

98] *Academy* School of art and principal museum of painting in Venice.

101] *Fenice* La Fenice (The Phoenix), the opera house of Venice.

119] *Hannibal Scratchy* Pun on Annibale Caracci (1560–1609), renewer of Italian painting in the late 16th and early 17th centuries from the tradition of Venetian painting. By the 1830s he was beginning to be downgraded as a mere academic painter, particularly by the advanced taste of the time, which the Nazarene painters and their German followers exemplified. (See also *Persons, Foreign Students*; I, 2, *Munich.*)

PART II [i]

Stage directions] *Over Orcana* Overlooking Orcana from Possagno. See *Introduction,* 131; I, 2, *Stage directions, Possagno.*

14] *Tydeus* See I, 2, 98n.

26] *Psyche* Heroine of the Greek legend of Cupid and Psyche; also a famous marble group by Canova. See also I, 2, 74n.
39] *Coluthus* Alexandrian poet of the 5th–6th centuries A.D. His only surviving work, *The Rape of Helen*, was discovered by Cardinal Bessarion (see l. 40n).
40] *Bessarion* A learned Cardinal (1389?–1472) who came to Italy in 1439 from Trebizond on the Black Sea. He was one of the transplanters of ancient Greek culture to the West.
46] *Antinous* The chief of Penelope's wooers in the *Odyssey* (22.5).
50] *Almaign Kaiser* German Emperor. Almaign, specifically, is Swabia, in SW Germany. Innsbruck, Austria, is the site of the 16th cent. monument to the Emperor Maximilian I, in the Court or Franciscan Church, built to house the monument. It includes 28 bronze statues of heroic size, a number of which are of German Emperors. B stopped at Innsbruck on his way back from Italy in 1838. Jules would have stopped there on his way from Munich to Italy.
54] *Hippolyta* Queen of the Amazons.
55] *Numidian* Numidia was an ancient country of N Africa, approximately coextensive with modern Algeria.
61] *Hipparchus* With his brother Hippias, he succeeded their father, Pisistratus, as joint rulers of Athens. He was assassinated c. 514 B.C. by Harmodius and Aristogiton, subjects of the famous statues by Kritios, set up in 477 B.C. Later copies are now in the National Museum, Naples. "The daggers with which the tyrant was killed were concealed in myrtle-branches borne by the assassins at the festival of Panathenaea" (P-C).
92] *Dryad* Tree-nymph.
258] *Kate the Queen* Caterina Corner (or Cornaro) (1454?–1510), a daughter of a great Venetian family who married the last King of Cyprus, James II of Lusignan. Widowed in 1473, she abdicated in 1489 and ceded Cyprus to Venice. The Venetian Senate granted her the lordship of Asolo, where she created a small but distinguished Renaissance court. She fled the troops of the invading Holy Roman Empire in 1509 and died in Venice.
289] *Psyche* See II, 1, 26n. The legend of Cupid and Psyche was allegorically interpreted as the search by the soul for the divine. The butterfly was the emblem for the soul.
306] *Ancona* A city on the Adriatic about 50 mi. S of Venice, until 1860 in the Papal States.

PART II [ii]

1] *Bluphocks* B's note is from Matthew 5:45.
2] *Intendant* It. *intendente*, manager, or steward, of estates.
8] *Armenian* The Armenian church, with distinctive beliefs and customs, has been autonomous since the 4th century.
9] *Koenigsberg* At this time the chief city of E Prussia, province of the

Kingdom of Prussia, it is now Kaliningrad, capital of the republic of the same name and part of Russia. It was the home of Immanuel Kant, the philosopher (1724–1804).

9] *Prussia Improper* Prussia Proper was old E Prussia.

11] *Chaldee* The Biblical Chaldee, in which portions of Ezra and Daniel are written; also applied to vernacular paraphrases of the Old Testament. It was supposed that this language was Babylonian, but it is now classified as Aramaic. This is perhaps a reference to "The Chaldee MS," a satire on Edinburgh notabilities published in *Blackwood's Edinburgh Magazine*, Oct., 1817. (Cf. *Persons, Bluphocks.*)

16] *Syriac* Aramaic language which replaced Hebrew as the language of the Jews after the Babylonian exile (see II, 2, 11).

17] *Celarent, Darii, Ferio* In traditional medieval logic the syllogism was conceived of as having 64 moods, of which 19 were said to be valid. These had various names for mnemonic purposes, and by the mid-17th century were remembered in the following verses: "Barbara Celarent Darii Ferioque prioris;/ Cesare Camestres Festino Baroco secundi;/ Tertia Darapti Disamis Datisi Felapton/ Bocardo Ferison habet: quarta insuper addit/ Bramantip Camenese Dimaris Fesapo Fresison."

20] *Moses* When Pharaoh refused to let the Israelites leave Egypt, the Lord sent a series of plagues, among others, flies and locusts (Exodus 8, 10).

21] *Jonah* Jonah was told to go to Nineveh, but fled to Tarshish to avoid the Lord's command (Jonah 1).

24] *Shackabrack, Boach* Shadrack, Meshach, and Abednego were cast into a fiery furnace for refusing to obey Nebuchadnezzar's religious commands (Daniel 3).

26] *Bishop Beveridge* A 17th-century bishop of St. Asaph, active in supporting the Society for the Propagation of the Gospel in New England. Here a pun on beverage; bishop is a hot punch of port wine heated, sweetened, and flavored with oranges and spices.

28] *Charon* The ferryman of the Styx in Greek mythology, paid with an obolos (small coin) in the mouth of the corpse.

29] *Hecate* Greek earth-goddess, queen of ghosts and of magic; hence of crossroads, a common site for incantations and other magic practices. Food was offered to Hecate at crossroads.

31] *zwanziger* Austrian currency: 1 kreutzer = 20 kronen. In the 19th cent. = 16/8 English; $4.05 U.S.

32] *Stygian* See II, 2, 8n.

39] *Metternich* Clemens, Fürst von. Austrian Prince (1773–1859) and the principal minister of Austria during the later Napoleonic era and after, until his overthrow in the Revolution of 1848. To the Italians, the architect and adminstrator of Austrian oppression.

44] *Panurge* The knavish companion of Pantagruel, the younger hero of *Gargantua and Pantagruel* by François Rabelais (1494?–1553). In Book III

(1546), Chap. 25, Panurge consults Herr Trippa (probably Cornelius Agrippa, 1486–1535, German philosopher, magician and praiser of women) about the possibility of marriage. He is told that he will be a cuckold.
45] *King Agrippa* Kings of Judea; Herod I (10 B.C.–A.D. 44) or II (A.D. 27–100).
63] *Carbonari* Charcoal burners, name of a number of loosely federated secret societies devoted to the liberation of Italy, probably offspring of the Freemasons. Their most recent attempt and failure had been in 1831 and 1832, when they staged a considerable uprising in the Romagna and the Marches (areas along the NE coast of Italy, S of the Po).
64] *Spielberg* An infamous Austrian political prison in Brünn, Moravia (now Brno, Czechoslovakia). Silvio Pellico, Italian dramatist and fighter for Italian liberty (1789–1854), and a Carbonarist (see preceding note), was imprisoned there from 1820 to 1830. In 1832 he published *Le mie prigioni* (*My Prisons*), which gave him and the Spielberg European fame.

PART III [i]

6] *Lucius Junius* Lucius Junius Brutus, who, according to legend, drove the Tarquins out of Rome and established the Roman Republic in 510 B.C. Thus he avenged the rape of Lucretia; later he is said to have put to death his own sons for attempting to bring the Tarquin kings back to Rome.
14] *Franz* Francis I, Emperor of Austria from 1804 to 1835. (As last Holy Roman Emperor, he was Francis II, 1792–1806.) Born in 1768, he died March 2, 1835. His minister was Metternich (see II, 2, 39n). The date of his death places the time of *Pippa Passes* in March, 1834, at the latest, if by New Year's Day B means March 25; otherwise January, 1835 (see Introduction, *Stage directions*), or not long after the abortive Carbonari uprisings in 1831 and 1832 (see II, 2, 63). But see I, 2, *Stage directions, Possagno* for the opening of the Canova Gipsoteca in 1836.
20] *Pellicos* See II, 2, 64n.
135–138] *Austrians, provinces, treaty* See note to *Persons, Austrian police*.
146] *Jupiter* The planet second only to Venus in brightness, named for the Roman ruler of the gods.
148] *I am the bright and morning-star.* Revelations 2:26–28. "And he that overcometh, and keepeth my works unto the end, to him will I give power of the nations: and he shall rule them with a rod of iron; as the vessels of a potter shall they be broken to shivers: even as I received of my Father. And I will give him the morning star."
163] *Titian* Venetian painter (c. 1490–1576). In the Chapel of the Annunciation of the Cathedral at Treviso (see Introduction, *Stage Directions, Asolo, Trevisan*) the altar-piece is an Annunciation by Titian, painted about 1520 (or perhaps 1503).
208] *Python* Ancient Greek serpent or dragon, frequently supernatural. Apollo slew the Python which guarded Delphi and founded his shrine there.

PART III [ii]

8] *Breganze* A village about 18 mi. W and a little S of Asolo.
22] *Deuzan* Deusan or applejohn, a variety of apple the flavor of which is improved by drying.
22] *junetings* Jenneting, an early apple.

PART IV [i]

3] *Benedicto benedicatur* "Blessings upon the blessed"; perhaps equivalent to "Bless my soul!"
6] *Messina* City on the E coast of Sicily.
7] *Assumption Day* A church-feast on August 15 to celebrate the taking up into heaven of the Virgin Mary.
14] *Ascoli, Fermo, Fossombruno* Cities in the Marches and the Abruzzi, inland from mid-E coast of Italy. Ascoli, the most distant, is about 210 mi. S of Asolo.
42] *Correggio* Italian painter (1494–1534), principally active at Parma, famous for his exquisite finish and sensuousness.
47] *Ideal* A traditional Renaissance conception of painting and sculpture which held that the task of the artist is to create a perfect exemplar of the real, earthly, attributes of whatever his subject was. A bit of art jargon, in the 19th cent. it took on a Transcendentalist coloring, so that the work became a means whereby divine truth became visible, or at least was symbolized.
62] *podere* It., farm; pl. *poderi*.
68] *Forlì* A town in Romagna, 110 mi. S of Asolo, across the Po.
70] *Cesena* A town 12 mi. SW of Forli (see IV, 1, 68n.)
86] *soldo* A small coin, no longer in use. Equivalent to halfpenny or cent.
116] *Pontiff* The Pope.
178] *Miserere mei, Domine*! "Lord have mercy on me!"

PART IV [ii]

70] *Brenta* The river Brenta runs through Bassano (10 mi. W of Asolo) S to Padua, and then E to the Lagoon of Venice.
96] *twats* "Dr. Furnivall explains that Browning got the word *twats* from the Royalist rhymes entitled 'Vanity of Vanities,' on Sir Harry Vane's picture, in which he is charged with being a Jesuit. ''Tis said that they will give him a cardinal's hat: / They sooner will give him an old nun's twat.' 'The word struck me,' Browning says, 'as a distinctive part of a nun's attire that might fitly pair off with the cowl appropriated to a monk' " (P-C). Browning was mistaken—that is, if he was being frank.

Editorial Notes

KING VICTOR AND KING CHARLES

The Text

King Victor & King Charles; A Tragedy was written after August 1, 1837, when B notified Fanny Haworth that he was "going to begin the finishing of *Sordello*—and to begin thinking a Tragedy (an Historical one. . .)" (Orr *Life* p. 96), and completed at least one draft before September 5, 1839, when Macready first read the play, found it to be "a *great mistake*," and called B in for an interview "and most explicitly told him so, and gave him my reasons for coming to such a conclusion" (*The Diaries of William Charles Macready 1833–1851*, ed. William Toynbee [London, 1912], 2:23). In the light of Macready's critical disapproval and B's desire to write a stageworthy tragedy it seems clear that the text was revised in the next two and a half years. The play was advertised in *Sordello* as "Nearly Ready" and published on March 12, 1842, as Number II of *Bells and Pomegranates*. B's information about the historical figures he depicts came largely from articles on "Charles-Emmanuel III," "Orméa," and "Victor-Amédée II" in Volumes XVIII (1813), XXXII (1822) and XLVIII (1827) of the Paris *Biographie universelle*. B's prefatory Advertisement, later called Note, alludes to four other accounts of the Sardinian succession of 1730 and its aftermath which are discussed below. It is apparent that B rejected the *Biographie's* version of European diplomatic history of 1727–1731 in favor of the Abbé Roman's; but B may have read elsewhere for views on the rivalry of Spain and Austria and the significance of the Infant Carlos.

B's Note

2] *Voltaire . . . "a terrible event without consequences;"* François Marie Arouet (1694–1778), the great writer and philosopher of the French Enlightenment who signed himself Voltaire, devotes a paragraph in *Précis du Siècle de Louis XV* (1768) to the abdication of King Victor Amadeus II of Sardinia in favor of his son Charles Emmanuel III in 1730, Victor's attempt to regain the throne, his imprisonment, and death in 1732. (See *Persons*, nn.) Attributing Victor's abdication to mere whim (*caprice*), Voltaire concludes:

"Ni l'abdication de ce roi, ni sa tentative pour reprendre le sceptre, ni sa prison, ni sa mort ne causèrent le moindre mouvement chez les nations voisines. Ce fut un terrible événement qui n'eut aucune suite" [Neither the abdication of this king, nor his attempt to regain the sceptre, nor his imprisonment, nor his death caused the least stir among the neighboring nations. It was a terrible event without consequence].

8] *Abbé Roman's Récit* Abbé Jean-Joseph-Thérèse Roman's *Mémoires historiques et inédits sur les révolutions arrivées en Danemarck et en Suède, pendant les années 1770, 1771, 1772; suivis d'anecdotes sur le Pape Ganganelli, et le conclave tenu après sa mort; et d'un récit historique sur l'abdication de Victor Amédée, roi de Savoie* (Paris, 1807) contains a detailed account of the Sardinian succession of 1730 and biographical sketches of the two kings (see pp. 253–83, 302–06); cited hereafter as "Roman, *Récit*, 1807." The Abbé Roman alone, among B's known sources, states that Victor abdicated because contradictory agreements he had signed with Austria and Spain placed him in an untenable position. Victor believed that his own diplomacy had led to political bankruptcy at Turin but that Charles, as king, might not be held responsible for the paternal obligations.

9] *fifth of Lord Orrery's Letters from Italy* The fifth letter reproduced in *Letters From Italy, in the years 1754 and 1755, by the late right honourable JOHN Earl of Corke and Orrery,* ed. John Duncombe (London, 1773; reprinted 1774), pp. 46–58, was sent to William Duncombe and dated from Turin, October 16, 1754. Lord Orrery holds that the "intriguing, ambitious temper" of Victor's second wife Contessa di San Sebastiano prompted his scheme to regain the Sardinian throne after his abdication, (see I, 1, 10n). Orrery's account of Victor and Charles is brief, historically inaccurate, and apparently based on gossip but it belongs to the "correspondence . . . of the time" as B indicates in his Note.

14–17] *Victor . . . Charles . . . D'Ormea* See *Persons,* nn.

19] *Condorcet* Antoine Nicolas, Marquis de Condorcet (1743–1794), French philosopher, mathematician, and revolutionist, wrote a biography of Voltaire and appended in an edition of *Précis du Siècle de Louis XV* a lengthy footnote to Voltaire's paragraph on Victor's abdication. See *Oeuvres complètes de Voltaire* ([Strasbourg] 1784 [1785]), 22:39–43. Condorcet, whom the author of the *Biographie universelle's* entry on d'Ormea attempts to refute, maintains that Victor never tried to regain the Sardinian throne after abdicating and that d'Ormea invented the story to drive the son from the father and seize power himself; see *Persons, D'Ormea, minister.*

Persons] *Victor Amadeus, first King of Sardinia* Victor Amadeus II (1666–1732), son of Charles Emmanuel II and Jeanne de Savoie Nemours, succeeded his father as Duke of Savoy at the age of eleven. He became King of Sicily when Philip V of Spain surrendered the island and kingdom in 1713 at the Peace of Utrecht, lost Sicily, and became the first King of Sardinia in 1720; his domain thenceforth included Sardinia, Savoy, the Piedmont, and

Montferrat. B in the play concentrates on the bizarre events of the last two years of his life. In 1730 Victor Amadeus II ("Victor" hereafter) made embarrassing contradictory agreements with the rival powers of Spain and Austria (see I, 2, 233–34n). In his sixties and weary of rule, he married his probable mistress, abdicated the Sardinian throne in favor of his son Charles Emmanuel III ("Charles" hereafter), and left the Turin court for Chambéry. Bored in retirement, and influenced by his second wife's ambition, he tried to revoke his abdication; this led to a bitter quarrel with the new king, Charles, who apprehended his father in a bedchamber and placed him under house arrest at Rivoli, and later at Moncalieri, where Victor died. For a full account of his career we recommend the Marchesa Vitelleschi, *The Romance of Savoy: Victor Amadeus II. and his Stuart Bride*, 2 vols. (London, 1905), referred to hereafter as "Vitelleschi, 1905." Most of the *Biographie universelle's* twenty-six column entry on Victor analyses his role in the complicated wars and foreign relations of Savoy from 1684 to 1720. Victor is seen as a shrewd, brave, but constantly intriguing figure, who ordered the arrest of his own mother when she was Regent. Yet as Duke of Savoy, he defied his first wife's uncle, Louis XIV of France and 18,000 troops under Catinat, for the benefit of Savoy; with allies he waged war against Louis for six years, switched sides, and drove a hard bargain at the Peace of Ryswick in 1697. Thickly involved in the War of the Spanish Succession after 1700, he emerged handsomely with the Kingdom of Sicily. As King of Sardinia from 1720, he founded a university at Turin, encouraged art and business, reformed the lower schools, beautified the capital, and kept state finances in "marvelous" order. The *Biographie*'s account of the critical years 1730–1732 is circumstantial and full. The writer denies that Victor abdicated because he was trapped by unfavorable treaties with France [*sic*] and Austria and wanted to get out of a mess; dispatches to his foreign ministers indicate nothing of the kind. Perhaps he was tired of ruling. Charles begged him to change his mind. Adamant, Victor retired with an income of 50,000 crowns to St. Alban near Chambéry. King Charles dutifully sent him reports about state affairs and visited him twice. Weary of idleness and inspired by the Marchesa di Spigno (that is, di San Sebastiano, whom he had married), Victor tried to repossess the Rivoli Palace in Charles's absence; but Charles arrived in the nick of time and thereafter set spies on his parent at Moncalieri. Since Victor's machinations persisted, Charles had him arrested and confined, almost insane with anger, at Rivoli, and after he calmed down, at the Moncalieri Palace where "everything was done to allay the bitterness" of his situation. There Victor died "piously" without having seen his son again. "He has remained in history the greatest prince of his race," the *Biographie* writer concludes.

Charles Emmanuel, his son, Prince of Piedmont Charles Emmanuel III (1701–1773), second son of Victor Amadeus II and Anne of Orleans (a niece of Louis XIV of France), became Prince of Piedmont at fourteen when his elder brother died, and King of Sardinia at twenty-nine when his father abdicated. In 1731 he imprisoned Victor, who had arranged Charles's marriages with Princess Christina (1722) and then Princess Polixena (1724) and otherwise regulated the young man's life. B read in the *Biographie* that in youth Charles deliberately concealed political and military talents so as not to arouse his father's touchy ambition; later when Victor schemed to regain the throne, Charles took coercive measures either because he had become fascinated by power or because public interest would not allow him to step down; he was also alarmed for his own safety. As king from 1730 to 1773 he devoted himself totally to the Sardinian state, led the allied armies of France and Spain against Milan, later sided with Austria, negotiated shrewdly, and was always abstemious, unostentatious, and brave and emotional in battle. The *Biographie* declares he was one of the "wisest" kings the Piedmont ever had.

Polyxena, wife of Charles Princess Polixena of Hessen-Rheinfels became Princess of Piedmont and the second wife of twenty-three year old Prince Charles Emmanuel of Sardinia in 1724. His first wife, Princess Christina, daughter of Theodore of Bavaria, Count Palatine of the Rhine, had died in 1723 after giving birth to a son, who was to die two years later. Though gentle and passive at first, Polixena resented her father-in-law's control of her husband and, especially after she became the Sardinian queen in 1730, helped to alienate Victor from Charles, and even to arrange the ex-king's arrest, according to Vitelleschi, 1905, 2:551–52. She is not very definitely characterized in B's chief sources.

D'Ormea, minister Charles François Vincent Ferrero, whose career began in the law, assumed successively the titles of Count of Roazio and Marquis d'Ormea as finance minister to Victor at Turin; he rose to direct home and foreign affairs in 1732 under Charles, accumulated the titles of "grand-chancelier de robe et d'epée" (Chancellor of the Law and the Army) in 1742, and died honorably in 1745, according to the four-column entry on "Orméa" B read in the *Biographie universelle*. B took most of his facts about the Minister General of the Finances from this outline. However, the *Biographie* writer aims to refute Condorcet's argument that d'Ormea, intent on gaining control of the Sardinian state, schemed to alienate Victor from Charles after Victor abdicated (see *B's Note*, 19n). Condorcet's most serious charge is that d'Ormea concocted a story to the effect that Victor planned to overthrow and perhaps murder his son to regain the crown; a search of Victor's papers revealed that he never planned a coup d'état, according to Condorcet. In short, B read conflicting estimates of d'Ormea—that he was a loyal servant of two Sardinian kings in turn (*Biographie*) and that he was a malicious scoundrel who lied to King Charles and virtually caused Victor's death (Condorcet). These sources (and later historians such as Vitelleschi and Vernon) agree that d'Ormea was subtle, patient, diplomatically brilliant at Turin and Rome, and very durable.

Scene] *Rivoli Palace* One of several palaces of French aspect and decor in NW Italy used by the kings of Sardinia and favorite residence of Victor; it is about 8 mi. W of Turin.
Turin Or Torino, city in the Piedmont on the Po River in NW Italy; it passed to the House of Savoy about 1280 and served as capital of the Kingdom of Sardinia from 1720 to 1798.
Time] *1730–1731* B's play interprets historical events of 1730–1732.

FIRST YEAR, 1730.—KING VICTOR PART I [I, i]

10] *Sebastian* Contessa di San Sebastiano, whom King Victor married in a clandestine ceremony on August 12, 1730, three weeks before he abdicated. A daughter of the Conte di Cumiana, she attracted Victor's attention as a maid of honor at the Turin court; probably she became his mistress. Her first husband died when she was in her forties. Blondel, French minister at Turin, reports that she was then still attractive and was known (curiously) for irreproachable conduct. Soon after abdicating, Victor revealed their marriage and conferred on her the Marquisate of Spigno. B's sources agree that she urged Victor to regain the throne; Lord Orrery heard in 1754 that she was "no longer dangerous, being very old, very infirm, and enormously fat" (*Letters From Italy*, ed. John Duncombe, p. 53). She died, aged ninety, at the Monastery of the Salesiane of Pinerolo in 1769.
21] *my brother* Victor's eldest and favored son, Victor Amadeus, Prince of Piedmont (1699–1715), deceased at the time of B's play.
24–25] *France... England... Spain... Austria* As Duke of Savoy Victor allied himself with England and Spain against Louis XIV in 1690, then in 1696 switched his allegiance to France a year before the Peace of Ryswick; in the War of the Spanish Succession (1700–1715) he began on the French side, but joined England, Austria, and Holland against Louis XIV and his grandson, Philip V of Spain, who ceded the Kingdom of Sicily to Savoy in 1713. Complex shifts in Victor's alliances continued.
36] *Philip* Charles's older brother who died of smallpox in 1715; see l. 21n. B apparently changed his name from Victor Amadeus to avoid confusion with the king's name.
77] *Savoy turns Sardinia* Savoy is the Alpine region of SE France ruled after Humbert the White-handed in 1034 by the dynasty of the House of Savoy; it merged with the Kingdom of Sardinia in 1720 and was annexed to France in 1792. Victor was the first of Savoy's princes to be crowned in nearly seven centuries. His titles had changed from Duke of Savoy to King of Sicily (1713) to King of Sardinia (1720).
83] *this mistress* Victor was notorious for liaisons with ladies of the Turin court such a Melle. di Saluzzo and Contessa di Verrua; he had several natural children.
96] *the Minister* D'Ormea.
97] *The Mistress posted to entrap you* Contessa di San Sebastiano, Victor's

favorite or latest mistress, whom he appointed lady-in-waiting to Princess Polixena around 1724. See l. 10n.

128] *Reduction of the Fiefs* A plan to gain property for the state; the Turin Ministry of Finance (under d'Ormea) investigated titles by which Piedmontese noblemen held fiefs, or heritable lands under the feudal system, in an effort to discover legal flaws. Fiefs held by flawed title were confiscated. Victor apparently packed the law courts with his own dependents to secure desirable verdicts and gained a sizable revenue from forfeited holdings; the *Biographie* alludes to bitter enemies he and d'Ormea made through this practice.

132] *Spanish Claims* Claims to the duchies of Parma and Tuscany pressed by Philip V of Spain and his second wife Elizabeth Farnese on behalf of their son, the Infant Carlos, from 1727 to 1731 (see I, 2, 523n).

158] *The Marquis* D'Ormea.

172] *Del Borgo, Spava* Marchese del Borgo, Turin Minister of Foreign Affairs and Attorney to the Crown, who read aloud Victor's act of abdication and later signed his death warrant; Count Spava is not mentioned in B's known sources but may have an historical counterpart.

186] *Fiefs* See l. 128n.

218–219] *Spain and Austria choosing / To make their quarrel up* The Treaty of Hanover in 1725 between France, England and Holland led Spain and Austria, old rivals, to a new secret agreement which included plans for a war against England. However, Spain and Austria were soon at odds again over the claims of the Infant Carlos.

224] *their friend* Victor.

272] *the Sebastian's child* Contessa di San Sebastiano may well have had a child by Victor before her marriage to him (see l. 10n).

307] *Piedmont* Region in NW Italy bounded along its Alpine crests by France and Switzerland, with Turin as its capital city, and under control of the House of Savoy from about 1280 to 1798.

311] *your Rhine-land* Princess Polixena (B's Polyxena) came from a ruling family of Hessen-Rheinfels in the former Prussian Rhine Province, commonly known as the Rhineland.

KING VICTOR PART II [I, ii]

Stage direction] *Regalia* Victor's crown and sceptre.

8–9] *Cyprus . . . / Jerusalem, Spain, England* The meaning of this passage involves the titular and actual holdings of the House of Savoy. From 1034 when Humbert was awarded the estate of Savoy and a feudal title by Conrad the Salic until 1713, princes of the House of Savoy had enjoyed ducal honors but not a kingship. After 1487, when the deposed Queen of Cyprus and Jerusalem, Charlotte of Lusignan, died and left her titles to the House, Savoy's dukes retained the title of "King of Cyprus." But they were kings with no kingdom. In 1713, Philip V of Spain ceded the Kingdom of Sicily to

Victor, who was crowned at Palermo in July; yet Victor's ability to defend the island was uncertain. Spanish troops returned to it. Victor, whose forces joined the Quadruple Alliance against Spain, lost Sicily, but after the Treaty of London in 1720 he was given in exchange the more tenable Kingdom of Sardinia. (England already had contributed to his hopes in August, 1718, when Admiral Byng destroyed Alberoni's powerful Spanish fleet off Sicily.) Cyprus and Jerusalem, Spain, and England thus mark the progress of the House of Savoy toward a genuine and secure crown.

21–24] *Europe... / means... / To crush the new-made King* Spain, France and the N Italian states were interested in the territories of Sardinia, the Savoy, and the Piedmont; Victor had reigned over them as "King" for ten years by this time (1730). The passage may also allude to European tension building up over the Spanish claims on Parma and Tuscany (see l. 523n).

38] *Annunziata* Knights of the Annunziata or Holy Annunciation, an honorary order of Savoyan noblemen, founded in 1360 by Amadeus VI but increased in size, status, and political significance by Victor in 1720.

40] *Del Borgo* See I, 1, 172n.

43–45] *Annulment of the Oaths ... / the Instrument* Legal forms of the state incident to Victor's abdication.

51] *the Spaniard and the Austrian* See ll. 233–34n.

52] *England, Holland, Venice* At various times, allies and enemies of Victor in his complicated military and diplomatic effort to defend Savoy from France and obtain a kingdom (see I, 1, 24–25n).

59] *Mondovi* Town in Cuneo province in the Piedmont of NW Italy; B read in the *Biographie* that when on a trip to Mondovi Victor first discovered d'Ormea (then Charles Ferrero), who was serving as a magistrate at nearby Carmagnola.

61] *quarrel with the Pope* Victor had made mortmain laws, claimed the revenue of vacant benefices in the Piedmont, and refused to ask for papal investiture of Sicily. Chiefly for these reasons papal investiture was withheld from the Kingdom of Sardinia. But Sardinians grew restive without bishops. Victor sent d'Ormea to Rome in 1724 to negotiate with Pope Benedict XIII. After three years of brilliant diplomacy, a Concordat (1727) was signed which gave Victor "the rights of disposing of ecclesiastical benefices of his States, with the exception of the bishoprics of Casal, Acqui, and Alexandria"; see Vitelleschi, 1905, 2:471. Later Pope Clement XII refused to honor this Concordat, and there was a diplomatic deadlock; but d'Ormea won investiture for the states of King Charles in 1738, and finally in 1742 helped to arrange a firm Concordat with Pope Benedict XIV.

67] *that great town* Ironically, Mondovi. See l. 59n.

71] *Toulon* Mediterranean port and naval base in SE France fortified by Vauban. Victor was nominally in command of the allied siege of Toulon in 1707, in the War of the Spanish Succession, but the attack was unsuccessful and the besieging naval forces were mainly British.

91] *Pianezze* Marquis de Pianezza, who was arrested by Victor at Turin after he warned of Victor's mother's intrigues in connection with a diplomatic marriage she was trying to arrange.
182] *Macchiavels* Cunning, unscrupulous politicians—after Niccolò Machiavelli (1469–1527), Italian author and statesman who analysed in *The Prince* methods by which political power is kept.
233–234] *"I began no treaty,"/(He speaks to Spain)* That is, if Charles were King of Sardinia he might protest that since not he, but his father, had agreed to support Philip V of Spain against Austria, the Kingdom of Sardinia could no longer be held responsible for that embarrassing treaty obligation. Victor was in very grave trouble. In 1730 he had agreed at Milan to support Austria against Spain, and at Turin, to support Spain against Austria in the event of war over the claims of the Infant Carlos (see l. 523n). Victor saw Charles's elevation to the Sardinian throne as a solution to this dilemma partly because, as B read, "Il pensa que les Bourbons étaient trop généreux pour faire tomber le poids de leur indignation et de leur vengeance sur un jeune prince nouvellement monté sur le trône. . ." [He thought that the Bourbons (of France and Spain) were too generous to bring the weight of their indignation and vengeance down upon a young prince newly crowned]. See Roman, *Récit,* 1807, p. 260.
254] *Chambery* Town in SE France, historically the capital of Savoy, with a fifteenth-century ducal castle; Victor spent much time in Chambéry and environs after abdicating. Lord Orrery found the town in 1754 well fortified, but dark, poor, and filthy.
256] *Count Remont* A fictitious name.
257] *Count Tende* Victor had assumed the fictitious name Conte di Tenda on a secret diplomatic mission to Venice in 1687. The name punningly suggests "Lord of the Mountain-Pass"—or specifically, of the Col de Tende, a 6,135 foot defile in the Maritime Alps on the French-Italian border, through which Victor had led troops against Louis XIV.
258] *Catinat* Maréchal Nicolas de Catinat (1637–1712), who repeatedly conducted Louis XIV's military campaigns against Victor and Victor's allies.
259] *Staffarde* Near the Abbey of Staffarda, on August 18, 1690, Catinat ambushed and defeated Victor's forces on marshy terrain; the *Biographie* states that Victor fought five hours in command of German and Spanish troops; a bullet pierced his clothes, his horse was shot, and he lost 5,000 men. Staffarda is about 7 mi. from Saluzzo in the Piedmont near the E foot of the Cottian Alps.
260] *Turin, where you beat the French* With the help of Prince Eugene of Savoy, and Austrian and Prussian forces, Victor routed some 40,000 French troops besieging Turin on September 7, 1706 in the War of the Spanish Succession.
261] *Montferrat* Region in the Piedmont of NW Italy; a marquisate after

the tenth century, it was invaded by Savoy in 1612 and came fully under Victor's control in 1713.

308] *Alps* Victor, retiring from Turin and Rivoli to the environs of Chambéry in Savoy, would virtually be living among Alpine ranges.

311] *Louis of the South* That is, Victor—who, like his former northern ally and enemy Louis XIV, the "Roi Soleil" of France, waged war, supported the arts, and ruled a kingdom.

312] *Janus* Two-faced Roman god, guardian of portals and patron of beginnings and endings.

322–323] *Victor / Imprisoned his own mother* Victor as a young man ordered the arrest of his mother, the Regent, but repented before she was imprisoned (*Biographie*).

338] *German soul* Polixena herself was German (see I, 1, 311n).

406] *how they fought in Greece* Ancient Greek infantry in close and deep ranks of the phalanx, with shields joined together and spears overlapping.

458] *Spanish claim* See I, 1, 132n.

499] *defile of Tende* See l. 257n.

503] *Spigno* The marquisate which Victor conferred on Contessa di San Sebastiano (see I, 1, 10n) included lands once belonging to his natural brother and the title of Marchesa di Spigno.

515] *House* The dynasty of Savoy, to which Victor belonged (see I, 1, 77n).

523] *Infant Carlos* The Bourbon Charles III (1716–1788), who became King of Spain in 1759. A son of Philip V by Elizabeth Farnese, his claim to the duchies of Parma and Tuscany kept Europe in expectation of war in the late 1720s. The Bourbons of France eagerly supported him; Austria feared the return and extension of Bourbon power to Italy; for Victor's involvement see ll. 233–34n.

524] *Tuscany* Hilly, fertile region of central Italy with Florence as its capital; created a grand duchy under the Medici in 1569.

SECOND YEAR, 1731. KING CHARLES PART I [II, i]

2] *Count Tende* Victor himself (see I, 2, 257n).

6] *Evian* Or Evian-les-Bains, a spa with famous mineral water on the S shore of Lake Geneva in the Haute-Savoie, 9 mi. SSW of Lausanne; as soon as Charles had left to visit Evian in 1731, Victor journeyed to Turin and thence to Rivoli to seize the state, according to the *Biographie*.

45] *Council Chamber* See B's note on the Scene at the beginning of the play.

61] *redress our nobles' grievance* Charles as King of Sardinia from 1730 not only abandoned d'Ormea's reduction policy but eased taxes on feudatories (see I, 1, 128n).

68] *a Treaty, Austria, Spain* The second Treaty of Vienna (1731), by which Austria permitted the Infant Carlos to take possession of Parma and Piacenza and garrison Tuscan fortresses with Spanish troops. Probably it would have absolved Victor, had he still been king, from the burden of contradictory agreements he had made with Spain and Austria; historically it may have motivated his desire to regain the Sardinian throne since it lessened the likelihood of war between two powers to whom he was equally committed (see I, 2, 233–34n).

73] *from Vienna* See the preceding note.

120] *pickthank* Tale-telling flatterer.

241] *Veneria, or Moncaglier* Magnificent country palaces within easy communication with Turin. The Véneria, erected by Victor's father as a shooting palace, is described in 1670 as "built in all perfection in a mountain of ill access" (see Vitelleschi, 1905, 1:72); Victor preferred Moncaglier or Moncalieri, where he celebrated his second marriage and was later imprisoned.

244] *Evian Baths* See l. 6n.

301] *Sicily . . . granted me/And taken back* See I, 2, 8–9n.

335] *Susa, and Veneria, and Superga* Scenes of former glories. Susa, 32 mi. WNW of Turin, was one of Victor's important forts; it briefly withstood a siege by Catinat in 1690 before it fell and was lost to the French again in 1704. For the Véneria Palace, see l. 241n. The Superga is a domed basilica, named after the steep hill 2,200 feet above sea level it surmounts near the Po River in N Italy; here Victor in 1706 vowed to defeat French troops besieging Turin, both the enemy and the city being visible in the plains below; after his victory he built the Superga to commemorate the event. Militarily Superga hill was important since Victor and Prince Eugene had been able to view from it "transparent disorder" in the enemy's ranks. See Nicholas Henderson, *Prince Eugen of Savoy: A Biography* (London, 1964), p. 132.

395] *Moncaglier* See l. 241n.

KING CHARLES PART II [II, ii]

36] *France—its King* The ineffectual relative of Victor's, King Louis XV (1710–1774), who succeeded his great-grandfather Louis XIV. Since he was only five when the latter died, Philippe II, duc d'Orléans, was regent for him until 1723, after which Cardinal Fleury dictated to him until 1743. His mistress, Mme. de Pompadour, guided most of his policies from 1743 to her death in 1764.

37] *Fleury's* André Hercule de Fleury (1653–1743), the astute French cardinal who as chief minister to Louis XV virtually ruled France from 1726 to 1743.

40] *Montorio* Here, a rich and powerful Piedmontese nobleman (and actually the name of two towns in S central Italy). It is not clear that B had an historical personage in mind.

45] *Count Spava* See I, 1, 172n.

62] *King of France* Louis XV, then twenty-one. See l. 36n.

71] *Rhebinder* Baron Othon de Rhébinder, appointed field-marshal of Victor's forces in 1730.

79] *Soccorso gate* An entrance to the citadel of Turin; the gate does not appear in contemporary maps though a Contrada del Socorso led to the Piazza Carlina in the city.

80] *San Remi* Commander of the Turin citadel.

112] *Forquieri's* The governor of Turin is mentioned by Condorcet as "Fosquieri," and as being among those arrested in 1731 for alleged conspiracy with Victor against King Charles.

113] *Rivarol* Marquis de Rivarol, another alleged conspirator who was arrested and soon released, according to Condorcet. His seat was probably at Rivarolo Canavese, 18 mi. N of Turin.

114] *Rabella* Another Piedmontese nobleman, but the name does not appear in B's chief sources for the play.

119] *St. George* The President of Chambéry's senate bears the name of the patron of England, in legend a dragon-slayer, and perhaps a soldier in the imperial army who died for the faith in Asia Minor in the fourth century; for the significance of this name to B see W. C. DeVane, "The Virgin and the Dragon," *YR*, NS 37 (1947): 33–46.

121] *Count Cumiane* The fief of Cumiane belonged to a family of Turin origin for over 400 years; Victor's second wife was born di Cumiana; her father, Grand Master at Court, was dead by 1730; her brother was the present count.

148] *baffled Alberoni and tricked Coscia* D'Ormea (and Victor) had baffled Cardinal Alberoni, chief minister to Philip V of Spain, by securing for Savoy in 1720 the Kingdom of Sardinia, which Alberoni's powerful Spanish forces had failed to hold. Victor might not have held the kingdom in tact had papal investiture been denied Sardinia; d'Ormea went to Rome in 1724, won over "with presents" (according to the *Biographie*) the corrupt Cardinal Coscia, and in 1727 obtained a satisfactory Concordat from Pope Benedict XIII (see I, 2, 61n).

173] *Perugia* The count bears the name of a province and provincial capital in central Italy with ancient Umbrian, Etruscan, and Roman associations.

174] *Solar* A chief officer of Charles; when Victor was under house arrest, the Cavaliere Solaro with two officers searched his room daily.

313] *D'Orleans* Philippe II, duc d'Orléans (1674–1723), regent for Louis XV of France from 1715 to 1723; he is said to have set the tone for licentiousness in the court of the regency. Victor had defeated him in 1706, when Orléans was nominally in supreme command of the French siege of Turin.

314] *Eugene's comrade, Louis's rival* Prince Eugene of Savoy (1663–1736), a general ranked by Napoleon as one of the seven greatest commanders in history, entered the service of Austria after Louis XIV refused him a commission; he helped Victor rout the French at Turin in 1706 and supported Savoy at other times; yet Victor plotted against him in 1717 to further his own territorial ambitions in Italy. Louis XIV, French king from 1643 to 1715, who had designs on Savoy, outshone Victor in every respect—except perhaps in diplomatic agility.

356] *When Louis reigned . . . Victor reigned* Their kingships barely overlapped in time. Louis XIV's reign and Victor's Sicilian reign coincided from 1713 to 1715.

Editorial Notes

ESSAY ON CHATTERTON

The *Essay on Chatterton* appeared anonymously in the *Foreign Quarterly Review* for July, 1842 (29:465–83). The July issue was the first under the editorship of John Forster, who had called upon other of his friends to help him with contributions of anonymous reviews for his initial number. Such "reviews," in the tradition of this journal and others of the time, were often independent studies without any great amount of attention to the works specified as being under review. Though Carlyle was too busy with his *Cromwell* to dare promise anything, Bulwer provided a lengthy article upon the Reign of Terror and Landor produced an extended study of the writings of Catullus for Forster's first issue and another on Theocritus for the second. B's essay was not acknowledged (so far as is known) or reprinted during his lifetime. In the spring of 1895, Katherine Bradley and her niece Edith Cooper, who had been friends of B in his last years, paid a fortnight's visit to B's sister Sarianna and his son Robert Wiedemann Barrett Browning at their home in Asolo, above Venice. In bringing out "heaps and heaps" of letters and other curiosities, including B's boyhood copy of Shelley and the proof sheets of *Paracelsus*, Sarianna apparently produced a copy of B's article for the *Foreign Quarterly*. Edith Cooper recorded in the two women's joint diary, *Works and Days*: "Now I am going to read 'the Old's' [Browning's] article on *Tasso and Chatterton* in the *Foreign Quarterly Review* for July 1842" (*Works and Days: From the Journal of Michael Field*, ed. T. and D. C. Sturge Moore [London, 1933], p. 208).

The *Essay on Chatterton* was first published as the poet's work in *Browning's "Essay on Chatterton,"* edited with Introductory Chapters and Notes by Donald Smalley, with a Foreword by William C. DeVane (Harvard University Press, 1948). Internal evidence of B's authorship is so strong that no serious question of the authenticity of the *Essay* has been raised. The Broughton, Northup, and Pearsall authoritative Browning bibliography lists it as "Browning's beyond a reasonable doubt."

It is unlikely that the manuscript of B's anonymous article has survived. The text of the *Foreign Quarterly Review* July, 1842, issue is given here, save where obvious errors have been corrected in the following eight instances:
Line 209 *Mayors* altered to read *Mayor's*.
Line 271 **βαπτιζετα** altered to read **βαπτιζεται**.

Line 392 *ballad* capitalized.
Line 393 quotation marks inserted after *face*.
Line 650 *Thistlewaites* altered to read *Thistlethwaites*.
Line 652 quotation marks inserted before *knowing*.
Line 720 *tergiversification* altered to read *tergiversation*.
Line 742 *must not not stay* altered to read *must not stay*.

8–9] *"If windows . . ."* "Then a lord on whose hand the king leaned answered the man of God, and said, Behold, if the Lord would make windows in heaven, might this thing be?" (2 Kings 7:2).

27] *Mr. Wilde* Richard Henry Wilde (1789–1847) had been attorney general of Georgia and had served five terms in Congress before he took up Italian scholarship during an extended visit abroad from 1835 to 1840 or early 1841. In addition to his study of Tasso Wilde wrote a treatise upon the life and times of Dante and another upon the Italian lyric poets, though neither of these last two was published. Wilde's work on Tasso is in good part an elaborate compilation of materials from Tasso's critics and biographers rather than an intensive independent study. He also translates at length (and rather well) from Tasso's verse.

33] *green-tree time* "For if they do these things in a green tree, what shall be done in the dry?" (Luke 23:31).

114] *Campbell* The passage quoted from Thomas Campbell's *Specimens of the British Poets* is given in the edition of Chatterton's works that B is purportedly reviewing (cf. B's note 2).

126] *"perish in the pride"* B is alluding, of course, to Wordsworth's famous lines in *Resolution and Independence*

> . . . of Chatterton, the marvellous Boy,
> The sleepless Soul that perished in his pride; . . .

147] *earliest and most partial biographer* Mrs. Newton, Chatterton's sister, who wrote a brief sketch of her brother's life for Sir Herbert Croft (for whom see note to line 373 below).

199] *Psalmanazar or Macpherson* George Psalmanazar (1679?–1763) was a French impostor who caused great excitement in London, 1703–1708, by posing as a native of Formosa and deceiving many eminent men with his translations into "Formosan" (a language of his own invention). It seems unfair of B to place the creator of Ossian in quite the same gallery.

252 ff.] *Bryant* Jacob Bryant (1715–1804) had laid stress upon Rowley's *Sermon on the Holy Spirit* as a work clearly beyond the powers of Chatterton to produce. His *Observations upon the Poems of Thomas Rowley, in Which the Authenticity of Those Poems Is Ascertained* appeared in 1781. He was later to publish *Observations upon a Treatise* . . . [on] *the Plain of Troy* (1795) and *A Dissertation concerning the War of Troy*, probably in 1796 (both of the later volumes, incidentally, are quartos, and the treatise on Rowley an octavo). Bryant argued that the Trojan War was a fiction and that Phrygian Troy had never existed.

256 ff.] *Hurrion* B may well have looked through the Reverend John

Hurrion's sermons in the Edinburgh edition of 1798 (which I have been unable to consult). He was right in his conjecture that Chatterton made extensive use of the first edition of Hurrion's six sermons on *The True Divinity of the Holy Spirit Proved Upon Scripture* (1734) and there found his materials, including his Greek quotation from Gregory Nazianzen and his quotation from Cyprian ready to his hand. For a full discussion of the process by which Chatterton created the *Sermon* from the pages of Hurrion together with an illustration showing Chatterton's curiously telltale copying of the Greek quotation, see the "Appendix" to *Browning's "Essay on Chatterton,"* pp. 177–87.

317] *"beauteous pieces . . ."* B is quoting from Chatterton's second letter to Dodsley, the eminent London publisher. Chatterton's attempt to interest Dodsley in the Rowley poems is again referred to in lines 424–428 below.

350–351] *Barrett and Catcott* William Barrett, a surgeon who was in process of writing a history of Bristol, and George Catcott, a pewterer, were Chatterton's principal patrons. For both of them Chatterton fabricated archaic documents and produced "originals" of these by means of a clever imitation of antique writing on ancient parchment or on parchment made to look antique through the use of various materials, including ocher and black lead powder.

373] *Sir Herbert Croft* Chatterton's first biographer worthy of the name. His account is still a major source for Chatterton biography. It appears as Letter XLIX in Croft's *Love and Madness, A Story Too True* (1780), a curious novel purportedly giving the love letters of Martha Ray and the Reverend James Hackman, who was hanged at Tyburn in April, 1779, as her murderer. Letter XLIX (pages 125–244), written within ten years of Chatterton's death on August 24, 1770, contains much material that Croft obtained by interview with persons who had known Chatterton, including Chatterton's sister.

493–494] *Gray and Mason's* William Mason (1724–1797), minor poet and dramatist, friend of Thomas Gray and later his biographer.

503] *doit . . . dead Indian* "Were I in England now . . . any strange beast there makes a man: when they will not give a doit to relieve a lame beggar, they will lay out ten to see a dead Indian." *The Tempest*, II.ii.28–32.

504] *spurious cardinal's hat* Walpole's famous Strawberry Hill collections were auctioned off in April and May, 1842. Charles Kean, the actor, had bid in what was offered as Cardinal Wolsey's hat for £21. There were many doubters of the authenticity of this relic, including a writer for *Punch* (April 16, 1842), who remarked that if the hat had been *"lying dormant"* from Henry VIII to the time of James II, as it was said to have done, it could boast of an unusually long nap and "we still think it will not be found worth much after having been exposed to so many REIGNS!"

506 ff.] Here, as so often elsewhere, B is surely quoting from memory. He manages to telescope three widely separated sentences from Walpole's *Letter.*

520–521] *Benedick's* Old Tale *Much Ado About Nothing*, I.i.219–20.

532] *"Walpoliana"* B quotes accurately, though the italics are his own. See John Pinkerton, *Walpoliana* (second edition; 1804), 1:105.

576 ff.] *The desire . . . Mr. Stephens* Chatterton's letter to his relative in Salisbury is indeed a strange piece of flattery and posturings that might well have made B question his interpretation of the marvelous Boy.

600] *Dr. Gregory* Dr. George Gregory in his *The Life of Thomas Chatterton, with Criticism on his Writings* (1789) had taken a stern view of Chatterton as a wild youth who, through reckless misuse of his genius came to a bad end that might serve as a lesson to later generations.

636] *Anticyra* Browning presumably has in mind the proverb *naviget Anticyram* and perhaps alludes specifically to Horace's *Satires*, ii.3.166. But the ancients sailed to Anticyras not for hemlock but for hellebore, the most popular remedy in antiquity for madness.

DRAMATIC LYRICS

Text and Publication

Dramatic Lyrics was published in November, 1842 as *Bells and Pomegranates* No. III. (For an explanation of the series title see *Text* n, *Pippa Passes*.) In a letter to Alfred Domett on May 22, 1842 (*Domett*, p. 36), B mentions "a few songs and small poems" which his publisher, Moxon, has advised him to publish "for popularity's sake." By mid-July he had decided on the title of the collection. The sixteen-page pamphlet, printed in very fine type in double columns divided in the center, contained sixteen poems arranged in ten groups, only one group of which had been published previously. The two poems of *Madhouse Cells*, probably written in the spring of 1834 during B's visit to Russia, appeared autonomously in the January, 1836 *Monthly Repository* under the titles "Porphyria" and "Johannes Agricola." In the collected edition of 1849, B yoked the *Dramatic Lyrics* with the *Dramatic Romances* of 1845, calling the collection *Dramatic Romances and Lyrics*. With the exception of *Cavalier Tunes* and *Madhouse Cells*, which remain in their original groupings, B broke up the old groupings in the 1849 edition, allowing the poems to stand as individual pieces. For the collected edition of 1863, B rearranged poems within the three collections of shorter poems which he had published by then, *Dramatic Lyrics* (1842), *Dramatic Romances* (1845), and *Men and Women* (1855). Of the original *Dramatic Lyrics* only the following poems appeared in the 1863 edition of the *Dramatic Lyrics*: *Cavalier Tunes*, "Through the Metidja," "Soliloquy of the Spanish Cloister," and "Cristina." Three poems—"Artemis Prologizes," "Rudel to the Lady of Tripoli," and "Johannes Agricola"—were placed in *Men and Women*. The following poems became part of *Dramatic Romances*: "My Last Duchess," "Count Gismond," "Incident of the French Camp," "Porphyria's Lover," "In a Gondola," "Waring," and "The Pied Piper." In the collected editions after 1863, *Dramatic Lyrics* consists of fifty poems, most of them borrowed from the original *Men and Women*. (Subsequent placement of an individual poem is given at the beginning of the variants to that poem.)

Part-Title] *Cavalier* The Royalist forces, mainly aristocratic, who supported

Charles I against the Puritans or parliamentary party in the Civil War, 1642–1651. They were dubbed Cavaliers by their enemies, after the brutal Spanish *cavaliero,* or trooper.

I. MARCHING ALONG

1] *Kentish Sir Byng* An aristocratic family settled for many centuries at Wrotham in Kent. In the eighteenth century they became connected with the Earl of Strafford through marriage. B is probably using the name simply for its strong Kentish and Royalist associations, for there does not seem to have been a Byng who took any noteworthy part in the Civil War. The Kentish were militant supporters of the crown throughout the revolutionary period. In March, 1642, a Kentish petition which supported the policies and views of Charles I, especially in regard to religious matters, was condemned by the parliamentarian House of Commons: "If any one moment can be selected as that in which the Civil War became inevitable, it is that of the vote of March 28, by which the Kentish petitioners were treated as criminals. From that moment the indignation of hundreds of high-spirited gentlemen came rapidly to a head, and it would not be long before they placed their swords at the services of a king who shared in their prejudices and their resolve" (S.R. Gardner, *History of England, 1603–1642* [London, 1884], 10:182).
2] *crop-headed Parliament* Parliamentarians, nicknamed Roundheads after the London apprentices, cropped their hair to distinguish themselves from the long-locked Royalists (see *Part-Title* n).
3] *pressing a troop* To conscript for military service.
7] *Pym* John Pym (1583?–1643), who successfully promoted the election of Puritans to the Long Parliament first assembled in November, 1640, was the aggressive leader of the parliamentary struggle against Charles I. Pym was the chief instrument for the impeachment of Thomas Wentworth, Earl of Strafford, Charles's advisor and public champion, though he did not support the Bill of Attainder by which Strafford was executed. He was also the leading supporter of the Grand Remonstrance which listed the grievances that had arisen in Charles's reign and which provoked the King to go to the Commons to arrest him and four others. Though they escaped, Charles's breach of privilege, a declaration of open hostility, became a prelude to war. See also II, *Strafford,* p. 345n.
7] *Carles* churls.
13] *Hampden* John Hampden (1594–1643), a first cousin of Oliver Cromwell, was a champion of the people against the right of Charles to exact a ship-money tax for the financing of foreign ventures. In the Long Parliament which convened in 1640, he was Pym's chief associate in attacking royal policies. A major supporter of the Grand Remonstrance and one of the five members of Commons whom the King tried to arrest for treason, he was the soul of the opposition to the monarchy as Pym was its sword. He is consid-

ered by many the noblest of the parliamentarian leaders. See also II, *Strafford*, p. 345n.

14] *Hazelrig, Fiennes, and young Harry* Sir Arthur *Hazelrig* (or Hazlerigg) introduced the Bill of Attainder responsible for the Earl of Strafford's execution. Another of the five Commons members Charles tried to impeach in 1642. Died in the Tower in 1661. See II, Strafford, p. 357n. *Nathaniel Fiennes* (1608?–1669), an important member of Parliament and a friend of Oliver Cromwell. Prominent in Long Parliament debates on ecclesiastical matters, he argued in favor of the complete abolition of episcopacy on the grounds of the dangerous political powers of the bishops. See also II, *Strafford*, p. 346n. *Sir Henry Vane*, the younger (1613–1662), whose father was Secretary of State to Charles I. Appointed joint treasurer of the Navy by Charles in 1639, he was dismissed during the Long Parliament, to which he was elected, when he revealed that he was an unrepentant Puritan and supporter of the "Root and Branch Bill." In August, 1642, he was appointed sole treasurer by Parliament, a post he held until 1650. Throughout the Civil War Vane was one of the most important parliamentary leaders, virtually succeeding John Pym in 1643. See also II, *Strafford*, p. 345n.

15] *Rupert* Prince Robert of Bavaria (1619–1682), also called Rupert of the Rhine or of the Palatinate, the son of Frederick V and Elizabeth, daughter of James I of Scotland, and nephew to King Charles I. He joined the king at Nottingham in August, 1642, just before the latter raised his standard to commence the Civil War. Charles had reserved the generalship of the cavalry for Rupert. A skillful and successful commander, Prince Rupert was one of the dominant figures of the war. His success was unbroken until the battle of Marston Moor in 1644. In November, 1644, he was appointed general of the king's army. He was relieved of his command and estranged from the king after surrendering to the parliamentary forces at Bristol.

22] *Nottingham* On the river Trent approximately 123 mi. NNW of London. On what has been named Standard Hill, King Charles I raised his standard on August 22, 1642, marking the outbreak of the English Civil War.

II. GIVE A ROUSE

3] *in hell's despite* A later period in the war, when the Royalists were losing the struggle.

13] *George* The Cavalier speaker's son, a fictional character.

16] *Noll's damned troopers* Oliver Cromwell's company, called Ironsides, a double cavalry regiment of fourteen troops famous for their discipline and courage.

III. BOOT AND SADDLE

10] *Castle Brancepeth* The Cavalier speaker's castle situated near Durham in N England.

MY LAST DUCHESS

Title] In his research for *Sordello* (1840), B read deeply in the history of Ferrara and its powerful rulng family, the Este. Though the period of the city's history which concerned him predates the time of the setting of this poem, there can be little doubt that he was thoroughly versed in Ferrara's later Renaissance history (see II, *Sordello, Text* n, pp. 361–66). Moreover, in the summer of 1842, B wrote a review (commonly known as the *Essay on Chatterton*, see pp. 159–179 this volume) of R. H. Wilde's biography of Tasso for which B possibly consulted the *Biographie universelle* and Muratori's *Della Antichita Estensi*, both of which contain portraits of Tasso and his patron, Alfonso II, fifth duke of Ferrara and last of the Este. That B's Duke of Ferrara is Alfonso II has been shown convincingly by Louis S. Friedland ("Ferrara and *My Last Duchess*," *SP* 33 (1936): 656–84). The son and heir of Ercole II and Renée de France, Alfonso was born in 1533. From 1552–54 he lived in France. In Paris he consulted the famous seer and astrologer, Nostradamus, who prophesyed that he would be married three times, that he would be childless by his first two wives, and that the third wife would produce for him the male heir necessary to perpetuate his family. As it happened, Nostradamus was accurate in the number of marriages; however the Duke died childless and his ancestral estate reverted to the Pope. In 1558, Alfonso married Lucrezia, the fourteen-year-old daughter of Cosimo de Medici. In all likelihood, she is the source of B's last duchess, for she was known to be pretty, devout, and of modest mental endowment. The Duke was known for his pride, egotism, and occasional cruelty. A characterization based on original sources is given by the Renaissance scholar, Kazimienz von Chledowski (*Der Hof von Ferrara*, trans. Rosa Shapire [Munchen, 1919], 311, quoted in Friedland, p. 673): "He was immoderately arrogant and conceited, and prided himself beyond measure upon his bravery, intelligence, and ancient descent. With all that he was vengeful and ever ready to pursue a feud." Lucrezia died mysteriously in 1561 when she was barely seventeen. Suspicions were aroused and it was widely rumored that she had been poisoned. Recent investigations indicate that she probably died of a chronic lung ailment. Alfonso's choice for a second duchess was Barbara, sixth daughter of Ferdinand I, King of Austria. During 1564 and 1565 emissaries passed between the courts of Vienna and Ferrara negotiating the match. Ferdinand I died shortly after agreeing to the marriage and unconcluded business fell into the hands of his sons, chiefly Ferdinand II, Count of Tyrol, whose seat was in the city of Innsbruck. In July, 1565, Alfonso travelled to Vienna to attend the obsequies of Ferdinand I, stopping on the way at Innsbruck where he met for the first time his promised bride, then in the guardianship of her brother, Ferdinand II. Maximillian II, the first son and successor of Ferdinand I, had several emissaries in Italy who were negotiating the marriage; yet, they were directly responsible to Ferdinand II. The chief emissary was Nikolaus Madruz, who delivered the message inviting Alfonso to Vienna and who was to lead the escort conveying Barbara to her new husband. It may be assumed that Madruz, the envoy reporting to his master the Count of Tyrol in Innsbruck, is the silent auditor of B's poem.

Subtitle] *Ferrara* A city in N Italy. Ferrara and Florence ruled respectively by the Este and Medici families were the rival seats of secular power in Italy throughout the Renaissance (see *Title* n and "Province of Veneto," II, *Sordello*, p. 363).

3] *Frà Pandolf's* Probably an imaginary painter. There are several Pandolfi in the annals of Italian art, though none appear to have had any connection with the Duke or Duchess of Ferrara. There is no record of a portrait of Lucrezia di Medici painted in Florence.

33] *a nine-hundred-years-old name* The House of Este, of Lombard descent, a branch of the tenth-century dynasty of the Obertenghi. The family derived its name from the township castle of Este 17 mi. SW of Padua. Its founder was the distinguished margrave Alberto Azzo II who died a centenarian in 1097. Thus, at the time the Duke is speaking the family name is roughly six hundred fifty years old. The Medici, Lucrezia's family and traditional rivals of the Este were, in comparison, upstarts since the family was only a few generations old, and its origin the mercantile class.

45] *I gave commands* B was once questioned about these commands by Hiram Corson (*An Introduction to the Study of Robert Browning's Poetry* [Boston, 1891], pp. vii-viii). He replied: "Yes, I meant that the commands were that she be put to death." A moment later he added, "Or he might have had her shut up in a convent."

49] *The Count your master's known munificence* The second duchess, through her brother, the Count of Tyrol, made Duke Alfonso a dowry said to be "cento mila Renani Fiorini" or one hundred thousand Rhine Florins (see *Title* n).

54–55] *Neptune . . . / Taming a sea-horse* It was common in Renaissance bronze sculpture to depict the sea-god Neptune in some connection with sea horses, the fabulous marine animals with the foreparts of a horse and the tail of a fish. Usually a team of sea horses are shown pulling Neptune's chariot. B visited Innsbruck and the Tyrol on his way home from Italy in 1838, four years before the appearance of "My Last Duchess." It is possible that at that time he saw a bronze sculpture such as he describes.

56] *Claus of Innsbruck* Probably an imaginary artist. For the first half of the sixteenth century Innsbruck was perhaps the greatest center for bronze sculpture in Europe. Emperor Maximillian of Germany, a great patron of art, commissioned the building of a large tomb-monument in the Court Church of Innsbruck. The ancestors and members of the Hapsburg house were to be represented in larger-than-life bronze statues. The Roman emperors and saints of the Church were to be cast in small figures. A private foundary was established for the project. Most of the work on this prodigious venture was executed between 1508 and 1533. After a lull, work was resumed under Ferdinand I in 1540 (see *Title* n). None of the statues were erected until after 1550.

COUNT GISMOND

Subtitle] *Aix in Provence* Aix-en-Provence, a city in SE France 19 mi. N of Marseilles. For centuries the roads from the N of France to Italy and from Marseilles to the Alps have crossed here. During the Middle Ages it was the capital of Provence, governed by the counts and dukes of Anjou, and a center of art and learning where the troubadours and chivalric culture developed and flourished.
87] *hauberk, on the fret* Defensive armor which, during the twelfth and thirteenth centuries, developed into a long coat of mail, or military tunic, usually of ring or chain mail held together with a variety of frets, or interlacings.
124] *tercel* Var. of tiercel. In falconry usually the male of the peregrine falcon and the goshawk, it was also called the falcon-gentle or tercel-gentle—a name sometimes used for a knight or gentleman of good estate.

INCIDENT OF THE FRENCH CAMP

Title] The background of this poem is probably historical, but research has not uncovered the particular incident paralleling the one here described. Innumerable stories relating to the devotion of Napoleon's soldiers (several of them similar to this one) circulated in the nineteenth century. Browning told Mrs. Orr (*Hbk*, p. 300) that the story was true, except that the hero was a man, not a boy. DeVane records an anecdote related by Cardinal Fesch, Napoleon's uncle, which may be based on the same incident B had in mind (Baron Karlo Excellmanns, *The Eventful Life of Napoleon Bonaparte*, [London, 1823] p. 3:196; quoted in DeVane, p. 112). At Ratisbon, exhausted by the battle of three days, Napoleon

> retired to a short distance in order to enjoy a few minutes repose, when, making his steed lay down, he stretched himself upon the turf, and reclined upon the belly of the animal. While in that situation one of his aide-de-camps arrived, to make known a position taken by the enemy, and, while in the act of explaining his errand, he pointed with the right hand, when on the instant a shot severed the limb from his body, the ball passing close to the Emperor's head. Napoleon manifested his sincere regret, and proceeded to assist his unfortunate aide-de-camp, without displaying the least personal fear, or quitting his dangerous position.

1] *French stormed Ratisbon* The battle at Ratisbon (the German Regensburg) in Bavaria took place on April 23, 1809 and was one of Napoleon's most brilliant military victories over the Austrians. The town, 82 mi. NNE of

Munich on the S bank of the Danube, was sacked and burned, the Austrians driven across the river.

11] *Lannes* Jean Lannes, Duc de Montebello (1769–1809), perhaps Napoleon's most courageous marshall, led the attack on Ratisbon. Less than a month later he was critically injured at the battle of Aspern-Essling. He died in the arms of Napoleon on May 31, 1809.

29] *flag-bird . . . vans* The heraldic device of Napoleon's regime, borrowed from Caesar, was the eagle which was placed on the top of the flag pole. Shortly after his coronation in 1804, Napoleon held a Fête de Aigles on the Champ de Mars in which he presented over a thousand eagles to his forces. The eagle seems to have been a more sacred symbol than the tricolor itself.

SOLILOQUY OF THE SPANISH CLOISTER

10] *salve tibi* Hail to thee.

14] *oak-galls* An oak button or nut gall used in making ink and black dye.

16] *Swine's Snout* B probably borrowed this image from Proverbs 11:22: "As a jewel of gold in a swine's snout, so is a fair woman which is without discretion."

31] *Barbary corsair's* A pirate of the Barbary Coast of N Africa.

39] *the Arian* A heretic and follower of Arius, a fourth-century theologian who attacked the orthodox doctrine of the Trinity by holding that Christ was created by and inferior to God the Father. The fundamental premise of Arius was that the godhead is unique and therefore cannot be shared or communicated, so that the Son cannot be God. Arianism was condemned by the Church at the Council of Nicea in 325 though it persisted until the 7th century.

49–56] *great text in Galatians . . . Manichee* The text generally cited is Galatians 5:19–21 which lists seventeen, rather than twenty-nine, "works of the flesh," such as adultery, fornication, uncleanliness. Arnold Williams, in "Browning's Great Text in Galatians," *MLQ* 10 (March 1949): 89–90, argues that the Speaker's plot involves a theological and not, as commonly believed, a moral trap for Brother Lawrence. The Epistle to the Galatians, which deals with the relationship of the old law and the new, is full of difficult texts, especially in the second and third chapters. One could easily deviate from orthodox interpretation of these texts and fall into a number of heretical errors, thus incurring "damnations." Williams speculates that B knew in a general way of the difficulties in Galatians and invented the text with 'twenty-nine distinct damnations.' However, there is always the possibility that somewhere in theological literature there is a document which lists exactly twenty-nine errors based on a misinterpretation of a text in Galatians.

Manichaeism was a dualistic gnostic religion taught from the 3d cent. to the 7th cent. by the Persian, Mani, and his followers. According to Mani, good (light, God, the soul) and evil (darkness, Satan, the body) are essentially separate and opposed principles which have become mixed in the world through the act of the evil principle. Thus, in a world characterized by conflict, there is no possibility of reconciliation of flesh and spirit. Salvation lies in the release of goodness and a return to the original state of separation. However, as Miriam K. Starkman points out in "The Manichee in the Cloister: A Reading of Browning's 'Soliloquy of the Spanish Cloister,'" *MLN* 75 (May 1960): 400–01, while the term Manichaean describes the heretic in the formal sense, the term Manichee in later times came to describe any dualist or gnostic. Both usages she finds significant to the poem. By misinterpreting a difficult text in Galatians, Brother Lawrence will reveal himself as a formal heretic, for Galatians, with its many ambiguities, lent itself to proofs of Manichaean principles. Also, "by his attitude to the very name of the epistle he will reveal himself in his true colors, a 'Manichee.'"

57] *scrofulous French novel* Williams (p. 89) sees this as a plot against Brother Lawrence's morals, as opposed to the preceding plot against his faith (see ll. 49–56n). For Starkman, the novel is only incidentally a moral trap, and primarily a theological one designed to expose Brother Lawrence's heresy. A Manichee in this situation would have been extremely vulnerable. He might be expected to reveal his theological beliefs through either his chastity or his licentiousness, since the former was strictly enforced on the Elect while the latter was commonly associated with certain dualist sects. For a full discussion of the question see Starkman's article.

60] *Belial* Hebrew abstract noun roughly meaning wickedness. The common Biblical and proverbial phrase "sons of Belial" and the personification of Belial (as a figure opposite of Christ) in 2 Cor. 6:15 encouraged the notion that it was a name. In medieval religious drama, Belial is represented as a devil of lewdness. Milton gave Belial a distinct character, portraying him as lustful: ". . . a spirit more lewd/ Fell not from heaven, or more gross to love/ Vice for itself" (*PL* 1. 490–92); "Belial the dissolutest spirit that fell, the sensualist . . ." (*PR* 2. 150–51). Clearly, B thought of Belial as having a definite character of lust. In the Epilogue of *Parleyings* (1887), Fust's second friend speaks of "Sir Belial," lurer of Helen of Troy. Guido in *The Ring and the Book* speaks of "Priests/ No longer men of Belial" (V, 2044–45).

69] *rose acacia* A shrub with bristly stems and large racemes of handsome rose-colored flowers. The durable wood was used for the woodwork of the Ark of the Covenant. It was also used in the construction of the tabernacle and the altars. See Exodus 25:10; 26:15; 27:1.

70] *Hy, Zy, Hine* One of several explanations is that these words are meant to echo the vesper bell—another that it is an incantation to a black mass. See also Gordon Pitts' "Browning's 'Soliloquy of the Spanish Cloister': 'Hy, Zy, Hine,'" *NQ* n.s. 13 [1966]: 339–40. Pitts conjectures that B, while doing research for *Sordello* [1840] in the British Museum, stumbled across the

Beauvais manuscript of *Orientis Partibus,* which contains "The Mass of the Ass." This text has been dated between 1217 and 1234, the period of *Sordello.* The refrain that runs throughout the Mass is "Hez hez sire asnes hez," which, in Old French, means "Heigh, heigh, Sir Ass, heigh." Another phrase that occurs in the mass is "Hinham, Hinham, Hinham." "Hinham" means "he-haw." It is possible that in the mind of the speaker [or the poet] these phrases became slurred into "Hy, Zy, Hine."

71–72] *Plena gratiâ / Ave, Virgo!* The ejaculation "Hail Virgin, full of grace" is the beginning of the prayer to the Blessed Virgin, generally recited during the ringing of the Angelus bell.

71] *Vespers* Evening prayer, or the sixth of the canonical hours of the breviary.

IN A GONDOLA

Title] In an undated letter to Miss Fanny Haworth written toward the end of 1841, B described the origin and composition of the poem: "I chanced to call on Forster the other day—and he pressed me into committing verse on the instant, not the minute, in Maclise's behalf—who has wrought a divine Venetian work, it seems, for the British Institution—Forster described it well—but I could do nothing better than this wooden ware (All the 'properties,' as we say, were given—and the problem was how to cataloguize them in rhyme and unreason)—I send my heart up to thee—all my heart. . . . Singing and stars and night and Venice streets in depths of shade and space are properties, do you please to see. And now tell me, is this below the average of Catalogue original poetry?" (Hood *Ltrs,* p. 7). In a letter to Furnivall in 1881, B added a detail to the story (ibid., p. 196): "I wrote the Venice stanza [the first stanza] to illustrate Maclise's picture ["The Serenade"],—for which he was anxious to get some line or two: I had not seen it, but, from Forster's description, gave it to him in his room *impromptu*. . . .when I did see it, I thought the Serenader too jolly somewhat for the notion I got from Forster—and I took up the subject in my own way." After seeing Maclise's picture at the British Institution, where it was exhibited in 1842, B was moved to add 226 lines to the original seven line illustration, creating an entirely original tale.

22] *the Three* Later identied as Paul, Gian, and "Himself" (ll. 204–09). "Himself" is undoubtedly the lady's husband, Paul and Gian relatives, perhaps brothers.

31] *the Arab sage* Not a specific personage.

33] *cruce* A crucible or melting pot.

34] *mage* A magician. In the transferred sense, a person of exceptional wisdom and learning.

44] *Pucci Palace* Perhaps one of Venice's 15,000 houses and palaces, though not a famous one. Possibly imaginary.

47] *wried* Wrung.
81] *millet-sheaves* A hardy cereal grass with profuse foliage.
106–07] *Paul's . . . / . . . Himself* See l. 22n.
113] *Lido* A long narrow island on the Adriatic side of Venice, it was the Jewish cemetery. Jews, being heretics, were buried here in exile from the consecrated Christian ground. The graveyard is flooded at high tide.
121] *ribbon-grass* A grass having long slender leaves.
127] *Guidecca* The great canal which separates the island of Guidecca from the main part of Venice. It is one mi. long and nearly a quarter mi. wide at its widest point.
148] *Smyrna peach* Smyrna, Turkey, is famous for its fruits, among them peaches.
150] *This coiled hair* Snakes were often kept as pets in ancient Rome.
176–177] *God's plagues . . . / guilty glorious Babylon* Babylon, the ancient capital of Babylonia, is situated on a branch of the Euphrates in S Iraq about sixty mi. S of present-day Baghdad. Under Nebuchadnezzar II, who reigned from c. 605–562 B.C. and established the Chaldean dynasty, Babylon reached its height of glory. The Babylonian Captivity and the sacking of Jerusalem took place during this period. Because of its wickedness toward Israel, Isaiah (13) and Jeremiah (50, 51) predict the doom of Babylon. Plagues, however, are not mentioned in either prophecy. B is possibly in mind of the ten plagues used to punish the Egyptians.
180] *limpet . . . lymph* A tiny mollusk usually found clinging to rocks near the water, the limpet comes out of its shell at the sound of water, or lymph.
186] *Shidone's eager Duke* Bartolomeo Shidone (1570–1615) of Modena was a painter of the Venetian school who formed himself on Raphael and Correggio. His works, mainly of religious personages and events, were extremely few in number because he wasted his time gaming. The only painting of his in Venice is "Descent From the Cross." The painting mentioned here is probably imaginary.
188] *Haste-thee-Luke* Luca-Fa-Presto, nickname of the Neapolitan artist, Luca Giordana (1632–1705). There was such a great demand for his drawings and sketches that his father continually urged him to hurry up by repeating "Luca, fa presto" (Luke, make haste).
190] *Bold Castelfranco's Magdalen* Giorgio Barbarelli (1478?–1510), usually called Giorgione. Born at Castelfranco near Venice, he was known by his contemporaries as Zorzo Da Castelfranco. He was a school companian of Titian and an enormously popular painter. Giorgione does not seem to have painted a Magdalen.
193] *Tizian* Titian (1477–1576), or Tiziano Vecellio, carried on the style of Giorgione and became the most famous painter of the Venetian school. There are over twenty paintings by Titian in Venice alone.
206] *Zorzi* The lover's servant.

207] *Zanze* The woman's servant.
222] *Siora* Venetian for Signora.

ARTEMIS PROLOGIZES

Title] According to Mrs. Orr (*Life*, p. 121), B attached the following note to the first proof:

> I had better say perhaps that the above is nearly all retained of a tragedy I composed, much against my endeavour, while in bed with a fever a few years ago—it went further into the story of Hippolytus and Aricia; but when I got well, putting only thus much down at once, I soon forgot the remainder.

B apparently intended to write a continuation of the *Hippolytus* of his favorite Greek dramatist, Euripides, using this poem as the prologue. In Euripides' play, Hippolytus dies of the wounds incurred from an unjust punishment by Poseidon; but, in the versions of the story told by both Virgil (*Aeneid* 7. 765–77) and Ovid (*Metamorphoses* 15. 530–46) the dying youth is gradually healed by Aesculapius and then carried to Italy by Artemis (Diana), where he falls in love with the nymph Aricia. It is undoubtedly this part of the story which B planned to take up in his sequel to Euripides. In B's prologue, Artemis has conveyed Hippolytus, who was dead, to a grove in the forest where he is to be restored to life by Aesculapius, the famous physician. The goddess relates the story of Hippolytus up to the present moment, following the plot of Euripides' play. The bastard son of Hippolyte and Theseus, Hippolytus was a pure and noble youth, devoted to Artemis, the goddess of chastity, and an open enemy of Aphrodite, the goddess of erotic love. The latter, in revenge, plotted to destroy Hippolytus. In the absence of Theseus, she strickened Hippolytus' stepmother, Phaedra, with an uncontrollable desire for her stepson, to which Hippolytus reacted with shock and disgust. Out of shame, Phaedra committed suicide, but tried to cover her guilt by leaving a note for Theseus claiming that Hippolytus had attempted to rape her. Confronted by his father, Hippolytus remained faithful to an oath he had made not to divulge his stepmother's evil. Theseus called on his father, Poseidon, to punish Hippolytus and then banished the youth. As Hippolytus was riding his chariot out of the city along the seacoast a monstrous bull charged out of the surf and caused the horses to panic. Hippolytus, caught in the reins, was dragged over the rocks and severely injured. Nearly dead, he was carried to Theseus where Artemis appeared to reveal the true story of Phaedra's death, the devices of Aphrodite, and the innocence of Hippolytus. Theseus and Hippolytus were reconciled and the son died in his father's arms. The peculiar spelling of Greek names in this poem, a practice B adhered to later in *Balaustian's Adventure* and his translation of the *Agamemnon*, was the result of dissatisfaction with the Latinization of these names and a desire to approximate the Greek sounds.

In the preface to *Agamemnon* B defends this practice.

1] *ambrosial courts* Olympus, a mountain in N Greece, the home of the gods in Greek mythology. Ambrosia is the fabled food of the gods.

2] *Here, Queen of Pride* Hera, the wife (and sister) of Zeus, was queen of the gods. She came to represent motherhood for the Greeks.

6] *I, caring for the creatures* Artemis was the divine protectoress of wildlife.

12] *Athenai* The city of Athens, on the plain of Attica about 3 mi. from the sea, was the center of ancient Greek culture.

13] *Asclepios* Aesculapius, the son of Apollo, was the first great physician. Trained by Chiron, whom he far surpassed in healing, he became famous throughout Greece. Aesculapius was such a skillful physician he occasionally raised dead men to life. Zeus, fearful that mortals might learn from him the art of reviving the dead, slew him with a thunderbolt.

19] *Aphrodite* Goddess of beauty and the patroness of love of all kinds, she was generally associated with sensual love. According to Hesiod, she rose from the foam of the sea where the bits of Uranus' genitals fell when he was castrated by Cronus.

21] *Gadbee* Gadfly, a small fly which bites and goads.

22] *Phaidra* See *Title* n.

23] *Theseus* See *Title* n.

24] *Hippolutos* See *Title* n.

27] *Amazonian stranger's race* Hippolyte, the former lover of Theseus and mother of Hippolytus, was queen of the Amazons. One of the twelve tasks of Heracles was to obtain Hippolyte's girdle. Some accounts say that Theseus, who assisted Heracles in this task, abducted Hippolyte.

35] *Poseidon* Olympian god of the sea (see *Title* n).

39] *ai ai* Greek exclamation of sorrow.

42] *Henetian horses* Henetia, a district near Paphlagonia in Asia Minor, was known for its fine horses.

44] *shingles* Coarse gravel on the beach.

82] *Olumpos* See l. 1n.

101] *Phoibos* Phoebus, or Apollo. (See also *Title* n.)

102] *my radiant brother* Apollo.

114–15] *Divine presenter of the healing rod, / Thy snake* Aesculapius always carried a rod—he is sometimes pictured leaning on it—which had curative powers. The serpent is his symbol. In his sacred precincts it was the emblem of his presence. It was thought to communicate health to the sick as they slept.

118] *sister-nymphs* Artemis was always surrounded by nymphs from whom she required a vow of chastity.

WARING

Title] The prototype for Waring was B's intimate friend, Alfred Domett. The name was borrowed from a king's messenger whom B met in Russia in

1834. In this "fancy portrait of a very dear friend," as Joseph Arnould, another of B's friends from Camberwell, called it, the poet has Waring depart suddenly for Moscow. Actually, Domett's departure was for New Zealand and, while somewhat suddenly arranged, was in full knowledge of his friends. The voyage was made around May 1, 1842, not in the "snowiest of all December." The poem is a clever mixture of fact and imagination so that a strict biographical reading is dangerous. However, the narrator's feelings toward Waring coincide with the strong affection and complete confidence in a friend's abilities expressed in B's letters to Domett, especially the ones written within the first few months of the latter's parting. (For these letters and a full account of the friendship see *Domett*, and Griffin and Minchin, chap. 5.) Alfred Domett, the son of a shipowner, was born in Camberwell in 1811. He went to Cambridge in 1829, but after four years residence left the university without a degree. In 1834, he published his first volume, *Poems*, which went unnoticed. The same year he visited Canada, then Italy and the Tyrol. In 1839, he published *Venice*, a small volume of poetic impressions. It is possible that this volume had something to do with his friendship with B which began sometime around 1840. Both belonged to a small club, the Colloquials, whose members were all native of Camberwell. Other members were the originator, Captain Pritchard, Joseph Arnould, Christopher and Joseph Dowson, and William Curling Young. Besides meetings, "the set," as they often referred to themselves, met for semiannual dinners. Arnould and Domett were called to the bar in 1841, but Domett, probably out of impatience with the law, disappointment over his failure to gain recognition through his writings, and a desire for movement, left for New Zealand in May. He became Prime Minister of New Zealand in 1863. In 1872, twenty-four years after his departure from England, Domett returned and renewed his acquaintance with B, who helped Domett publish his own verse.

54–55] *Monstr'-inform'-ingens-horrend-ous/Demoniaco-seraphic* Probably a parody of Virgil's concatenated description of the Cyclopes (Polyphemus) as a horrible monster, misshapen and huge (see *Aeneid* 3. 658).

61] *Some lost lady* This incident, probably real, remains obscure.

99] *Ichabod* See 1 Samuel 4:21. "And she named the child Ichabod, saying the glory is departed from Israel." Ichabod (meaning "no glory") was the son of Phinehas and grandson of Eli. He received his name from the great catastrophe which befell Israel at the time of his birth—the capture by the Philistines of the Ark of the Covenant, which was Israel's glory.

108] *Vishnu-land what Avatar* India, where Vishnuism, one of the main forms of modern Hinduism, is practiced. The god Vishnu, considered by his cult the preserver and protector of the world, dates from the first century B.C. He is always associated with the idea of avatars, or incarnations, of which his are said to be uncountable, though in practice ten are generally considered.

122] *lambwhite maiden* Before departing for the Trojan War, Agamemnon, king of Mycenae, killed a sacred hind of Artemis. In revenge, the goddess sent storms to prevent the voyage. Agamemnon learned that he could not obtain fair winds until his daughter, Iphigenia, was sacrificed on the altar of Artemis. Overcome by the command, and afraid to take the maiden from her mother, Agamemnon gave the task to Odysseus, king of Ithaca, who brought her away by claiming that she was to become the bride of Achilles. Just as she was about to be sacrificed on the altar, Artemis put a deer in her place and bore her away unseen to the barbarian land of Tauris, where she became a priestess in the temple of Diana.

131] *Scythian strands* Scythia, an ancient country lying partly N of the Black Sea and partly E of the Aral Sea, was inhabited by warlike nomadic tribes.

152] *Caldara Polidore* An Italian painter (ca. 1500–43) influenced by Raphael and Hellenistic art. First hired as a hod carrier during the decoration of the Vatican galleries, he was later employed as a frescoe painter.

155] *Purcell . . . Rosy Bowers* Henry Purcell (1659–95), the most important English composer of his time, was also well known for his song-writing. He was composing "From Rosy Bowers" at the time of his death.

190] *Garrick* David Garrick (1717–1779), the most famous actor and producer in the history of the English stage. The mark of his style was a natural ease and he was considered a master at interpretation of character. Devoted to Shakespeare and manager of the Drury Lane Theater, he made Shakespeare's plays accessible to eighteenth-century audiences. Hamlet was one of his favorite and most famous roles. He is buried beside Shakespeare's statue in Westminster Abbey.

195–196] *Chatterton . . . / Rowley* Thomas Chatterton (1752–70), the most precocious of English poets, was born at Bristol, close to the Church of Saint Mary Redcliffe, where his father had been sexton. In 1764, at the age of twelve, he wrote a mock Chaucerian poem, *Elinoure and Juga,* which he claimed to have found among the papers of William Canning, the founder of St. Mary's. The work was ascribed to an imaginary poet, Thomas Rowley (a name he found on a brass at St. Jon's Church), whom he represented as a fifteenth-century monk, possibly modelled on John Lydgate. He applied to Horace Walpole for patronage with *The Ryse of Peynctynge yn Englande, wroten bie T. Rowleie, 1469 for Mastre Canynge* (March, 1769), but was unsuccessful. After a few acceptances which brought little money, Rowley's *Balade of Charitie* was rejected by his publisher. Desperate for money, Chatterton was turned down for the post of surgeon to a Bristol slave ship. Refusing to take handouts, he starved for three days before committing suicide. Chatterton's Rowley poems are his best works. There authenticity was a matter of controversy after his death. He probably did not intend to reveal their true authorship. "Waring" was probably written, says DeVane (*Hdbk,* p. 107), in the early summer of 1842, that is, within a few weeks of B's anonymous review of R. H. Wilde's biography of Tasso, commonly known as the *Essay on Chatterton* (see *Browning's Essay on Chatterton,* ed. Donald Smalley [Cambridge, Mass., 1948]. Smalley speculates that the essay was written in the five weeks preceding July 1, the date on which it was published in *The Foreign Quarterly Review,* edited by B's close friend John Forster. The *Essay on Chatterton* derives its name from the fact that B devoted all but the first seven paragraphs of the review to a discussion of Chatterton.

213] *Triest* Trieste, a port of Italy situated on the NE angle of the Adriatic Sea, seventy mi. ENE of Venice.

221] *lateen sail* Latin sail; a triangular sail commonly used on the Mediterranean.

228] *Lascar's* An East Indian sailor.

RUDEL TO THE LADY OF TRIPOLI

Title] B's exact source for this poem is unknown since the story of Rudel, a twelfth-century troubadour, had been dealt with often. Mrs. Jameson, who later became B's friend, had told the story in her *Loves of the Poets* (pp. 27–32), but others, notably Petrarch, Carducci, Uhland, Heine, and Leopardi, had also used the legend. Later, Swinburne was to use it in *The Triumph of Time.* It appears in all standard histories of troubadour literature, including those of Nostradamus, Tiraboschi, and Sismondi with which B was intimately familiar. Geofrey Rudel, Prince of Blieux, near Bordeaux, was a troubadour of Provence. Pilgrims from the Holy Land talked at his table one evening of the beauty, grace, and piety of Odierna, wife of Raimon I, and Countess of Tripoli, whom they had seen on their journey home from Antioch. The small Syrian duchy of Tripoli, ruled by the Crusaders, was located N of Palestine on the Mediterranean. Though he had never seen her, Rudel was so taken with the lady from the pilgrims' account, that he fell deeply in love. Some of his best songs are in her honor. At last, dressed as a pilgrim, he set out for Tripoli. On the voyage he contracted a fatal illness and, just as the ship reached port, it appeared to his companions that he was dead. The Countess, hearing the story of Rudel, came to the vessel (in some accounts, an inn to which he had been removed) and took his hand. Rudel recovered for a moment, then, giving thanks for having lived long enough to see his beloved, died in the lady's arms. The Countess had him buried in a lavish tomb in the Temple house of Tripoli. In some accounts, the lady, out of grief, becomes a nun the very day of Rudel's death. M. Gaston Paris, in *Jaufré Rudel* (Paris, 1904), expressed what has become the accepted scholarly opinion on the story of Rudel—that the tale has no foundation beyond vague allusions in Rudel's verse to a "distant love," the fact that he went to Palestine on the Second Crusade, and the probability that he died there in 1147. Upon these few facts the romance was constructed by a series of jongleurs.

CRISTINA

Title] The monologist in this imaginary incident is speaking of Maria Christina (1806–78), Queen Regent of Spain from 1833 to 1840 during the minority of her daughter, Isabella. Dissidents who opposed the succession of Isabella launched the Carlist War. The royal party was successful against this faction, but Christina was exposed in a scandal which forced her to abdicate in September, 1840. Having concealed with difficulty repeated pregnancies, Christina's morganatic marriage with an exsergeant, Fernando Muñoz, was discovered. Christina lived in exile in Italy and France until the installation of Isabella II in 1843 when she returned to Spain and again took part in political life. She was forced to go into exile again in 1854. Christina's greed led her to private engagement in the illegal Cuban slave trade. To build up her private fortune, she even sold the state silver services, replacing them with pewter. However, she was chiefly notorious for her love affairs and her constant, open flirtation.

JOHANNES AGRICOLA IN MEDITATION

Headnote] B slightly altered the text of this excerpt from Daniel DeFoe's *Dictionary of All Religions* (1704). Moreover, the date actually given by Potanus in his *Catalogue* is 1538, not 1535.

Title] DeVane (p. 124) points out that B was probably influenced by material on Johannes Agricola he found while researching *Paracelsus.* In a section on the lives of German lawyers (*Vitae Germanorum Jureconsultorum*, pp. 179ff.) added to Melchior Adam's *Vitae Germanorum Medicorum* is a full account of John Schnitter (1492–1566), who, according to custom, took the classical name Johannes Agricola. He is generally described as having been gifted, but vain and ambitious, cooperating with Martin Luther in founding the Reformation before parting with the latter over the doctrine of antinomianism. Agricola had studied under Luther at Wittenburg and accompanied him to the Leipzig Deputation in 1519. In 1536, Luther welcomed him as a fellow teacher at Wittenburg, but a year later, Agricola, in a public deputation, proclaimed the antinomian principles he had been secretly propagandizing since 1527. A bitter dispute with Luther followed, Agricola claiming that his doctrine represented the true Lutheran teaching which Luther had abandoned. Antinomianism was a direct attack on the moral law of the Old Testament in the interest of the new freedom of the Christian and the testimony of the spirit. Agricola denied that Christians were bound by any part of the Law of Moses, even the Ten Commandments. He went beyond the Reformation principle of justification through faith alone by declaring that works are indifferent, that a man is saved by faith alone, regardless of his morals: "Art thou steeped in sin, an adulterer or a thief? If thou believest, thou art in salvation. All who follow Moses must go to the devil." Luther immediately characterized this teaching as "antinomian" (against the Law) and identified it, in principle, with the moral anarchism of the Anabaptists. In 1540, Agricola moved to Berlin, where he published a recantation. Though he was partially reconciled with Luther, the doctrine was carried on by some of his followers. One of these, Ammsdorf, declared that good works actually imperiled salvation. It has been argued that the poem may be seen as a satire on the Calvinistic doctrine of election, and thus that it was influenced by the thought of W. J. Fox, B's friend. Fox, a progressive Unitarian minister, was the editor of the *Monthly Repository*, the magazine in which the poem originally appeared.

THROUGH THE METIDJA TO ABD-EL-KADR

Title] Abd-Al-Kadir (1808–1883), the emir of Mascara and Sultan of the Arabs, was the leader of the Algerian resistance movement against the French which began in 1830 after France occupied Algiers. A first holy war was fought from 1832 to 1837 and ended with the Treaty of Tafna. War broke out again in 1839 and Abd-Al-Kadir attacked the Mitidja, the great plain stretching behind Algiers, and harried the French army. In 1840, the French gave General T. R. Bugeaud the command of a reinforced army of 106,000 men which, by 1842, reversed the trend of the war by gradually pushing back the Arabs. In the same year Mascara was taken. By 1842 the Muslims were driven back to Morocco. Abd-Al-Kadir finally surrendered in 1847. At the time this poem was written—early summer, 1842—Abd-Al-Kadir was trying to unite the different Muslim brotherhoods in order to maintain his authority. Throughout June, the *Times* reported the leader's attempts to organize into a solid army the contingents of troops furnished by the various tribes. The speaker of this poem is an Arab tribesman crossing the Mitidja to meet his leader. In the summer of 1842, B was riding horseback every day to improve his health. It is generally believed that the gallop of his horse, York, suggested the anapestic meter of the poem.
38] *Prophet and the Bride* Mohammed, the Prophet of Islam, and his wife, Khadija. Their marriage, considered by Muslims the perfect union, lasted until her death. Many years older than her husband, she was his truest confidant, the first to believe in his prophecy, and the first convert to Islam.

THE PIED PIPER OF HAMELIN

Title] The problem of B's sources for his version of the Pied Piper legend has never been completely solved. The most thorough and convincing argument remains that of Arthur Dickson in "Browning's Source for *The Pied Piper of Hamelin*," *SP*, 23 (1926): 327–36. He questions B's own statement to the bibliographer, Furnivall, that his source was Nathaniel Wanley's *Wonders of the Little World*, bk. 6 (London, 1678) and the authorities cited by Wanley. B's version is, as Dickson sees it, much closer to the prose account of the story given in Richard Verstegen's *Restitution of Decayed Intelligence* (Antwerp, 1605), an account B claimed not to have seen before his poem was written. The following details in B's version appear only in the Verstegen account: the date assigned to the incident (July 22, 1376); the invitation to the piper, at the climax of the controversy, to "do his worst"; the statement that there was a little boy that was lame and couldn't keep up with the rest; the statement that no tavern was allowed in the street; and the concluding remarks about the possibility of the children's having been carried off to Transylvania. There is the possibility that when B, then an old man with a faulty memory, talked to Furnivall about the sources for a poem he had written forty years earlier in the spring of 1842, he forgot about having read Verstegen. Since the Pied Piper legend was very popular with B's family, there is an equally good possibility that the poet received the Verstegen account or a similar one from his father. By coincidence, the latter had composed his own Pied Piper in 1842, not knowing that his son had just completed a poem on the same subject. There are, however, a few details in B's poem not found in Verstegen, but provided by Wanley and the three sources the latter cites—Johann Wier, *De Presdigiis Daemonum* (1564); G. Schott, *Physica Curiosa* (1622); James Howell, *Epistolae Ho-Elianae* (1645). Dickson concludes that possibly a composite of details from all these accounts, but mainly from Verstegen's, was embodied in an account given the poet by his father. DeVane (pp. 128–29) offers the possibility that B, having earlier encountered some author's repetition of Verstegen's account, used Wanley and his sources to refresh his mind when it came to writing the poem in 1842. The historical basis for the incident which, according to most sources, took place in 1284, has never been verified. One theory supposes an exodus of the young men of the town in connection with German colonization of the East. That the legend concerns plagues of rats carrying the Black Death and the infection of children, who, naturally, would be highly susceptible to the disease, is suggested by D. Wolfers in "A Plaguey Piper" (*The Lancet*, 3 April, 1965, pp. 756–57; summarized by J. L. Winter in "Browning's Piper," *NQ*, n.s. 14 [1967]: 373). The disappearance of the children in the mountain is explained by the hypothesis that the dead children, victims of the plague, were buried in a mass hillside grave. The point is made that the piper in motley is a variation of the symbolic Death of medieval tradition leading a *danse macabre*, or dance of death. He is pied because the "red, yellow, black, and white patches of the fool represent the buboes, haemorrhagic spots and patches, and pallor of the victim of bubonic plague."

Inscription] To William Macready (see l. 300), the eldest son of the great tragedian, William Macready, who was associated with B in the production of *Strafford* (1837) and *A Blot in the 'Scutcheon* (1843). In May, 1842, the child was confined to his room with a bad cough. B knew of his interest in drawing and so composed two poems—*The Cardinal and the Dog* and *The Pied Piper of Hamelin*—for illustration. The illustrations for "The Pied

Piper" are now in The Armstrong Browning Library at Baylor University, Waco, Texas.

1] *Hamelin Town's* A town in NW Germany, situated on the right bank of the Weser River in a hilly region twenty-four mi. SW of Hanover. The medieval town was a market center dependent on a nearby abbey. The territory, or region, in which Hamelin was located is Hanover, not Brunswick.

2] *Hanover city* A German city of the northern Lowlands, chartered in 1241, it is situated near Hamelin in the valley of the Leine River.

3] *river Weser* One of the chief rivers of Germany, it rises in central Germany and flows northward to Bremerhaven on the North Sea. Hamelin is situated on the middle Weser.

89] *Tartary . . . Cham* A large region of central Europe extending eastward from the Caspian Sea was inhabited by the Tatars or Tartars. Cham is an obsolete form of khan formerly applied to the rulers of the Tartars and Mongols.

91] *Nizam* An abreviation of the title "nizān-al-mulk," or "orderer of the kingdom." The only ruler of Iran who actually held this title in the Middle Ages was Abu Ali Hasan Ibn Ali (1018–92). Nizam became the hereditary title of the ruler of Hyderabad, India in the early eighteenth century.

123–125] *Caesar . . . manuscript* When Caesar's ship was taken in the siege of Alexandria in 48 B.C., he swam to shore holding above his head the manuscript of his *Commentaries on the Gallic Wars.*

133] *train-oil-flasks* Flasks containing whale oil.

139] *nuncheon* A light refreshment taken between meals; a snack.

141] *sugar-puncheon* A large cask of sugar.

158] *Claret, Moselle, Vin-de-Grave, Hock* German wines, with the exception of Claret, a red Bordeaux.

160] *Rhenish* Any of a variety of Rhine wines.

177] *Bagdat* Baghdad, situated on the Tigris River, is the capitol of present-day Iraq.

179] *Caliph* The title given in Mohammedan countries to the chief civil and religious leader.

182] *bate a stiver* Bate: to lower or lessen. Stiver: a small coin of the Low Counties. Stiver, like penny, signified a coin of small value.

220] *Koppelberg Hill* Hardly a mountain, Koppelberg Hill is no more than a slight elevation among higher hills to the north of Hamelin.

258] *A text* Matthew 19:24.

290] *Transylvania* A remote and mountainous region of what is now NW and central Rumania. From the 11th cent. until 1920 Transylvania formed part of Hungary. It is contained on the N, E and S by the Carpathian, and on the W by the Bihor Mountains. It is a region of fertile soil, extensive forests, and abundant mineral resources.

EDITORIAL NOTES

THE RETURN OF THE DRUSES

Composition and publication] Under its original title, *Mansoor the Hierophant, The Return of the Druses* was advertised as "Nearly Ready" on p. [255] of *Sordello*, published in the first week of March, 1840. Macready read it on August 3, 1840, deciding against production. By then the title had been changed. It was published as No. IV of *Bells and Pomegranates* in January, 1843.

Occasion] The Lebanese Muhammadan sect, the Druzes, were of some interest to the British public. Lady Hester Stanhope, the niece of the younger William Pitt, his hostess and secretary, had gone to live among them, making her home in an almost inaccessible mountain area NE of Sidon. She exercised great influence over the Druzes, and to the neighboring Arabs was known as the Queen of Palmyra. Among other oddities of behavior, she kept a horse ready for the Messiah. In 1831 the viceroy of Egypt, Muhammad Ali, who had begun the modernization of Islam after the withdrawal of Napoleon, invaded Syria; the ruler of Lebanon, Bashir Al-Shihabi, who had begun the modernization of that country, sided with him in his struggle against the Turkish sultan. Lady Hester was considered sufficiently important to be asked for her neutrality in the struggle. The affair aroused international attention, since British, French, and Russian interests were all at stake. The European powers, chiefly England, forced the Egyptian viceroy to cease his attacks on the sultan, but in 1840 he was left in control of Syria. Lady Hester had died in 1839, and her home and garden subsequently became an attraction for English tourists. As early as 1834 there was rebellion against the Egyptians. Although Bashir sided with Egypt, the population of Lebanon sided with the Turks, principally because of Egyptian forced conscription. On June 8, 1840, insurgents of various sects—Druzes, Christians, Matailah, and Moslems—swore an oath to stick together in the struggle to restore their independence or die. News of the struggle and possibly of the oath itself may have been responsible for B's change of title and inclusion in it of the then well-known word "Druse." At any rate at this time England was cooperating with Austria and Turkey in fleet operations against the Egyptians. Bashir was forced to leave Lebanon in October, departing in a British ship. The decade of Egyptian occupation brought Lebanon to the attention of Europe and opened it to foreign influence, both missionaries and merchants.

Sources] For B the most recent discussion of the Druzes was Silvestre de Sacy, *Exposé de la Religion des Druzes, Tiré des Livres Religieux de cette Secte, et Précédé d'un Introduction et de la Vie du Khalife Hakem-Biamr-Allah* (Paris, 1838). However, there is little about the Druzes in the play which he could not have learned from other sources, although he used Silvestre. The most recent and picturesque account was in Lamartine's *Souvenirs, Impressions, Pensées et Paysages pendant Un Voyage En Orient, 1832–33, ou Notes d'un Voyageur* (Paris, 1835). Since this included a long account of an interview with Lady Hester Stanhope, the book was bound to be of interest to the British, in addition to the fact that during the 19th cent. almost any book about Syria and the Holy Land was certain to command a wide audience. It was the first interview Lady Hester had ever granted, and Lamartine was a very famous man. Popular French works were commonly imported into England. Lamartine includes two accounts of the Druzes, one in which he retails what he knows of their history, and one in which he describes his trip throughout Mt. Lebanon and his encounters with the Druzes. As for his knowledge of the Druzes and their religion, his principal source was C.-F. Volney's *Voyage en Égypte et en Syrie* (Paris, 1787) and republished several times in his *Oeuvres Complètes* (Paris, 1821, 1825, etc.). In his account of the famous Fakhr-al-Din B probably found the idea for his play. In 1516 the Ottoman Turks met the Egyptian Mamluks and destroyed Arab power. Thus Syria, including Lebanon, passed under Turkish control. At the end of the 16th cent. Fakhr-al-Din established virtually independent control over Lebanon and surrounding areas. In 1613 the Turks moved against him and he fled to Tuscany (where he was royally received by the Medici duke) and several years later, to Sicily. In 1618 he returned to Lebanon and reestablished his power, doing much to modernize Lebanon and open it up to European influence. In 1633, however, the Turks were again strong enough to move against him. As in 1613 he attempted to get Italian aid, but his efforts were ineffectual. He was defeated and captured in 1635, taken to Constantinople and there strangled. Volney has the following to say about his impact on the European scene in 1613:

> The arrival of an Oriental prince in Italy did not fail to arouse public interest: it was asked what his nation was, and the origin of the Druzes was inquired into. The historical facts and the character of the Druze religion were found to be so equivocal that there was some uncertainty as to whether they were moslims or christians. The crusades were recalled, and it was hazarded that a people that had sought refuge in the mountains and were enemies of the natives, must be of a race of the Crusaders. This presumption was too favorable to Fakr-el-din for him to discredit it; he had the presence of mind, on the contrary, to claim an imaginary relationship to the house of Lorraine: he was supported by missionaries and merchants, who saw the promise of a new theater of con-

> versions and commerce. Everyone improved the proofs of a fashionable opinion. Those learned in *origins*, struck by the resemblance of names, proposed that Druzes and Dreux [the ducal family of Brittany] could only be identical, and they built on this foundation the system of an imaginary colony of French Crusaders, who, led by a Count of *Dreux*, established themselves in Lebanon.

In summarizing Volney, Lamartine says more distinctly, "The clever adventurer spread this opinion [on the origin of the Druzes] in order to interest the sovereigns of Europe in his fate." In Chapter LVII of Gibbon is to be found in an account of the founder of the Druze religion, Hakim, Khalif of Egypt (see *Title* n), the statement, "at the present hour a free and warlike people, the Druses of Mount Libanus, are persuaded of the life and divinity of a madman and tyrant." In a note he refers to the French translation of the Danish Carsten Niebuhr's journey to Arabia and neighboring countries, published in Copenhagen in 1772, 1774, and 1778, and Hamburg in 1837. The earlier volumes were translated into English and published in Edinburgh in 1792 as *Travels through Arabia and Other Countries of the East*. Niebuhr has a chapter on the Druzes. This chapter, however, was not included in the Edinburgh translation. Nevertheless it was available in the French translation, *Voyage en Arabie & en d'autres Pays circonvoisins* (Amsterdam & Utrecht, 1776). Certain passages (pp. 348–363) suggest that B was familiar also with this work:

> The French have assured us that the Druses of Mt. Lebanon are descended from their compatriots, who remained in the mountain regions of the Holy Land, after the Europeans were driven out of that region. That this is not true one can prove, because Benjamin de Tudela had already mentioned them while he still traveled in these regions when the Europeans were still masters of the Holy Land. The Druses are certainly by appearance Syrian in origin; but they received their religion from the celebrated Mohammed Ibn Ismael El Darari, who made such a stir in Egypt at the beginning of the fifth century of the Hegira.
>
> The Druses are divided into Akals, that is Ecclesiastics, and Dsjahbels, or seculars. . . . The Akals distinguish themselves from the seculars by their white clothing. . . . They scorn all the honorable titles of the world; but perhaps they make a virtue of necessity; because in what follows one will see that after the return of their Hakem, they hope to become Kings, Visiers, and Pashas.
>
> The grand passions of the secular Druses are hospitality, ambition, courage, which often degenerates into foolhardiness and also sometimes avarice. . . . A Sheik, that is, a noble, would be greatly humiliated if he should be seen with tears in his eyes. . . . They are also of so stoic a character that they account death for nothing, and stab themselves or shoot themselves on the least word that they think dishonors them. The right of the strongest is still among them of great worth; even the Christians of Mt. Lebanon still observe that law and hereditary vengeance.
>
> Since the Druses often kill themselves because of a single imprudent word,

> ordinary people behave with the greatest circumspection and with great politeness and many compliments. They never speak evil of an absent enemy. Since the Druses do not wish the Turks to have any knowledge of their Religion and even to be ignorant that there is one, since otherwise there would be a religious war against them, they call themselves Mahometans. The reigning Emir and other principal men who sometimes have business with the Pasha and other important Turks, are circumcised. They also learn the prayers and the ceremonies which belong to it, in order to prove their Mahometanism. Otherwise they have no regard for the Mahometan religion. . . . Should they live in a village where there are Maronites, they often go to church, especially the principal Druse women; and if by chance a monk or a bishop of the Maronites wants to baptize the son or daughter of an Emir, he is granted that honor.

Niebuhr was able to come by a MS found by a Jesuit in the corner of a Druze home where he had spent the night. This was the first Druze text, apparently, that any European had been able to examine. The following passages are based on Niebuhr's examination of the MS:

> El Dursior, the Druses, as we Europeans call them, follow the doctrine of Mahomed Ibn Ismael and adore Hakem as God. . . . They believe that in the year 400 of the Hegira (1009 of the Christian Era) the godhead entered into Hakem, but it was not made manifest to men until 408, that is, when Mahomed Ibn Ismael began to spread the new doctrine. The Druses call the year 409 a year of affliction, because the Godhead abandoned Hakem that year; but they maintain that from the beginning of the year 410 until the beginning of the year 412 (when he died) God again lived in him. . . . God has appeared ten times in human form . . . 9) under the name of El Mansur, 10) under the name of Hakem and as King of Egypt. The principal apostles of Mahomed Ibn Ismael were Hamsa, Ismael, Mohammed el Kilme, Abu el Chair, and Behd Eddin or Ali ibn Mohammed esse Muki. Hamsa ben Ali appeared seven times in the world, 1) first at the time of Adam, under the name of Schat, 2) at the time of Noah, under the name of Pythagoras, 3) at the time of Abraham, under the name of David, 4) at the time of Moses, under the name of Schaib (Jethro), 5) at the time of Jesus Christ, under the name of Eleazar, 6) at the time of Mohammed under the name of Salman the Persian, and 7) at the time of Said under the name of Salech. . . . They maintain that Hamsa was the true Messiah.
>
> They believe further that Hakem is to appear one more time in human form, and that one can expect that advent when the Christians have won great victories over the Mahometans. Then Hakem is to conquer the world by the sword, and raise the Druze above all religions. However, the Christians will be the happiest and the Mahometans the worst off of all the other sects.

Title] *Druses* (or Druzes, Arabic Duruz). The Druzes are of mixed Persian and Arabic stock, the latter having settled in Mesopotamia and there mingled with the Persians. Their religion is one of many Muhammadan heterodox or heretical sects, frequently, like the Druze religion, a consequence of amalgamating Muhammadan and pre-Muhammadan religious beliefs and practices. The Druze religion, however, is fundamentally a sect of the Shiite branch of Islam. Unlike the Sunnite branch, the Shiite believed that the true *imam* or religious heir of Muhammad was an incarnation of the divine. A subbranch, the Ismailites, was even more stringent in this belief, particularly in the return or reincarnation of the divine in the Mahdi, or savior. The Qarmatians, who have been called "the Bolsheviks of Islam," intensified the tradition and even founded a state on the Persian Gulf. Though destroyed, the Qarmatian doctrines were passed on to the Fatimids of Egypt, from whom both Druzism and the Assassin movement sprang. In the early 11th cent. an eccentric, reformist, and possibly insane Khalif of Egypt, Hakim-Biamr-Allah (also Hakeem, Hakem, and more correctly al-Hakim) (996–1021) declared himself divine. (His original name was Mansour.) The first to acknowledge and teach that divinity was a Persian, al-Darazi. Forced to flee from Egypt, he went to Lebanon and converted some of the mountaineers of Mt. Hermon (at the S end of the Anti-Lebanon, a range of mountains parallel to Mt. Lebanon, which lies to the W, across the R. Litani). In Cairo another prophet, Hamzah al-Labbad al-Zuzani, also known as al-Hadi, also a Persian, was more successful in his worship of the divinity of Hakim, who disappeared mysteriously in 1021 on Mt. Mokattam (more correctly Gebe el Muqattam) a few mi. SE of Cairo. Although torn to death by a mob, Hamzah transmitted his beliefs to a disciple, Baha'-al-Din, the author of the principal Druze texts and chief Druze propagandist. He denied the death of Hakim, declaring that he had gone temporarily into supernatural withdrawal but would return triumphantly. He also announced that pending the "absence" of Hakim nothing of the new religion should be divulged. Much is still unknown. A small percentage is initiated, or wise, but the majority is ignorant of much of the religion. As a result of conflict with another heterodox Muhammadan sect the Druzes moved NW to Mt. Lebanon, E of Beirut, where the Crusaders found them, and where they still flourish. The mountain they also occupy in Syria is called Jabal al-Daruz, or Mt. of the Druzes.

Persons] *Grand-Master* The ruler of the Knights of the Order of the Hospital of St. John of Jerusalem. About 1070 a group of merchants from Amalfi, Italy, built a vast hostel for pilgrims to the Holy Land. In the course of time there arose from the individuals who devoted themselves to the care of the pilgrims, particularly the sick, a military monastic order, which eventually attained enormous power and wealth throughout the Crusader kingdoms of Palestine and Cyprus, and in Europe as well. Their great rivals were the Templars, or Poor Knights of Christ and the Temple of Solomon, and the less powerful Teutonic Knights of St. Mary's Hospital at Jerusalem. When, in 1312, the Templars were dissolved after a trial of stunning scandal, the Hospitallers were the official heirs, although most of the property remained in the hands of the kings and nobles who had been instrumental in the dissolution of the Temple. In 1291, the Crusaders were thrust from Palestine by the Mamluks, then the rulers of Egypt. The various Crusader institutions, including the Hospital, were reestablished in the Kingdom of Cyprus, where the Hospital already held possessions. Between 1308 and 1310 the Hospitallers seized the Island of Rhodes from the Byzantine Empire and made it their headquarters. In 1523 the Turks forced them out of Rhodes, and after seven years in Crete they moved to Malta, granted them by the Emperor Charles V. The order still survives.

Prefect The local commander of any establishment of the Hospital.

Patriarch In the Roman Catholic, or Latin, church a Patriarch ranks only after the Pope. He is the ecclesiastical governor, administering both religious matters and Church property, for some area. When the Crusader Kingdom of Jerusalem was founded in 1101, the Latin patriarch attempted to make it into a church state, like the Papal states in Italy, but he was outwitted by Baldwin and never, apparently, recognized by the Pope. Thereafter he was merely the Papal surrogate in a secular state. When the Crusaders were driven out in 1291 the Patriarchate also was transferred to Cyprus and became known as the Patriarchate of Jerusalem and Cyprus (acquired by Venice in 1489 and taken by the Turks in 1571). Thus the Patriarch was the ecclesiastical control over the Religious Order of the Hospital.

Nuncio Diplomatic envoy or representative of a Patriarch.

Republic's Admiral The Admiral of the Cretan navy of the Republic of Venice.

Dreux The family which ruled as Dukes of Brittany from the early 13th cent. to the end of the 15th, when Brittany was joined by marriage to the crown of France. The Brittany Dukes were almost royal in their power and independence, and Brittany continued to maintain certain unique political rights until the French Revolution.

Initiated Druses Only a minority of Druzes were admitted to the inner and esoteric doctrines of their religion. They were distinguished by white turbans.

Time] Placing the poem in the 15th cent. is anachronistic, for B has the Druzes flee from Osman, that is, the Ottoman Turks, who did not invade Lebanon until 1516 (see I, 86n).

Place] *Sporades* A group of islands off the SW coast of Asia Minor, for the most part running NW from Rhodes.

Lebanon] See *Title* n.

Knights Hospitallers of Rhodes] See *Persons, Grand-Master*.

ACT I

3] *incarnate mystery* In Druze religion God, his essence unknowable, was made flesh in the person of Ḥakim (see *Title, Druses*), had disappeared, was in hiding, and would again be incarnated. The coming incarnation would be

the last one. The Druze religion would be established as the world religion.
5] *Hakeem* or Hakim. See Title, *Druses.*
7] *Mokattam* The mountain SE of Cairo from which Hakim vanished or, according to orthodox Islam historians, was murdered by order of his sister, who feared that he was about to disinherit his son.
11] *Mother-mount* Either Mt. Hermon, at which the Druzes first appeared, or Mt. Lebanon, to which they later moved. See *Title, Druses.*
16] *disguise* It was a belief of the Druzes that they had a right and a duty to conceal their true religion, pretending to hold the faith of any place in which they found themselves.
21] *world's secret* See I, 3n).
40] *Rhodian cross* The eight-pointed Maltese cross, which took its name from the fact that the Hospitallers, after leaving Rhodes, went ultimately to Malta. It was silver on a black ground.
81] *Return* It was a Druze belief that on the reappearance of Hakim all Druzes would be returned to Lebanon.
86] *Osman* Presumably Osman or Othman (also Uthaman) I (1259–1326), the founder of the Empire of the Ottoman Turks, who in the 15th cent. were in conflict with the Knights of Rhodes. However the Mamluk Sultans of Egypt controlled Syria, including Lebanon, into the 16th century. B probably based his anachronism on the fact that in his own time the Ottoman Turks were losing control of Syria to their Egyptian viceroy and that the Lebanese quasi-independent ruler had sided with the Egyptians (see *Sources* n). The Turks had a reputation for savagery. In 1584, for example, they slaughtered, it is said, 60,000 Druzes in a punitive expedition; the Druzes were believed to have pillaged a caravan bearing tax-moneys.
87] *Syria's ridge* Mt. Lebanon (see I, 11n and *Title, Druses*).
110] *White-cross Knights . . . Isle* The Knights Hospitallers of Rhodes.
116] *Sheikh* An Arabian or Muhammadan term, referring to either a religious or a political leader. Roughly, noble.
140] *Khalif, King of Prodigies* Correctly *khalifah,* "deputy" or "successor" to Muhammad (570?–632). After Muhammad's death one of the leading converts to Muhammadism was created khalif (or caliph, and calif). The early caliphates were succeeded by the Umayyad and Abbasid dynastic caliphates. From the beginning, however, some felt that the proper successor to Muhammad was Ali, his cousin and son-in-law. This group was known as the Shiites, the name being derived from the Arabic for "the party of Ali." In the tenth century a branch of this group, the Ismailites, had gained sufficient power to capture Cairo and there establish the first Shiite caliphate, the Fatimids; al-Hakim, or Hakeem, was a Fatimid. The Druzes believe many prodigies or miraculous wonders of Hakim.
152] *Candia* the Venetian capital of Crete, on the N coast of the island. The Venetians held Crete from 1204 to 1669.
202] *Frank* Since the Crusades, the common Arabic name for any European.

217] *Crossed-keys* The papal insignia, the keys of heaven and hell.
224] *sombre groves* The famous cedars of Lebanon.
244] *Tu Dieu!* French equivalent of "Thank God."
284] *Rennes* Capital of the Dukes of Brittany, though rarely their residence in the 15th cent.
285] *Duke my father* Loys, a nonhistorical character, could have been the son of John IV (1365–1399), John V (1399–1442), Francis I (1442–1450), Pierre II (1450–1457), Arthur III (1457–1488), or Francis II (1458–1488).
291] *Bretagne* Brittany. In 826 Louis the Pious created the first Duke of Brittany. He rebelled against Charles the Bald and established an independent Duchy in 850. A Dreux married a descendant of Conan de Tort (d. 992), the founder of the ducal line; but he was descendant of the first duke. Thus the Breton ducal family was older than the royal line of France, though in the female line. See *Persons, Dreux*.
303] *Chapter* The official assembly of any religious order; here, of the Knights.
347] *Synod* Used loosely here as equivalent of Chapter (see I, 303n).
359] *Count Dreux* The first Dreux to marry into the Breton ducal line was Pierre de Dreux, who married Alix, duchess of Brittany in 1213. From them were descended the subsequent Dukes. The family name of Pierre was Mauclerc. He died in 1250 during his return from a crusade. Louis VI of France gave the countship of Dreux to his own son, Robert.
360] *Bouillon's war* Godfrey of Bouillon, one of the leaders of the first crusade, which set out from Europe in 1097 and captured Jerusalem in 1099. Godfrey was the first ruler of Jerusalem as Advocate of the Holy Sepulchre, having refused the crown. He had an enormous task before him in establishing European rule in Palestine, but died in 1100.

ACT II

166] *Mage-king* Such as the three wise men, or kings of the East who followed the star to Christ's birth. "Referring to the Oriental superstition that the ashes of magicians exhale perfume revealing tombs where treasures lie hid" (P-C; no authority given; questionable).
183] *khandjar* khanjar, or kandjar, a short curved Arabian dagger. Both Volney and Lamartine refer to it as part of the national Druze costume.

ACT III

164] *Cedars* The cedars of Lebanon, of which a few survive.
172] *new expiatory form* The Druzes believed in metempsychosis, the transmigration of souls after death into animal form, if they were evil, or some excellent human form if they were good. Strictly, only the uninitiated Druzes believed this.
271–72] *San Gines / By Murcia* Murcia is a city and province in SE Spain. S of Murcia on the coast is Cartagena; a few miles to the E is Cape Palos, and

the village of San Ginés de la Jara is near the Cape but on a virtually landlocked lagoon, Mar Menor, W and N of the Cape.

300] *red-cross rivals of the Temple* The Knights Templars, see *Persons, Grand-Master.*

ACT IV

64] *Bahumid the Renovator* Silvestre de Sacy, in his second volume, discusses the complex system of the Druze Ministers. Their task was to spread the doctrine. The first was Hamzah himself, whose ministerial or divine name was the Intelligence. Others were the Soul, the Word, the Follower, the Application, the Opening, the Phantom, and so on. P-C think that Bahumid the Renovator was Baha'-al-Din, known as the Follower or the Left Wing, because his writings circulated the beliefs of Hakim throughout the Islamic world from Constantinople to India. Another spelling is Baha-ud-Din. This does not seem sufficient to establish his identity with B's Bahumid. Rather, it seems likely that B took the idea of the Renovator for the purposes of his play from the general idea of the ministerial names, and invented Bahumid as a vaguely Arabic name.

ACT V

6] *Hamza* One of the first followers of Hakim. See *Title, Druses.*

8] *Copht* Copt, a member of the Egyptian Christian church.

10] *Biamrallah! Biamreh!* The first is a title received by Hakim when he ascended the throne; it means "he who judges or governs by the command of God." The second, given to Hakim by a follower, means "he who governs by his own order." The second epithet comes from Volney, apparently; the first is to be found in both Volney and Silvestre de Sacy.

38] *Fatemite* See I, 140n. Hakim was actually the sixth Fatimid calif but the third to reign in Egypt.

52] *Romaioi, Ioudaioite kai proselutoi* Greek. See Acts 2:9–11. The account of the Day of Pentecost, on which the eleven remaining disciples under the inspiration of heaven began to speak in the tongues of various nations: "Parthians, and Medes, and Elamites, and the dwellers in Mesopotamia, and in Judaea, and Cappadocia, in Pontus, and Asia, Phrygia, and Pamphlia, and Egypt, and in the parts of Libya about Cyrene, and strangers of *Rome, Jews and Proselytes,* Cretes and Arabians, we do hear them speak in our tongues the wonderful works of God."

104] *winged lion* The lion of St. Mark, the heraldic emblem of Venice.

160] *Stamboul* The center of Constantinople.

160] *Luke* The given name of the Nuncio. L. 161, 1843 variant, gives his name, which is Greek, to suggest his wiliness.

240] *God's sepulchre* The Church of the Holy Sepulchre at Jerusalem, for the control of which the Crusades were undertaken. Although the Europeans had been long since driven out of the Holy Land, the idea of another crusade to rescue it was still being revived in the 15th and even in the 16th century.

Cumulative Index of Titles

(Titles of long poems or of collections of short poems are indicated in bold type)

Cumulative Index of First Lines